AF574138

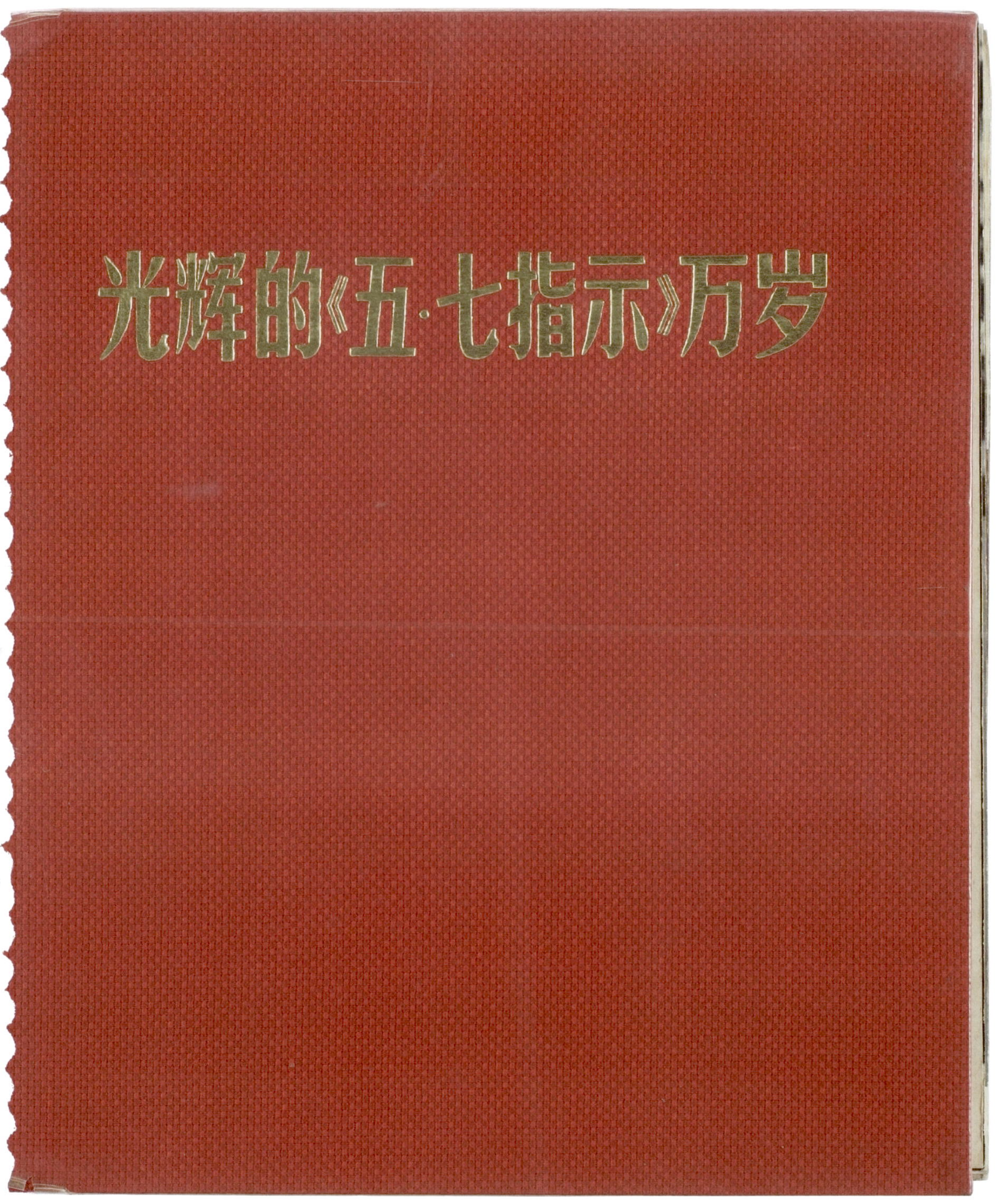

plate 1

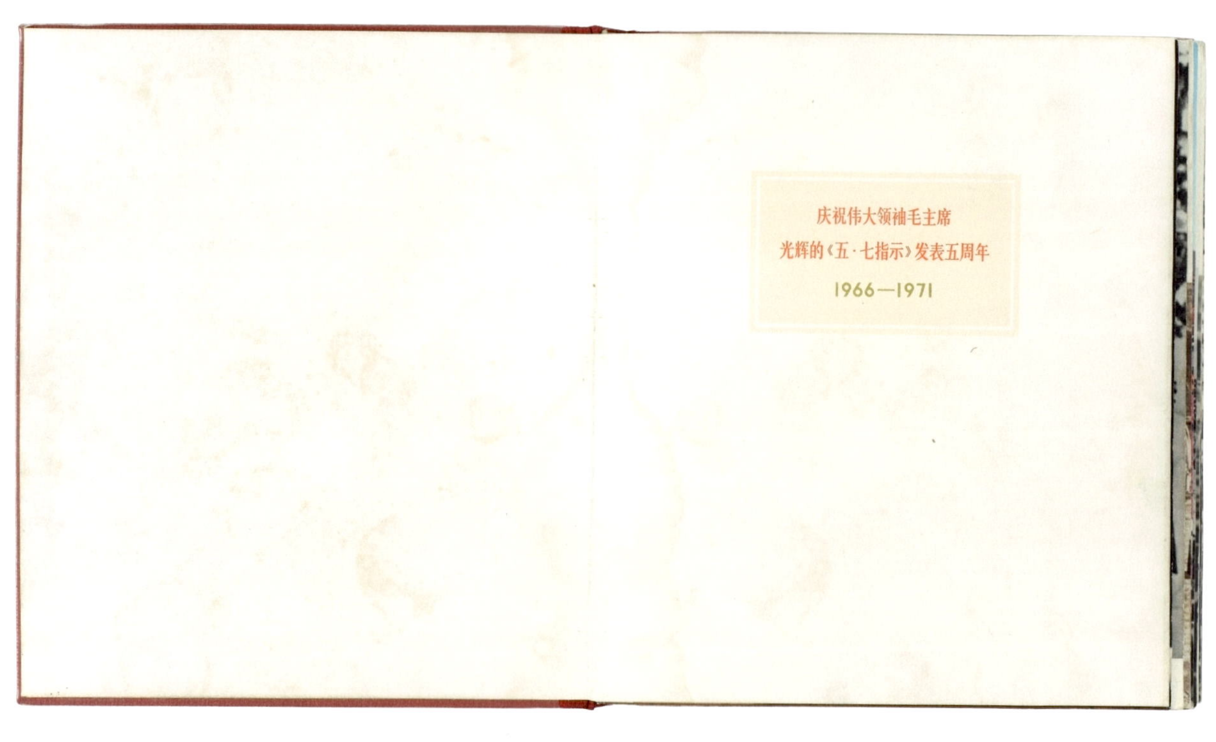

plate 2

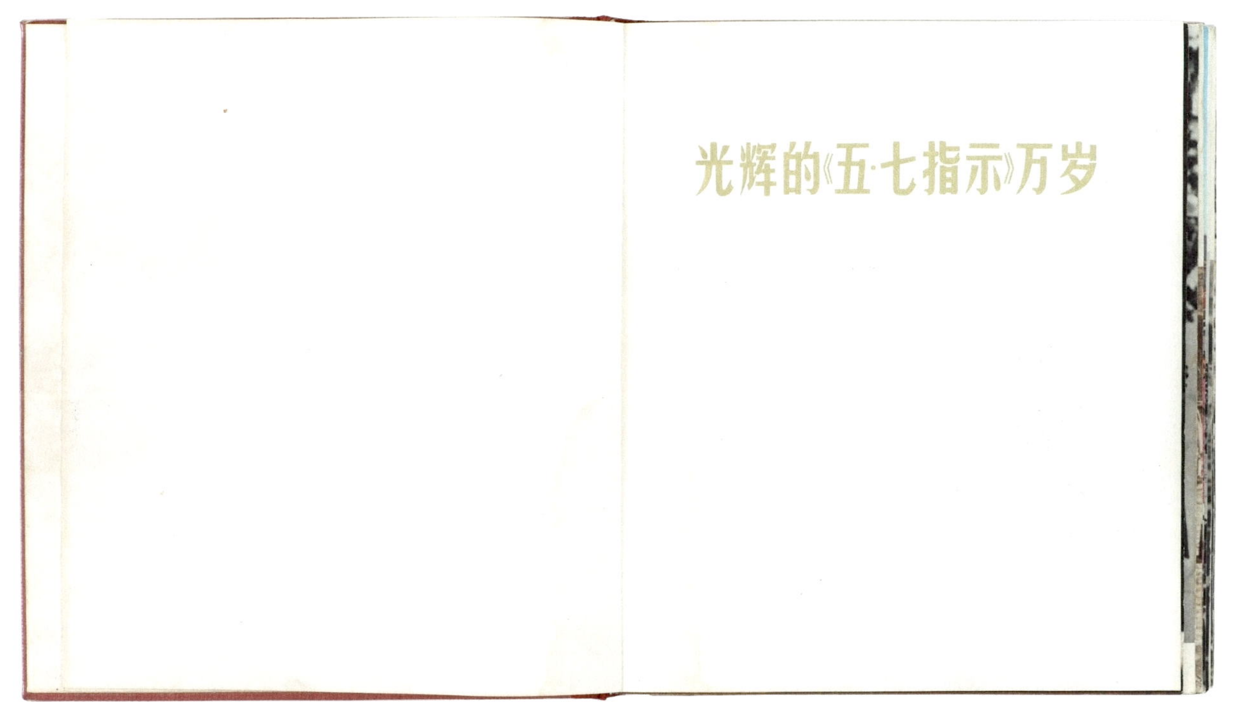

plate 3

plate 4 伟大 统帅毛主席 - The Great Commander-in-Chief Chairman Mao

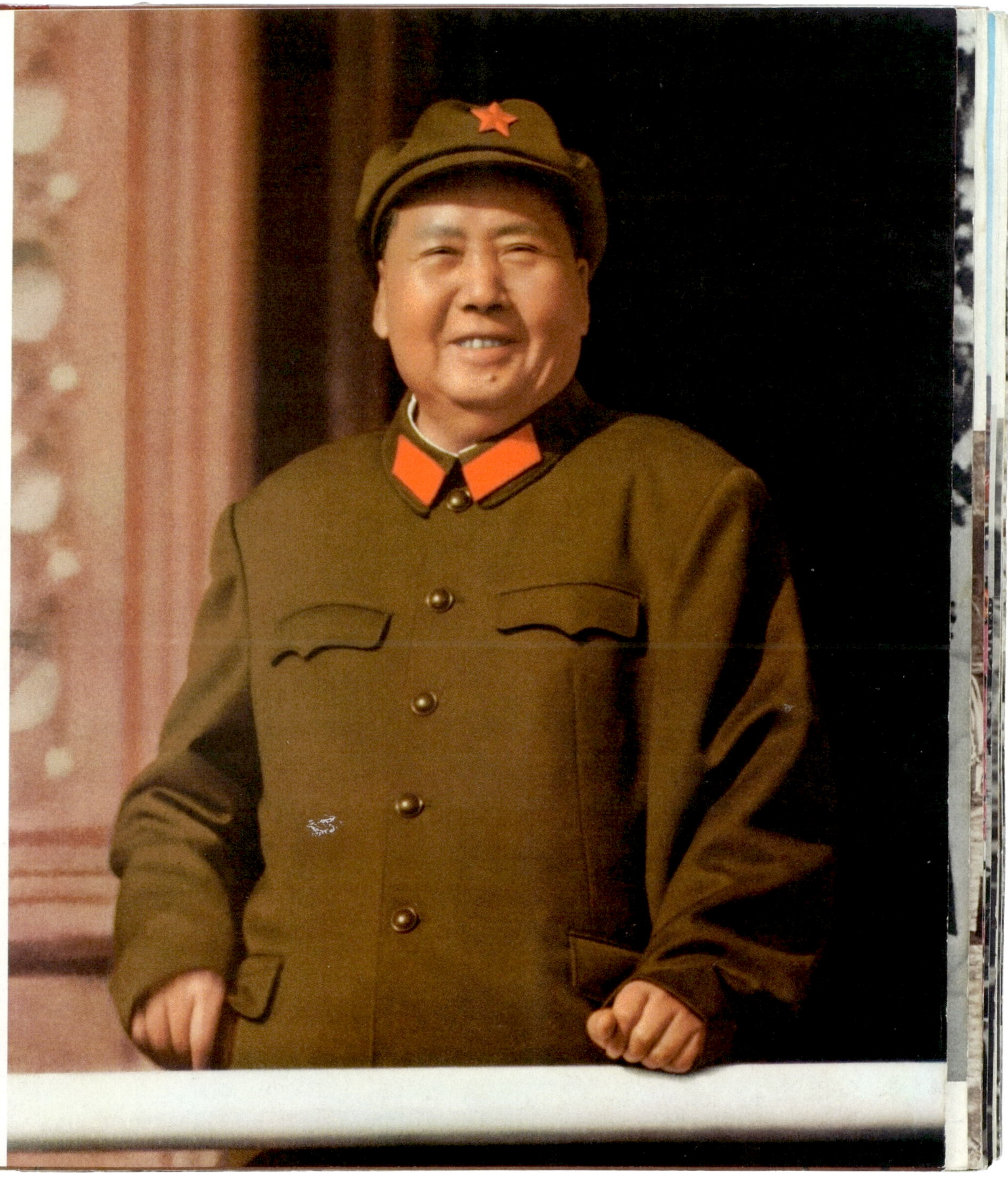

plate 5 伟大领袖毛主席在中国共产党第九次全国代表大会上 - The Great Leader Chairman Mao at the Ninth National Congress of the Communist Party of China

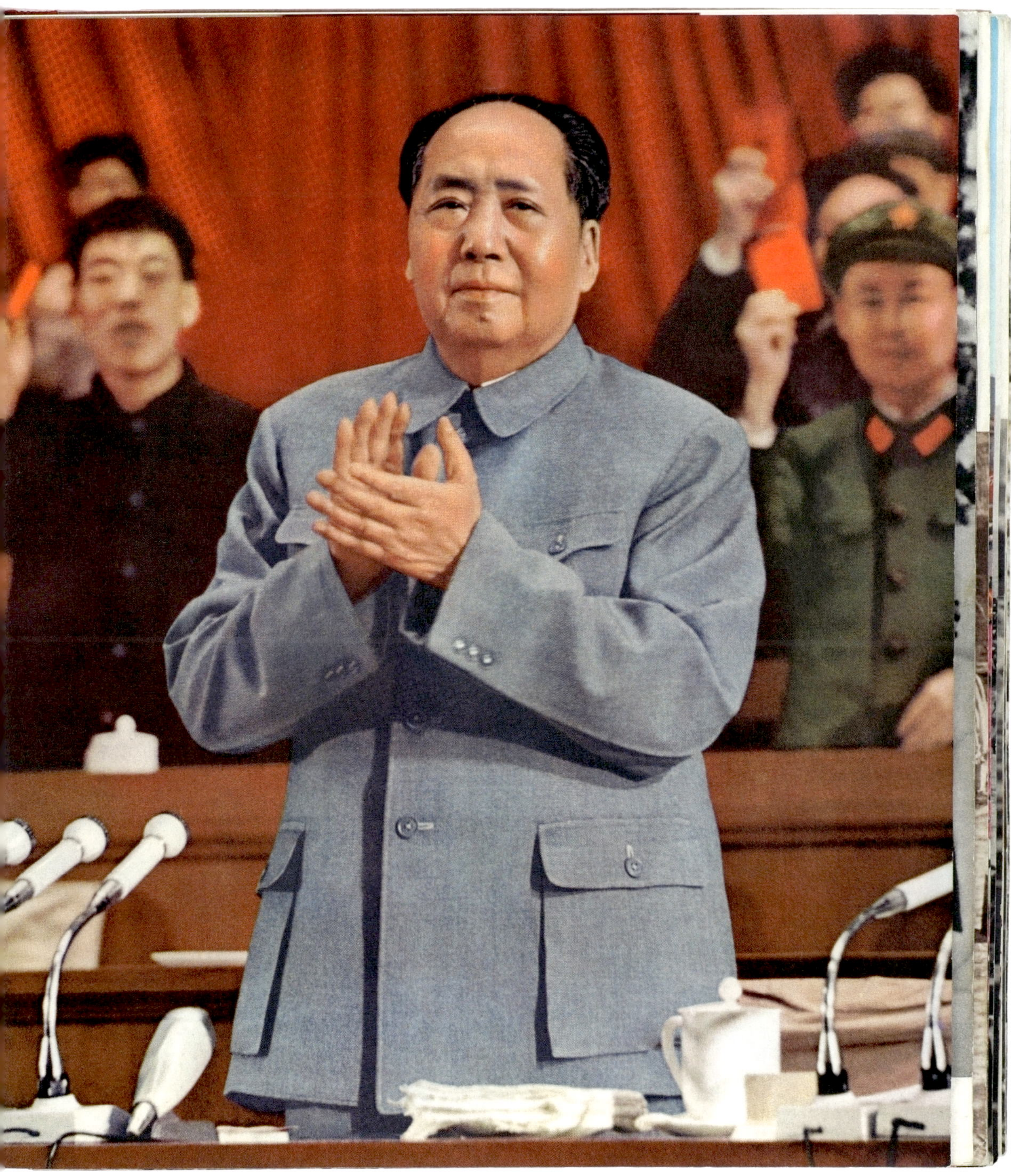

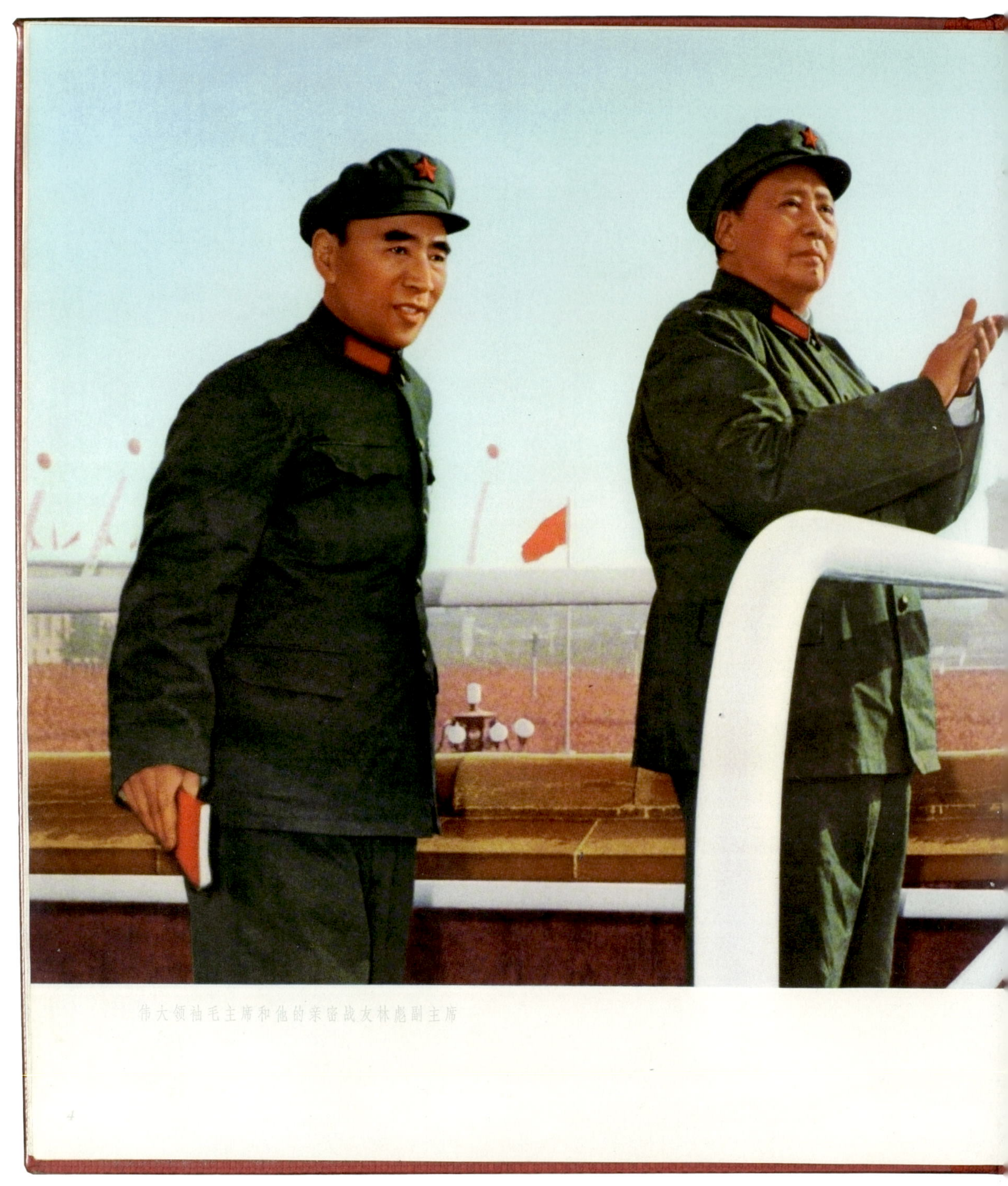

plate 6 伟大领袖毛主席[和他的亲密战友林彪副主席 - The Great Leader Chairman Mao [and His Closest Comrade-in-Arms, Vice-Chairman Lin Biao]

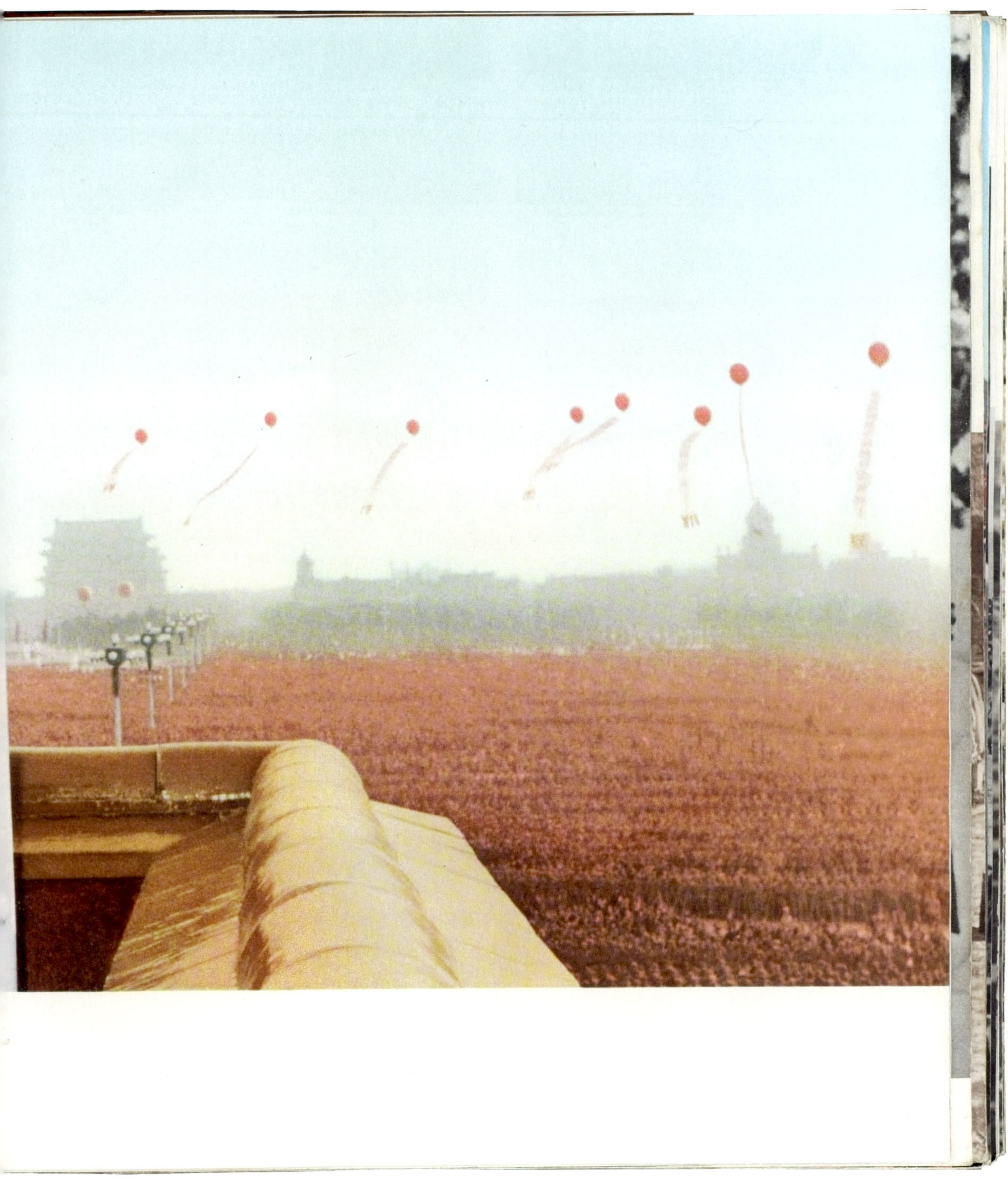

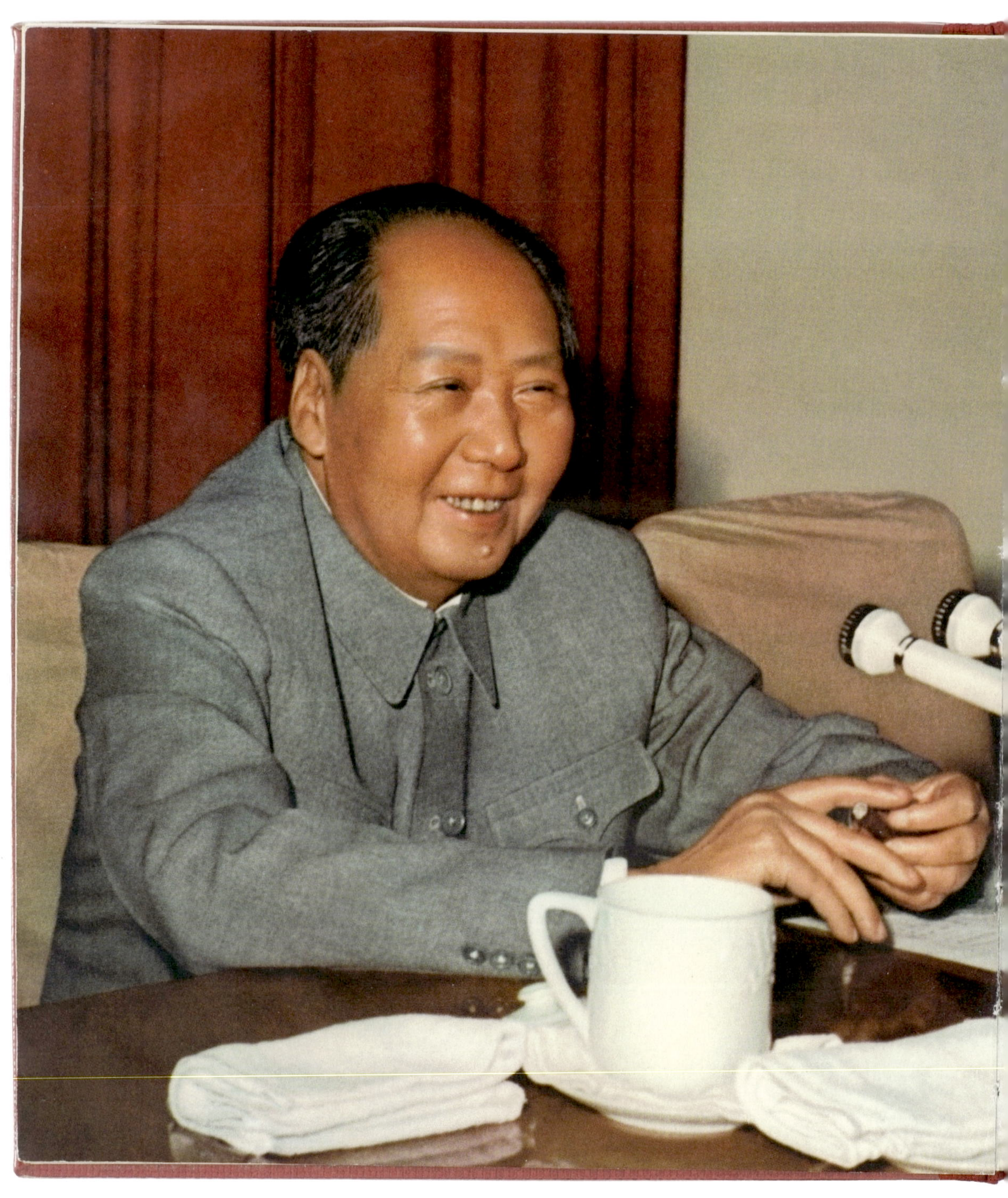

plate 7 毛主席[和林副主席]在中国共产党第九届中央委员会第一次全体会议上 - Chairman Mao [and Vice-Chairman Lin Biao] at the First Plenary Session of the Ninth Central Committee of the Communist Party of China

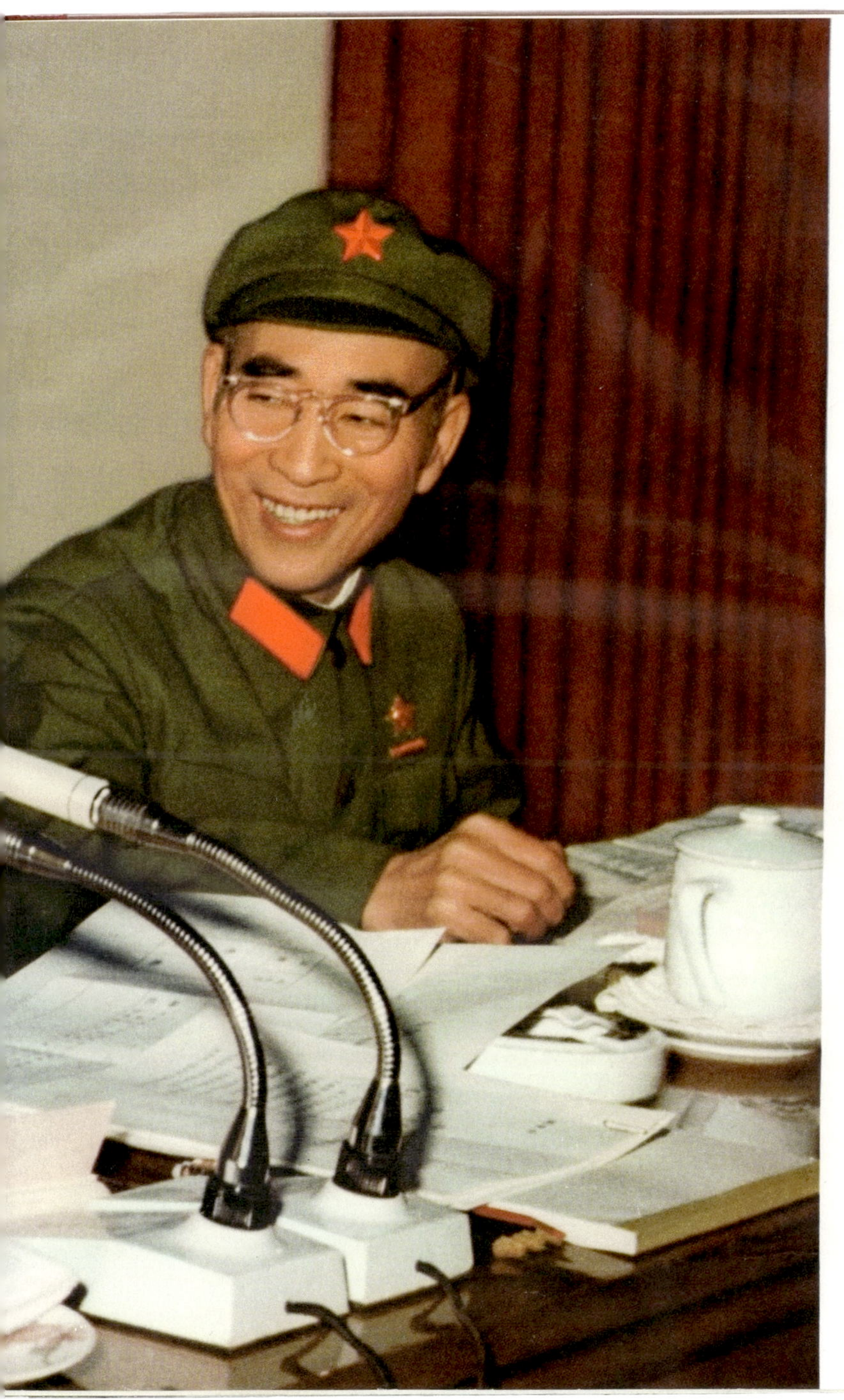

毛主席和林副主席在中国共产党第九届中央委员会第一次全体会议上

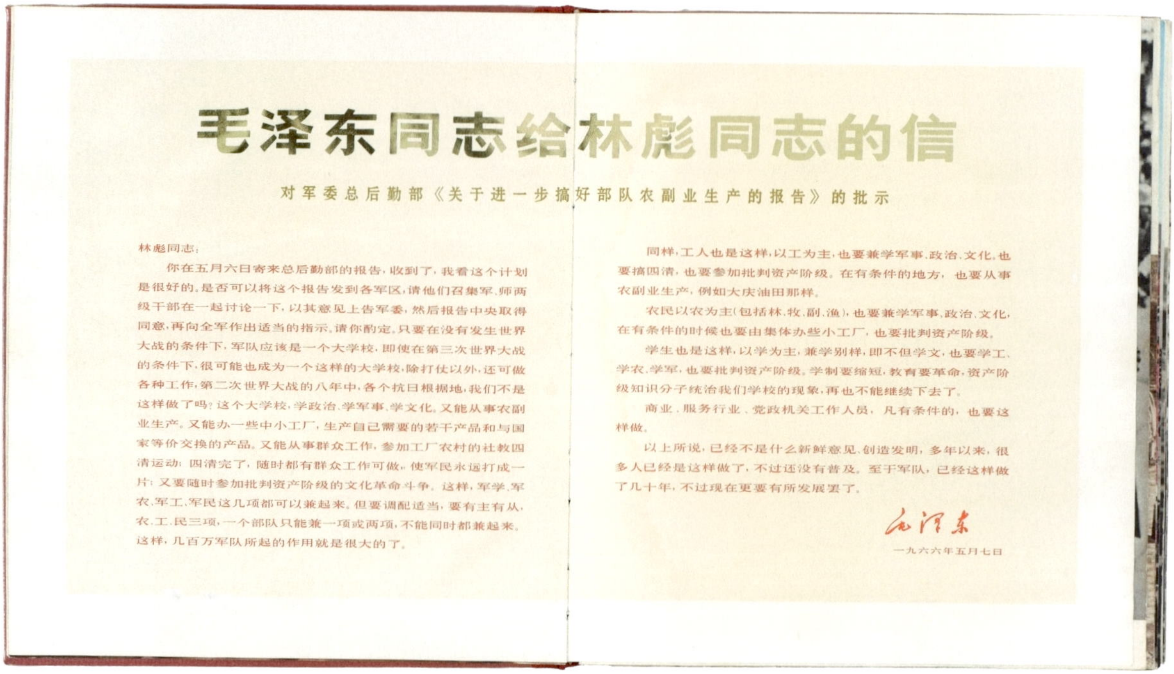

毛泽东同志给林彪同志的信

对军委总后勤部《关于进一步搞好部队农副业生产的报告》的批示

林彪同志：

你在五月六日寄来总后勤部的报告，收到了，我看这个计划是很好的。是否可以将这个报告发到各军区，请他们召集军、师两级干部在一起讨论一下，以其意见上告军委，然后报告中央取得同意，再向全军作出适当的指示。请你酌定。只要在没有发生世界大战的条件下，军队应该是一个大学校，即使在第三次世界大战的条件下，很可能也成为一个这样的大学校，除打仗以外，还可做各种工作，第二次世界大战的八年中，各个抗日根据地，我们不是这样做了吗？这个大学校，学政治、学军事、学文化。又能从事农副业生产。又能办一些中小工厂，生产自己需要的若干产品和与国家等价交换的产品。又能从事群众工作，参加工厂农村的社教四清运动；四清完了，随时都有群众工作可做，使军民永远打成一片；又要随时参加批判资产阶级的文化革命斗争。这样，军学、军农、军工、军民这几项都可以兼起来。但要调配适当，要有主有从，农、工、民三项，一个部队只能兼一项或两项，不能同时都兼起来。这样，几百万军队所起的作用就是很大的了。

同样，工人也是这样，以工为主，也要兼学军事、政治、文化。也要搞四清，也要参加批判资产阶级。在有条件的地方，也要从事农副业生产，例如大庆油田那样。

农民以农为主(包括林、牧、副、渔)，也要兼学军事、政治、文化，在有条件的时候也要由集体办些小工厂，也要批判资产阶级。

学生也是这样，以学为主，兼学别样，即不但学文，也要学工、学农、学军，也要批判资产阶级。学制要缩短，教育要革命，资产阶级知识分子统治我们学校的现象，再也不能继续下去了。

商业、服务行业、党政机关工作人员，凡有条件的，也要这样做。

以上所说，已经不是什么新鲜意见、创造发明，多年以来，很多人已经是这样做了，不过还没有普及。至于军队，已经这样做了几十年，不过现在更要有所发展罢了。

毛泽东

一九六六年五月七日

plate 8 毛泽东同志给林彪同志的信 - A Letter from Comrade Mao Zedong to Comrade Lin Biao

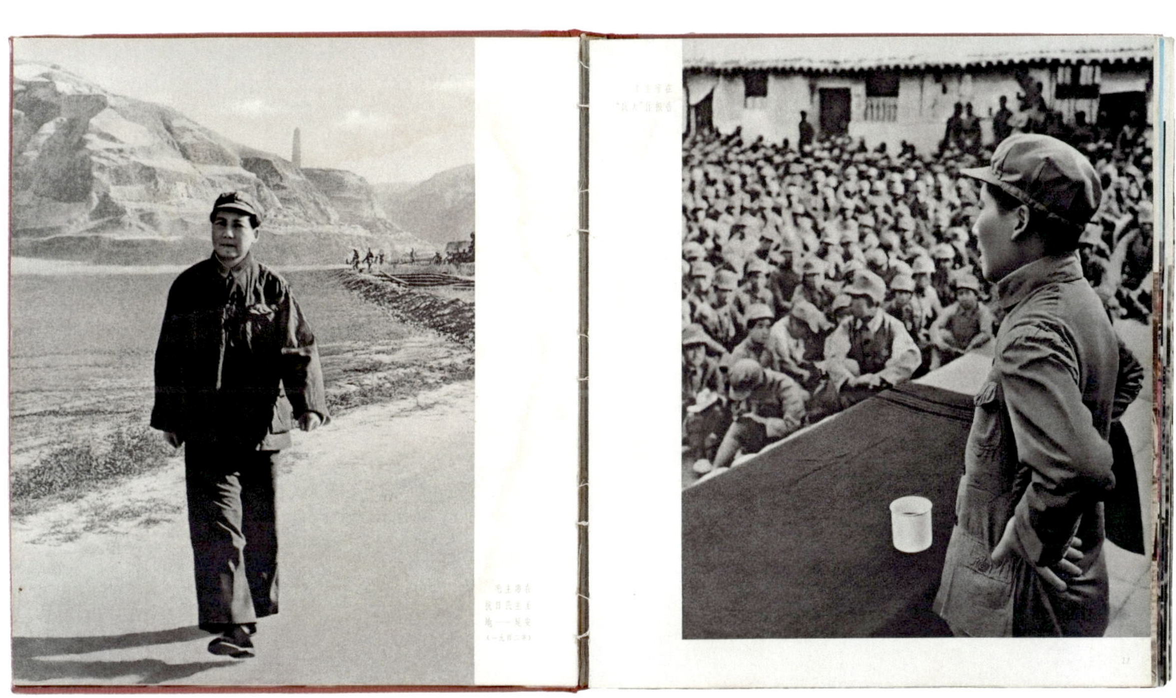

plate 9 (Left) 毛主席在抗日民主圣地 - 延安 (一九四二年) - Chairman Mao in the Anti-Japanese Sacred Democratic Land: Yan'an (1942) (Right) 毛主席在“抗大”作报告 - Chairman Mao Is Making a Report in the Chinese Counter-Japanese Military and Political University

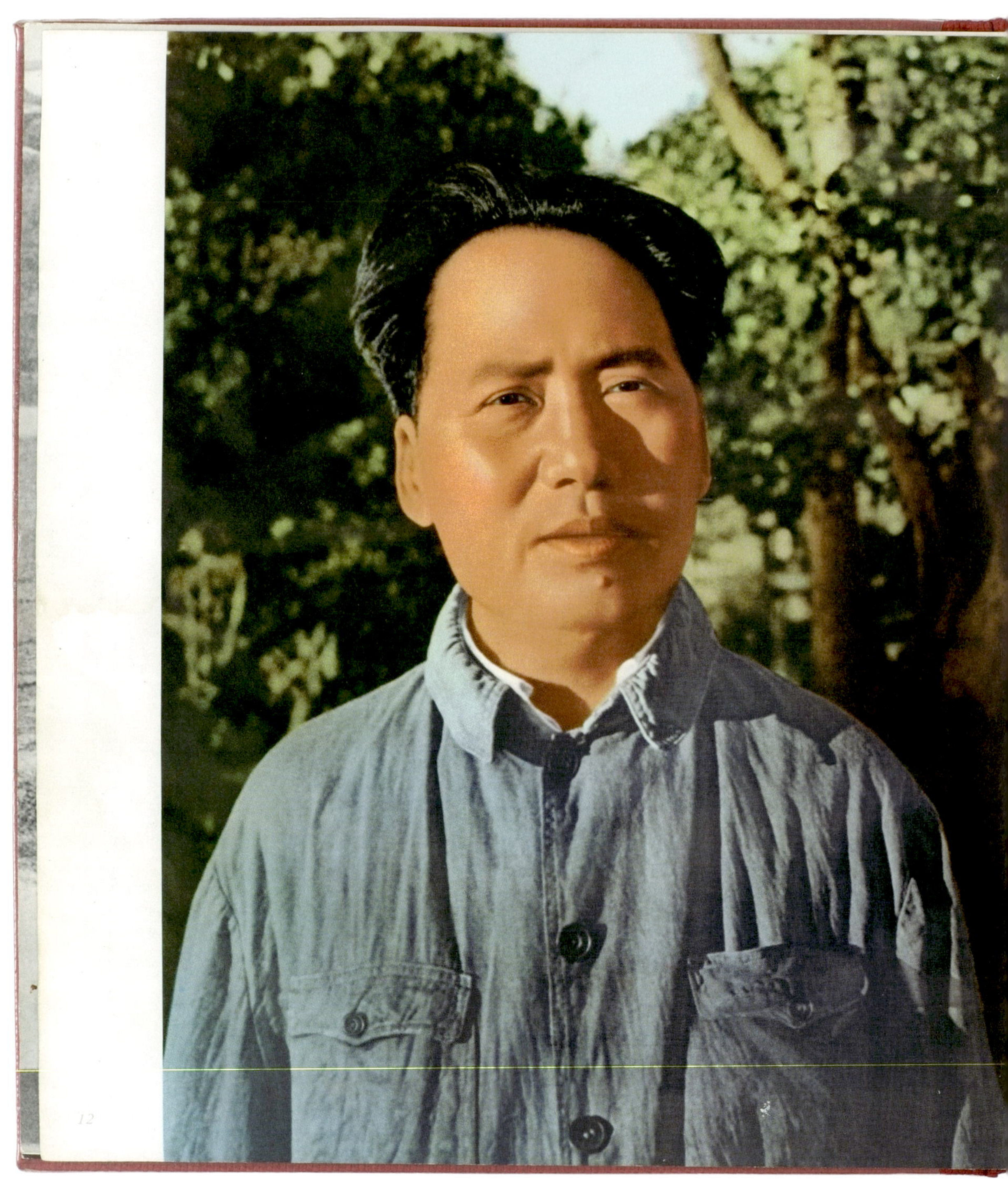

plate 10　毛主席[林彪同志]在延安（一九四五年）- Chairman Mao [and Comrade Lin Biao] in Yan'an (1945).

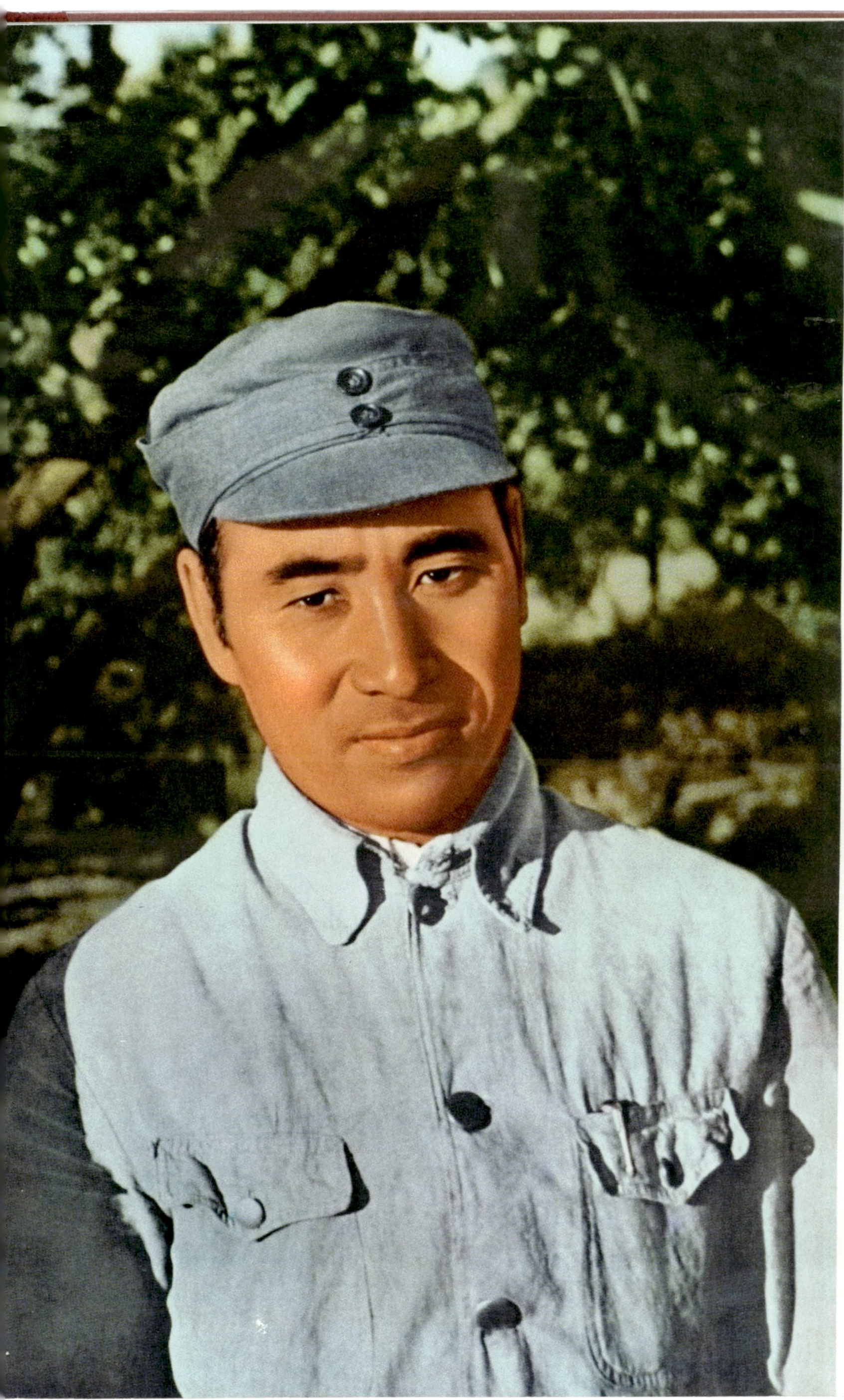

毛主席和林彪同志
在延安（一九四五年）

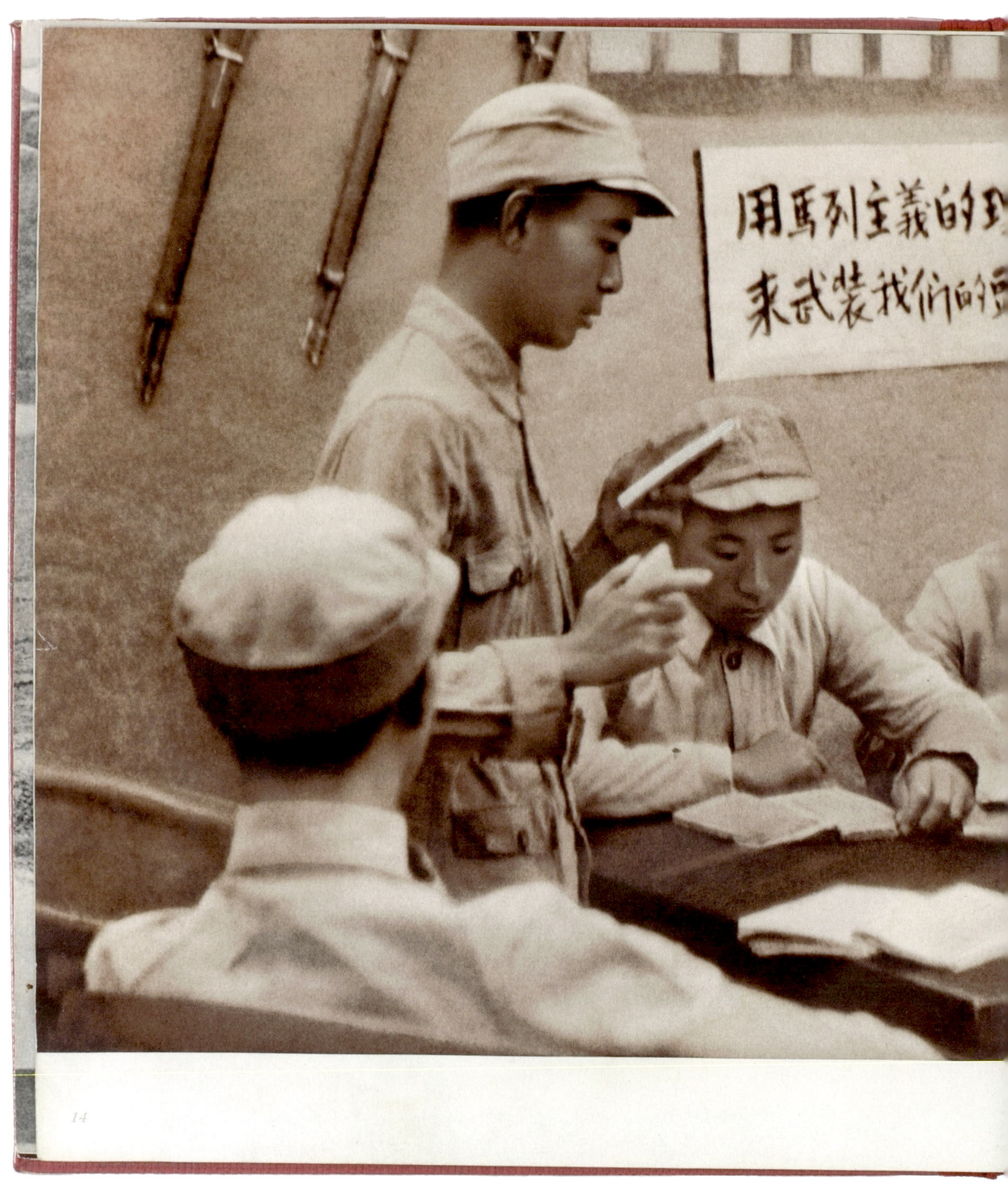

plate 11　认真学习马克思主义，列宁主义，毛泽东思想 - Conscientiously Studying Marxism, Leninism, and Mao Zedong Thought

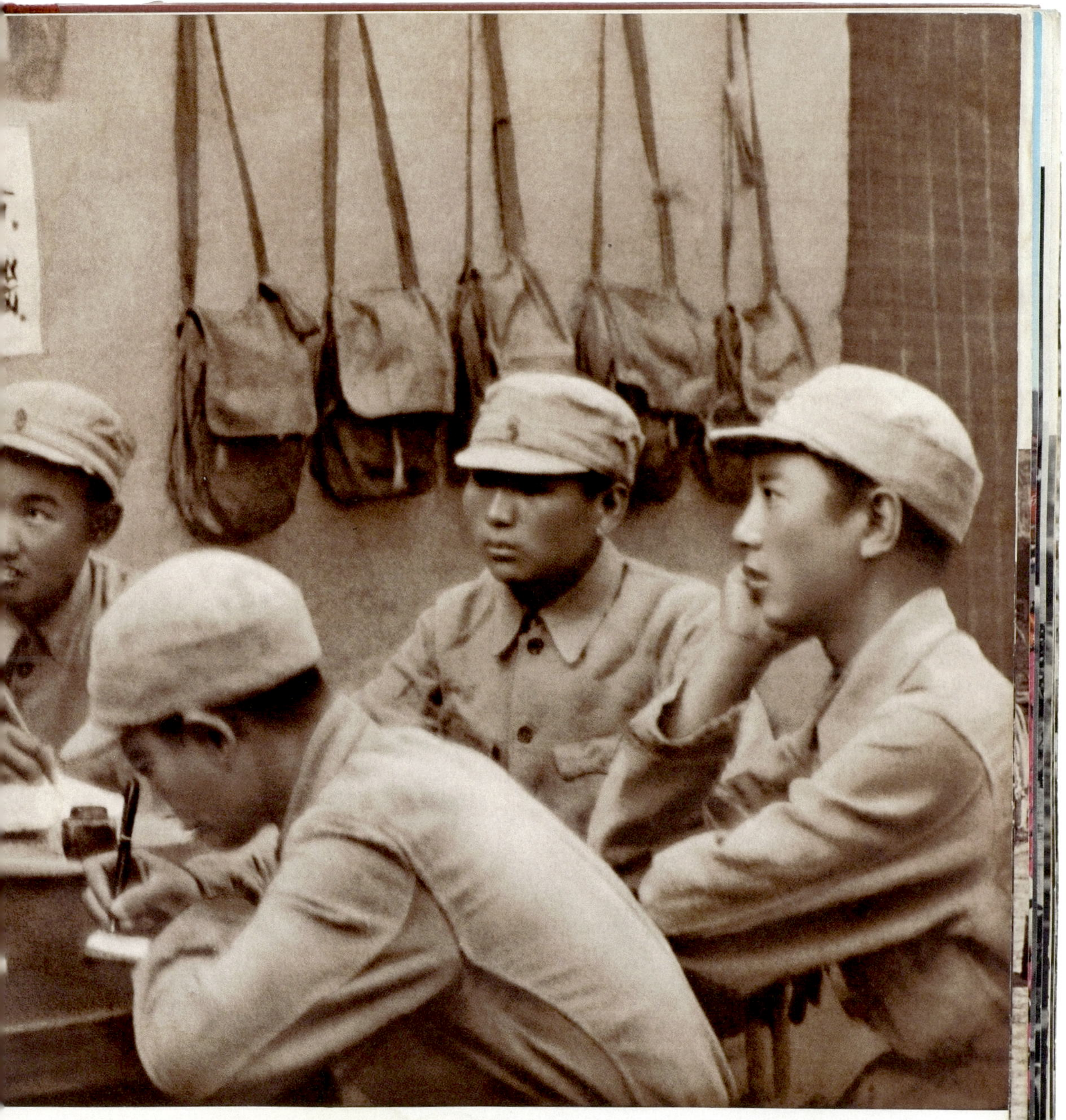

认真学习马克思主义、列宁主义、毛泽东思想

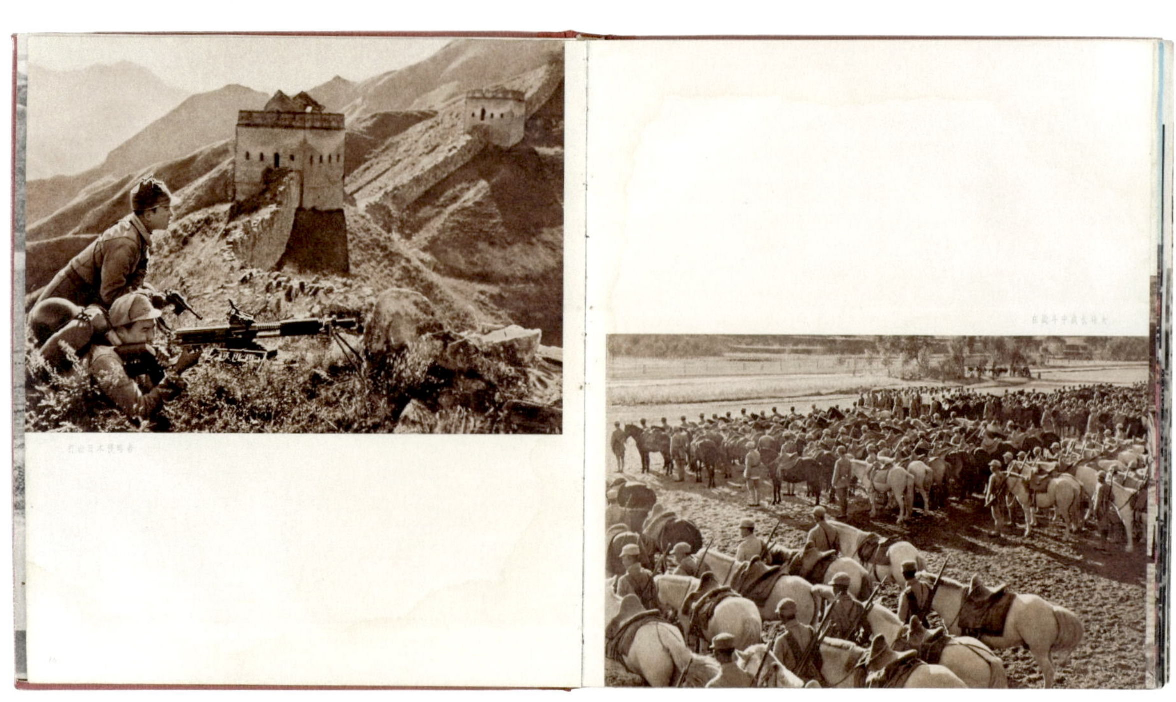

plate 12 (Left) 打击日本侵略者 - Fight Against the Japanese Invaders (Right) 在战斗中成长壮大 - Growing Strong During the War

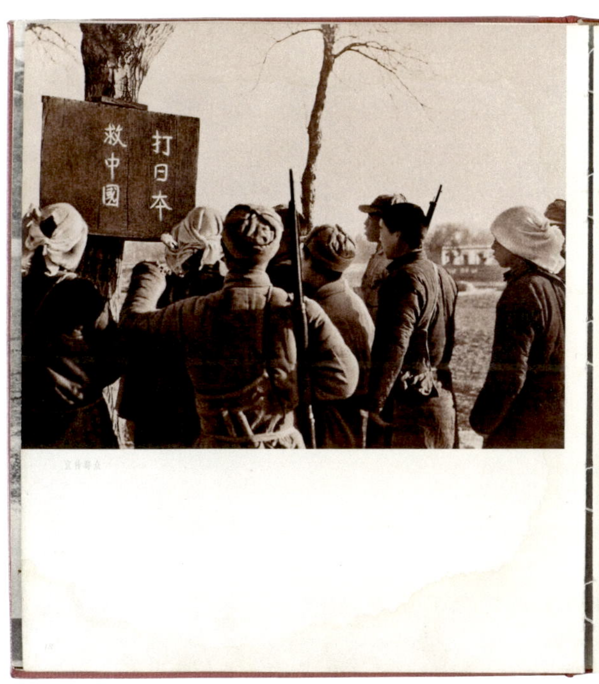

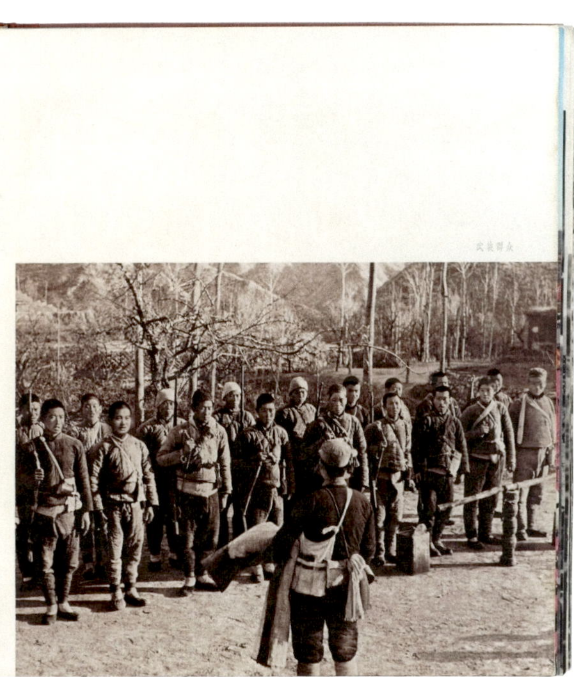

plate 13 (Left) 宣传群众 - Propagandize Among the Masses (Right) 武装群众 - Arming the Masses

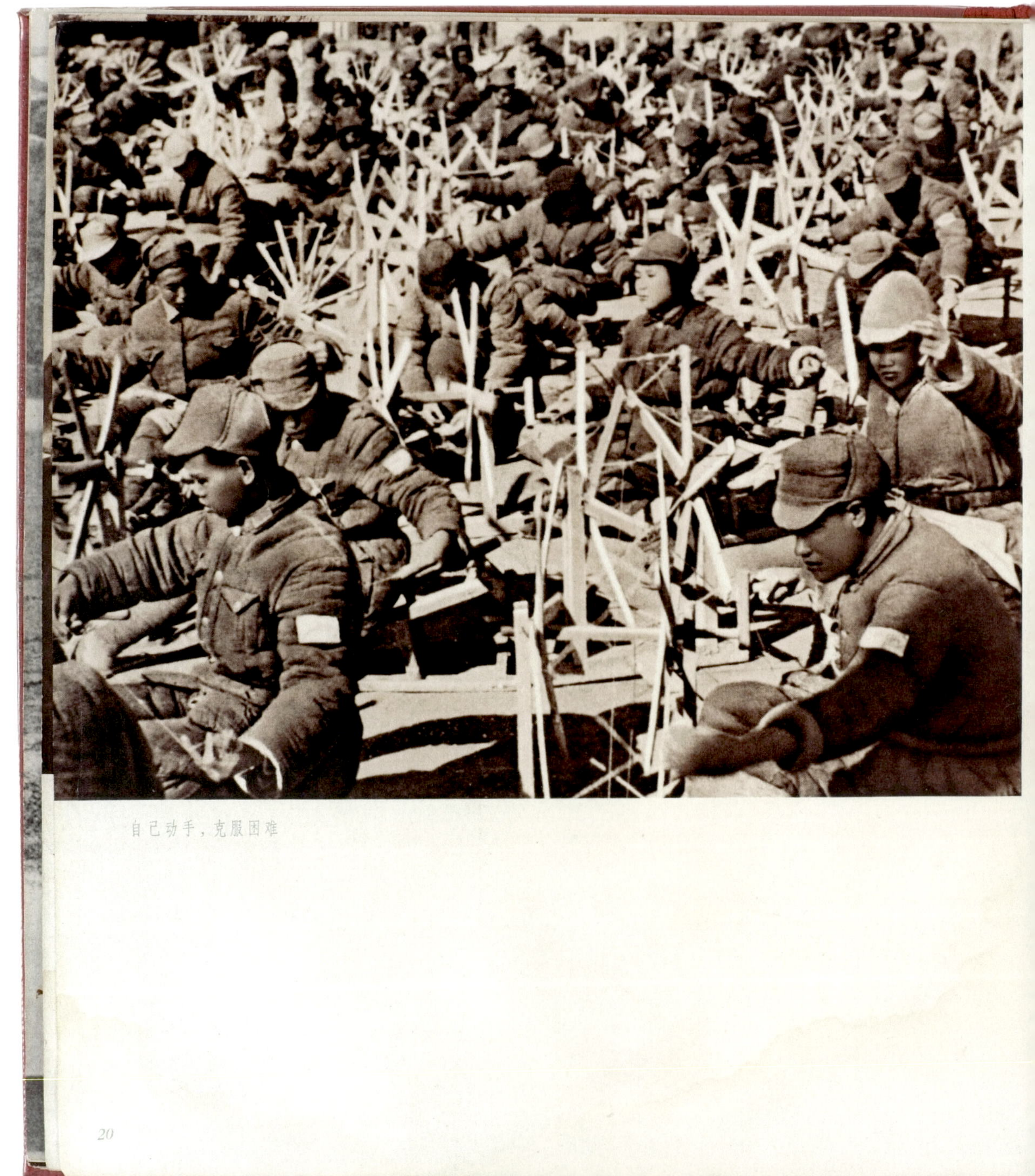

plate 14 (Above) 自己动手, 克服困难 - Do It Yourself and Overcome Hardship (Opposite) 自力更生, 制造武器 - Produce Weapons Through Self-Reliance

自力更生，制造武器

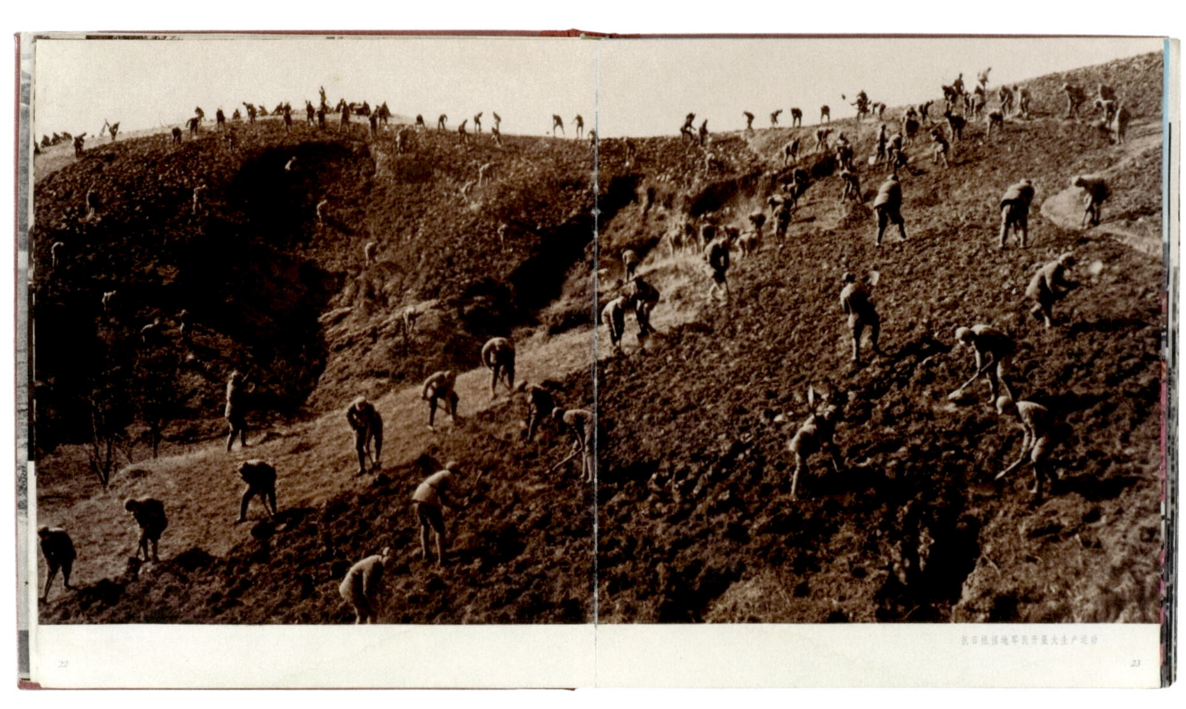

plate 15 抗日根据地军民开展大生产运动 - The Soldiers and the People Are Carrying Out the “Large-Scale Production Campaign” at the Anti-Japanese Base Area

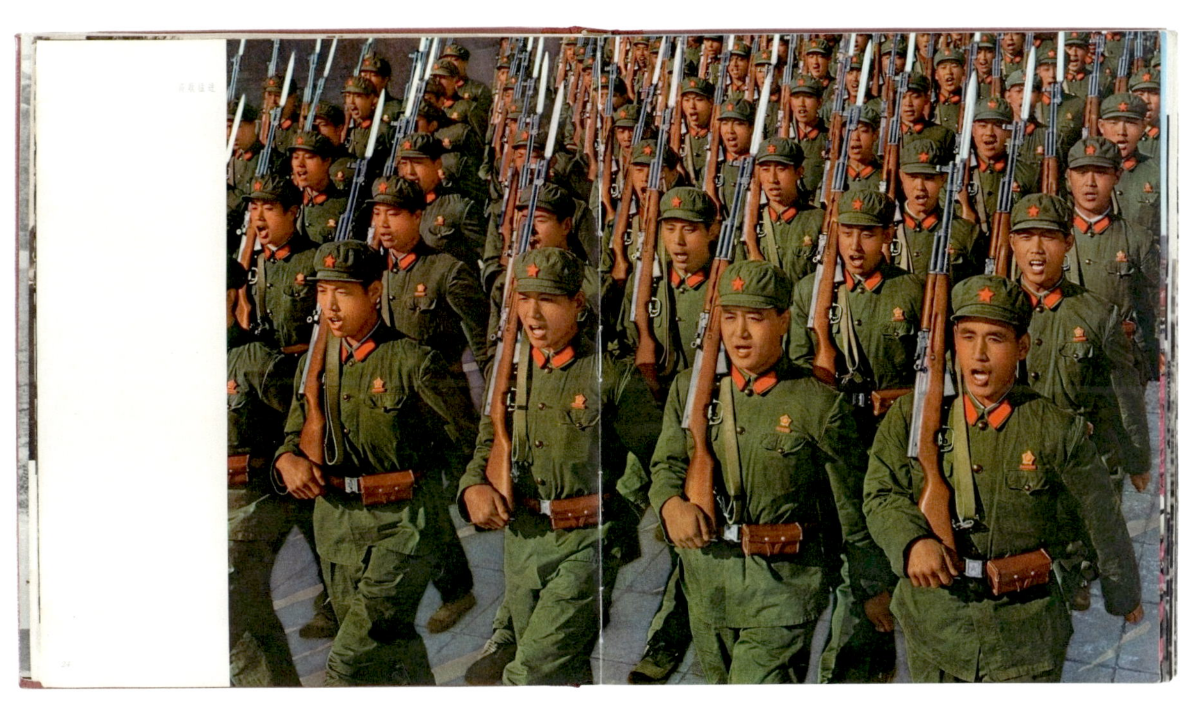

plate 16　　高歌猛进 - Advancing Triumphantly

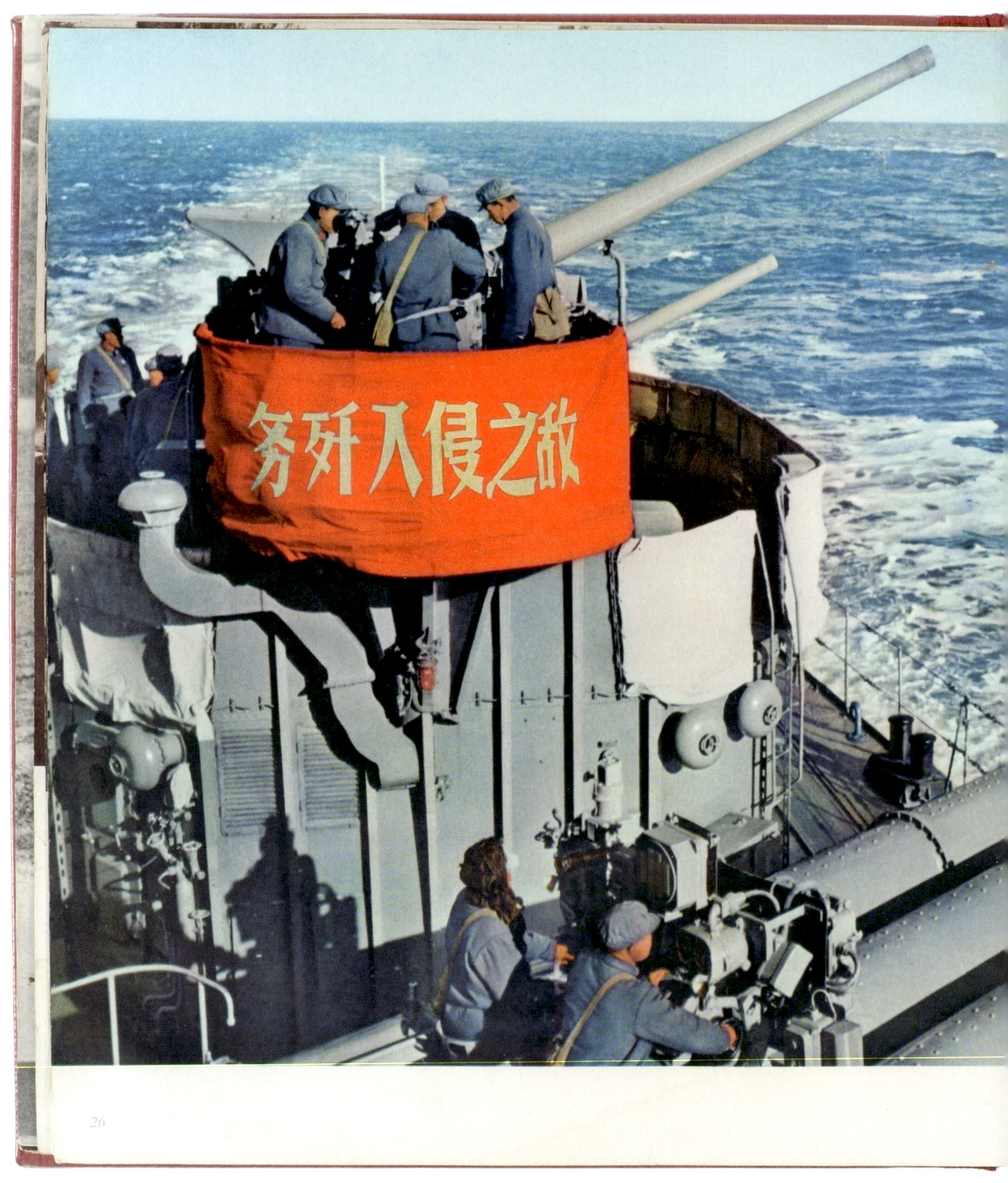

plate 17 乘风破浪 - Braving the Wind and the Waves

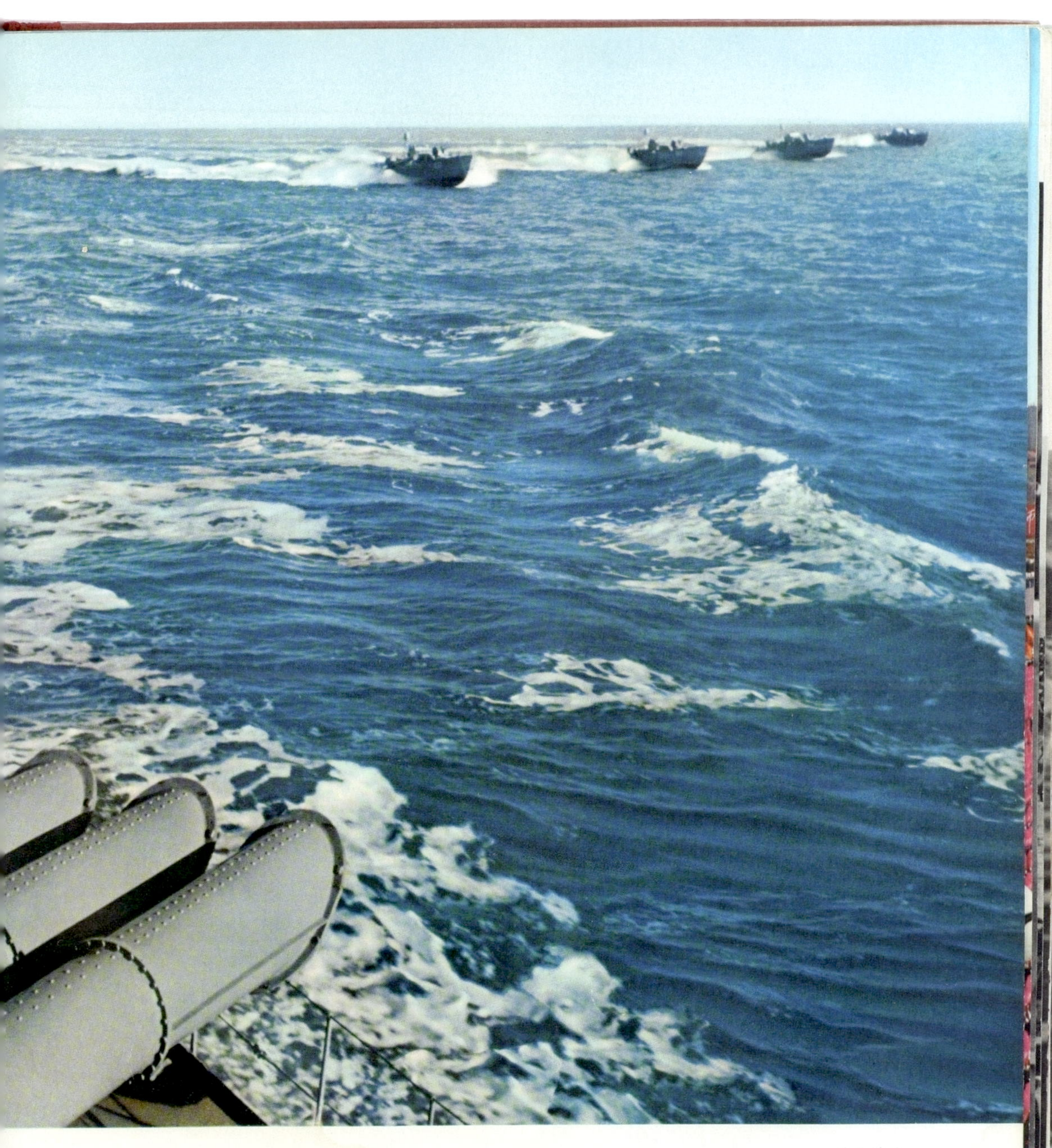

乘风破浪

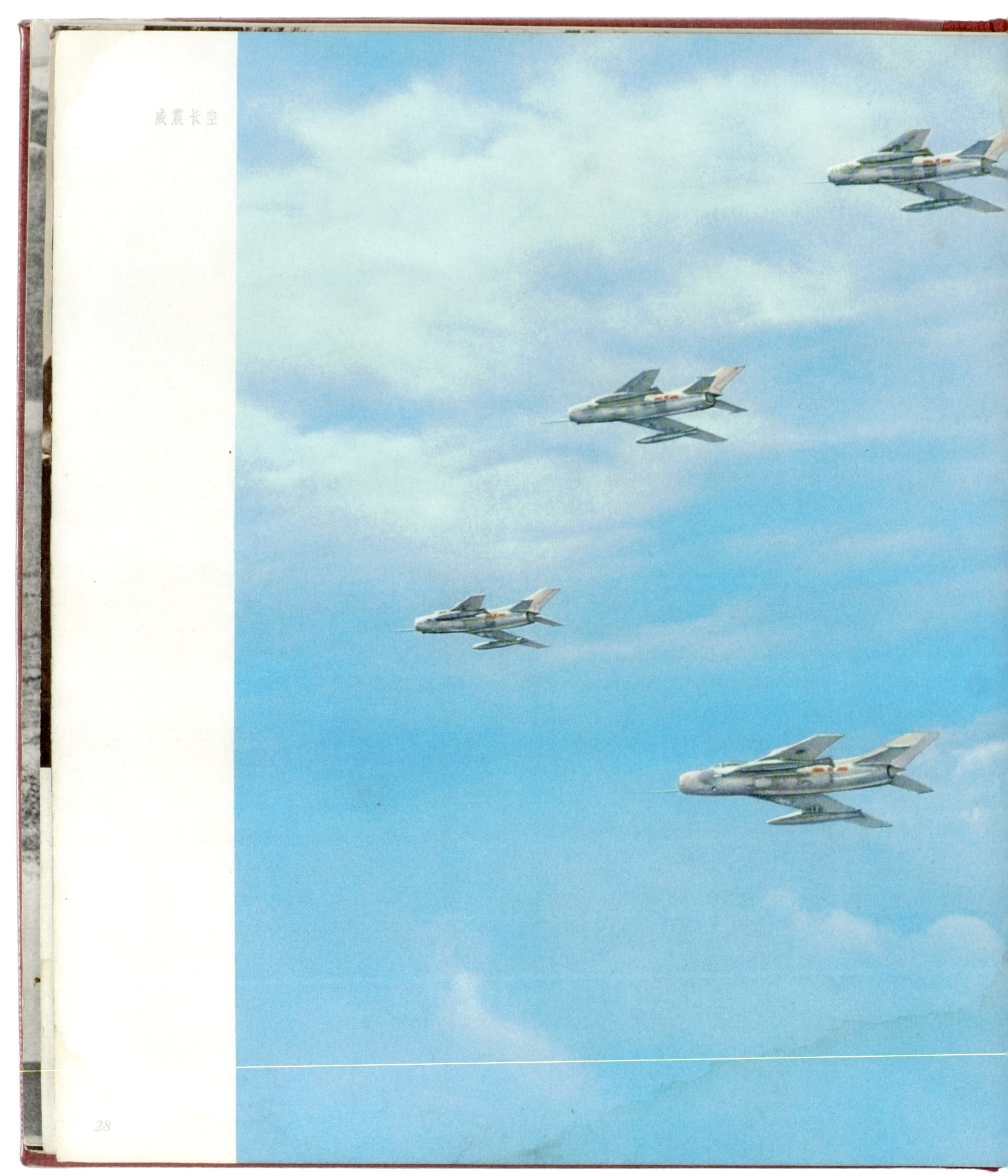

plate 18　威震长空 - Shock the Sky

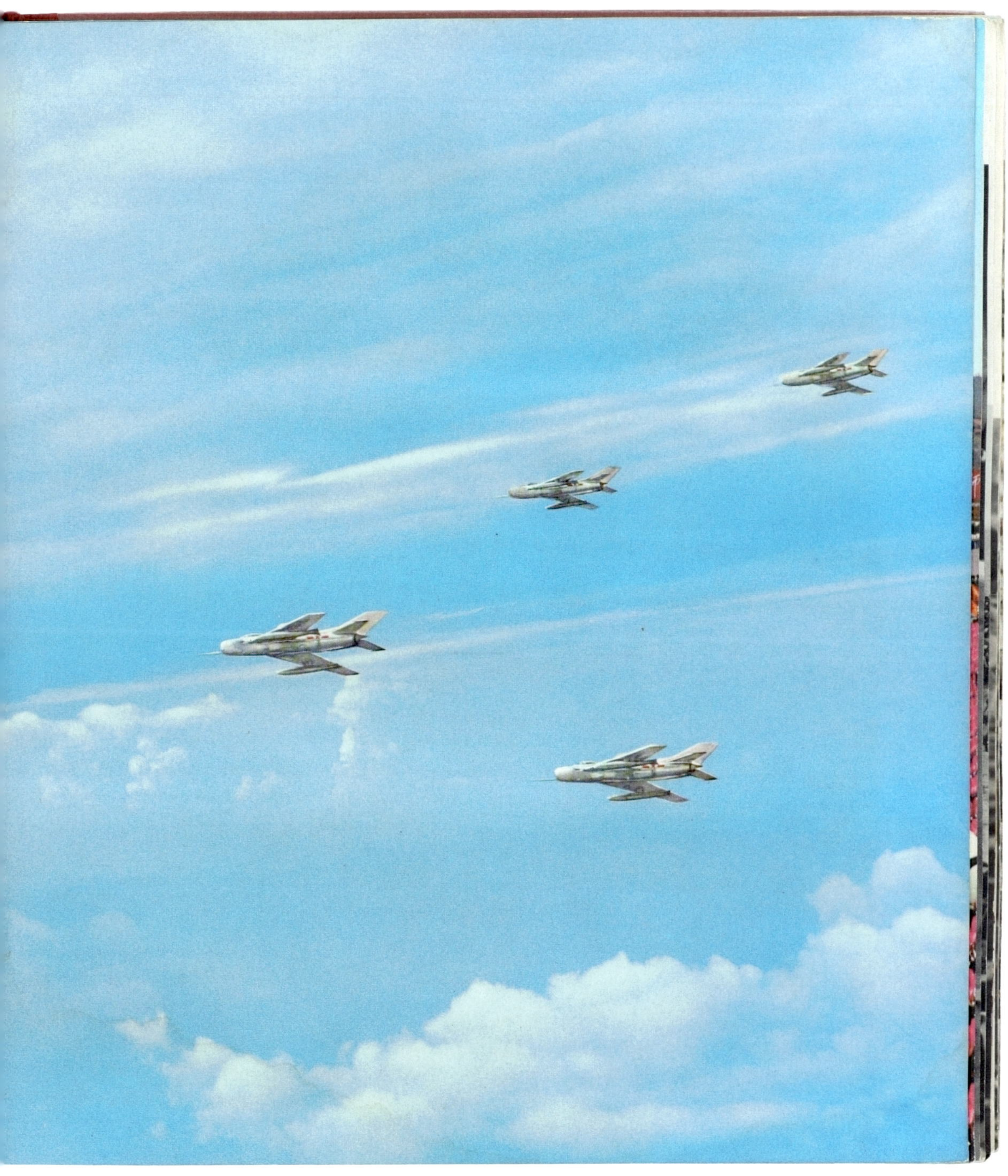

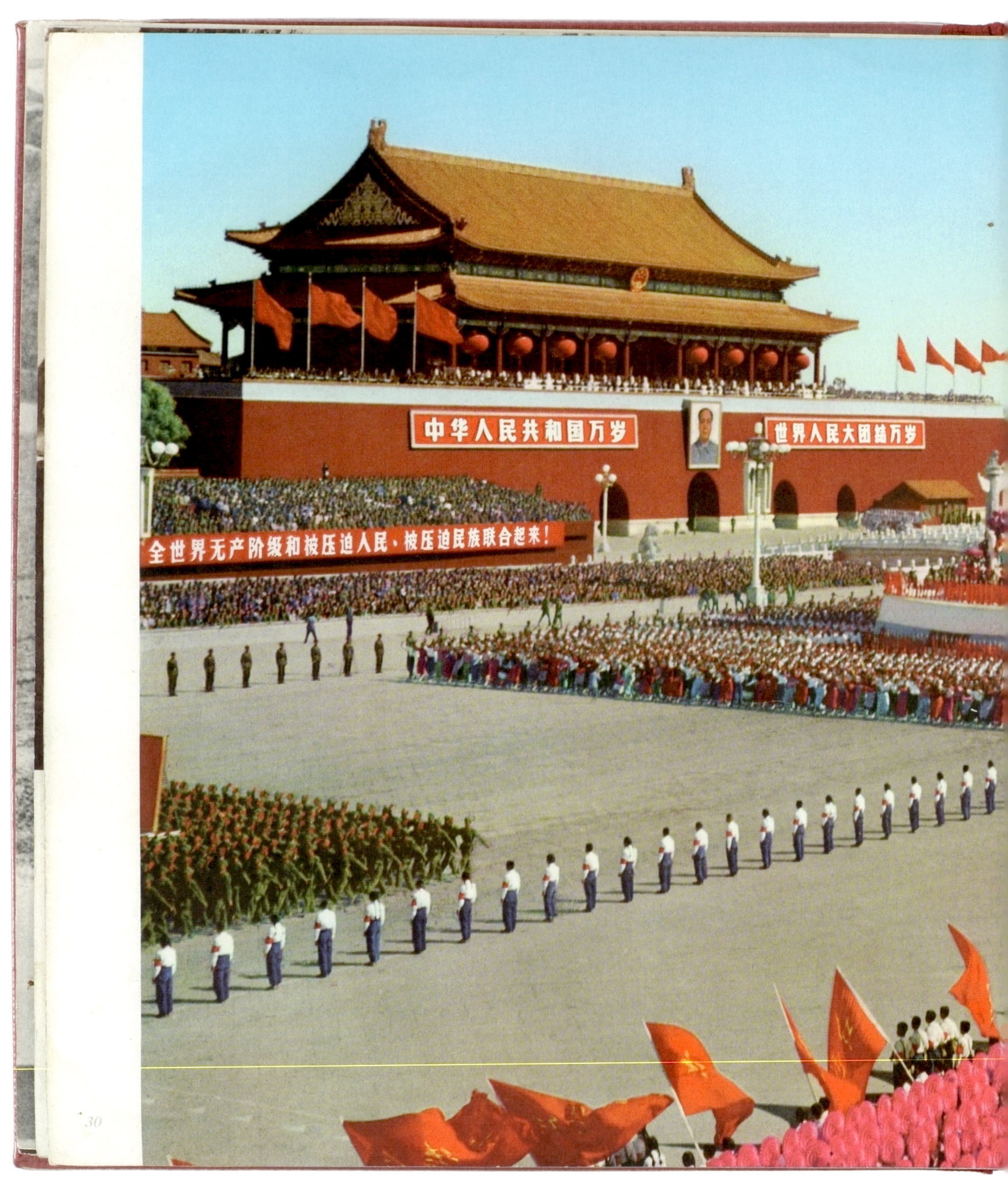

plate 19 高举"九大"团结胜利的旗帜，奋勇前进! - Hold High the United Victory Banner of the Ninth National Congress of the Communist Party of China and Forge Ahead!

高举"九大"团结胜利的旗帜，奋勇前进！

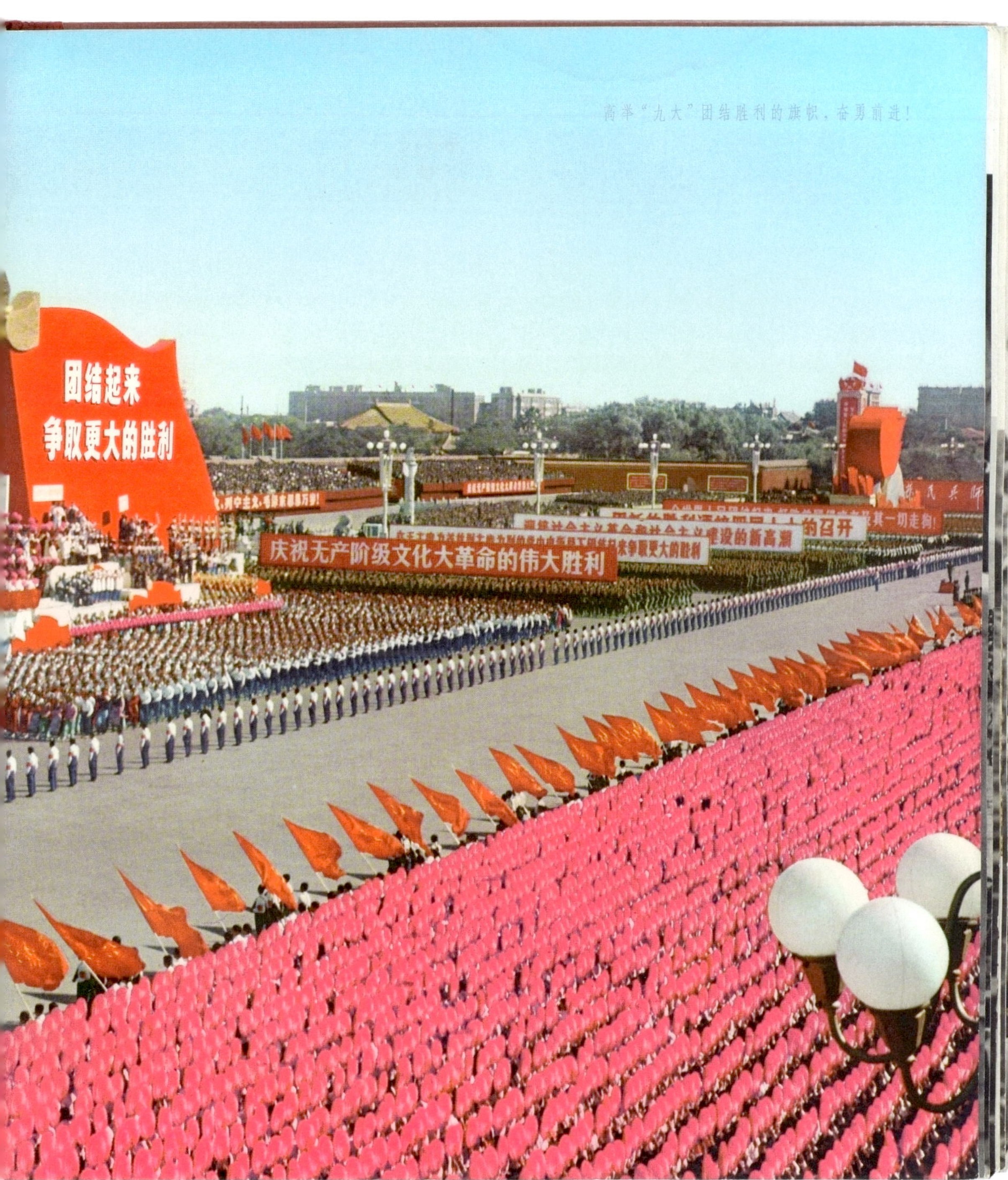

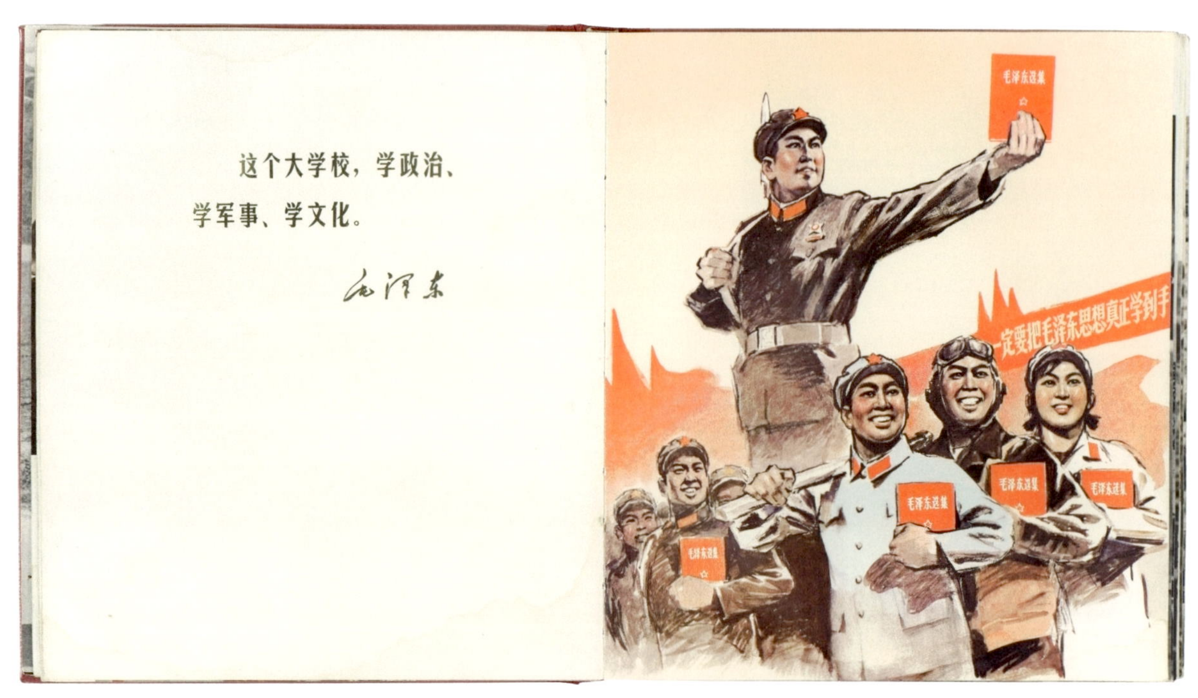

plate 20　这个大学校, 学政治, 学军事, 学文化 - In this great school, troops study politics, military affairs and culture.

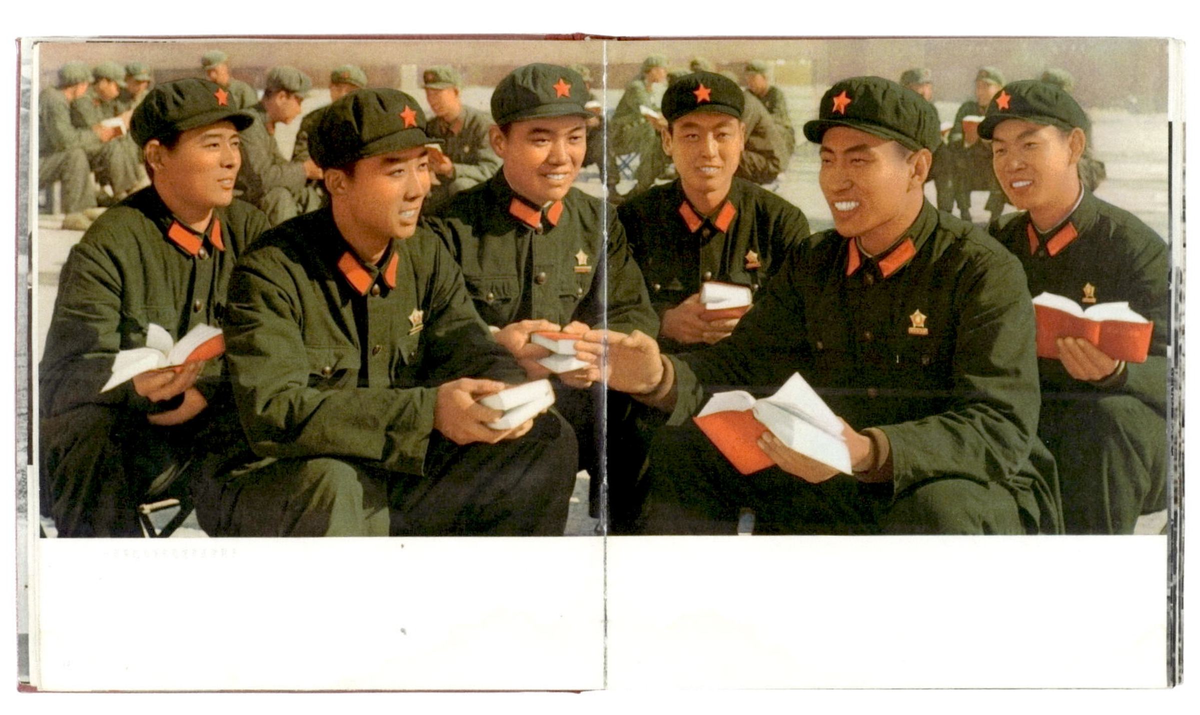

plate 21　　一定要把毛泽东思想真正学到手 - Be Determined to Master Mao Zedong's Thought

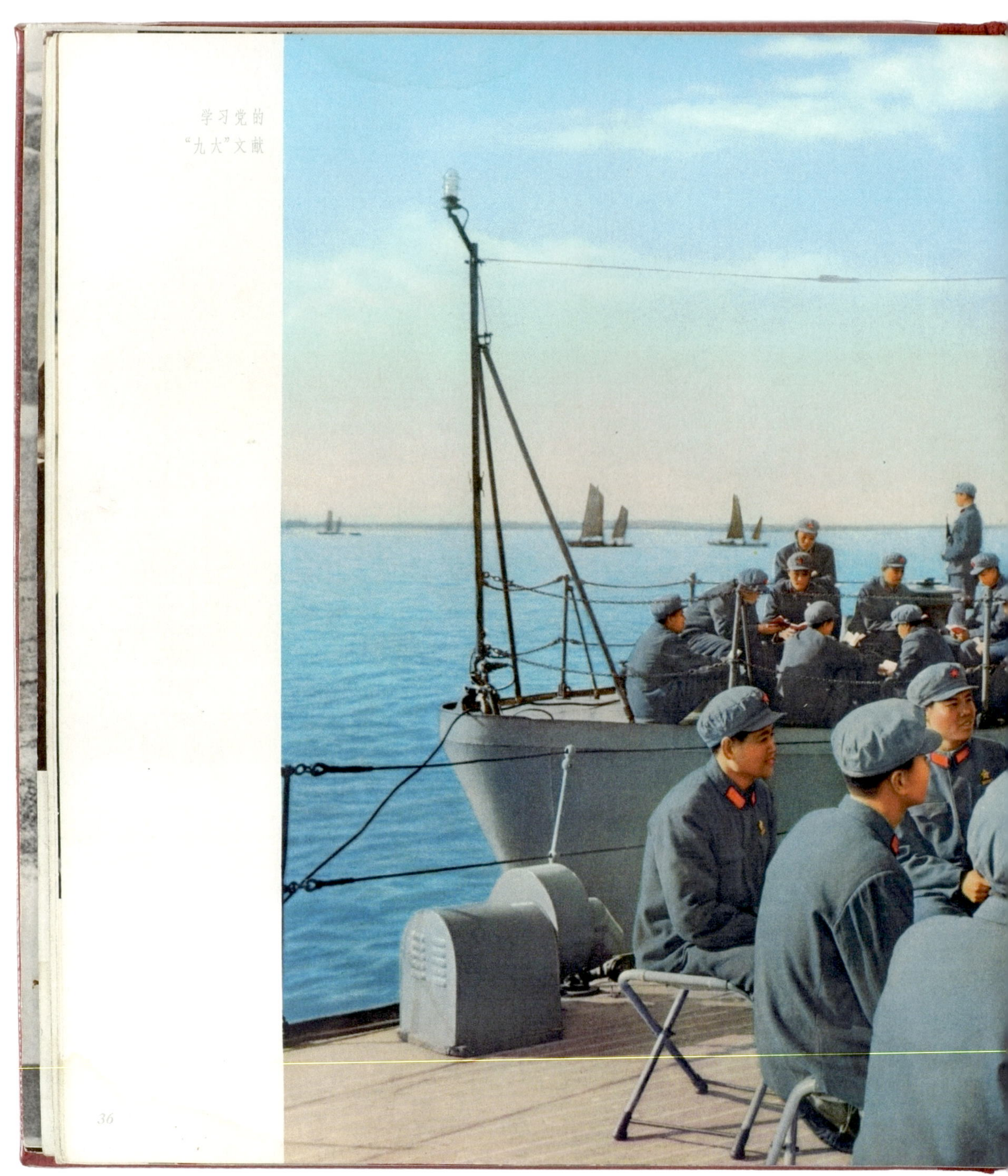

plate 22　学习党的“九大”文献 - Studying the Archive of the Ninth National Congress of the Communist Party of China

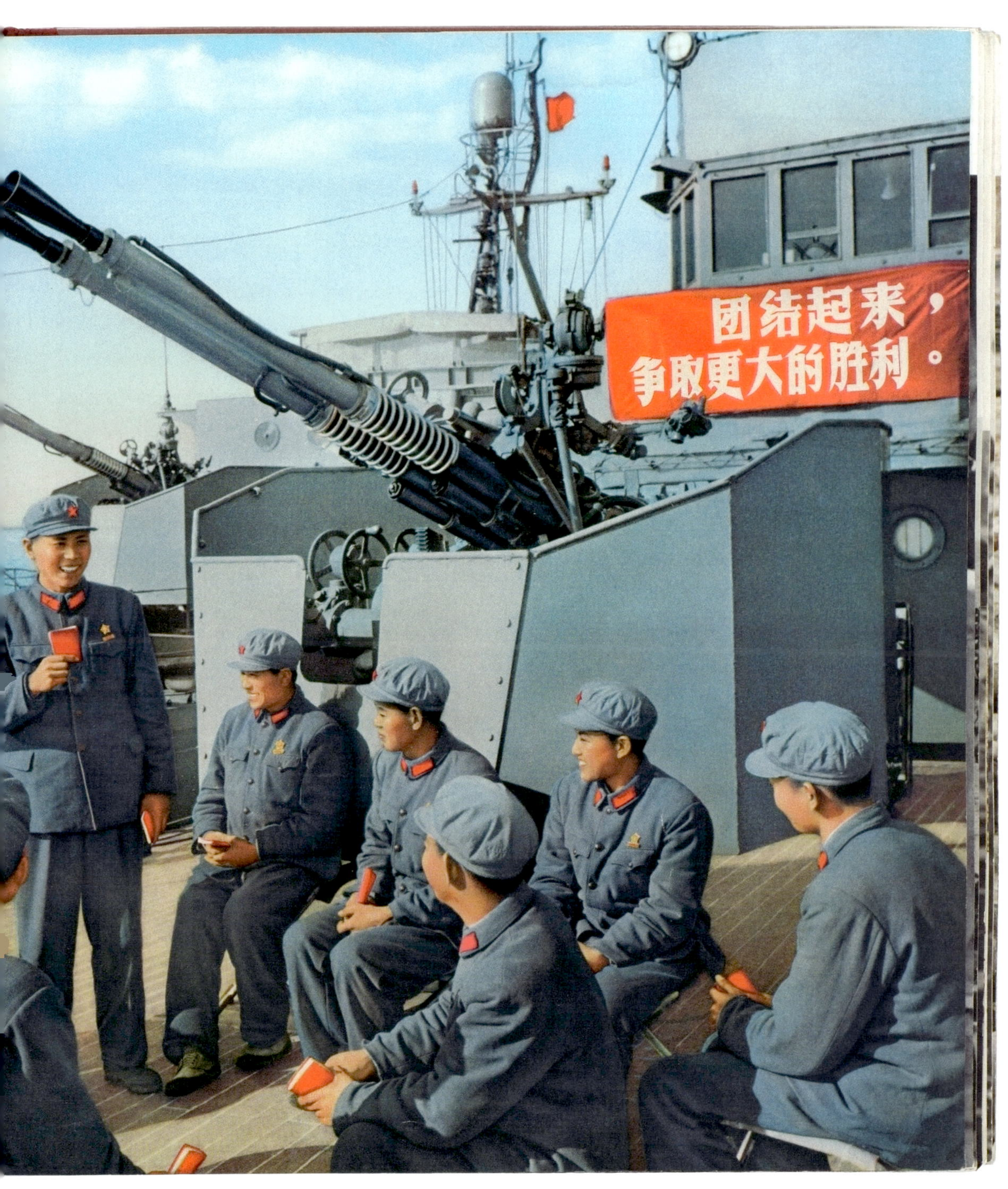
团结起来，
争取更大的胜利。

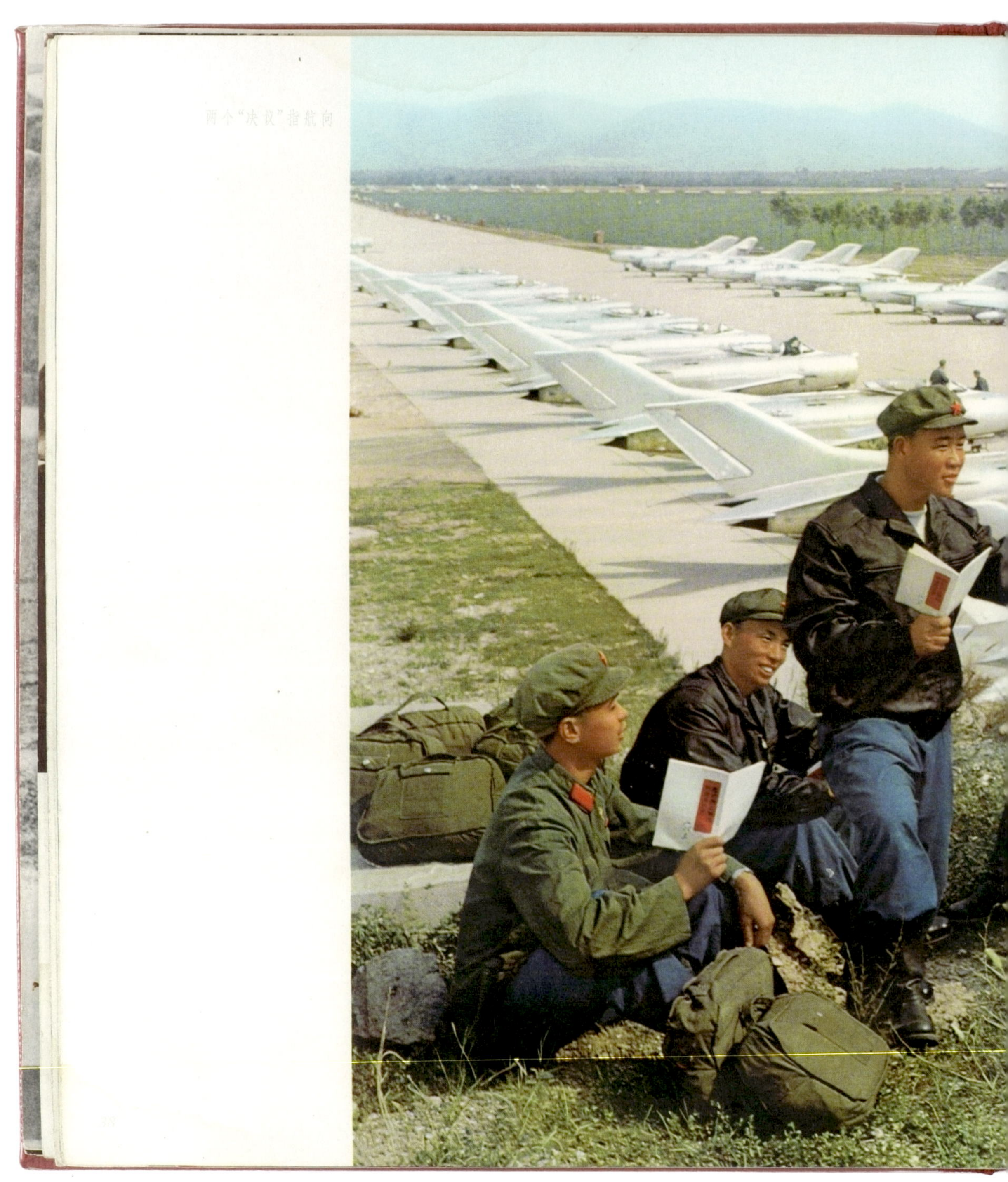

plate 23　两个"决议"指航向 - Two Resolutions Point the Way

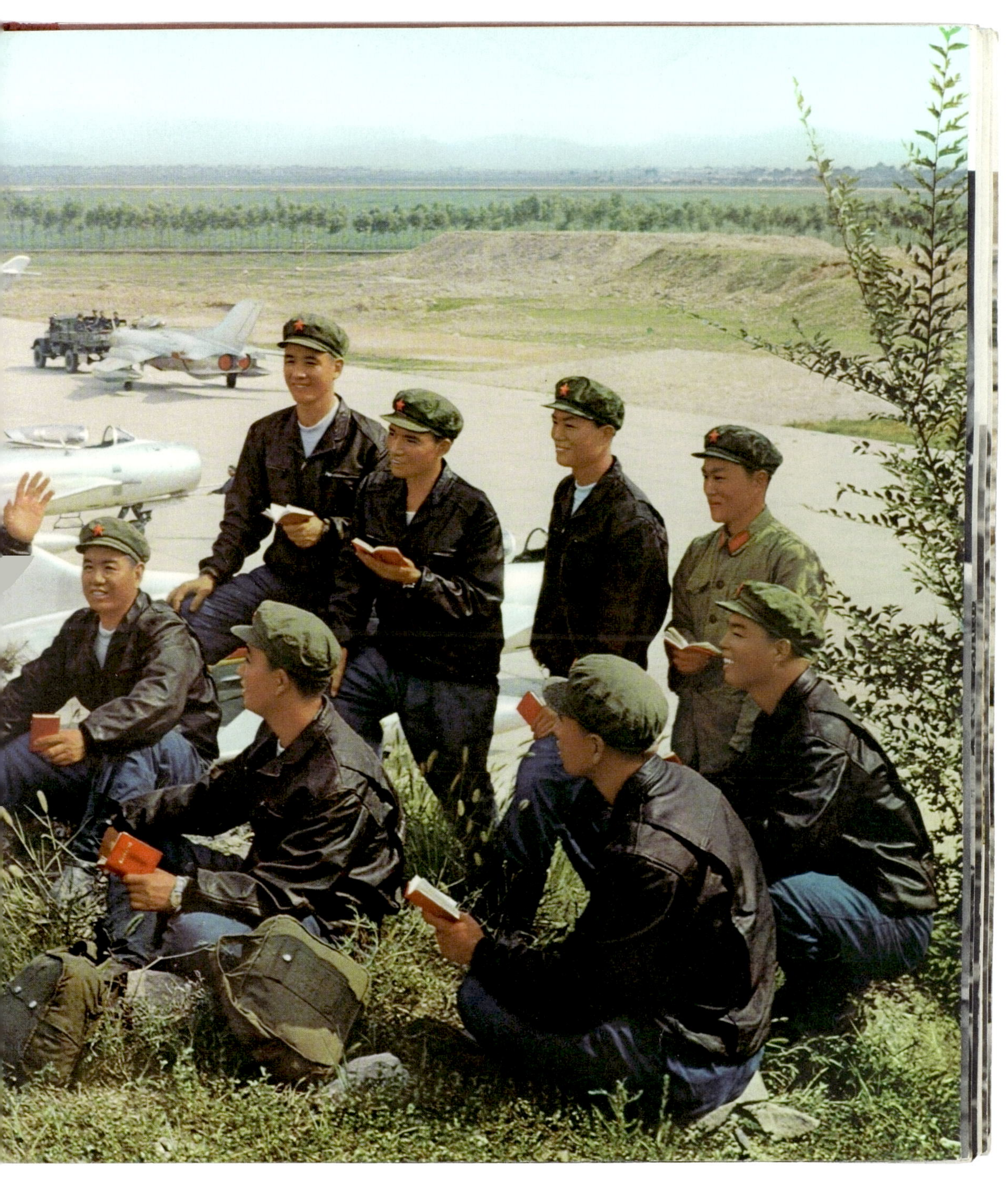

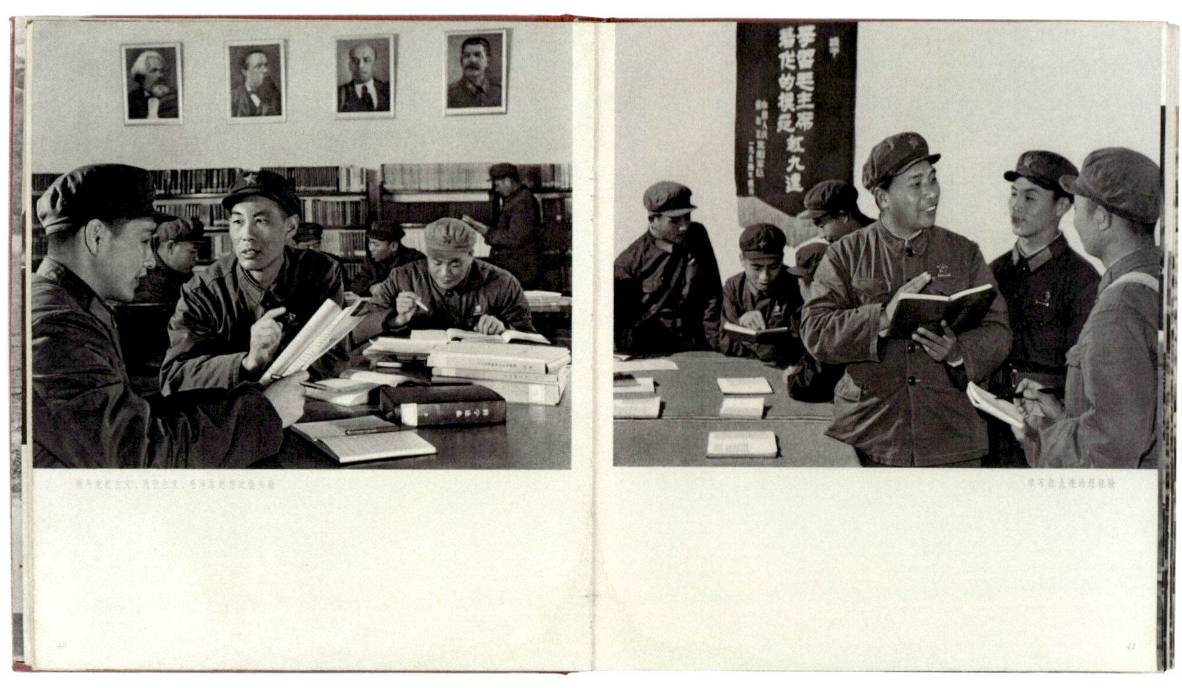

plate 24 (Left) 用马克思主义, 列宁主义, 毛泽东思想武装头脑 - Use Marxism, Leninism, and Mao Zedong Thought to Arm the Mind (Right) 学习红九连的好经验 - Studying the Good Experience of the Red Ninth Company

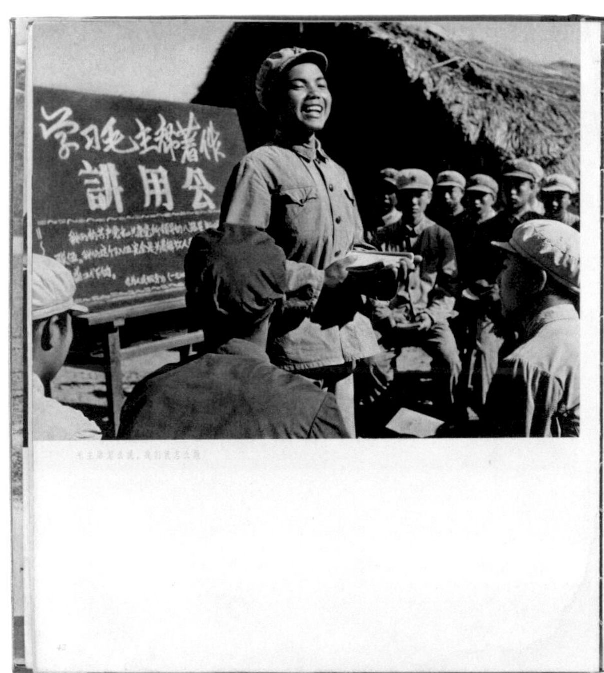

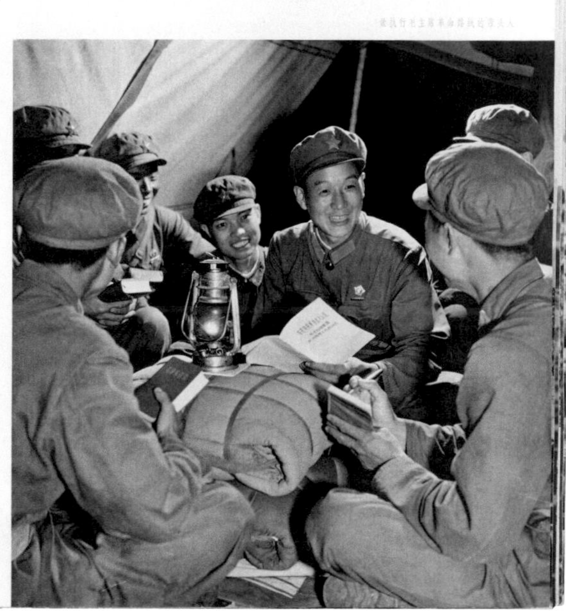

plate 25 (Left) 毛主席怎么说，我们就怎么做 - We Do Just as Chairman Mao Says (Right) 做执行毛主席革命路线的带头人 - Be a Leader in Executing Chairman Mao's Revolutionary Line

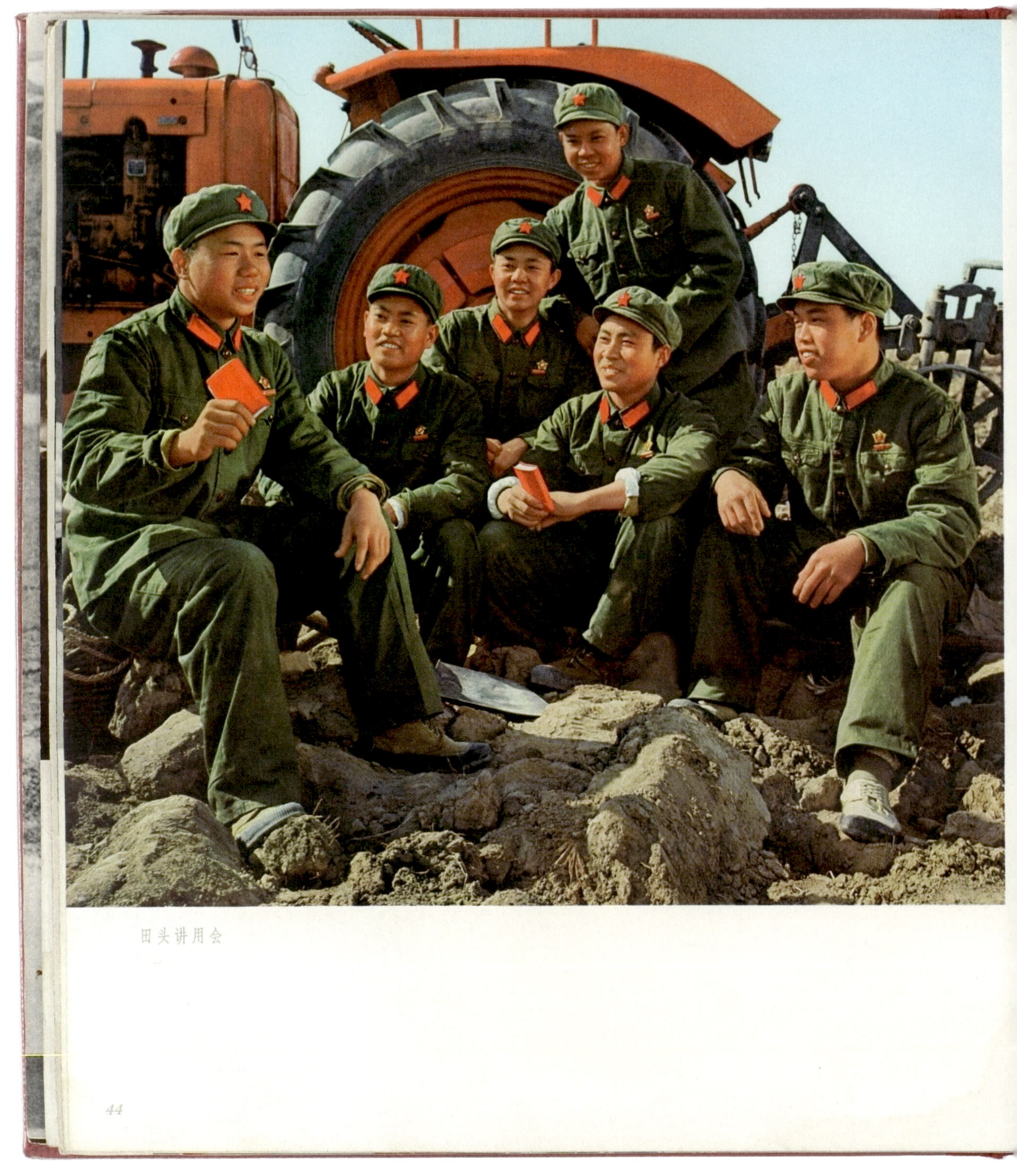

plate 26 (Above) 田头讲用会 - "Experience Exchange Meeting" in the Field (Opposite) 毛主席语录随身带, 随时学, 随时用 - Carry Chairman Mao's "Little Red Book" Wherever You Go, That You May Study It Whenever, and for All Occasions

毛主席语录随身带，随时学，随时用

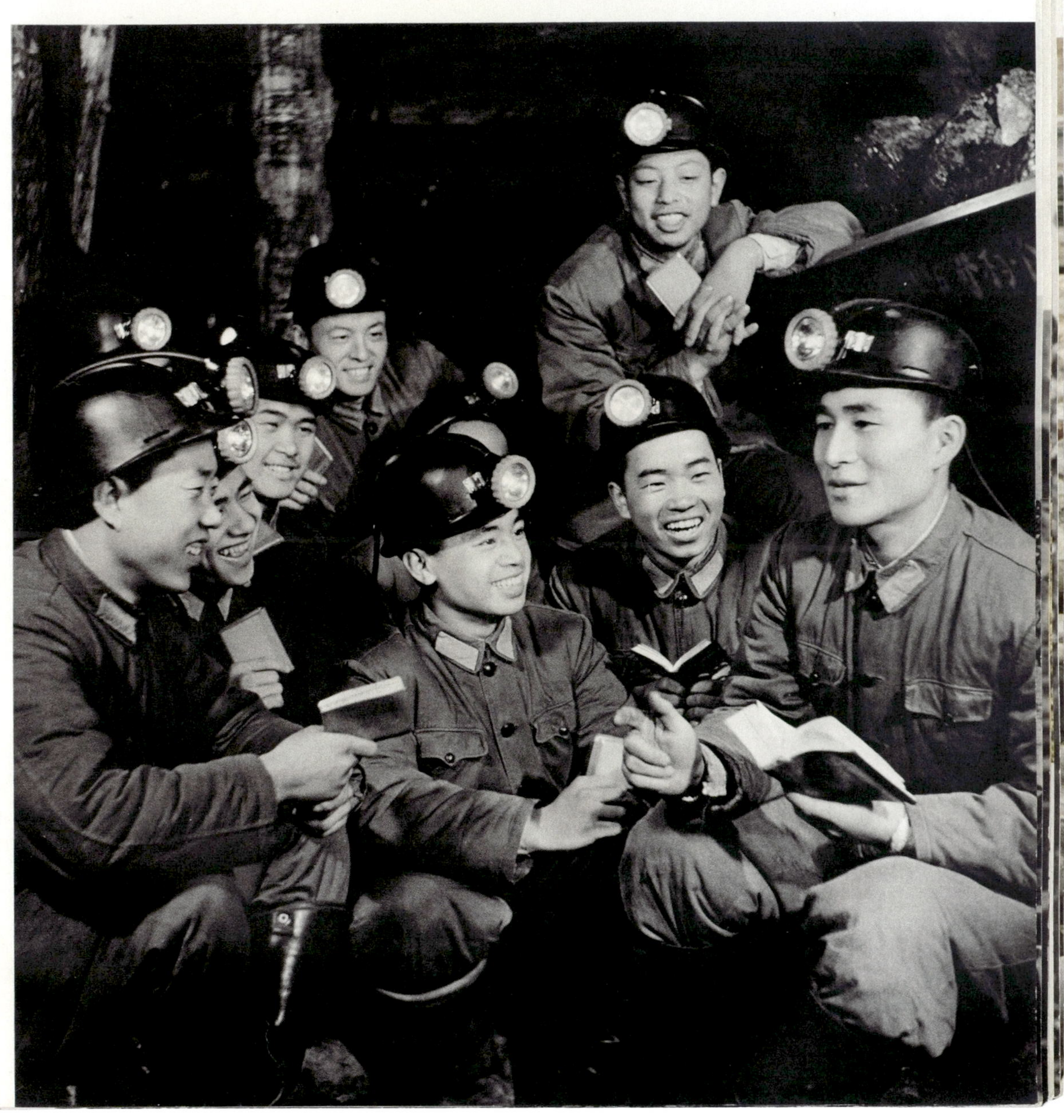

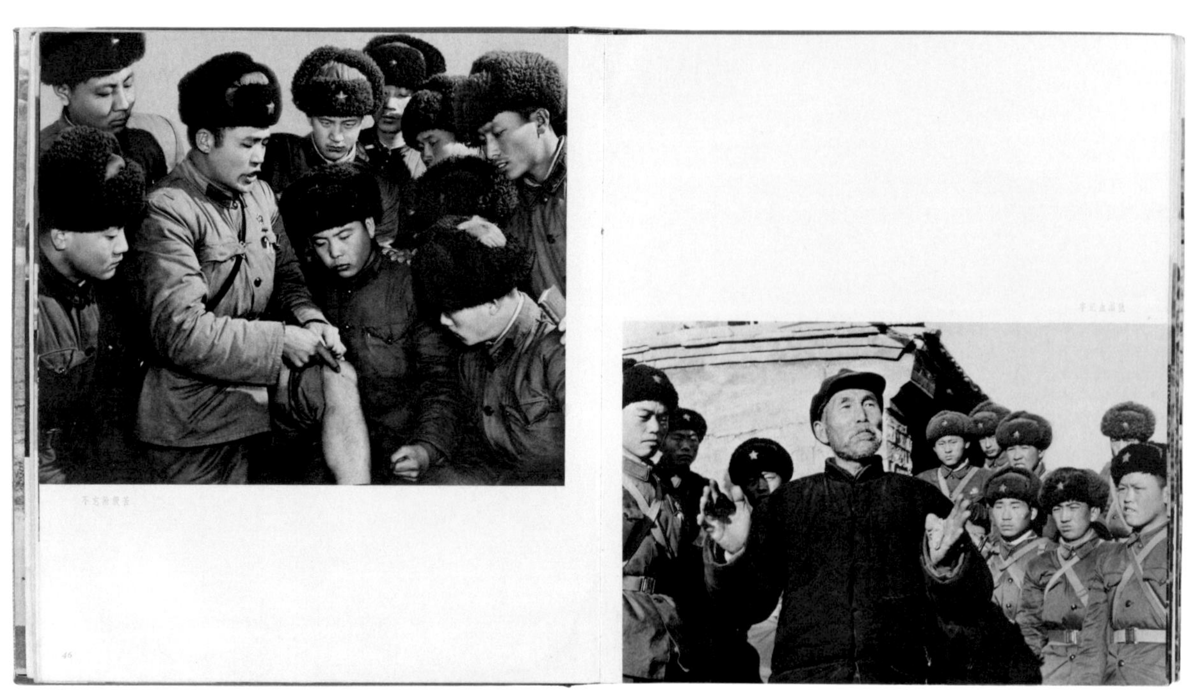

plate 27 (Left) 不忘阶级苦 - Never Forget Class Hardship (Right) 牢记血泪仇 - Always Remember the Enmity of Blood and Tears

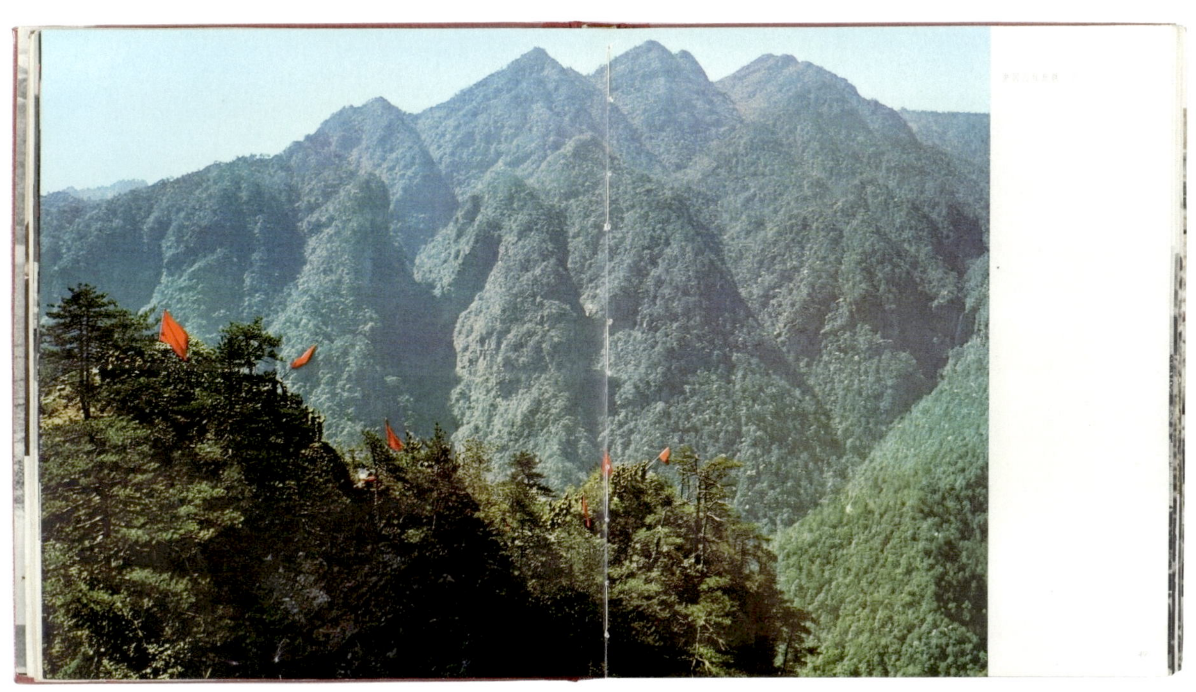

plate 28 井冈山红旗飘万代 - The Red Flags on Jinggang Mountain Flutter Forever

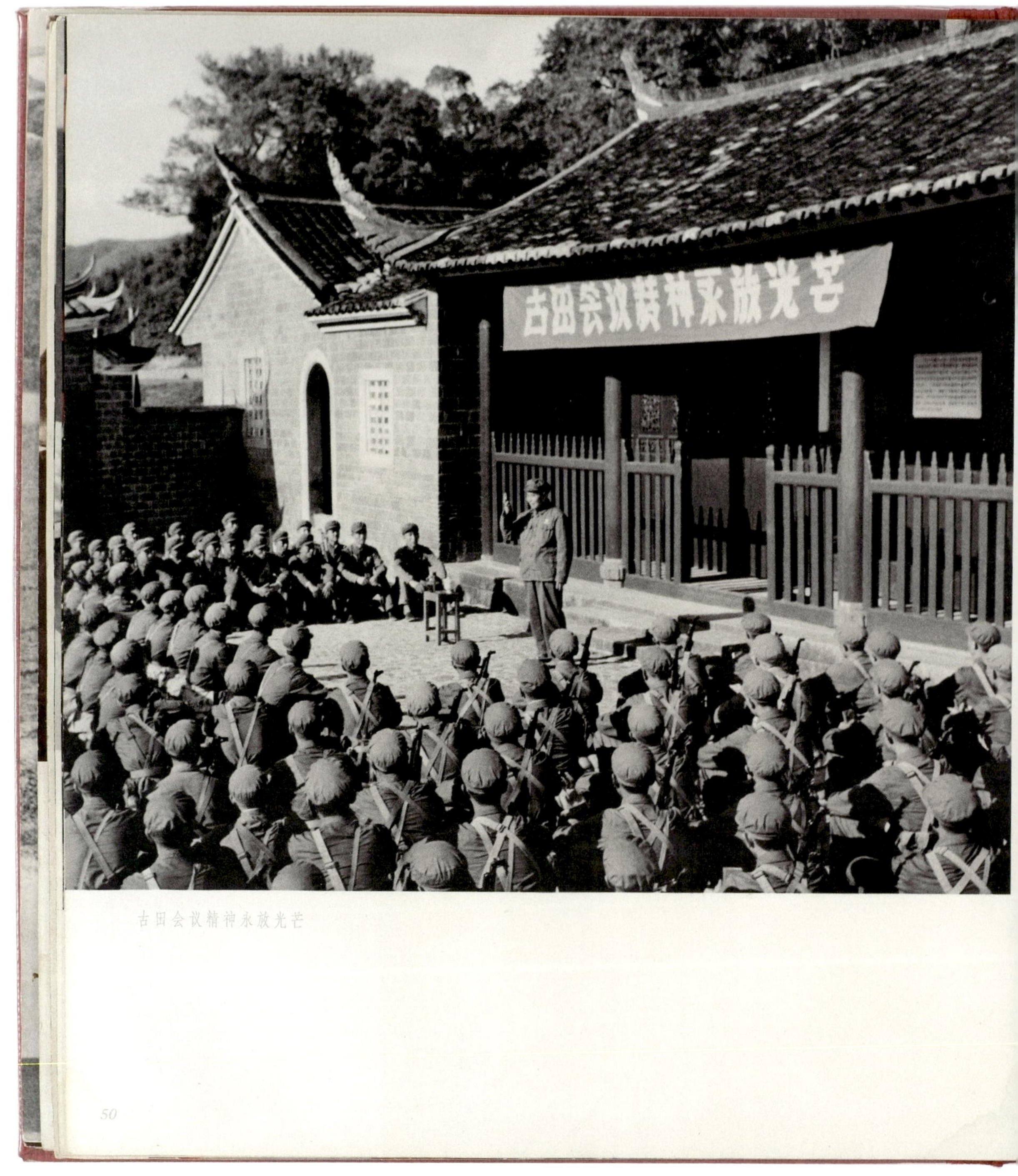

古田会议精神永放光芒

plate 29 (Above) 古田会议精神永放光芒 - The Spirit of the Gutian Meeting Shines Forever (Opposite) 老民兵讲革命传统 - An Old Militiaman Talks About the Revolutionary Tradition

老民兵讲革命传统

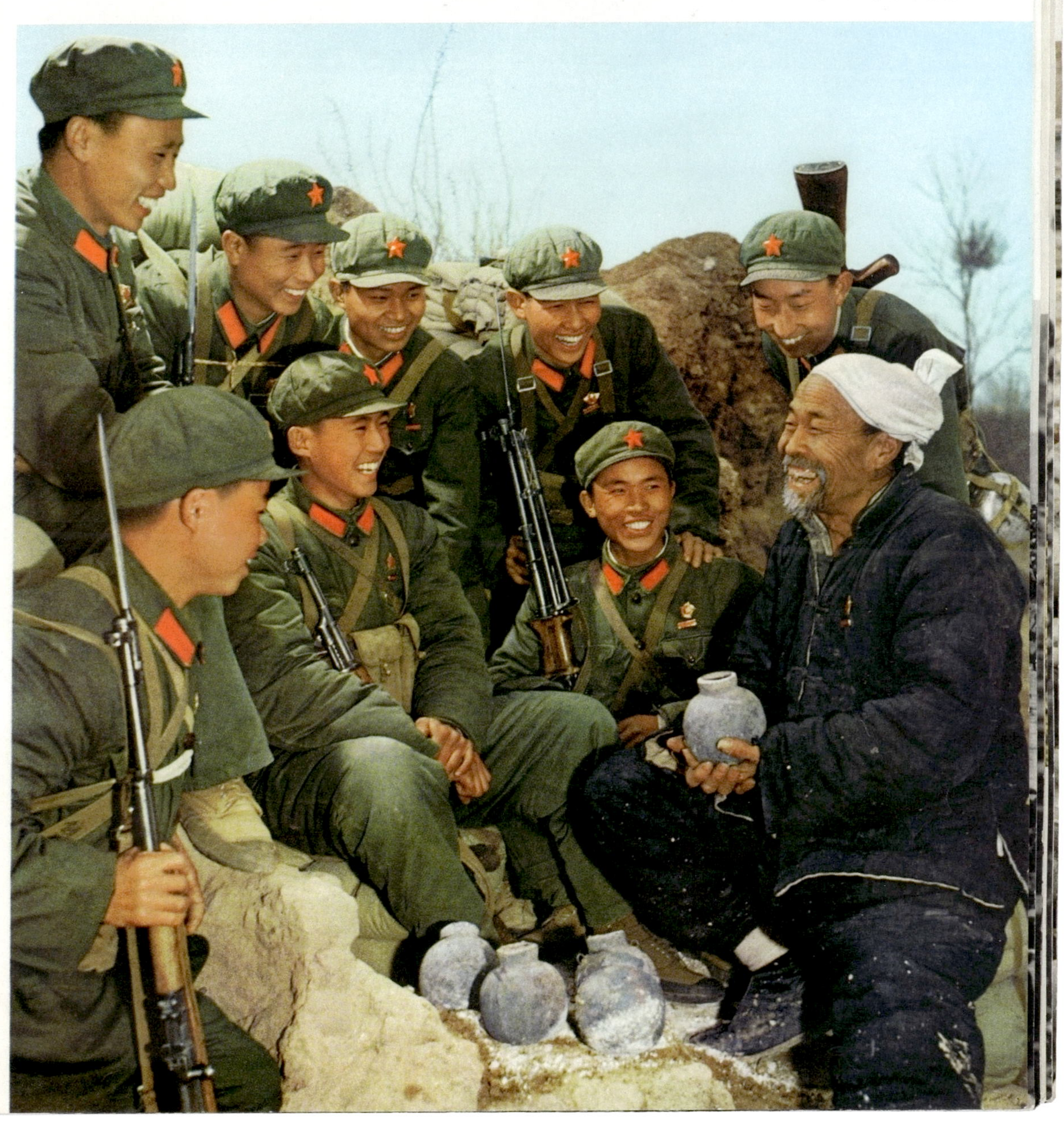

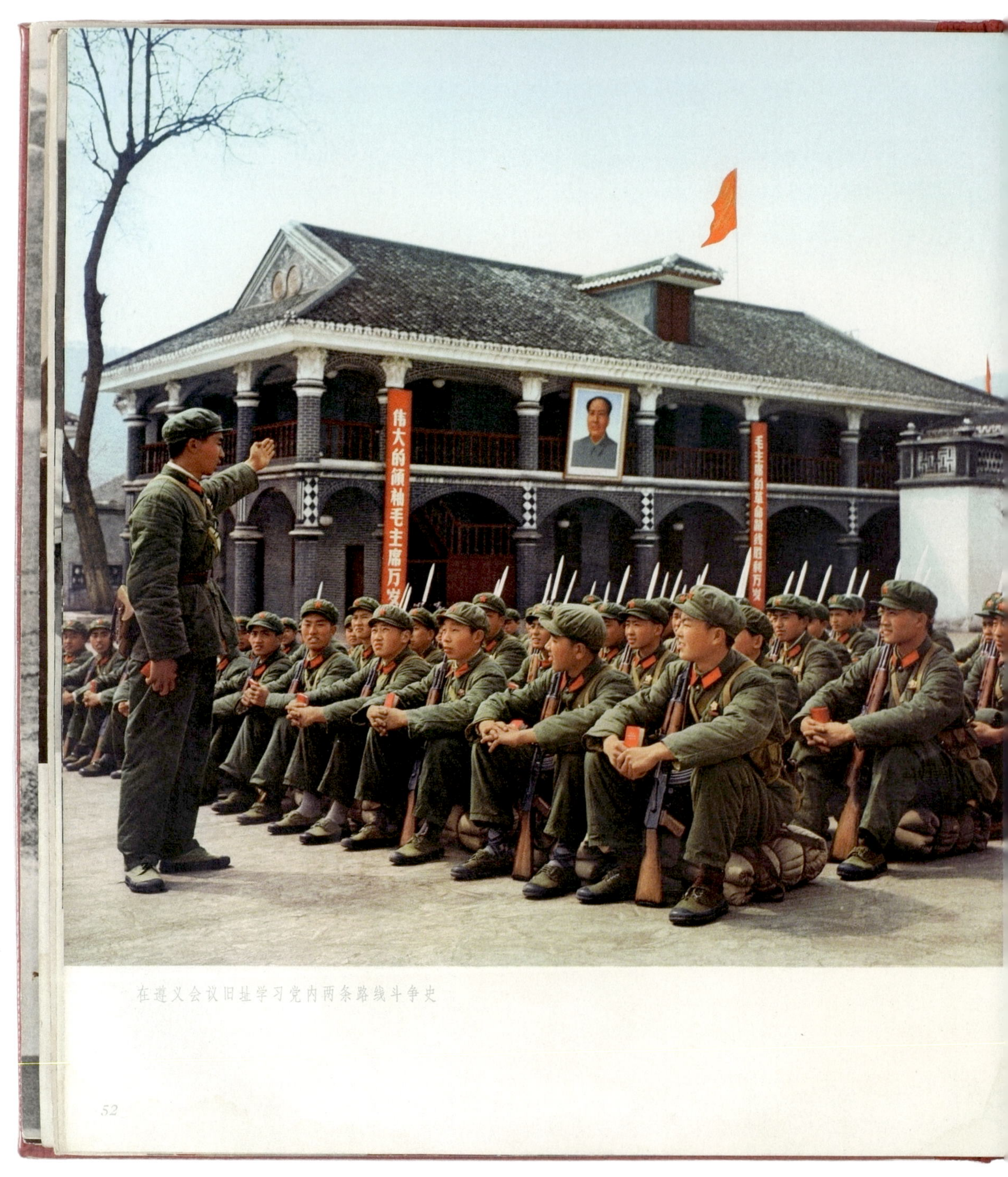

plate 30 (Above) 在遵义会议旧址学习党内两条路线斗争史 - Studying the History of the "Two Line" Struggle Within the Party at the Site of the Zunyi Meeting (Opposite) 誓攀新高峰 - Vow to Reach New Heights

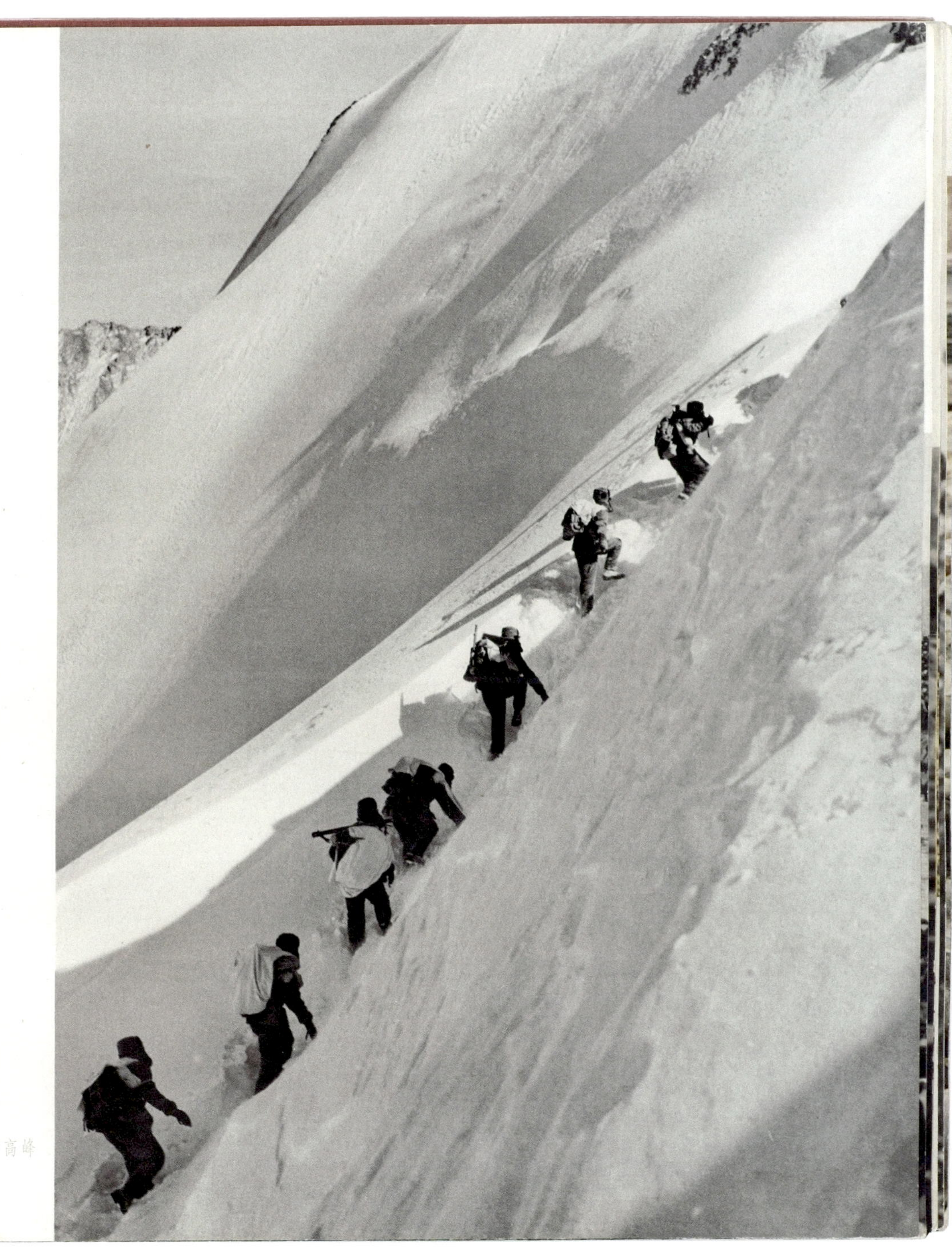

誓攀新高峰

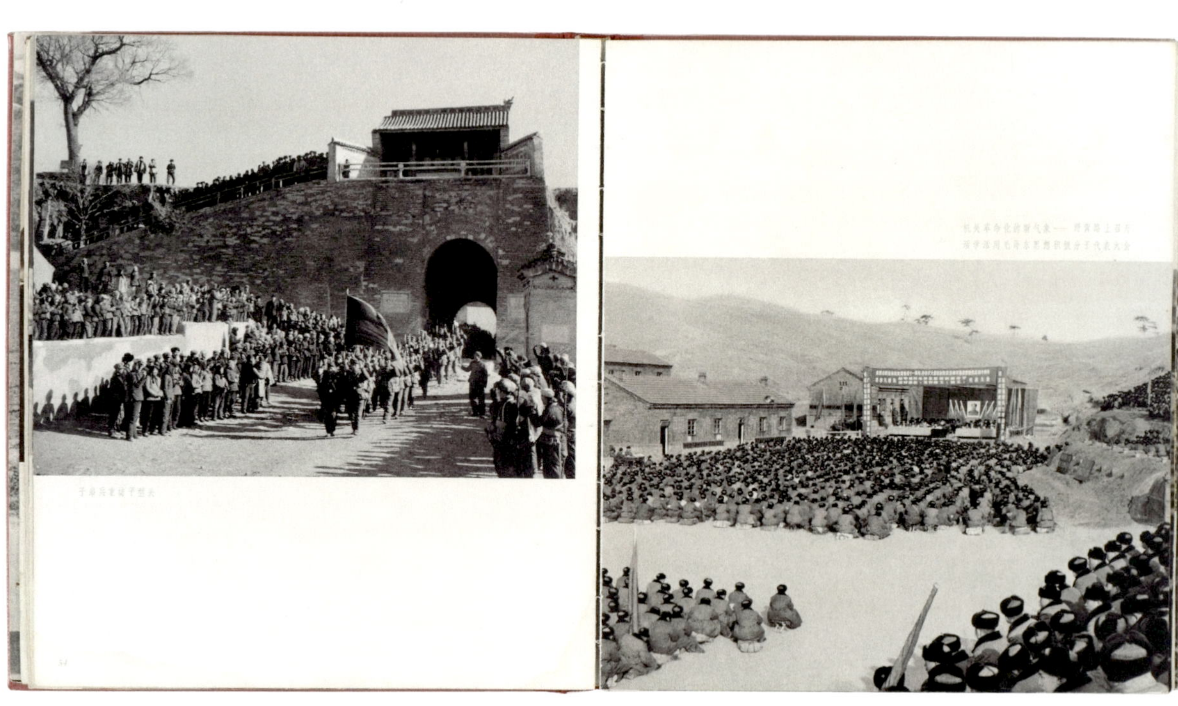

plate 31 (Left) 子弟兵重访平型关 - PLA Soldiers Revisit Pingxing Pass (Right) 机关革命化的新气象 - 野营路上召开活学活用毛泽东思想积极分子代表大会 - New Phenomenon in the Revolutionized Unit: A Meeting Is Convened on the Road to Camp for Those Exemplary Enthusiasts Who Actively Study and Apply Mao Zedong Thought

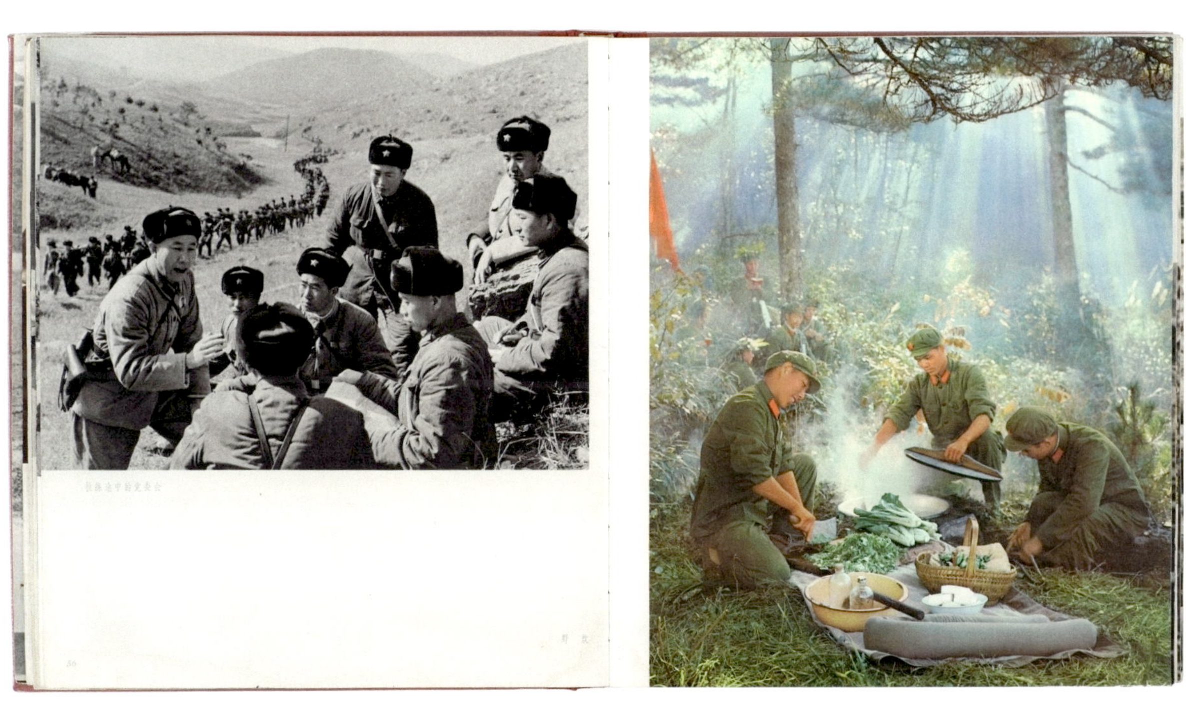

plate 32 (Left) 拉练途中的党委会 - A Party Committee Meeting on the Way to Military Training (Right) 野炊 - A Picnic

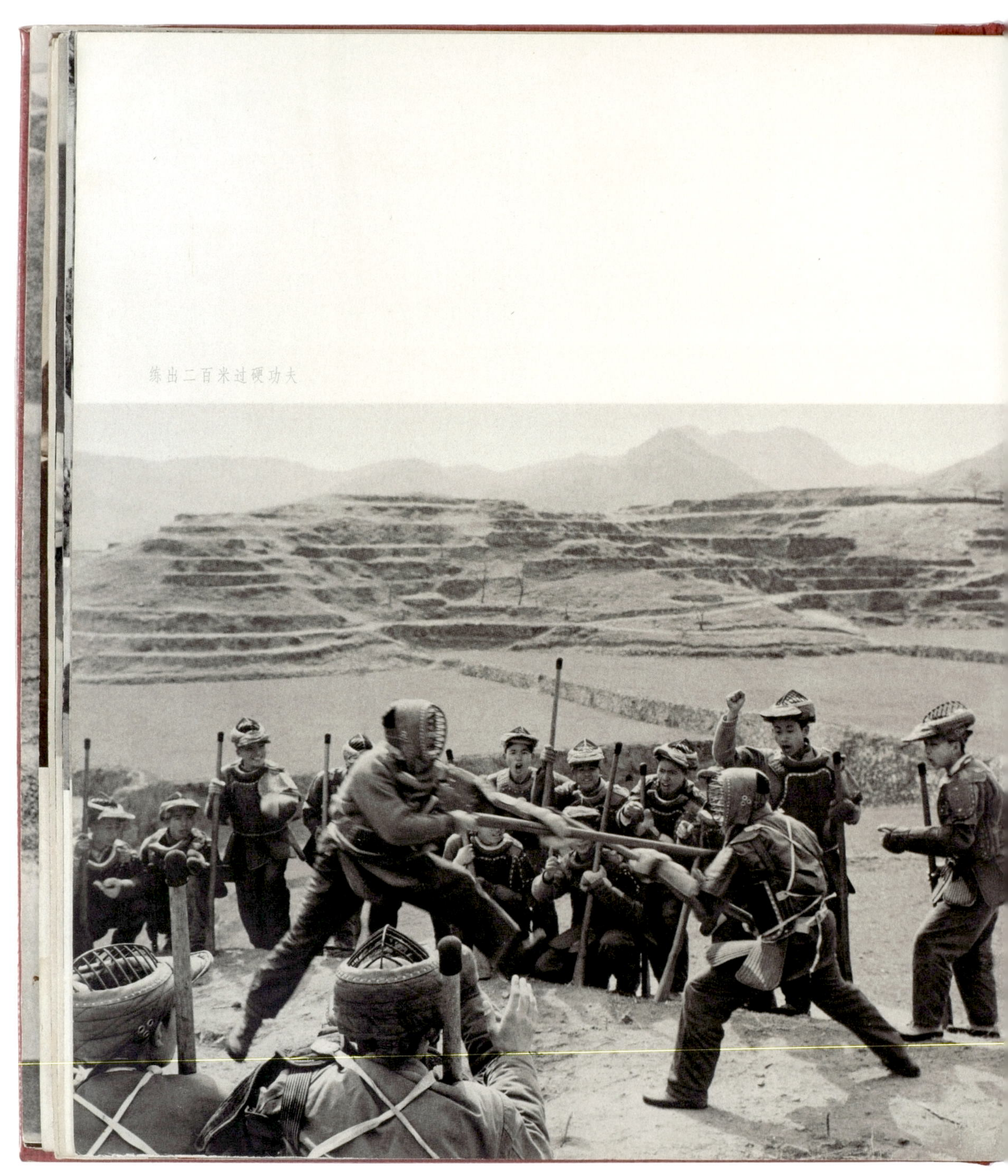

plate 33 (Left) 练出二百米过硬功夫 - Practice to Perfection (Right) 苦练打得准 - The More Grueling the Practice, the More Accurate the Shot

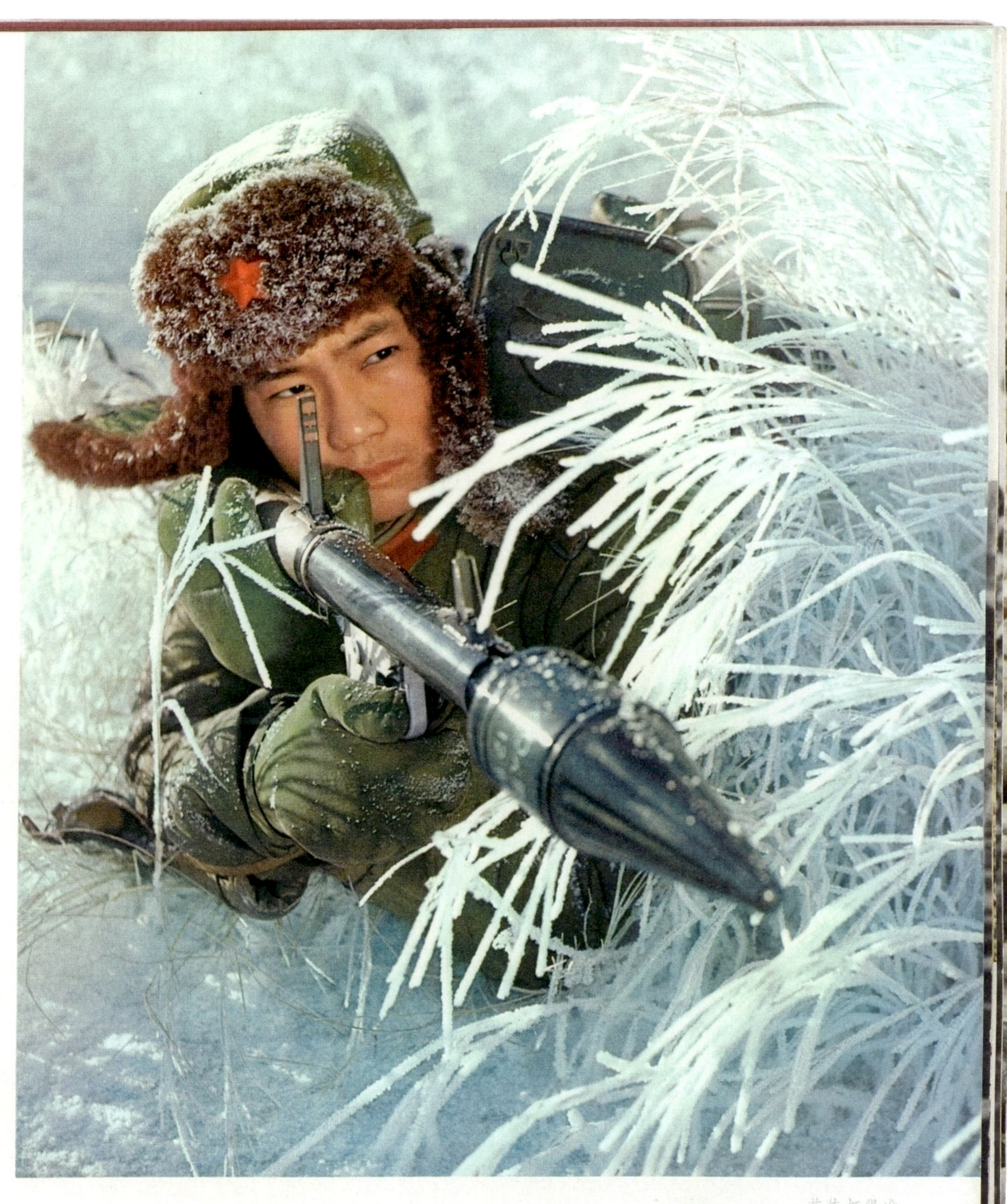

苦练打得准

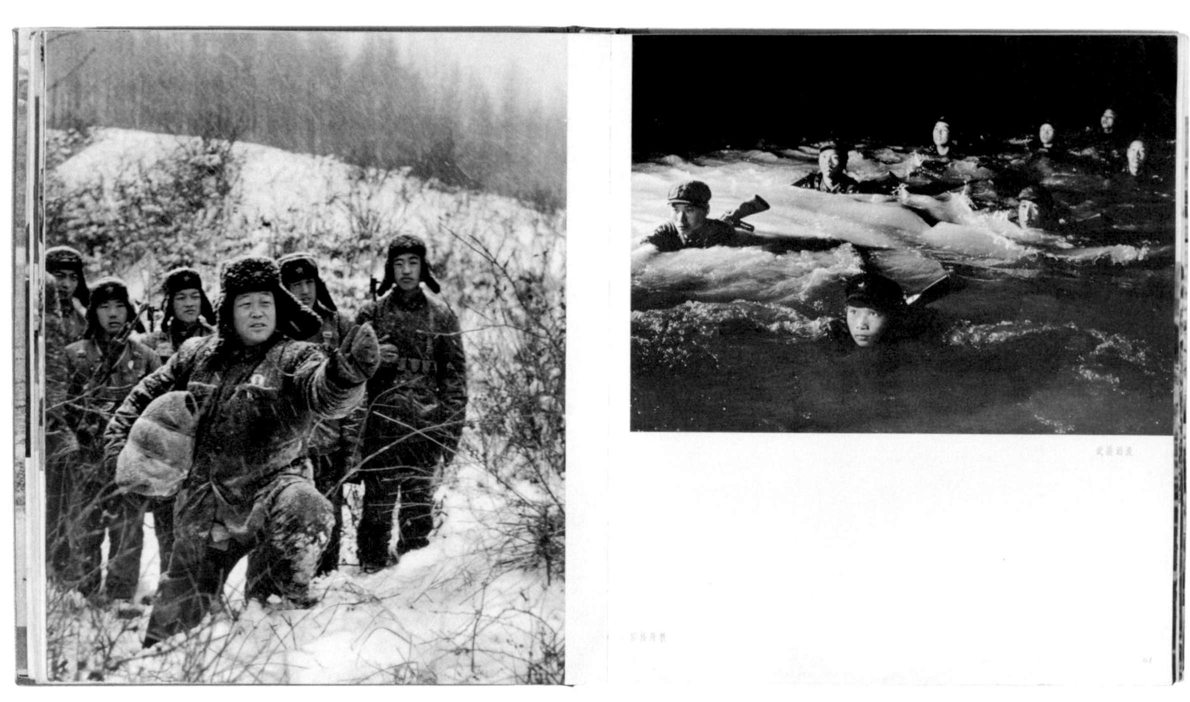

plate 34 (Left) 言传身教 - Teach by Precept and Example (Right) 武装泅渡 - Military Swimming Training

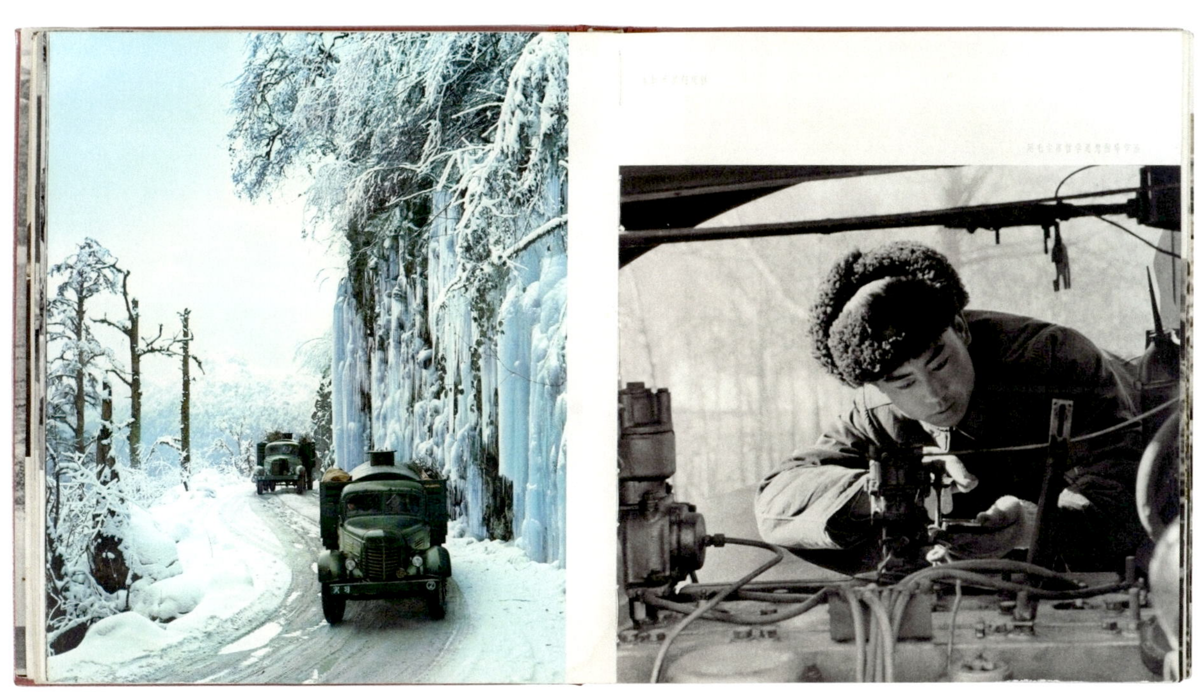

plate 35 (Left) 冰封千里何所惧 - No Fear When Facing the Frozen World (Right) 用毛主席哲学思想指导节油 - Save the Patrol Under the Guidance of Chairman Mao's Philosophical Thought

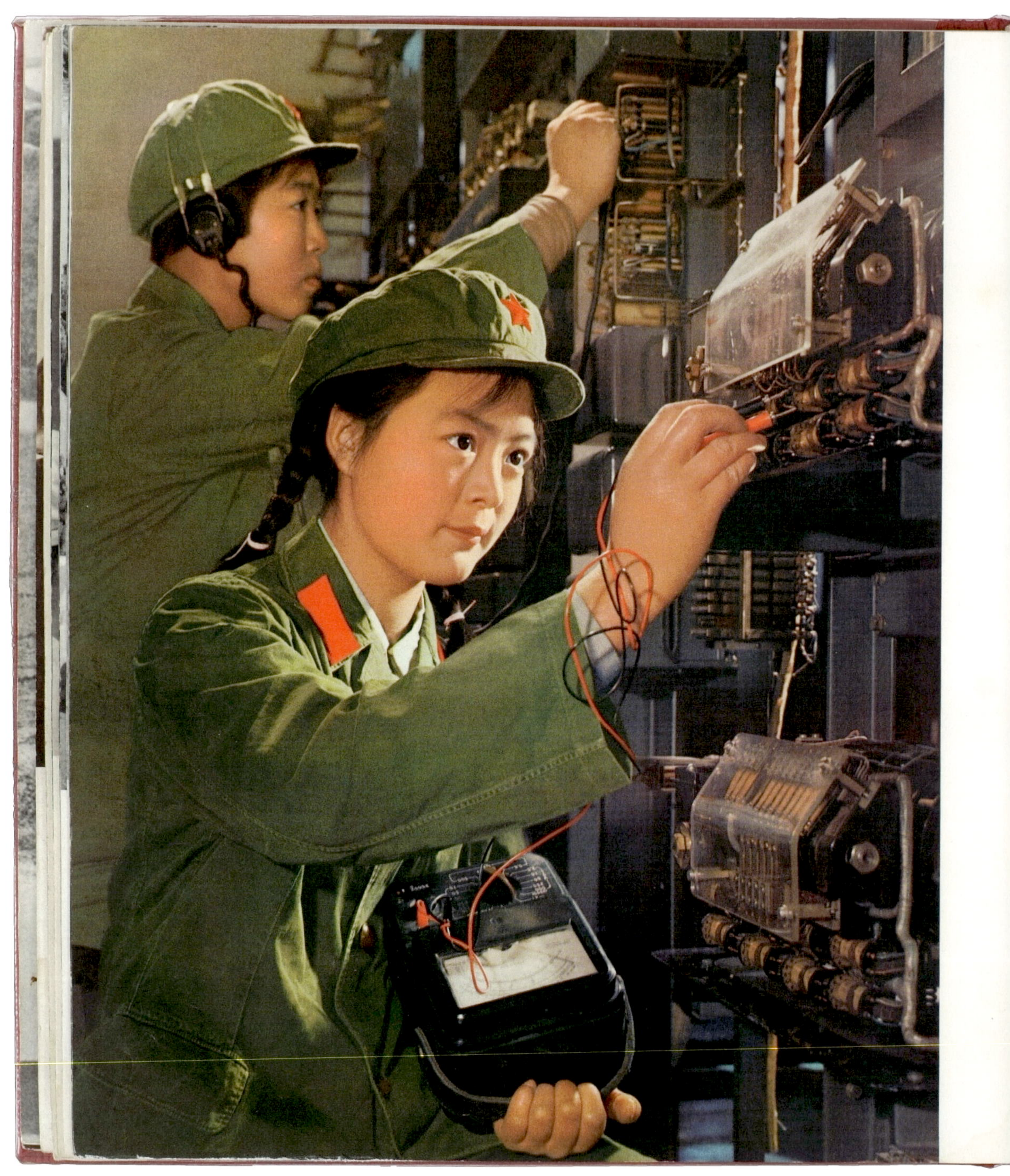

plate 36 (Above) 认真检修，精益求精 - Careful Examination for Perfection (Opposite) 万水千山架银线 - The Telephone Lines Reach Across the Mountains and Seas

认真检修，精益求精

万水千山架银线

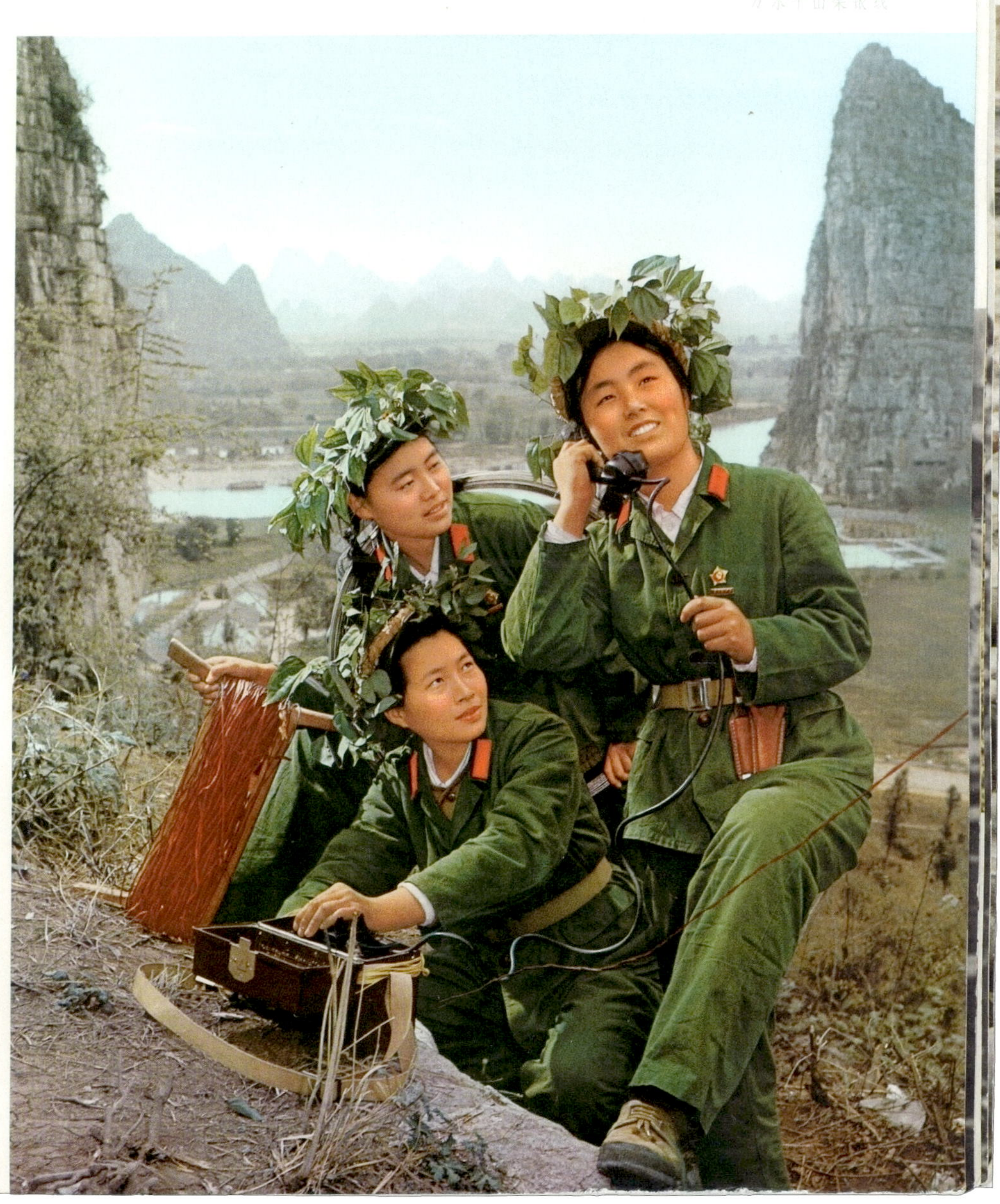

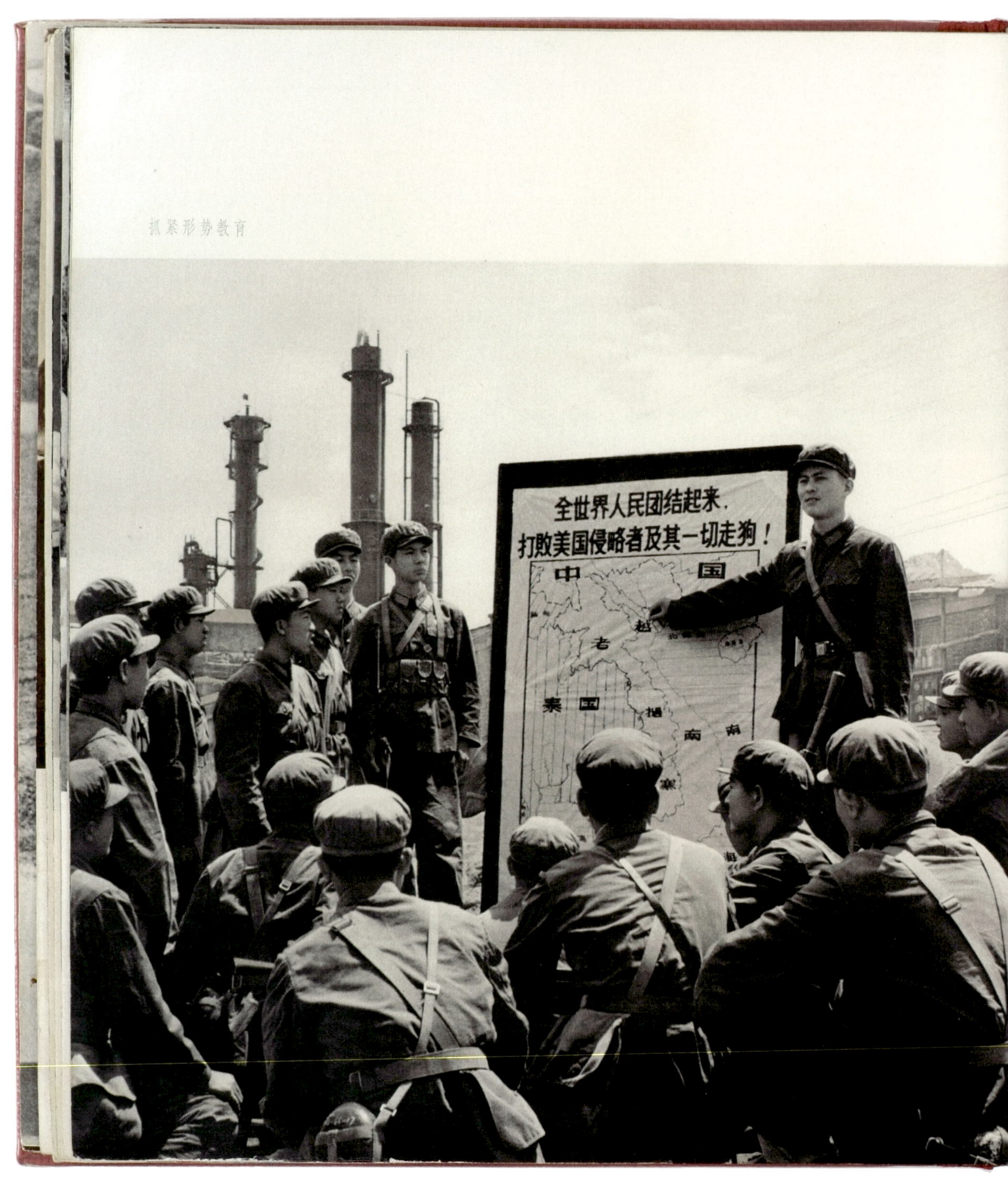

plate 37 (Above) 抓紧形势教育 - Pay Close Attention to the Situation Education (Opposite) 常备不懈 - Be Ever Vigilant

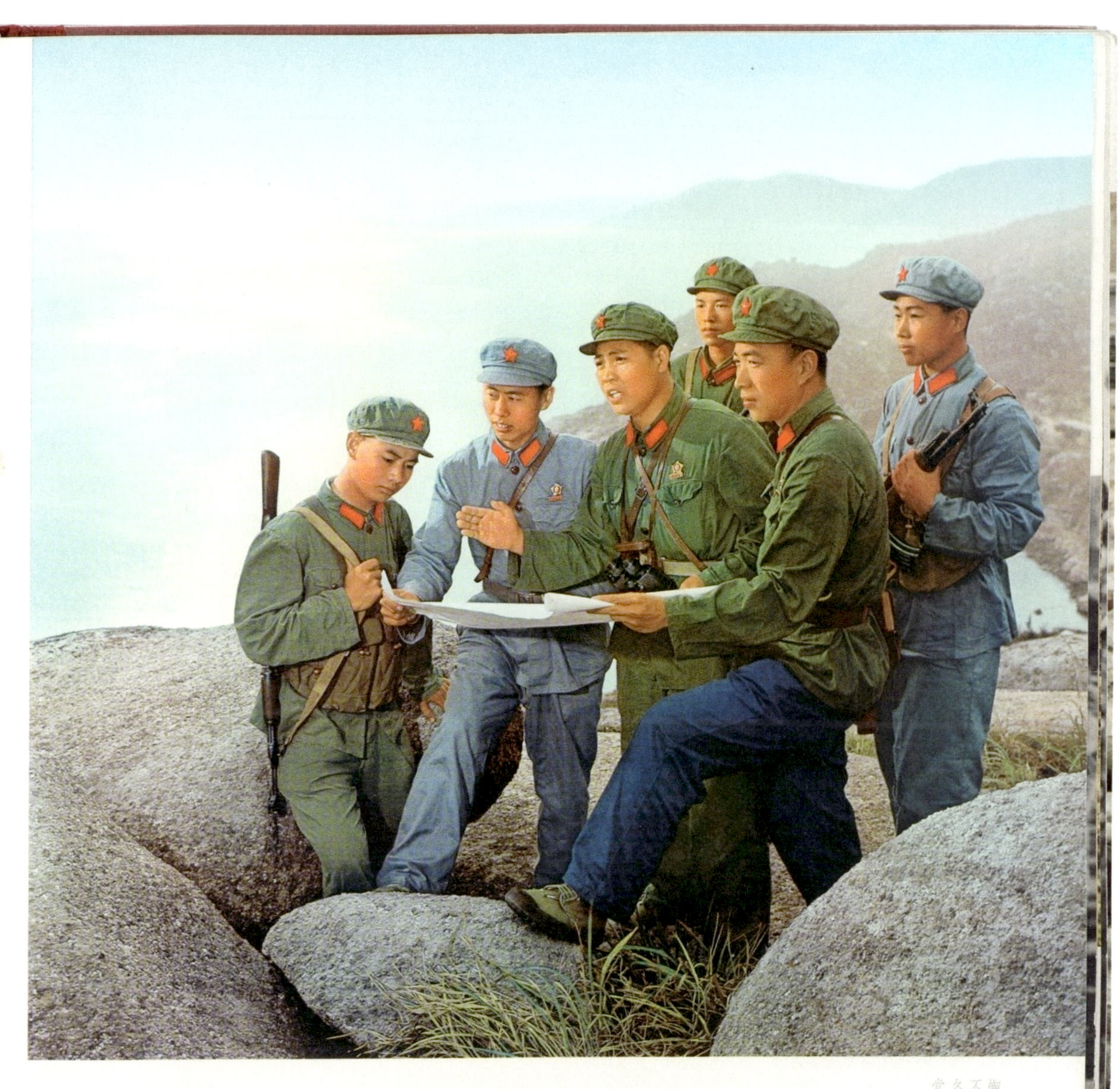

常备不懈

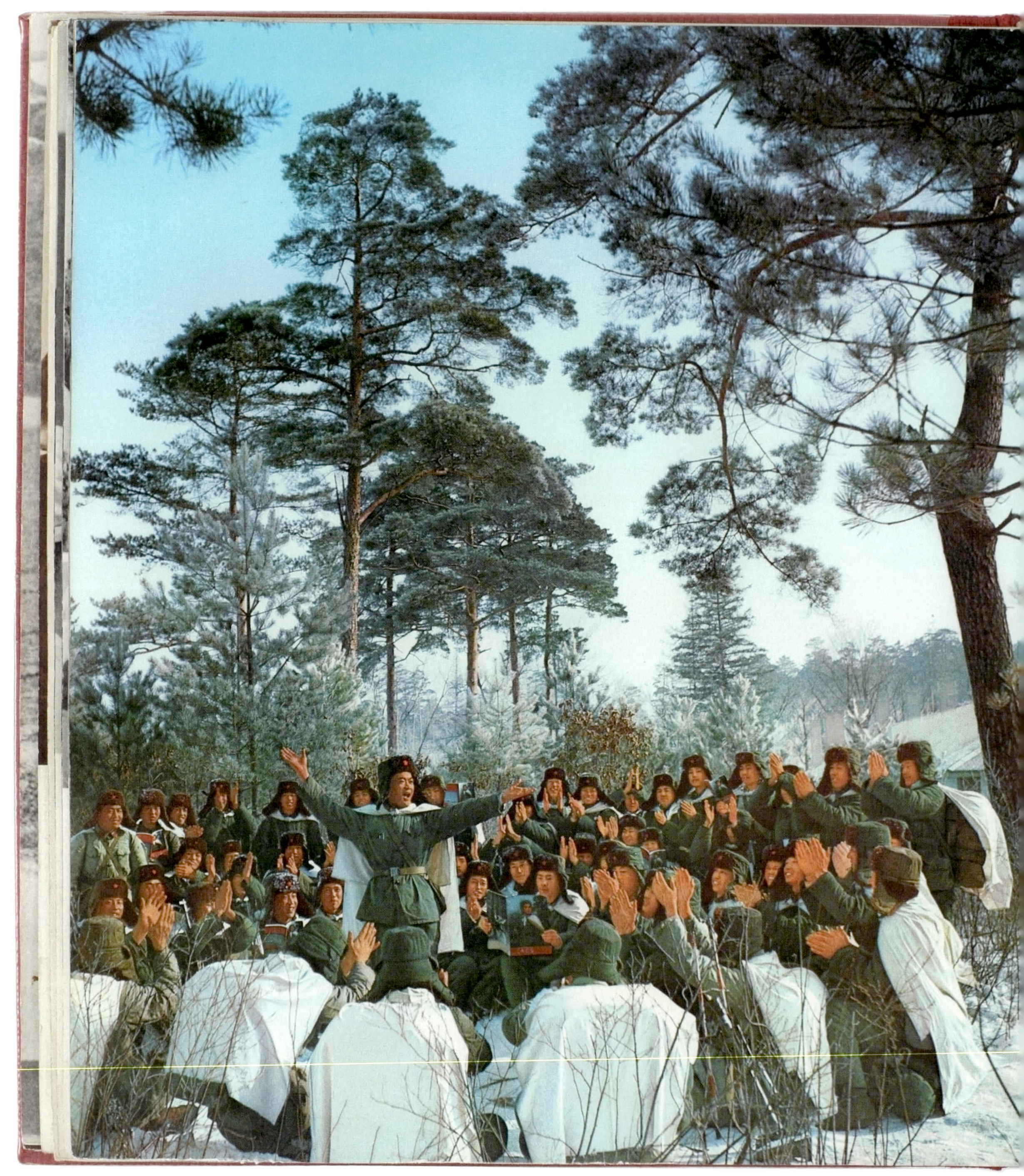

plate 38 (Above) “胸有朝阳” - “The Sun is always in One’s Heart” (Opposite) 战歌嘹亮 - Resonant Battle Singing

"胸有朝阳"

战歌嘹亮

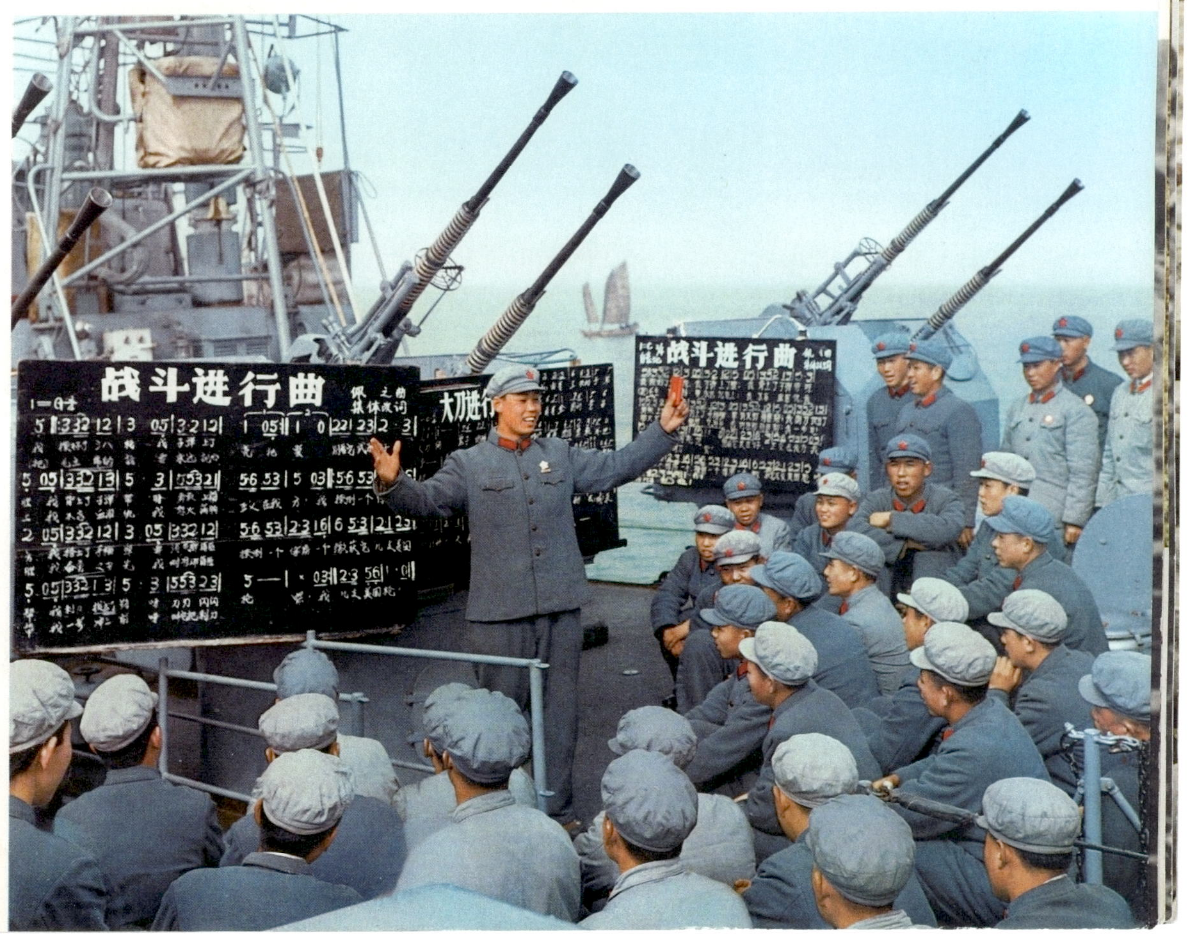

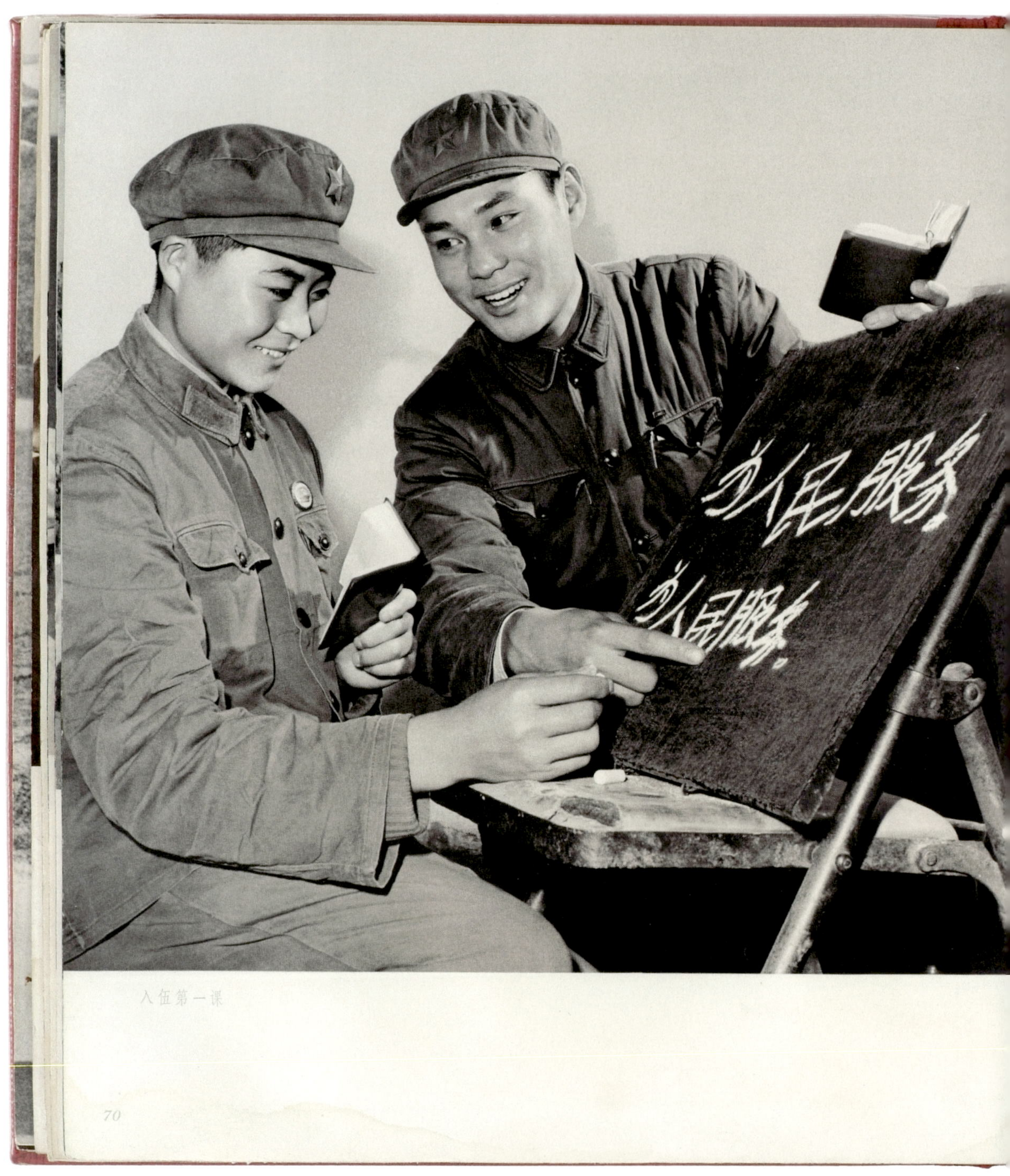

入伍第一课

plate 39 (Above) 入伍第一课 - The First Class After Enlisting (Opposite) 开展体育活动 - Promoting Sports Activities

开展体育活动

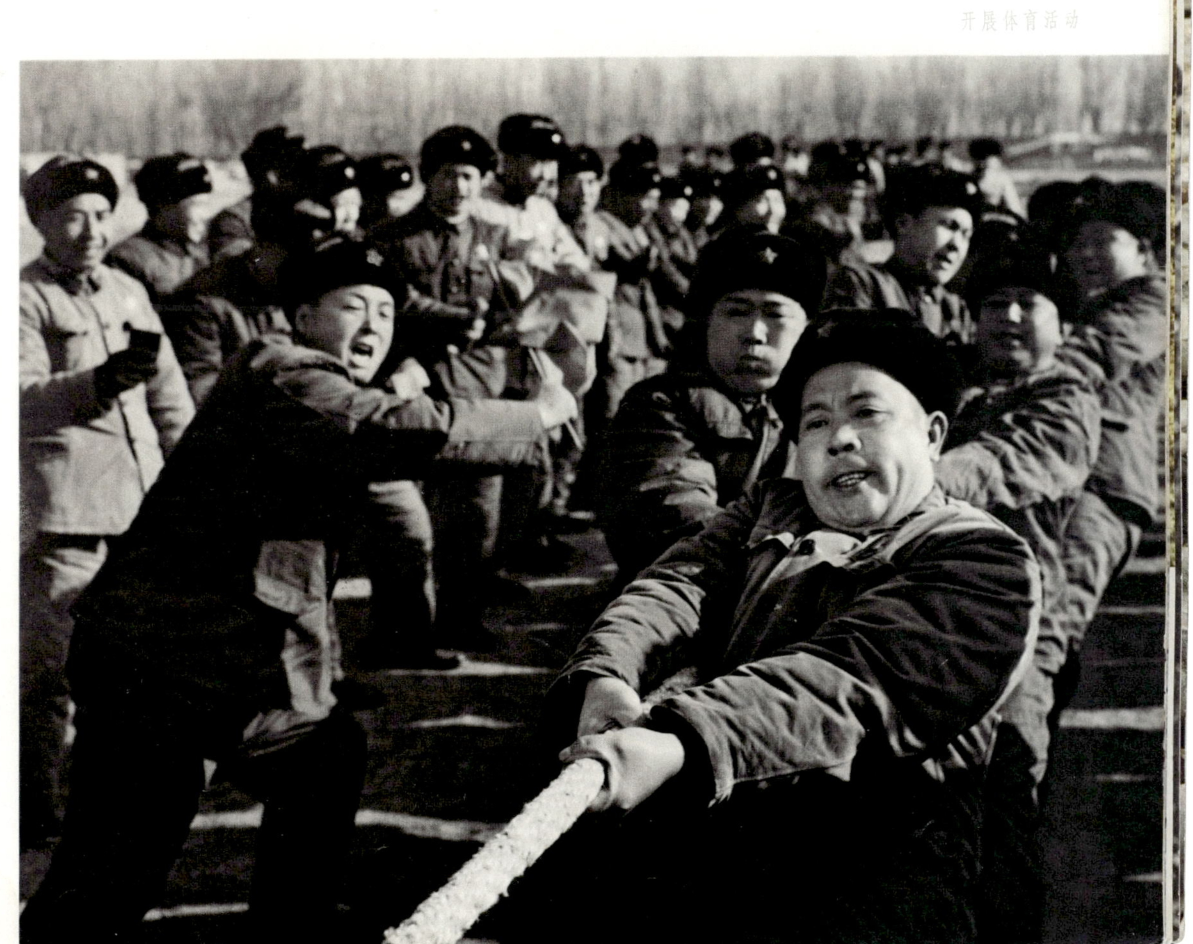

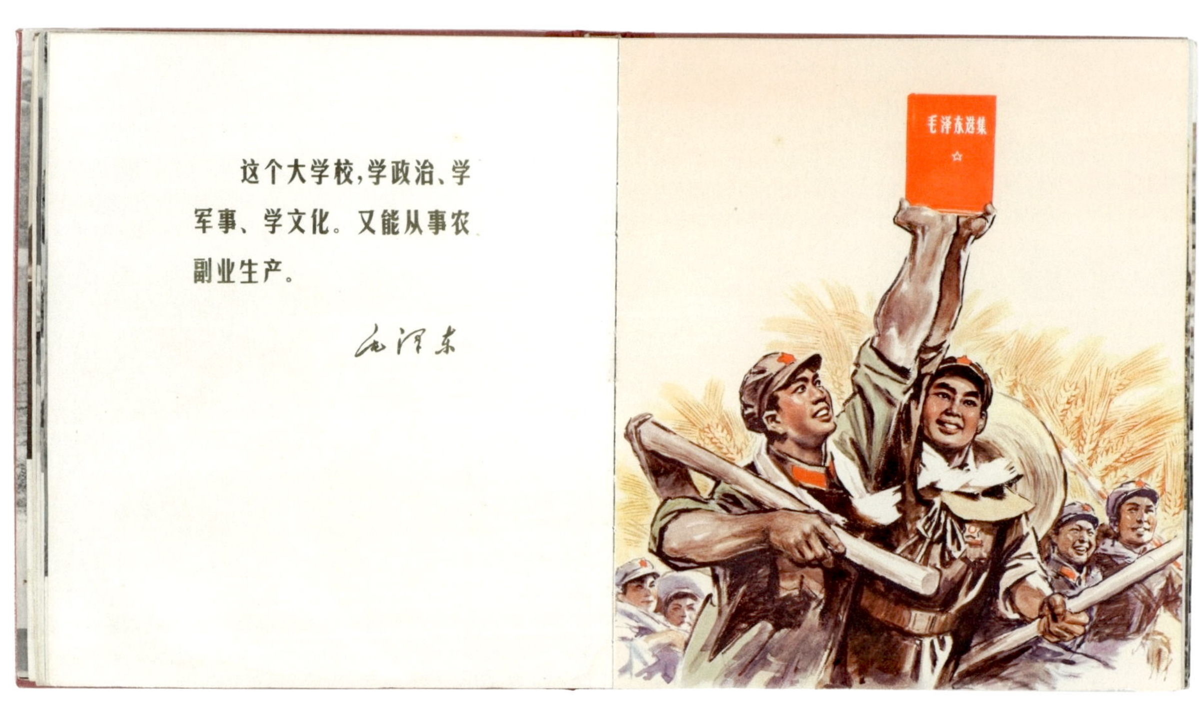

plate 40 这个大学校，学政治，学军事，学文化，又能从事农副业生产 - In this great school, troops study politics, military affairs and culture. They can engage in agricultural production and related occupations.

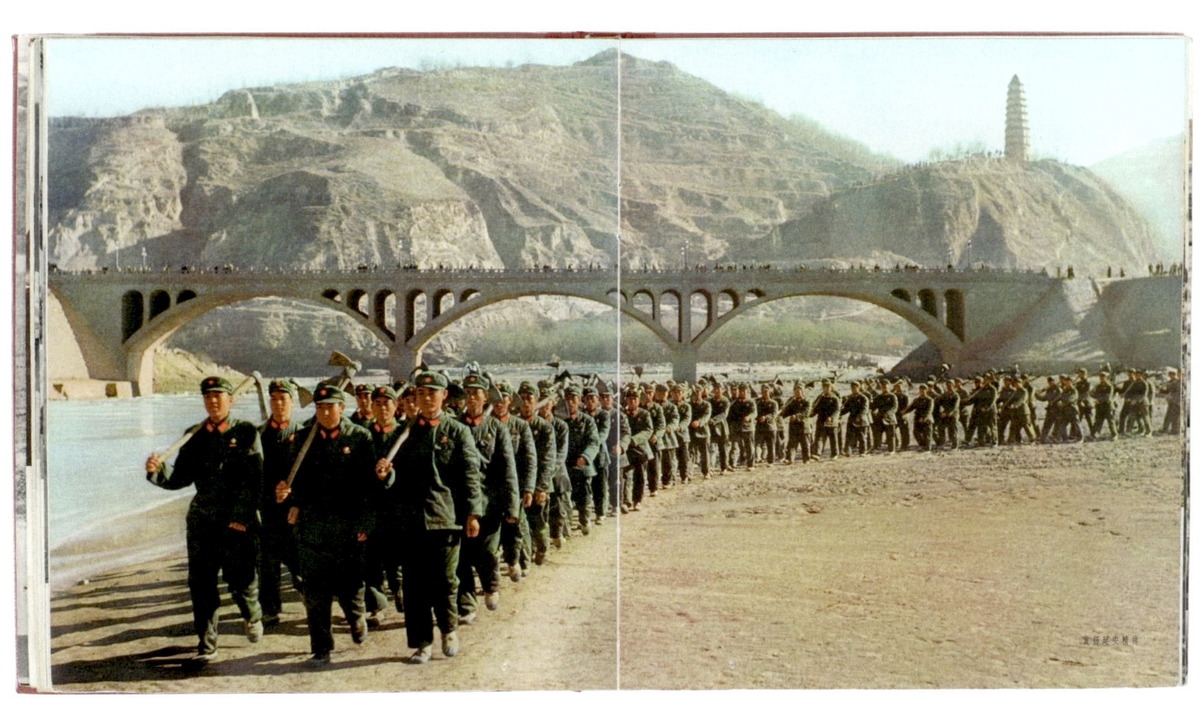

plate 41　　发扬延安精神 - Advocate the Spirit of Yan'an

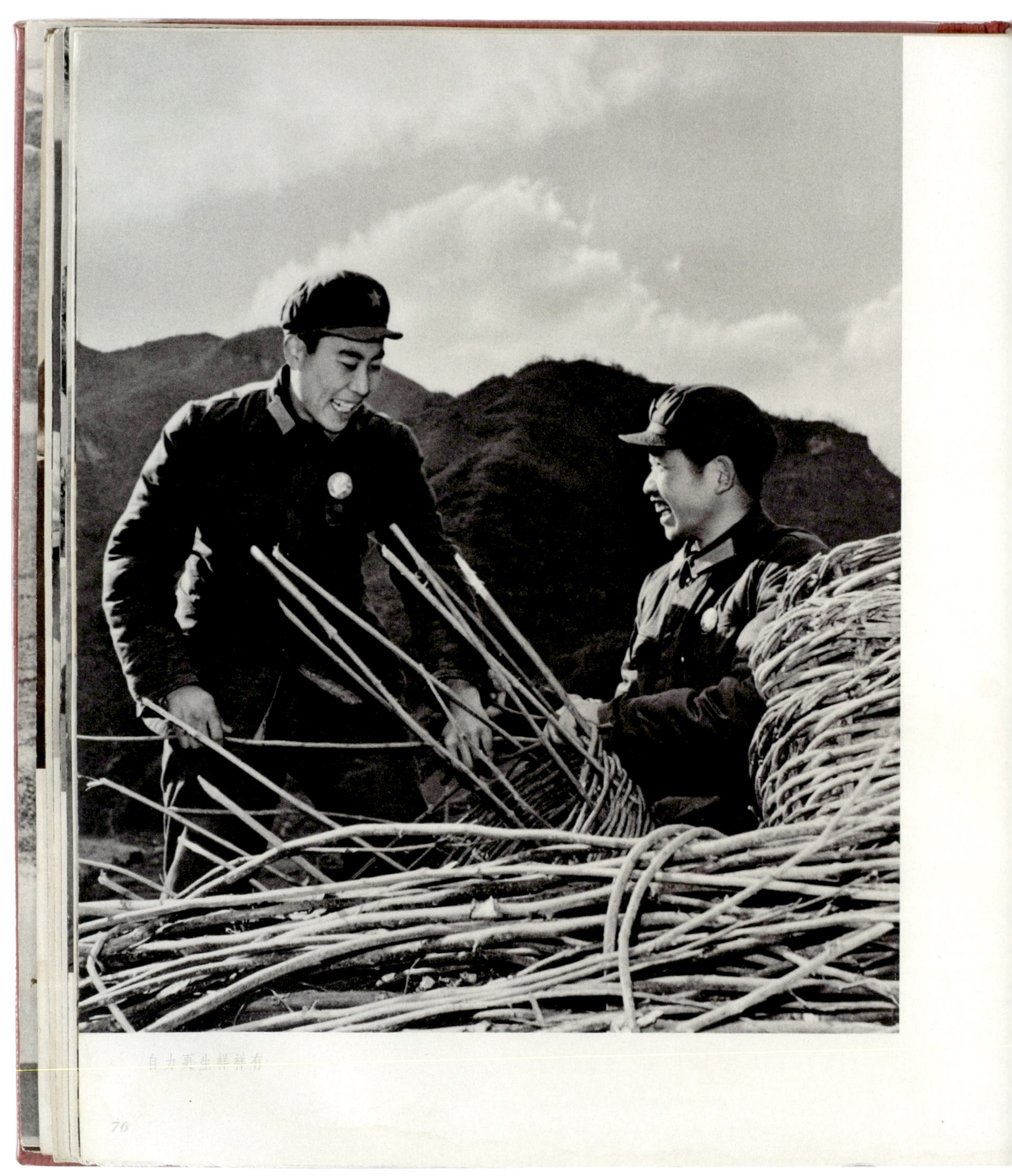

plate 42 (Above) 自力更生样样有 - Self-Sufficiency in All Things (Opposite) 劈山造田 - Turn the Hilltops into Fields

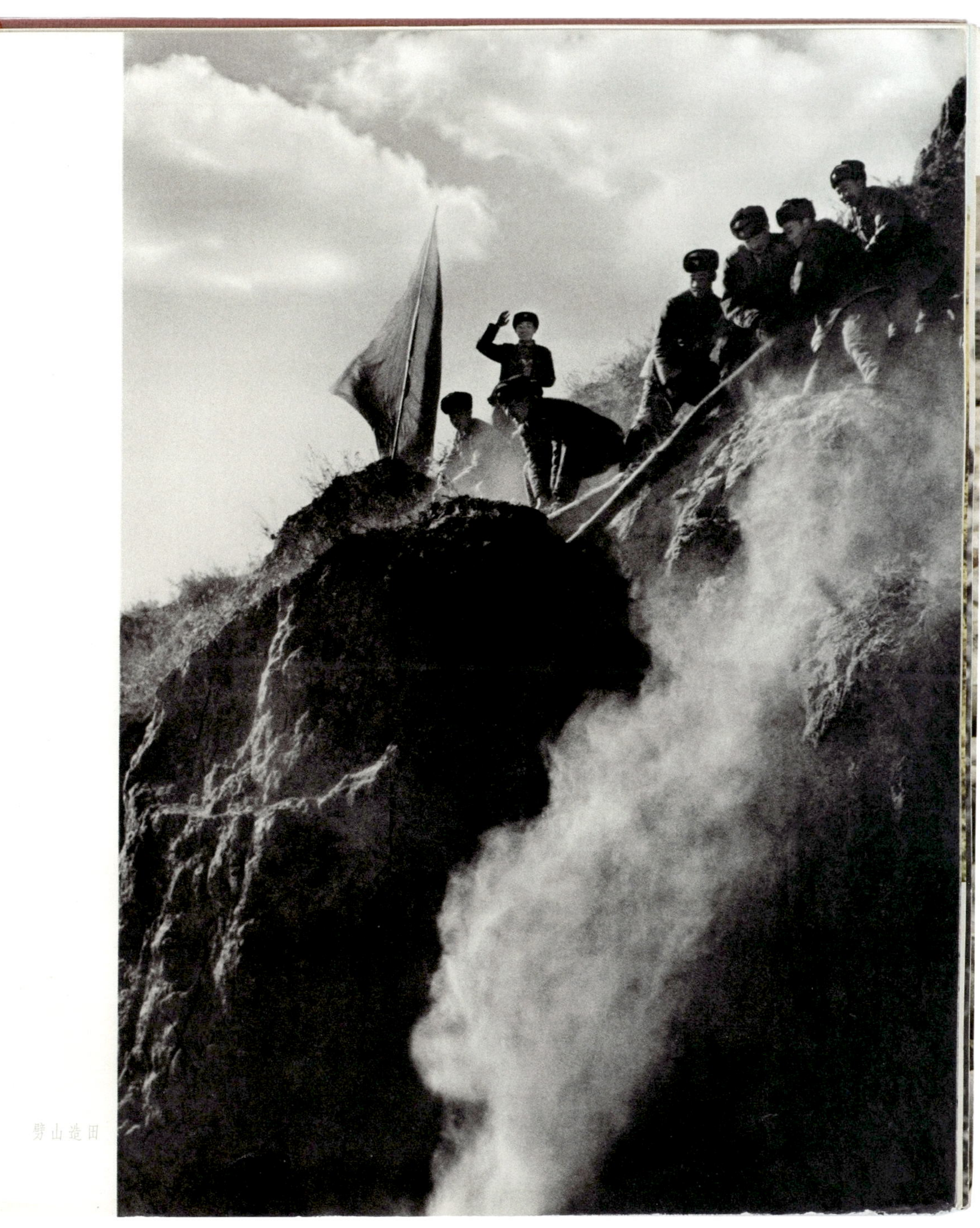

劈山造田

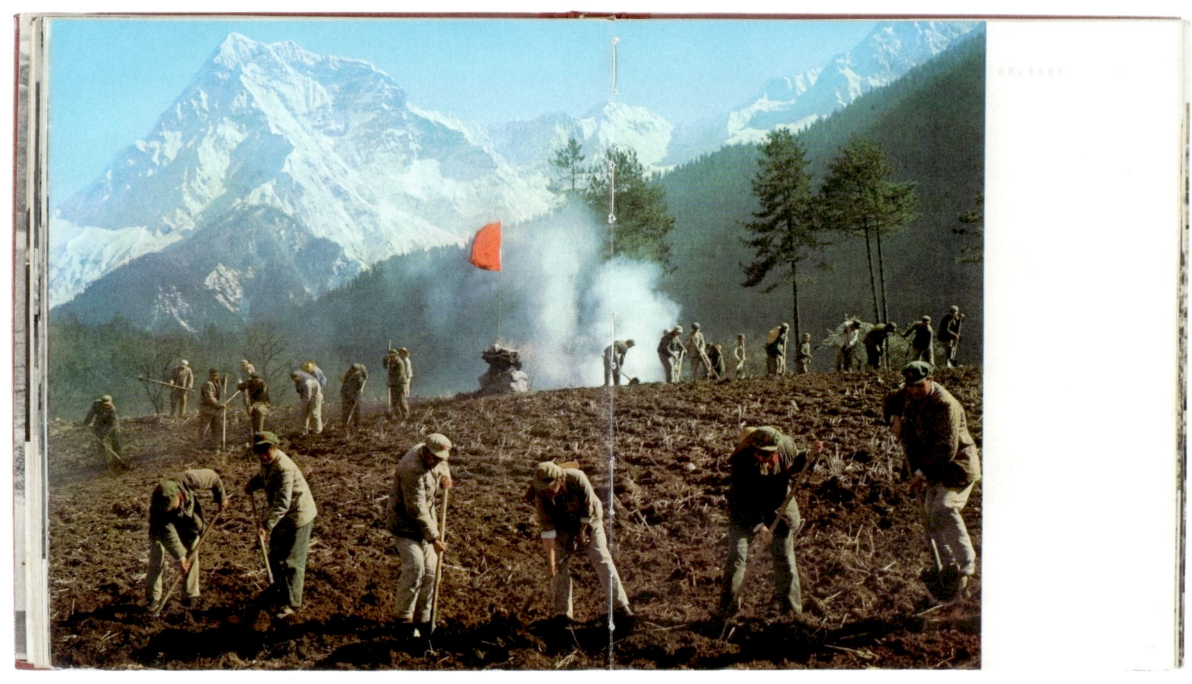

plate 43　西藏高原春来早 - Spring Arrives Early on the Tibetan Plateau

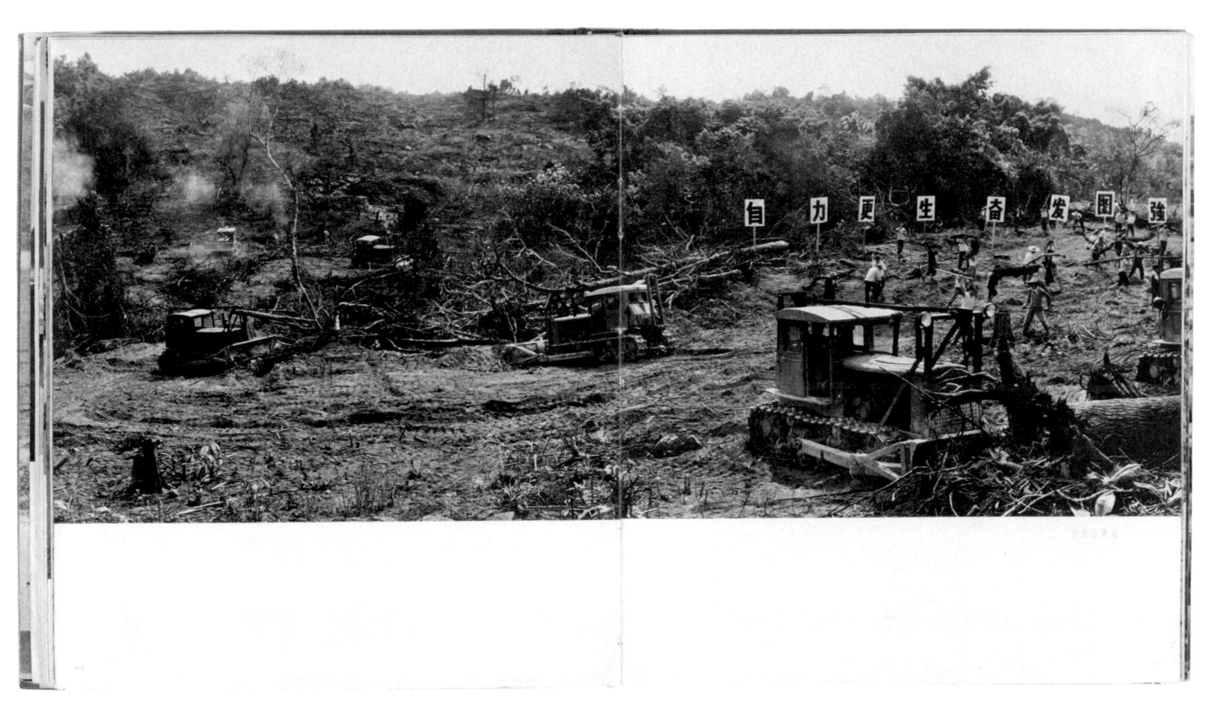

plate 44　向荒山要地 - Turn Barren Land into Fields

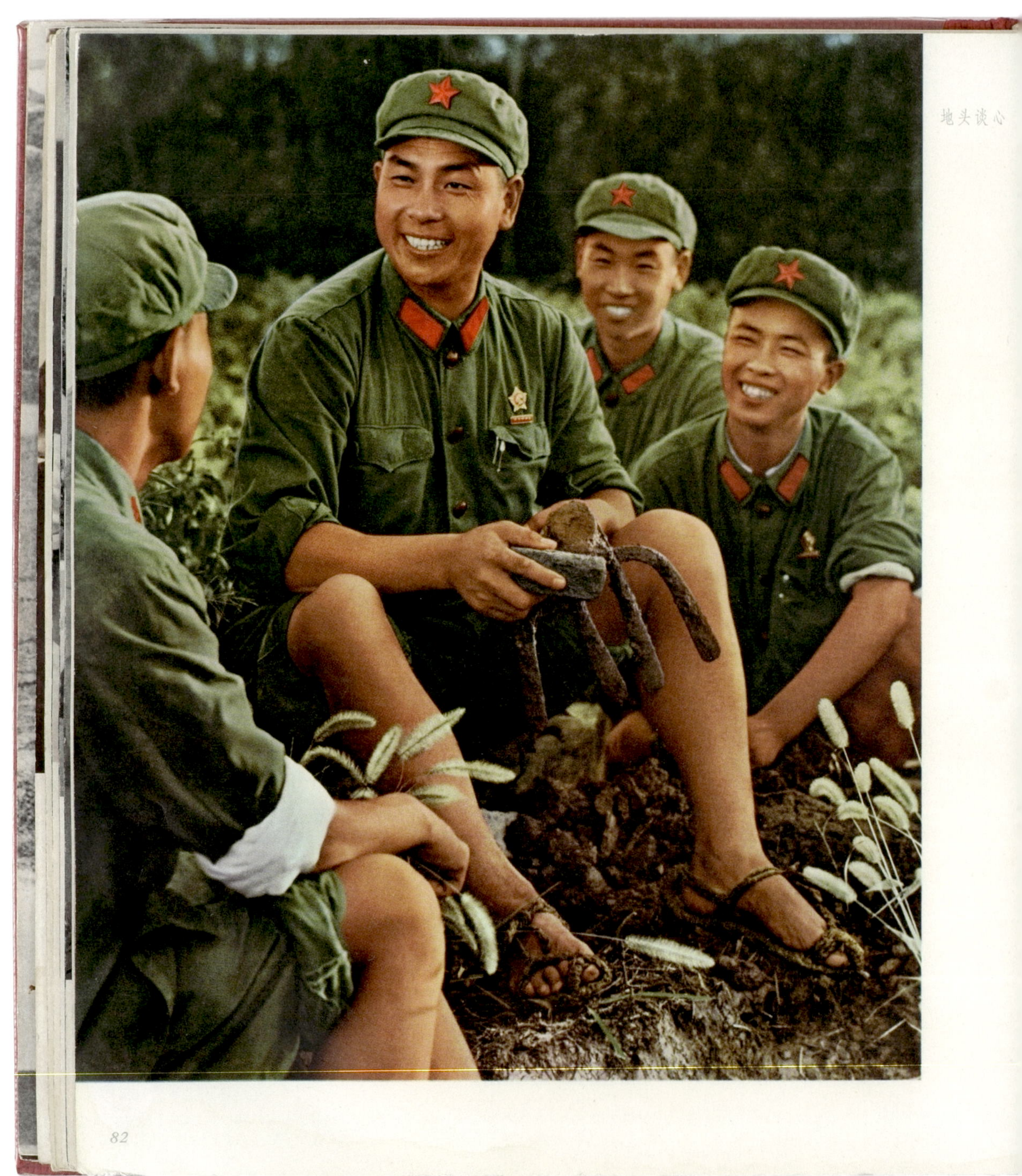

plate 45 (Above) 地头谈心 - A Chat in the Field (Opposite) 深翻土地 - Deep Plowing

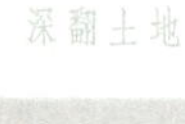

深翻土地

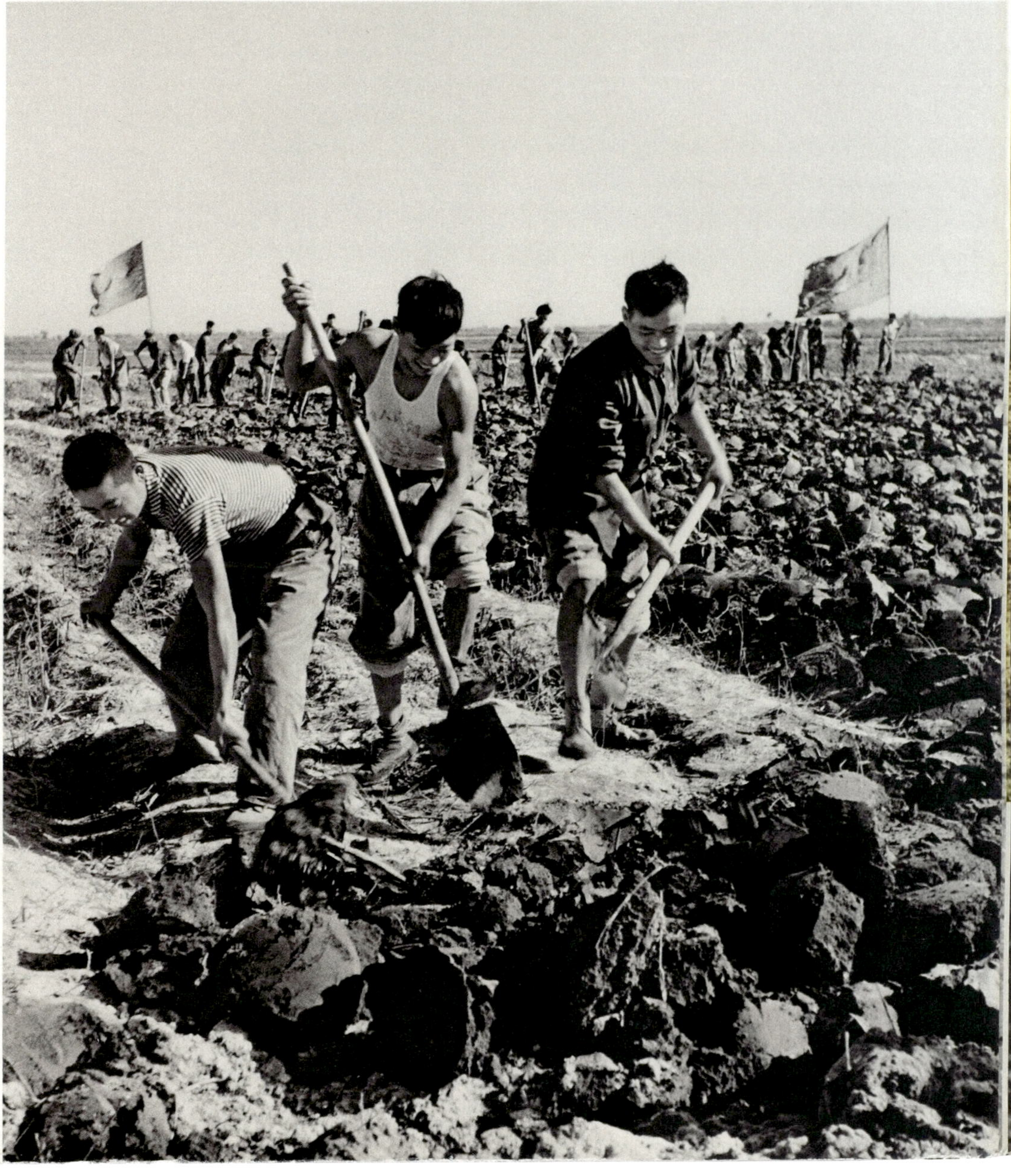

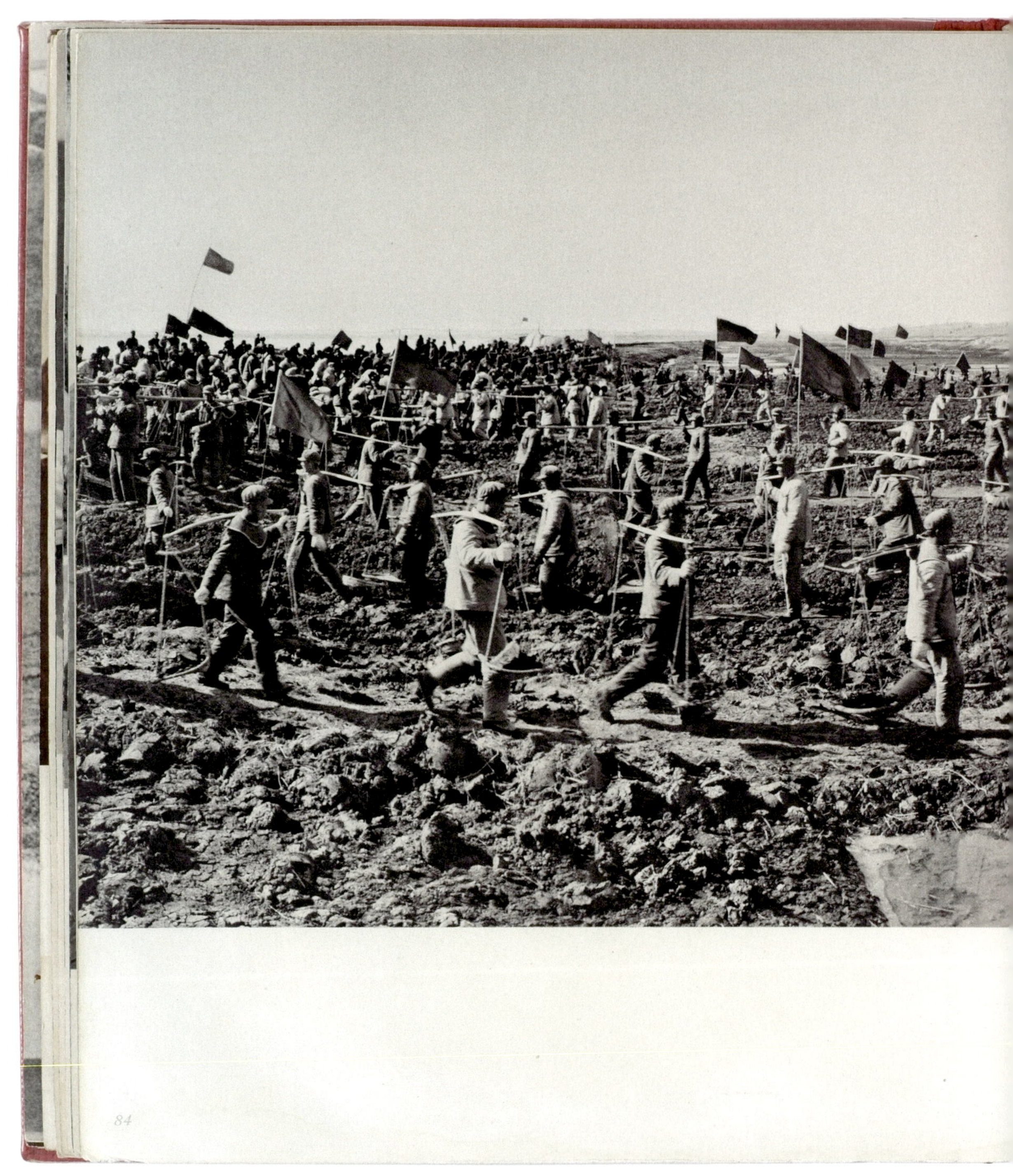

plate 46　围垦“城西湖” - Inning the “West Town Lake”

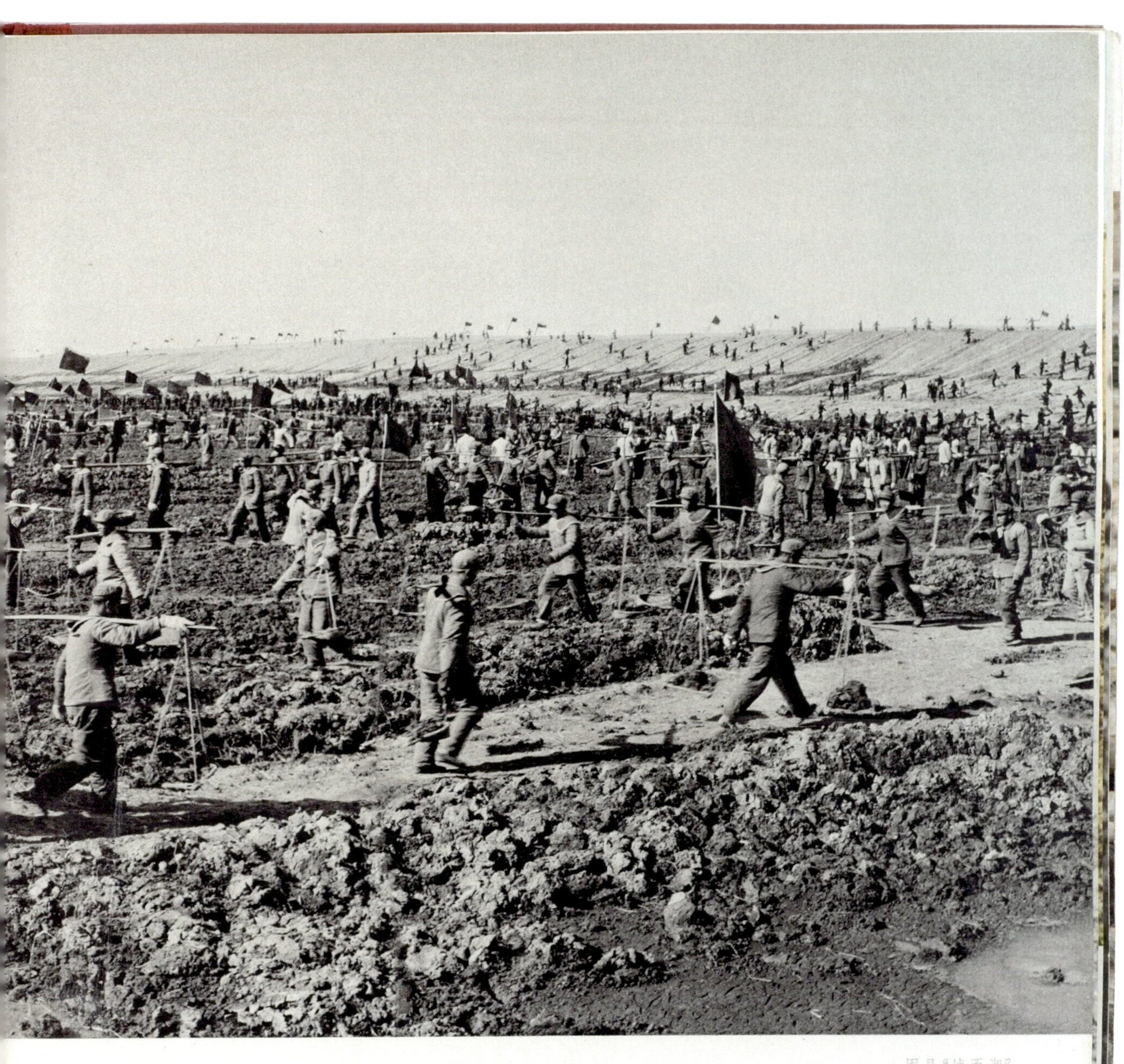

围垦“城西湖”

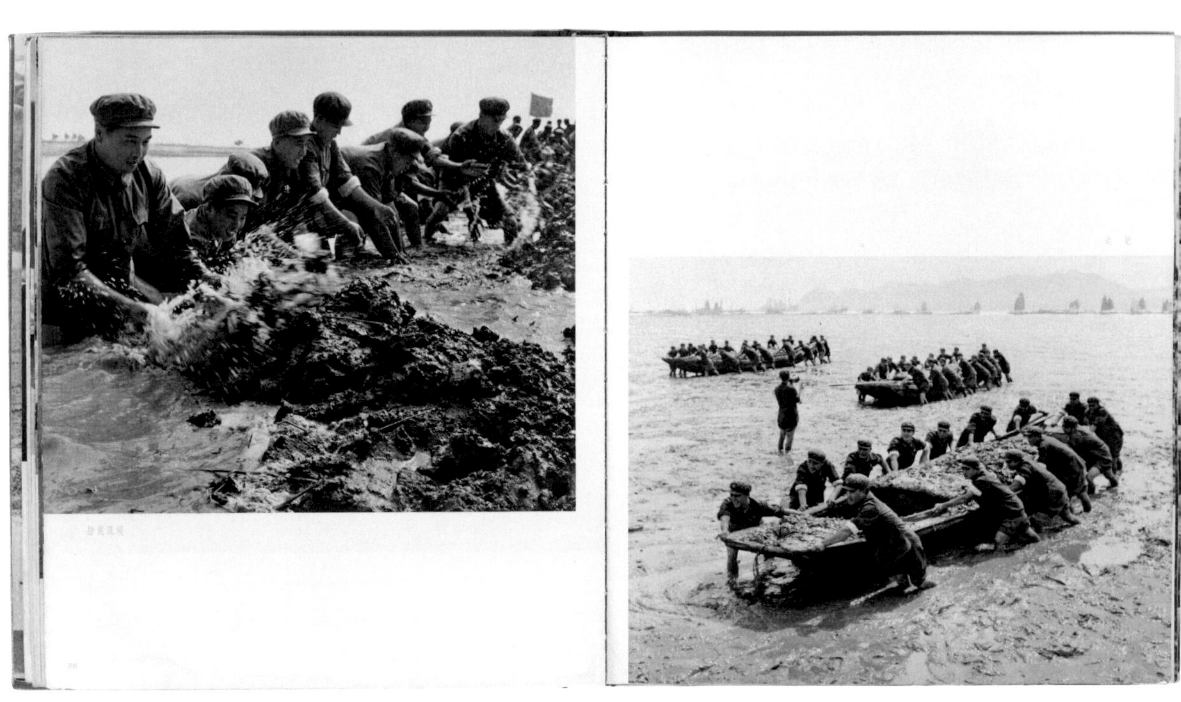

plate 47 (Left) 捞泥筑堤 - Digging Mud for the Embankment (Right) 运肥 - Transporting Fertilizer

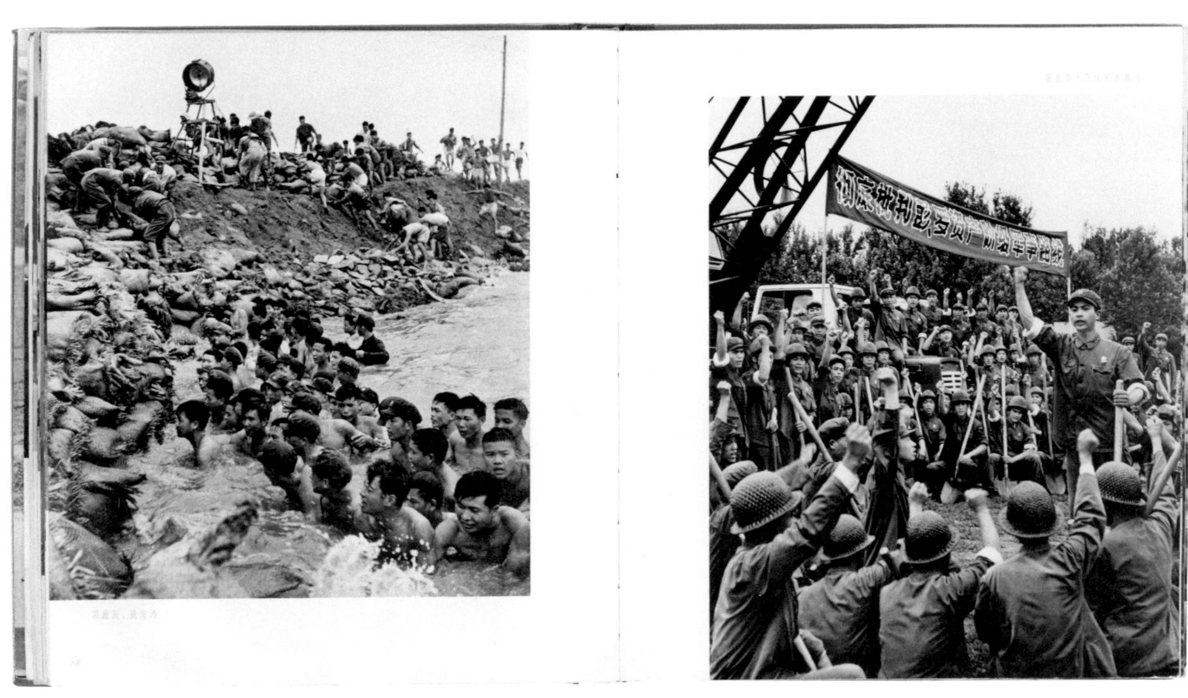

plate 48 (Left) 顶激流, 战海涛 - Braving the Rapids, Fighting the Waves (Right) 狠批资产阶级军事路线 - Severely Criticize the Bourgeois Military Line

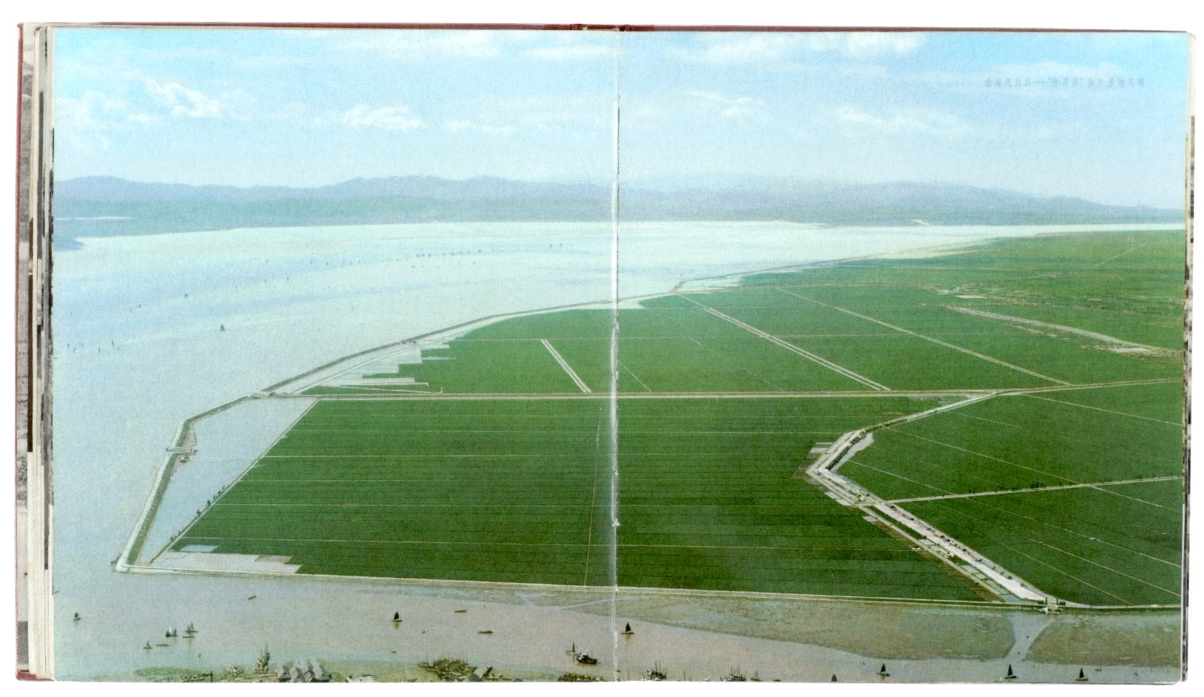

plate 49 沧海变良田—“牛田洋”生产基地鸟瞰 - Deep Oceans Become Fertile Fields – A Bird’s-Eye View of the Niutianyang Production Base

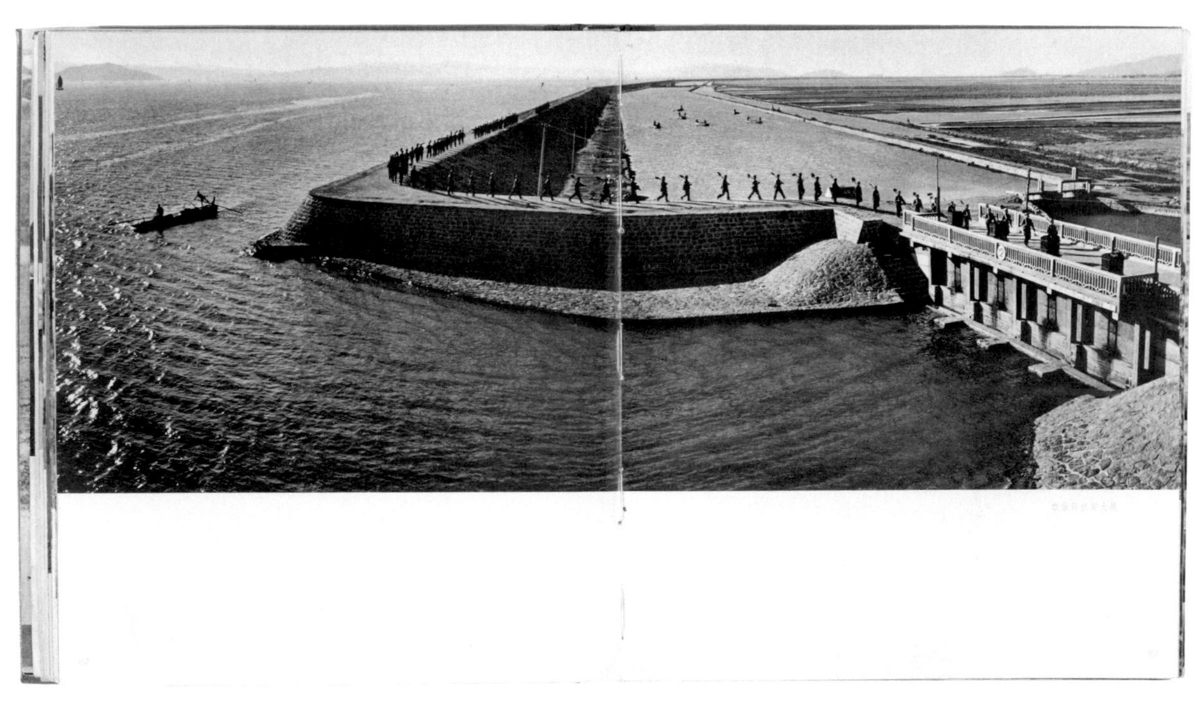

plate 50　雄伟的拦海大堤 - The Magnificent Sea Embankment

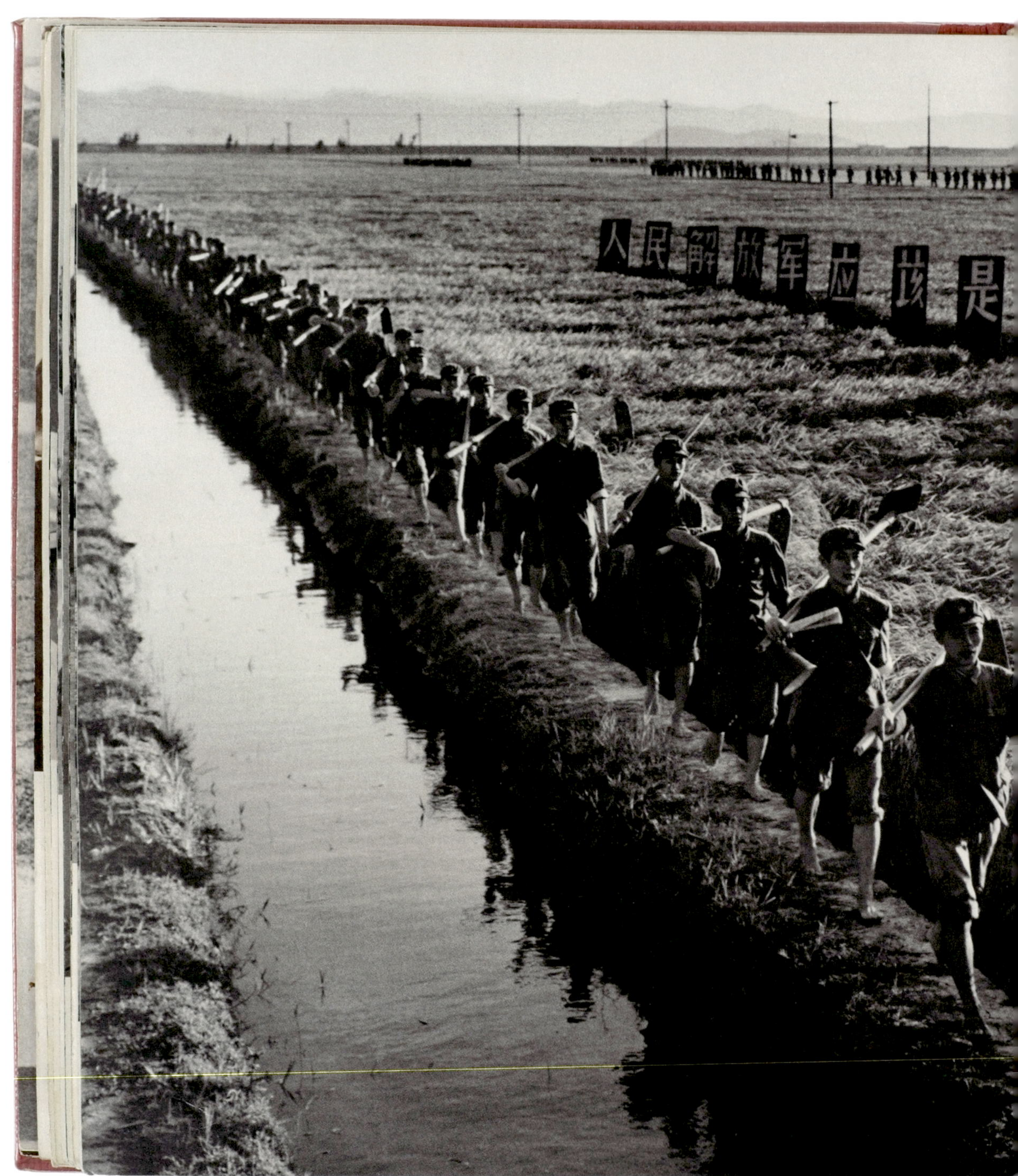

plate 51　　劳动归来 - Returning from Labour

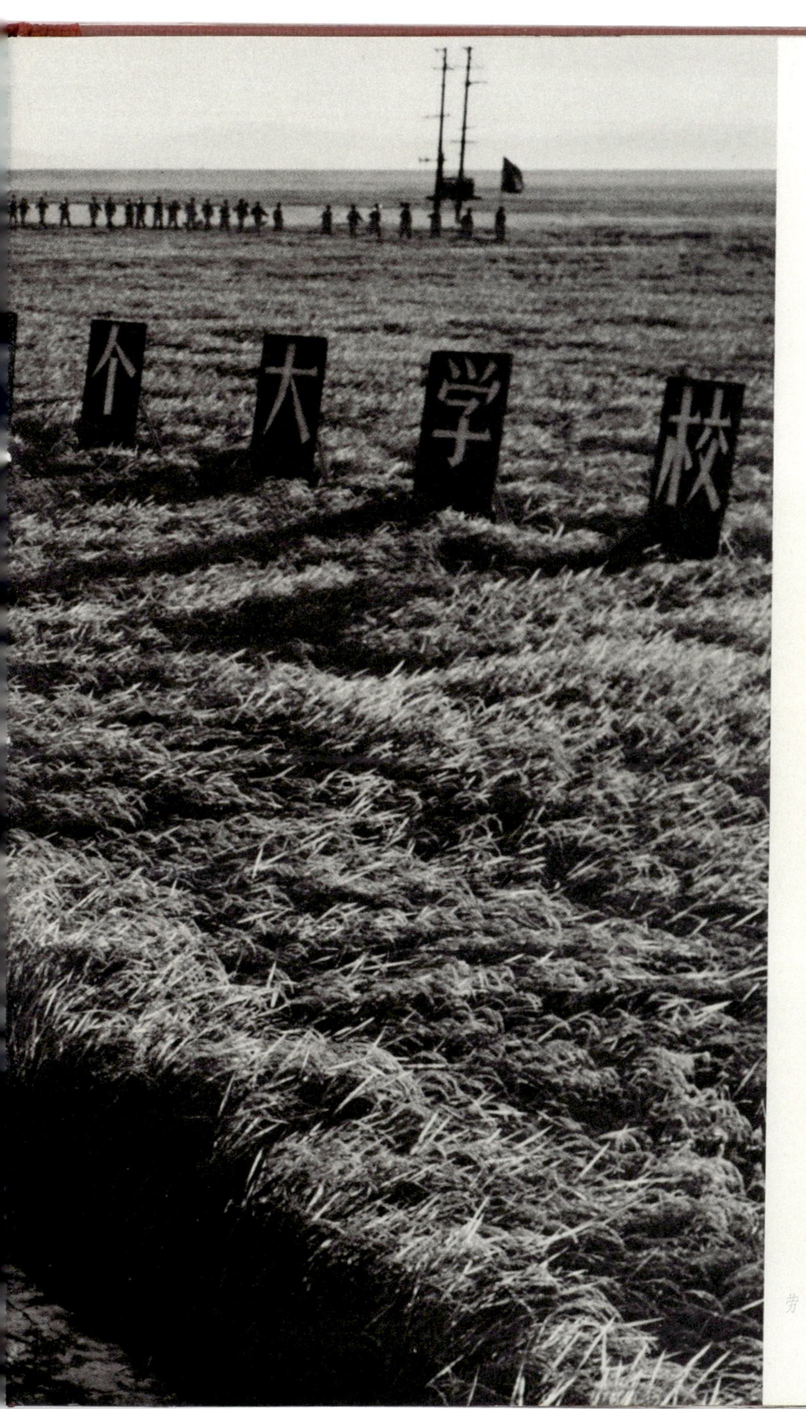

劳动归来

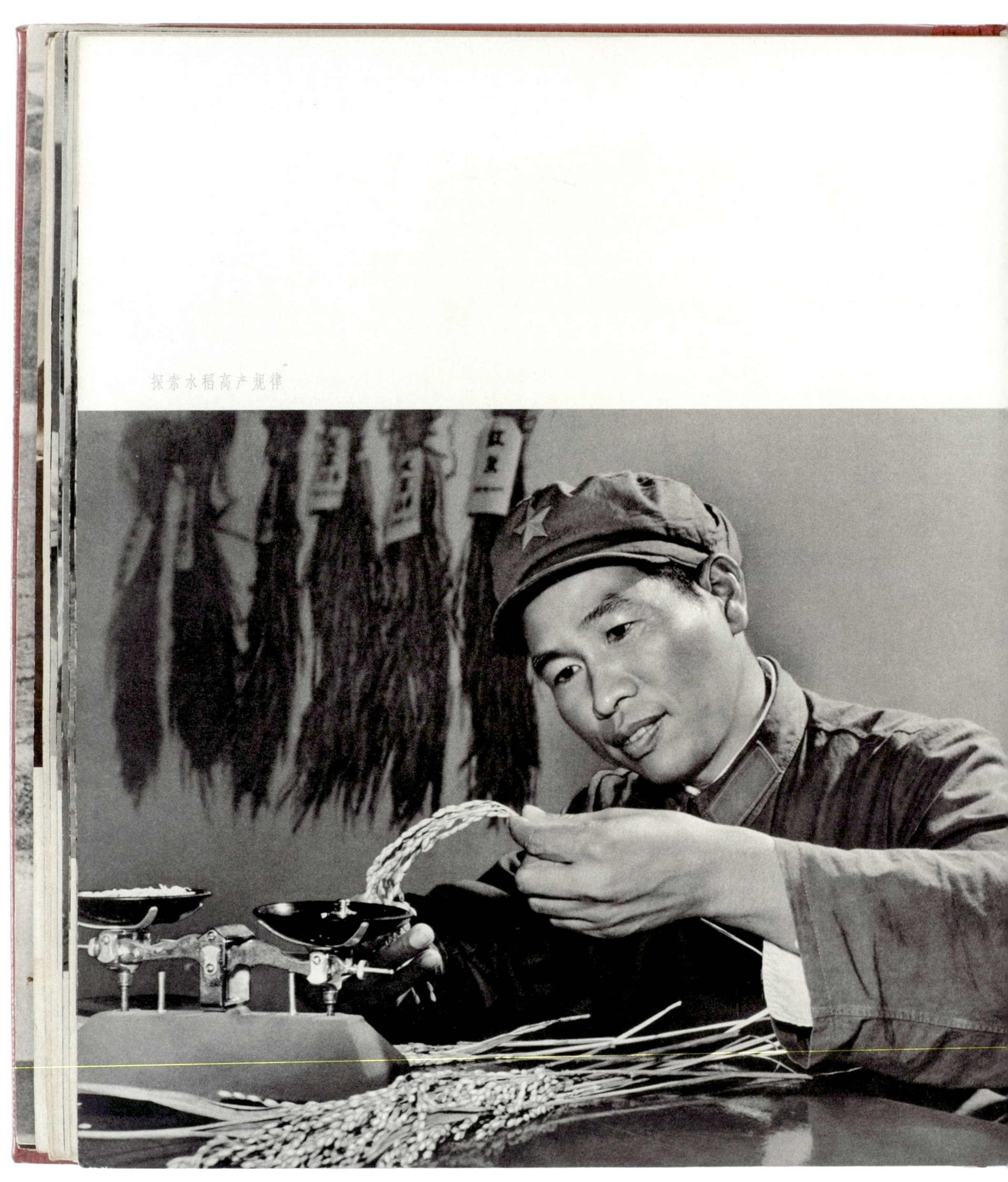

plate 52 (Above) 探索水稻高产规律 - Exploring the Regulations for the High Yield of Rice (Opposite) 丰收的喜悦 - The Happiness of Harvest.

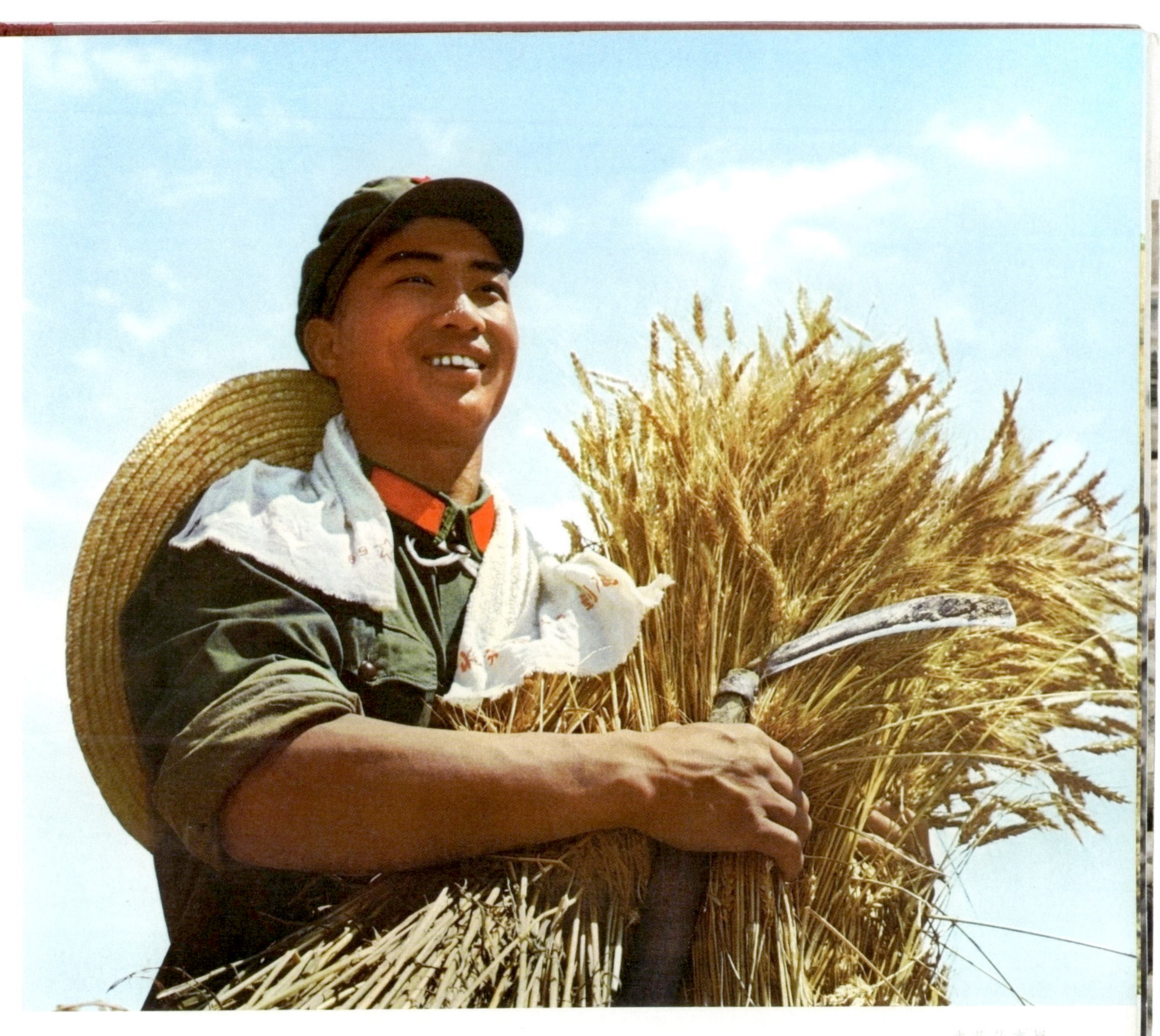

丰收的喜悦

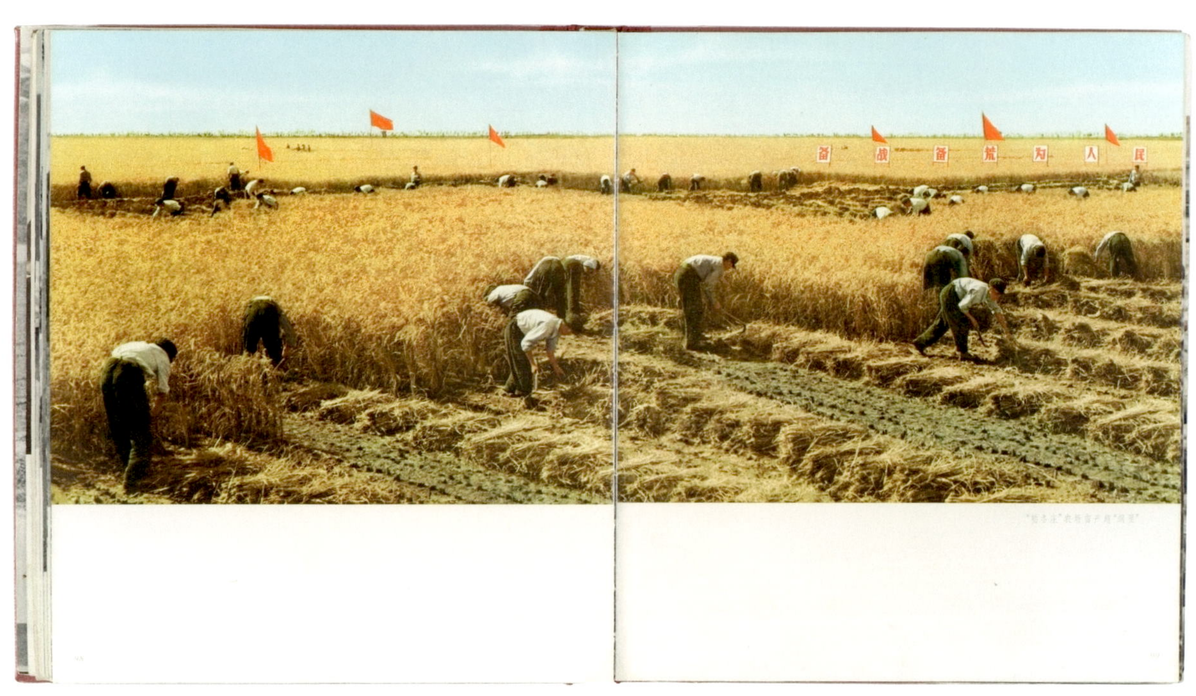

plate 53 “柏各庄”农场亩产超“纲要” - The Per *Mu* Yield of Baigezhuang Farm Exceeds the Requirement

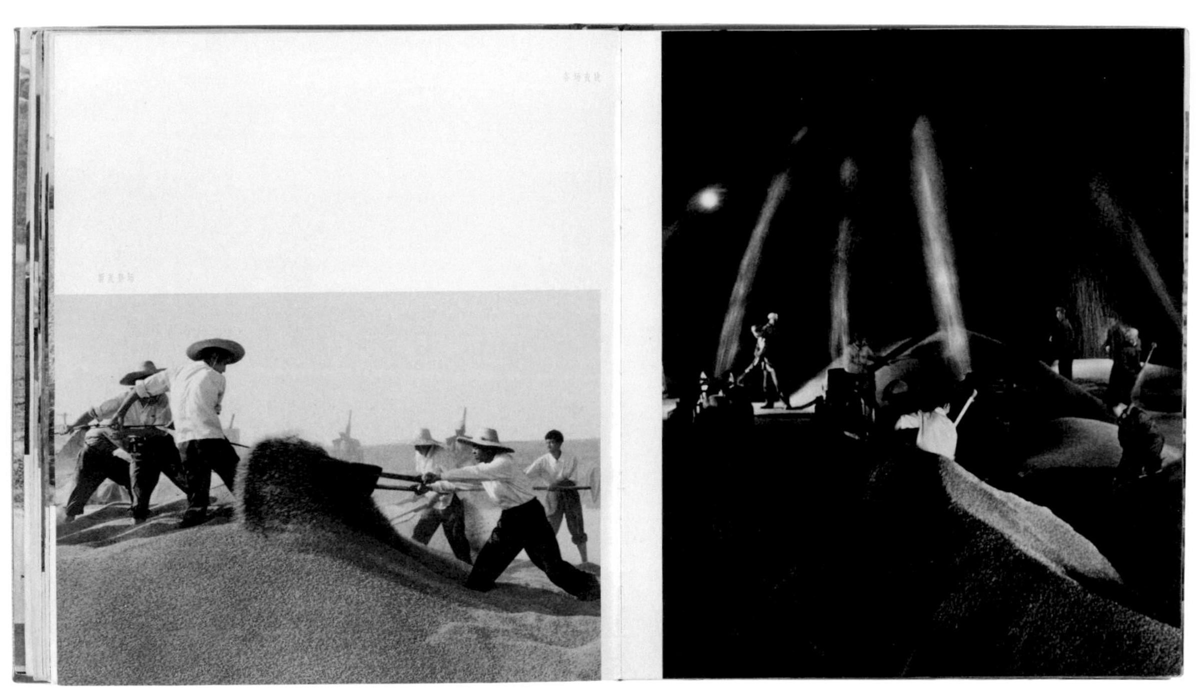

plate 54 (Left) 新麦登场 - Launching the New Wheat (Right) 谷场夜战 - Night Battle in the Threshing Field

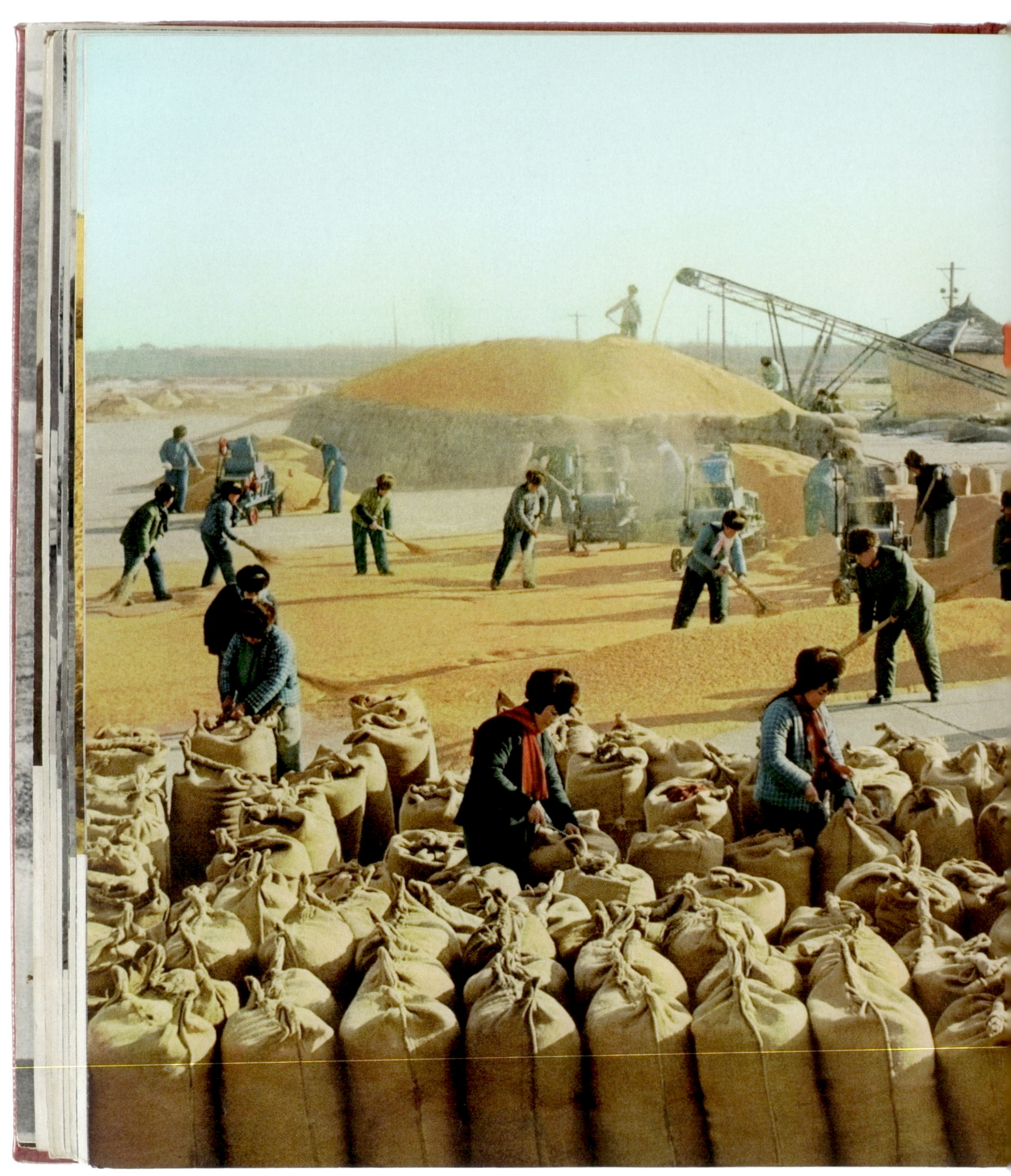

plate 55　为革命多打粮 - Threshing for the Revolution

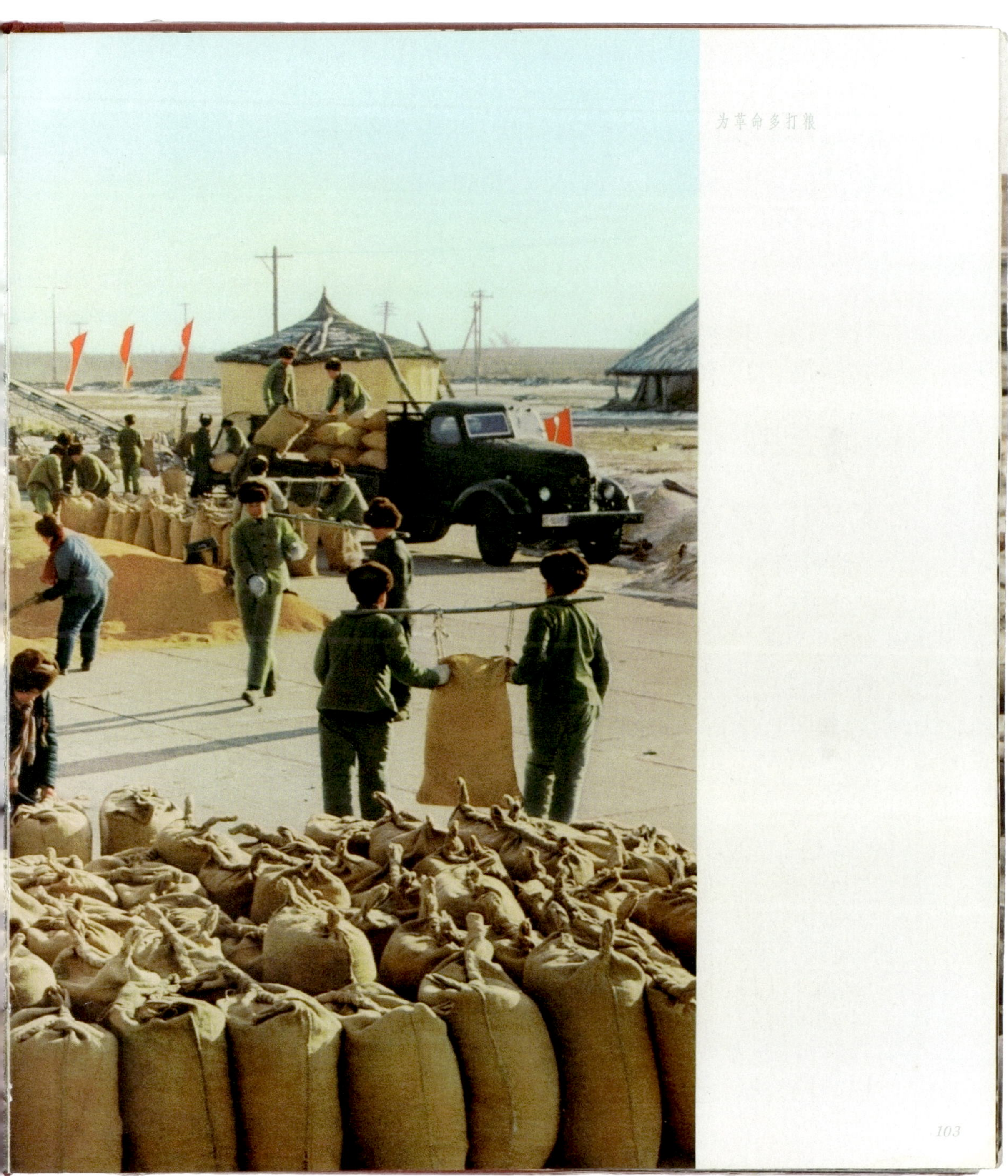

为革命多打粮

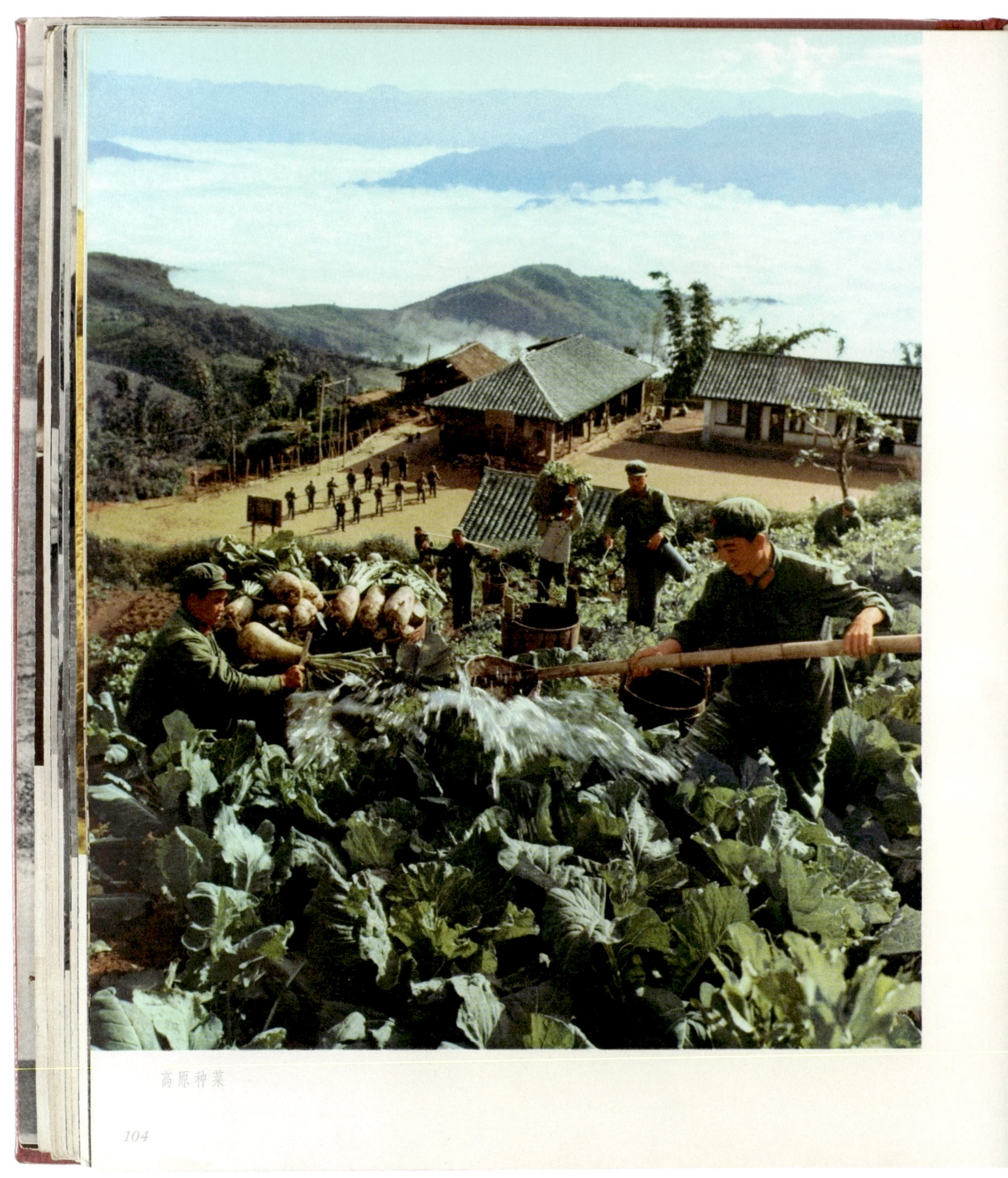

高原种菜

plate 56 (Above) 高原种菜 - Farming the Plateau (Opposite) 科学育秧 - Scientific Seedling

科学育秧

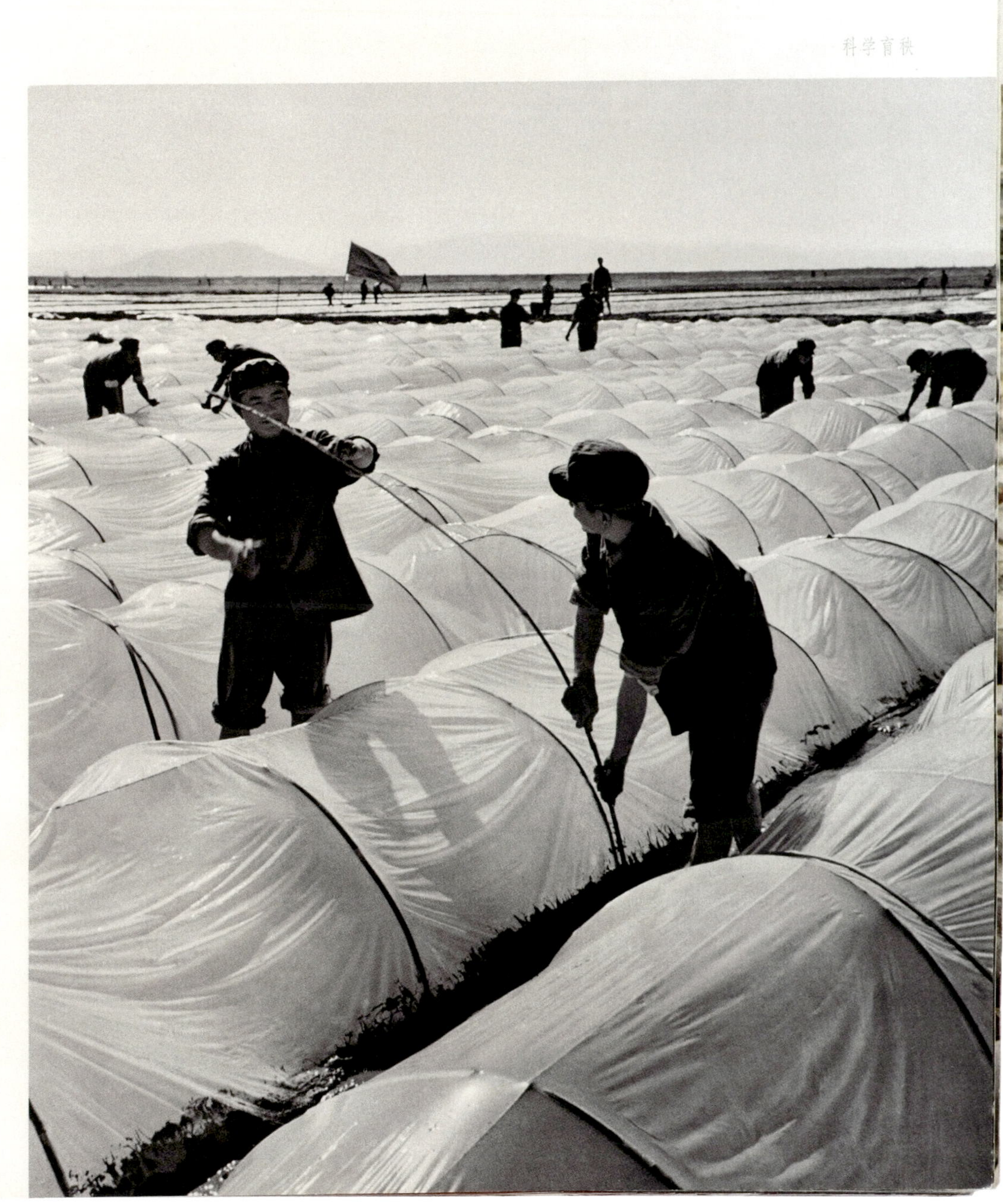

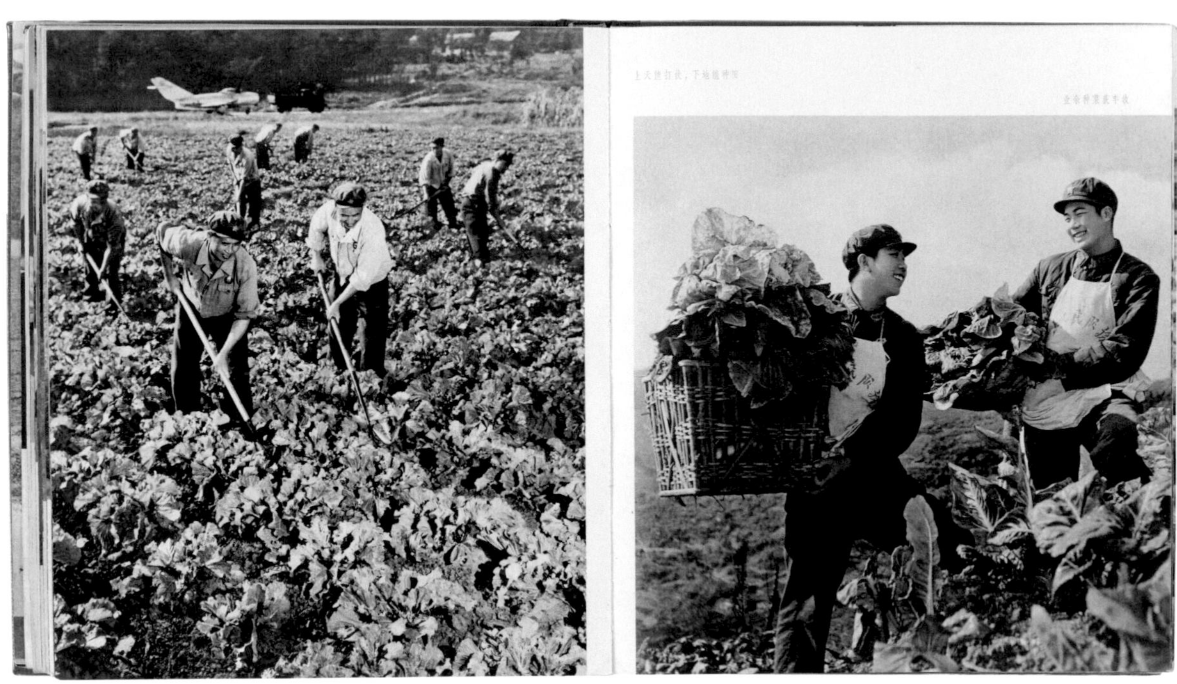

plate 57 (Left) 上天能打仗，下地能种田 - One can Fight in the Sky and Farm in the Field (Right) 业余种菜获丰收 - The Harvest of Amateur Farming

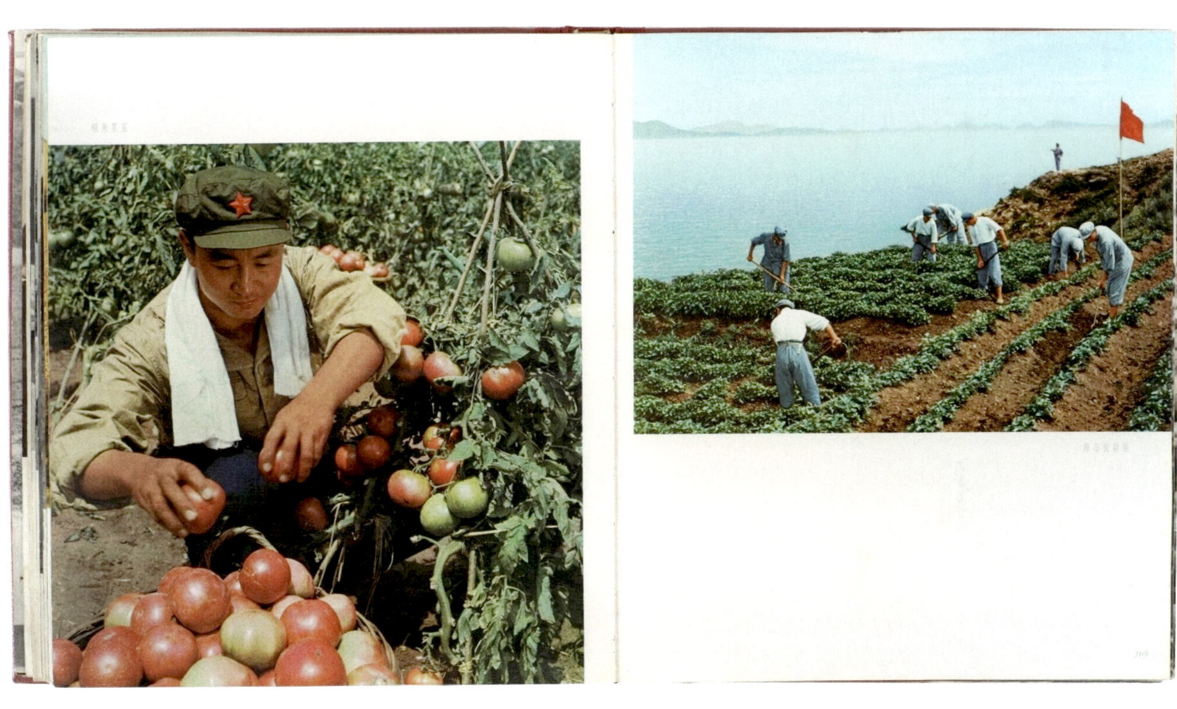

plate 58 (Left) 硕果累累 - Fruitful (Right) 海岛披新装 - The Island Has a New Look

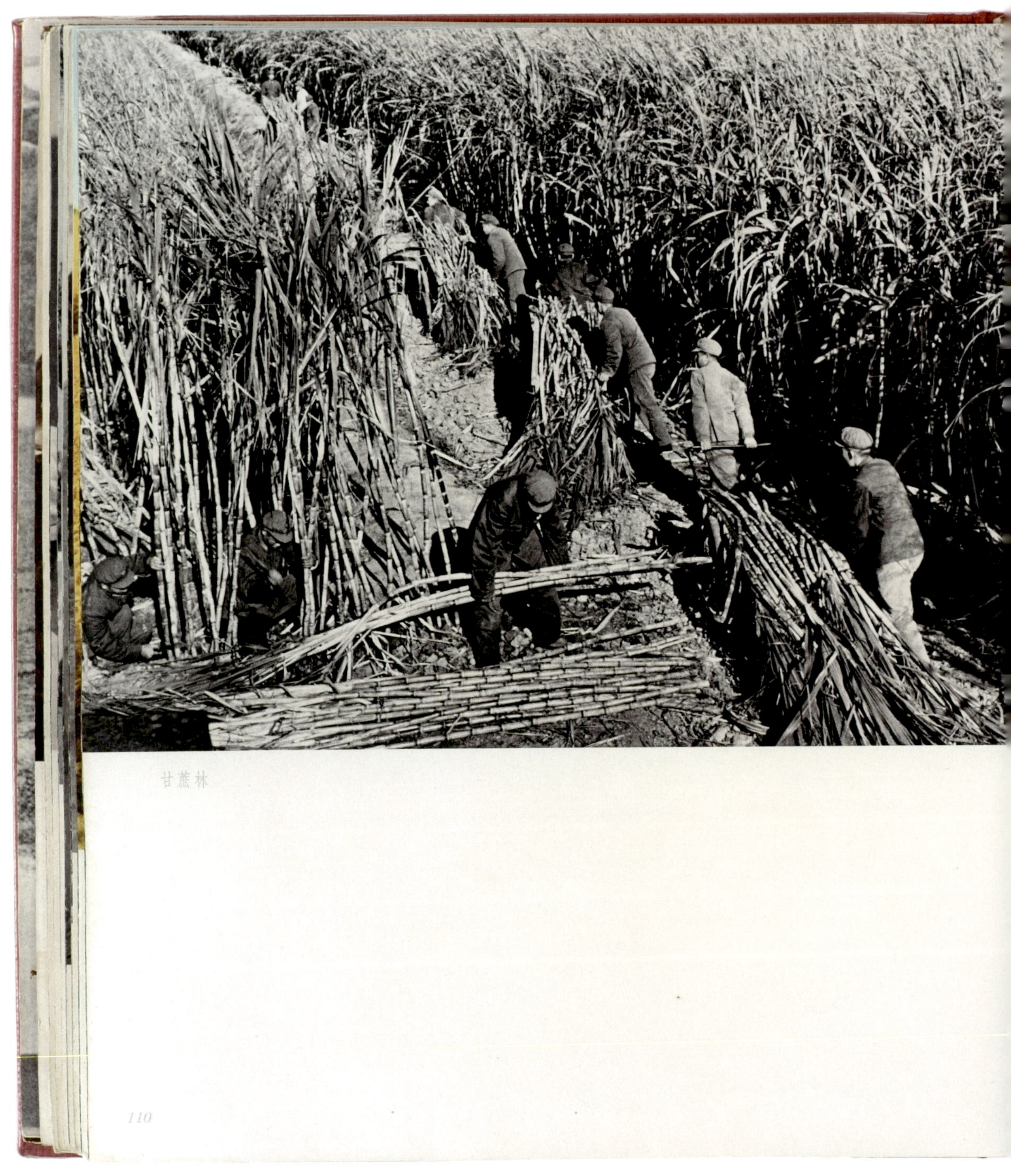

plate 59 (Above) 甘蔗林 - Forests of Sugarcane (Opposite) 高粱熟了 - The Ripe Sorghum

高粱熟了

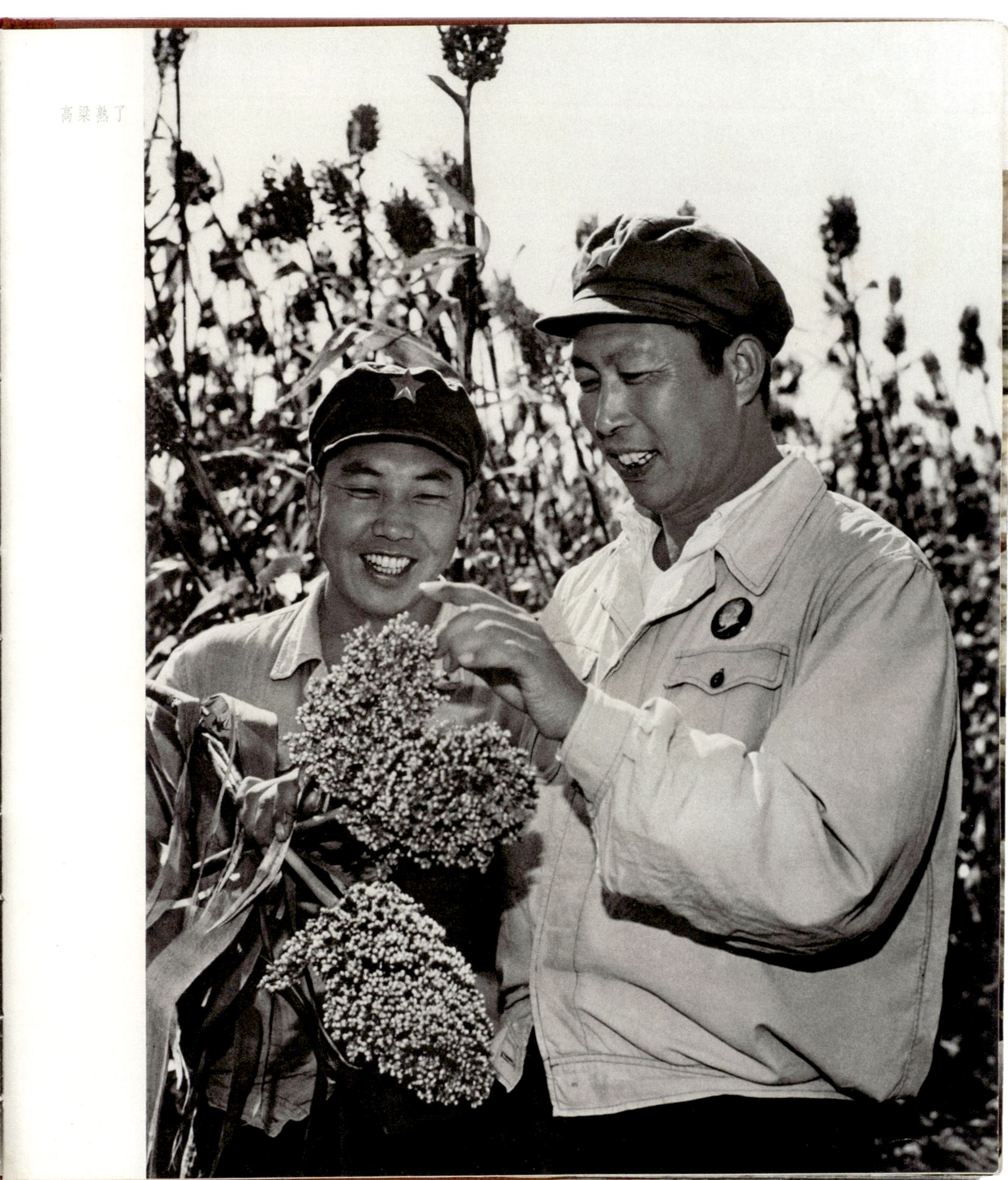

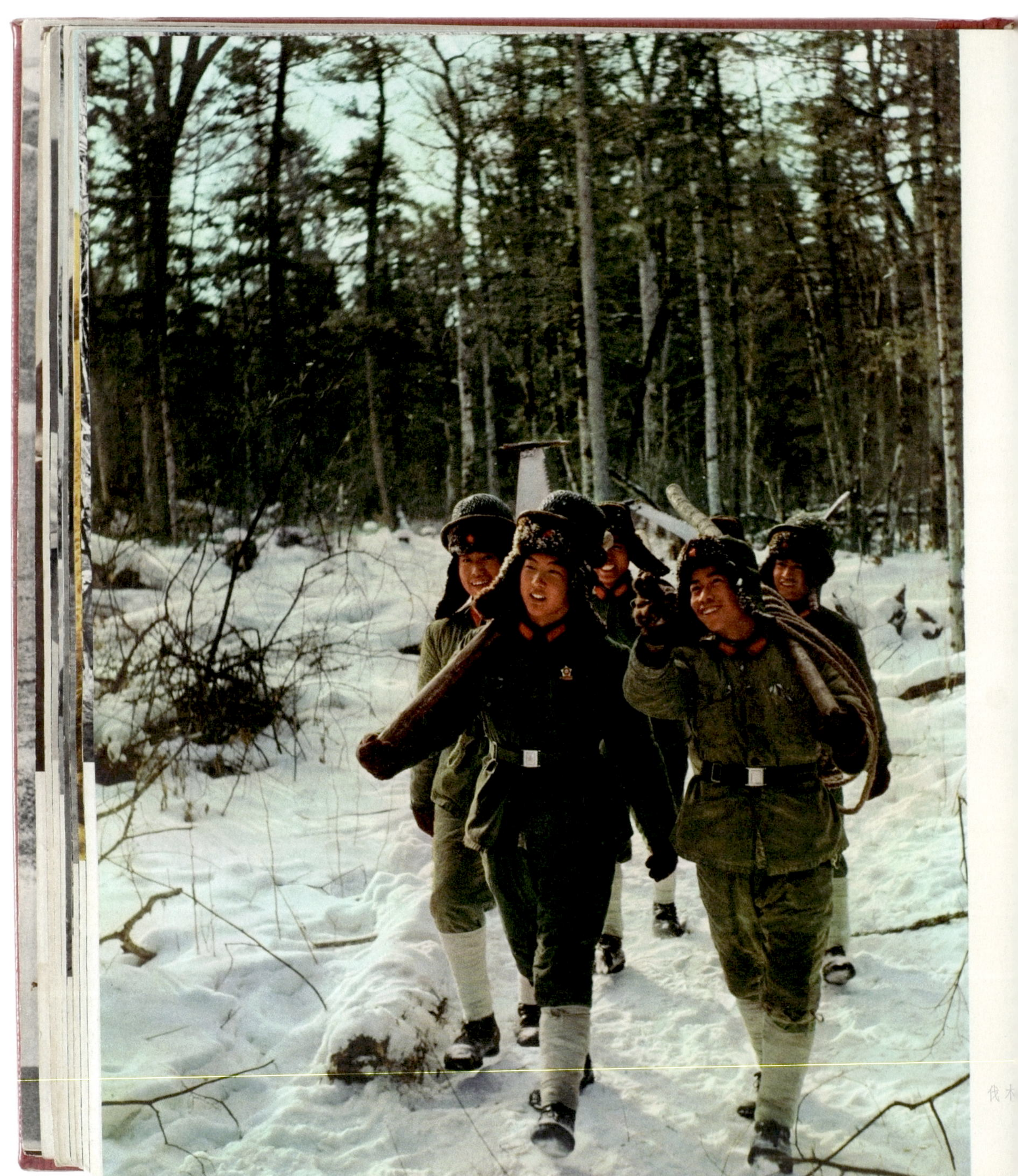

plate 60 (Above) 伐木路上 - On the Way to Lumbering (Opposite) 割橡胶 - Tapping Rubber

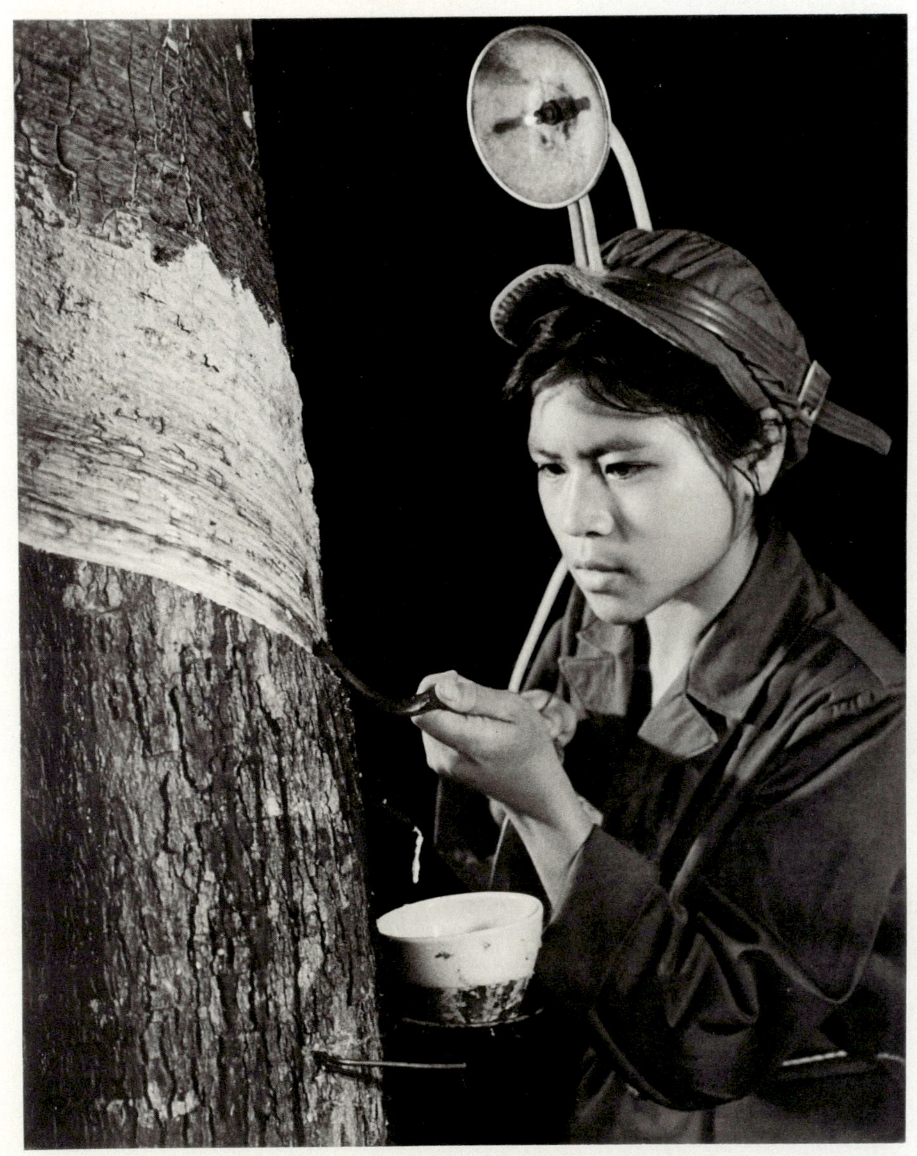

割橡胶

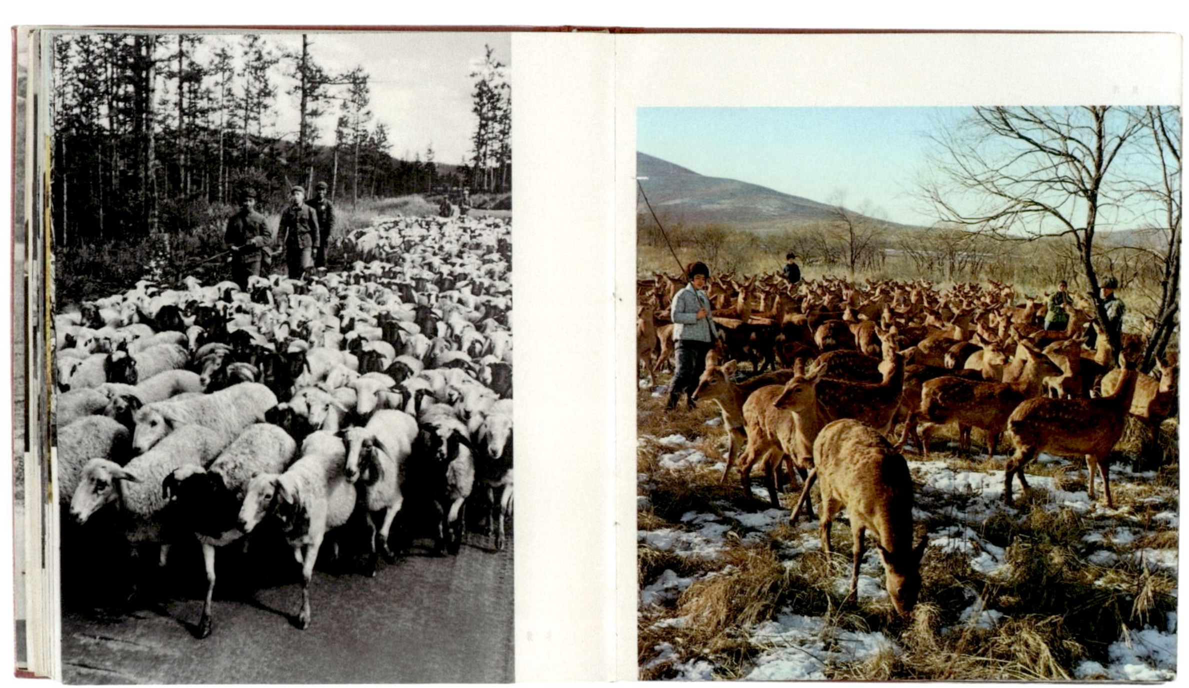

plate 61 (Left) 牧羊 - Herding Sheep (Right) 驯鹿 - Taming Deer

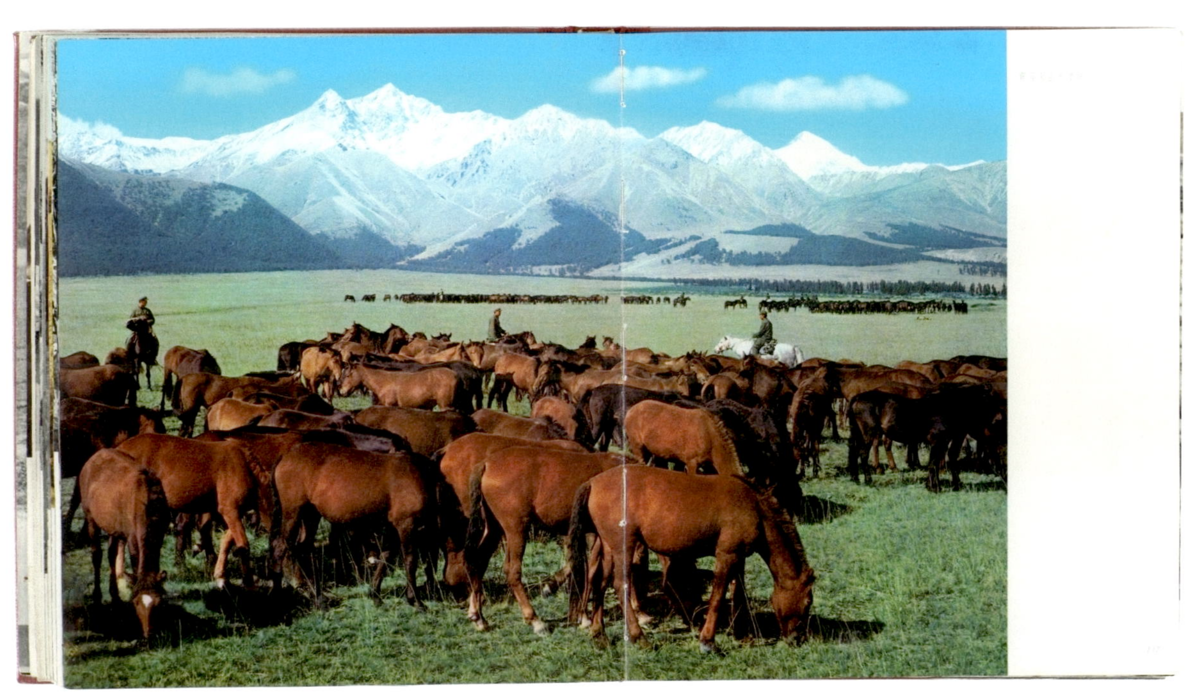

plate 62　育马天山为革命 - Breeding Horses on Mount Tian for the Revolution

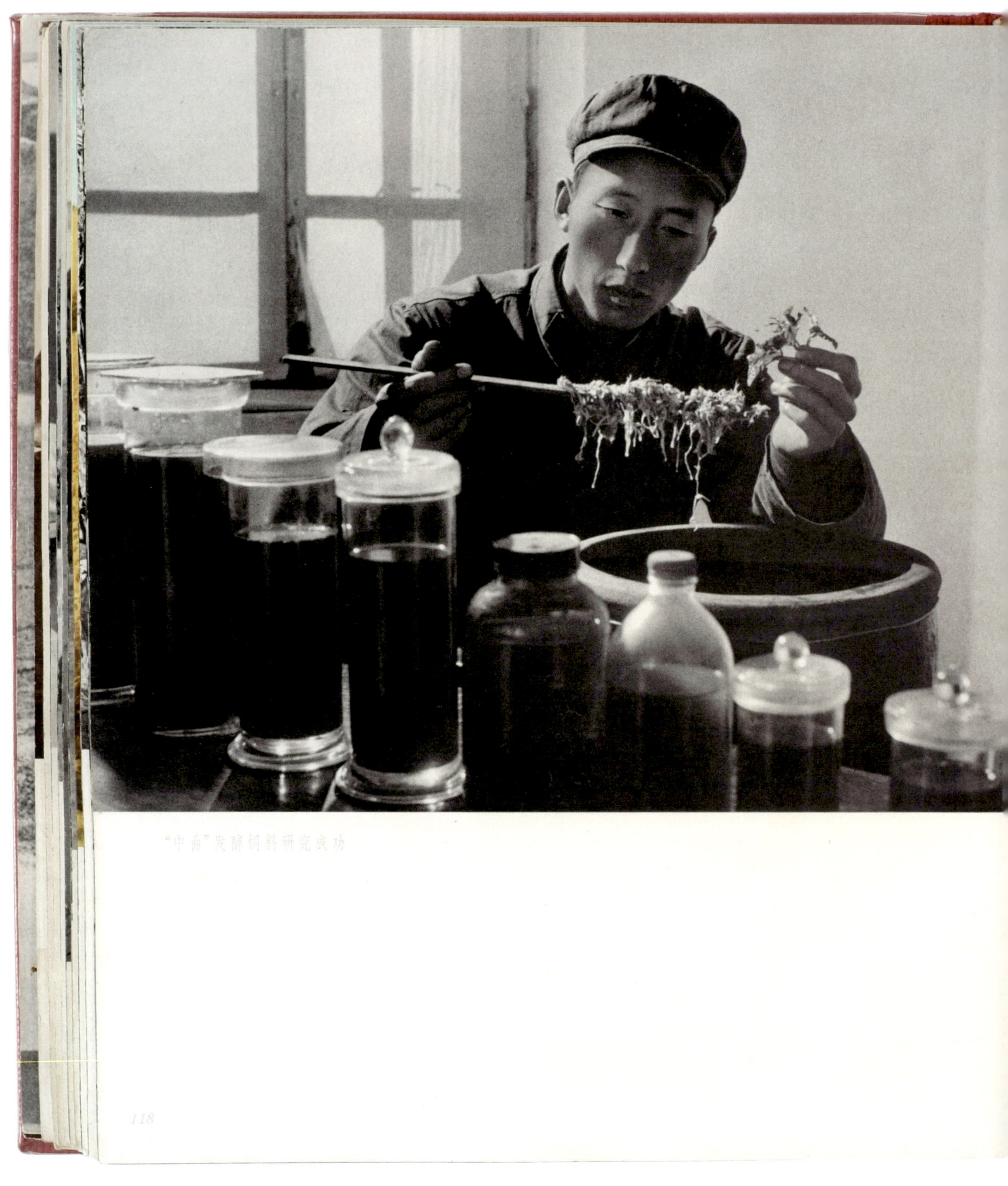

plate 63 (Above) "中曲" 发酵饲料研究成功 - The "Zhongqu" Fermented Feed Research is a Success (Opposite) 发展养猪事业 - Develop Pig Farming

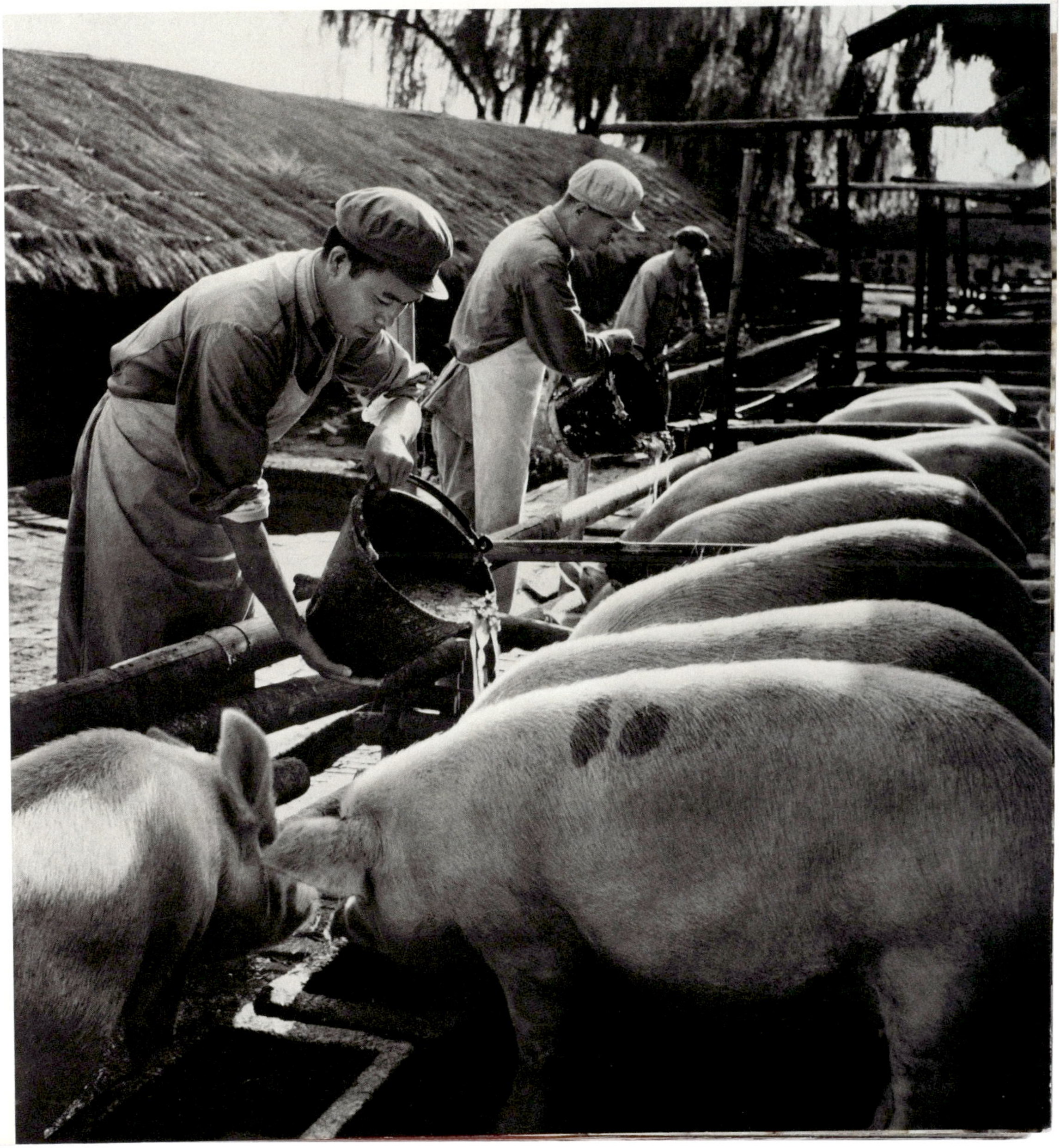

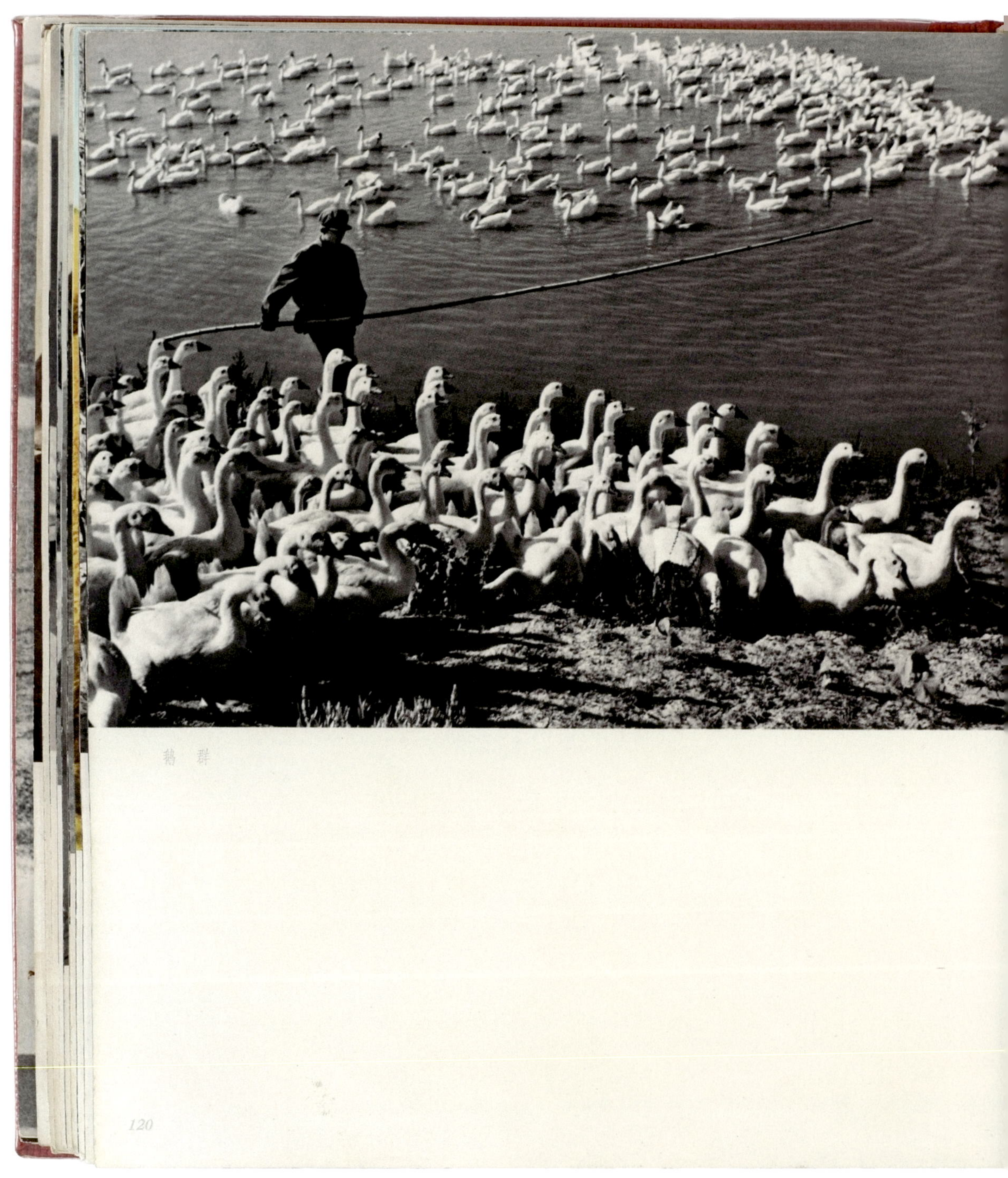

plate 64 (Above) 鹅群 - A Gaggle of Geese (Opposite) 蛋品丰产 - The Egg Yield

蛋品丰产

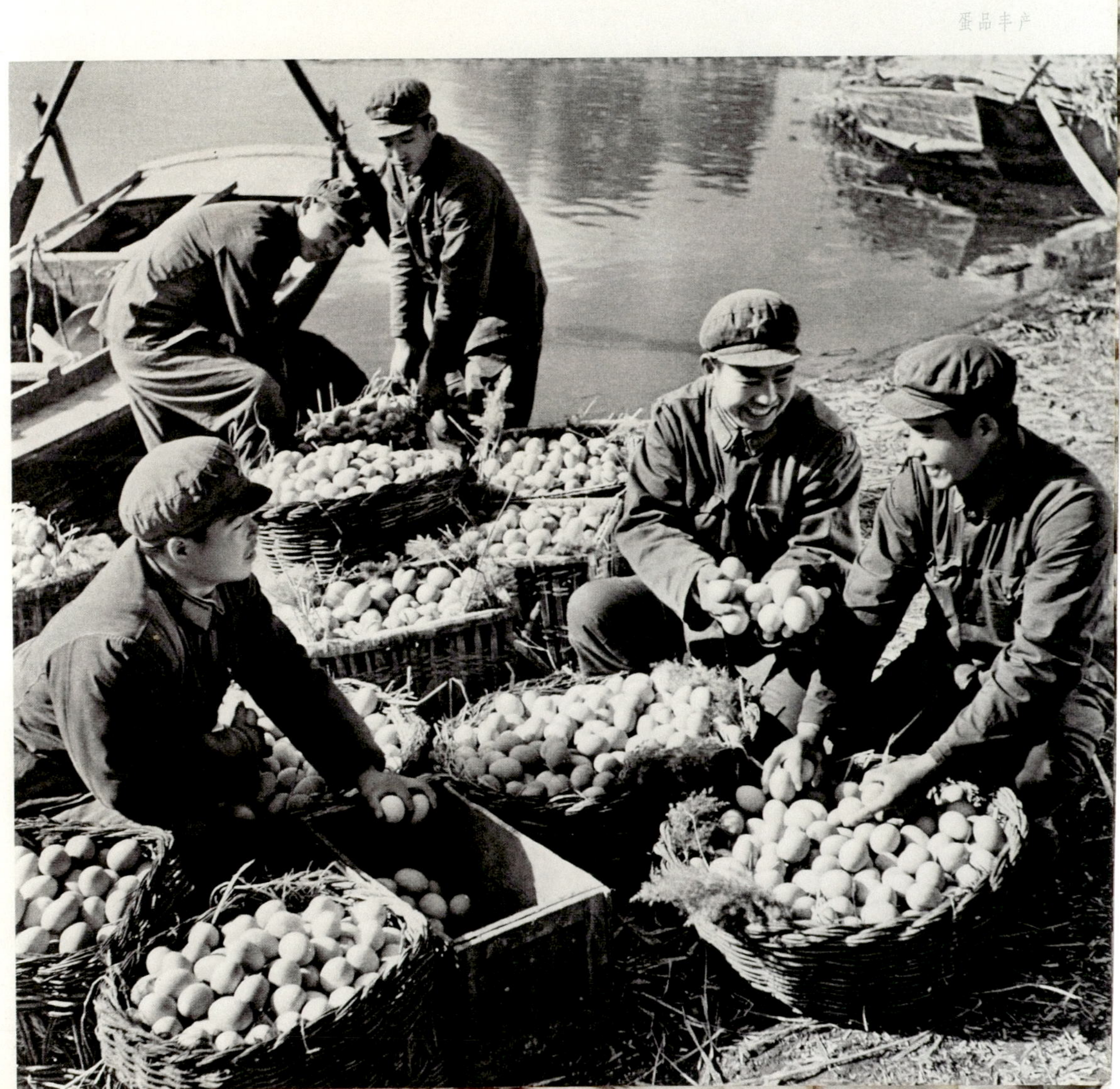

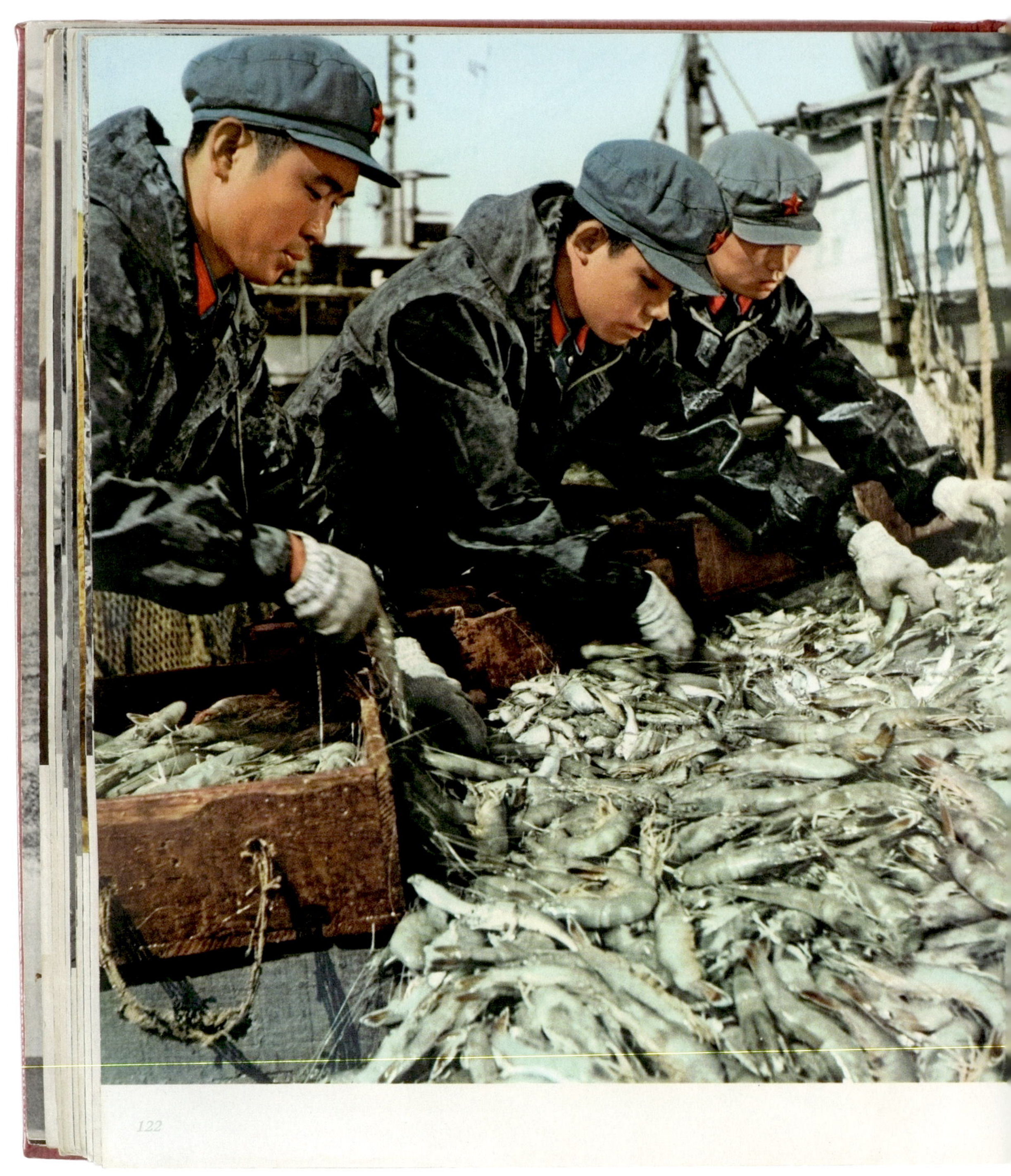

plate 65 (Above) 捕虾 - Catching Shrimp (Opposite) 乌苏里江鲑鱼肥 - Trout in the Ussuri River

捕　虾

乌苏里江鲑鱼肥

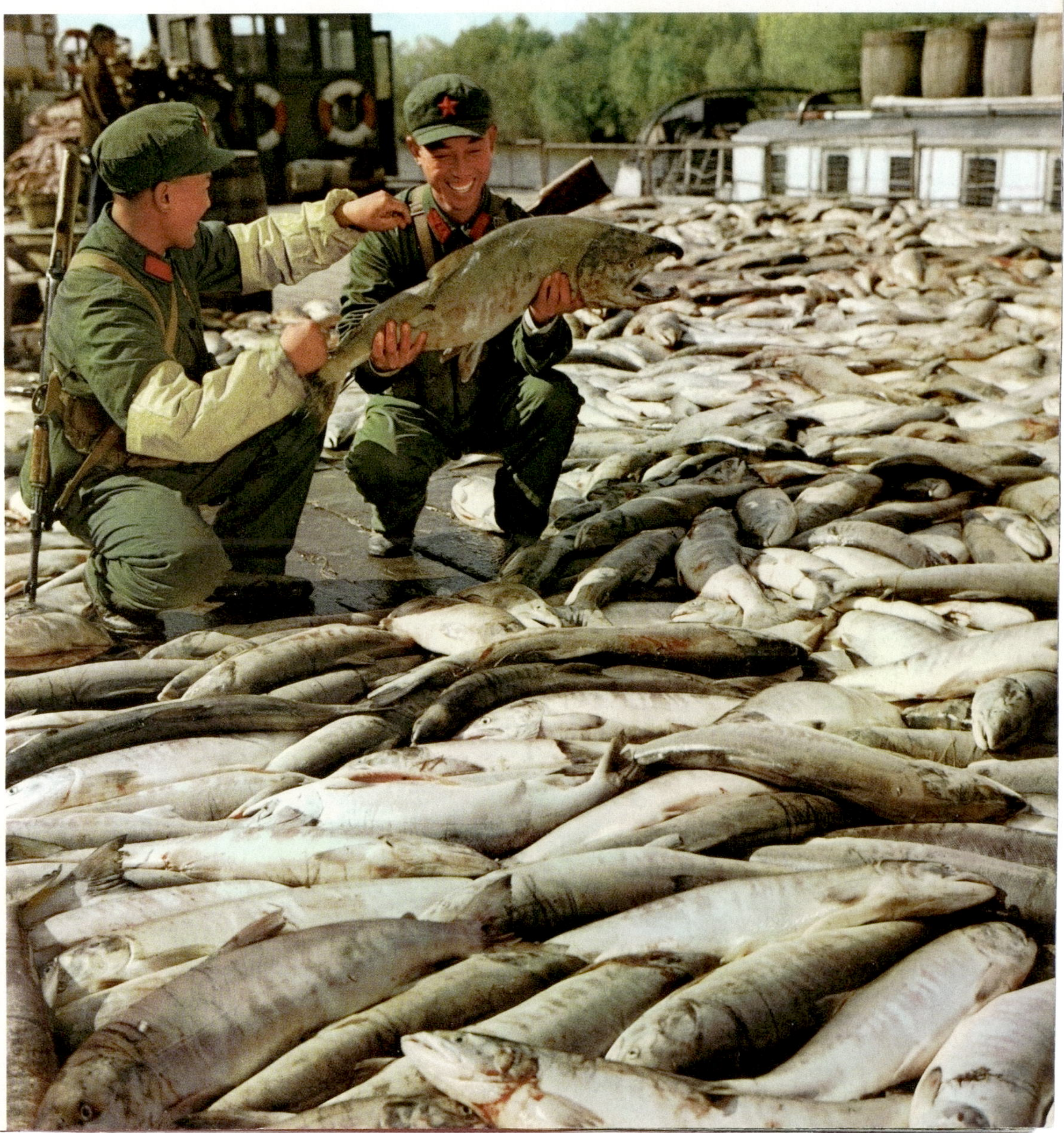

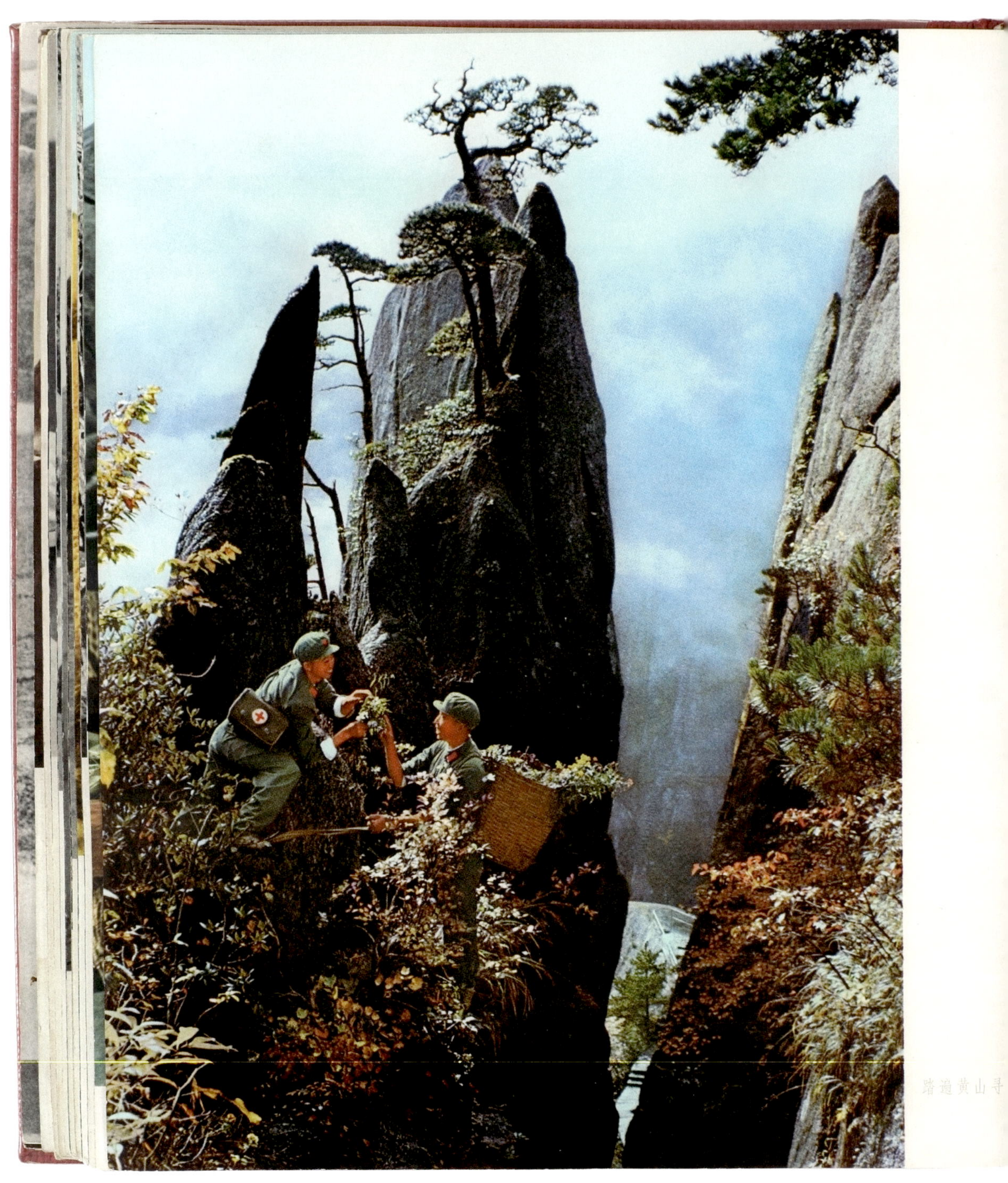

plate 66 (Above) 踏遍黄山寻草药 - Looking for Herbal Medicine on Mount Huang (Opposite) 漓江边上采药归 - Returning from collecting Herbal Medicines from the Lijiang River bank.

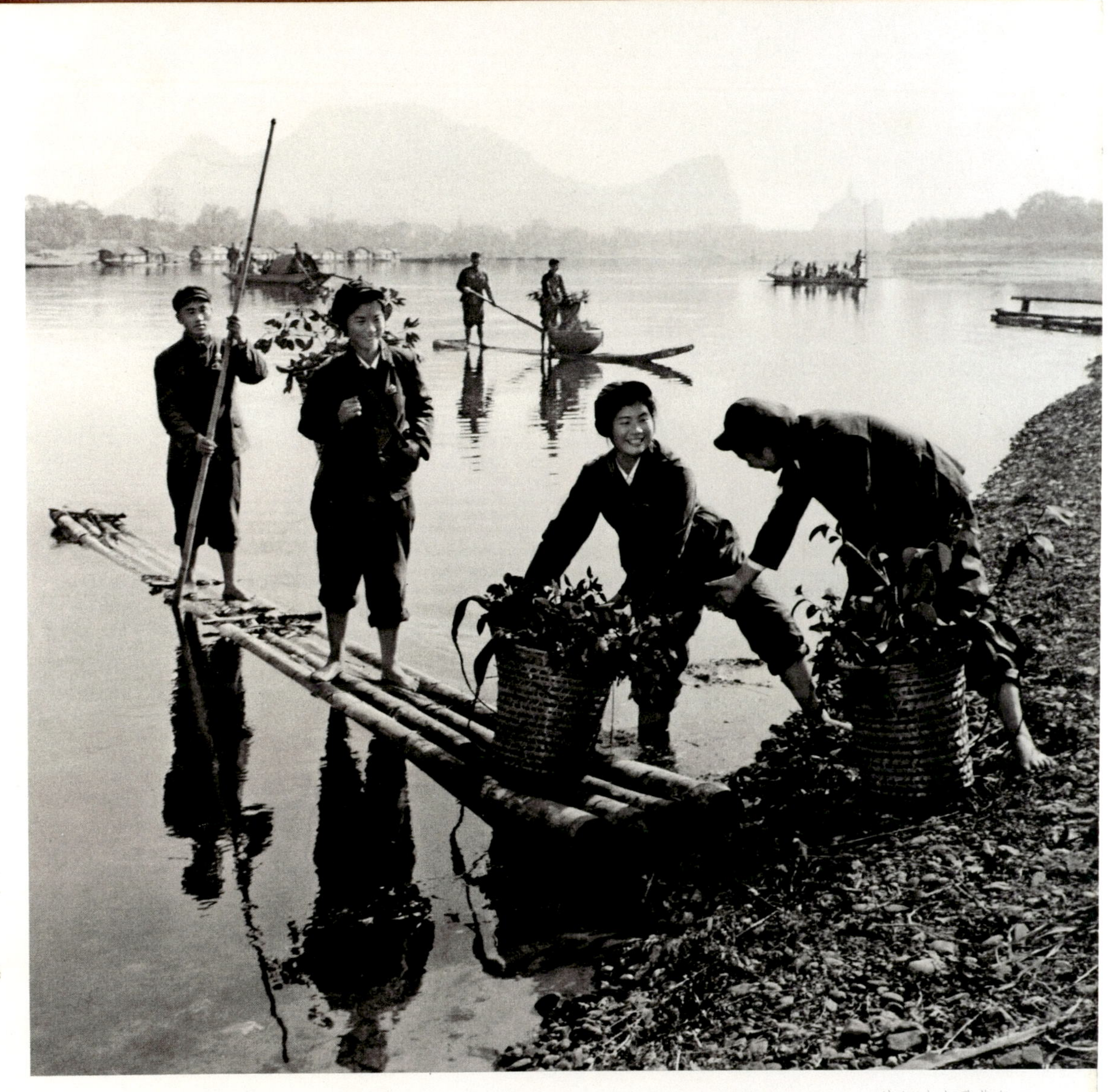

漓江边上采药归

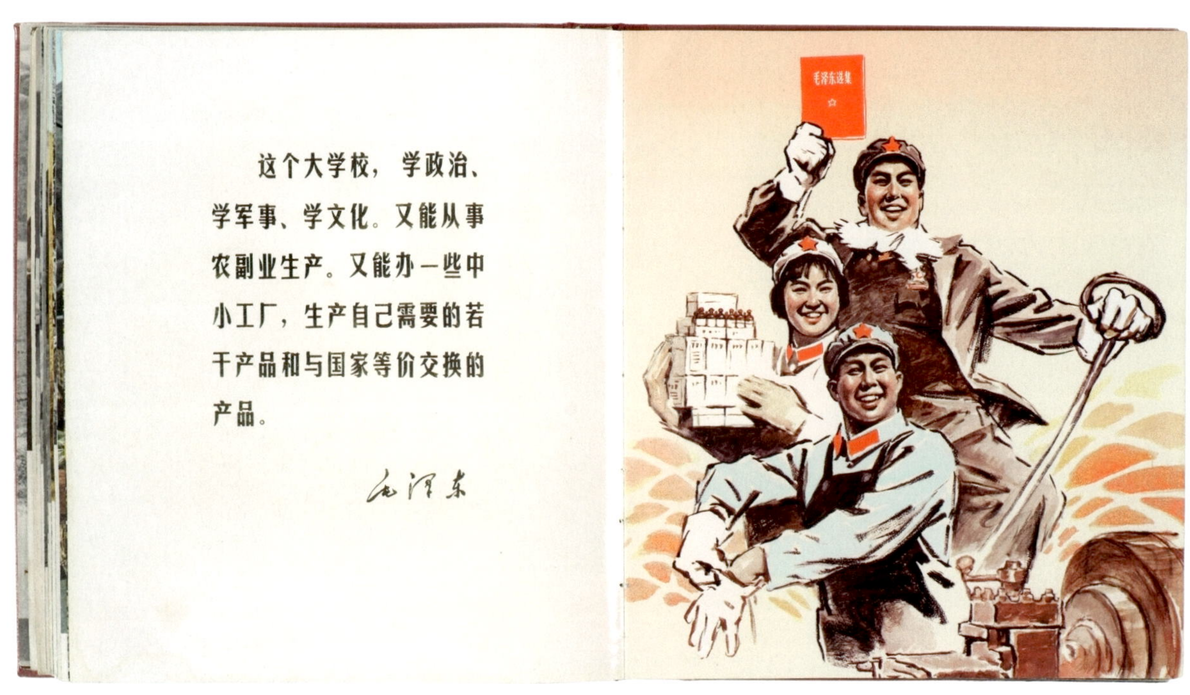

plate 67 这个大学校, 学政治, 学军事, 学文化. 又能从事农副业生产. 又能办一些中小工厂, 生产自己需要的若干产品和与国家等价交换的产品. - In this great school, troops study politics, military affairs and culture. They can engage in agricultural production and related occupations. They can also run some small or medium-sized factories to make certain products for their own needs or for exchange with the state at equal value.

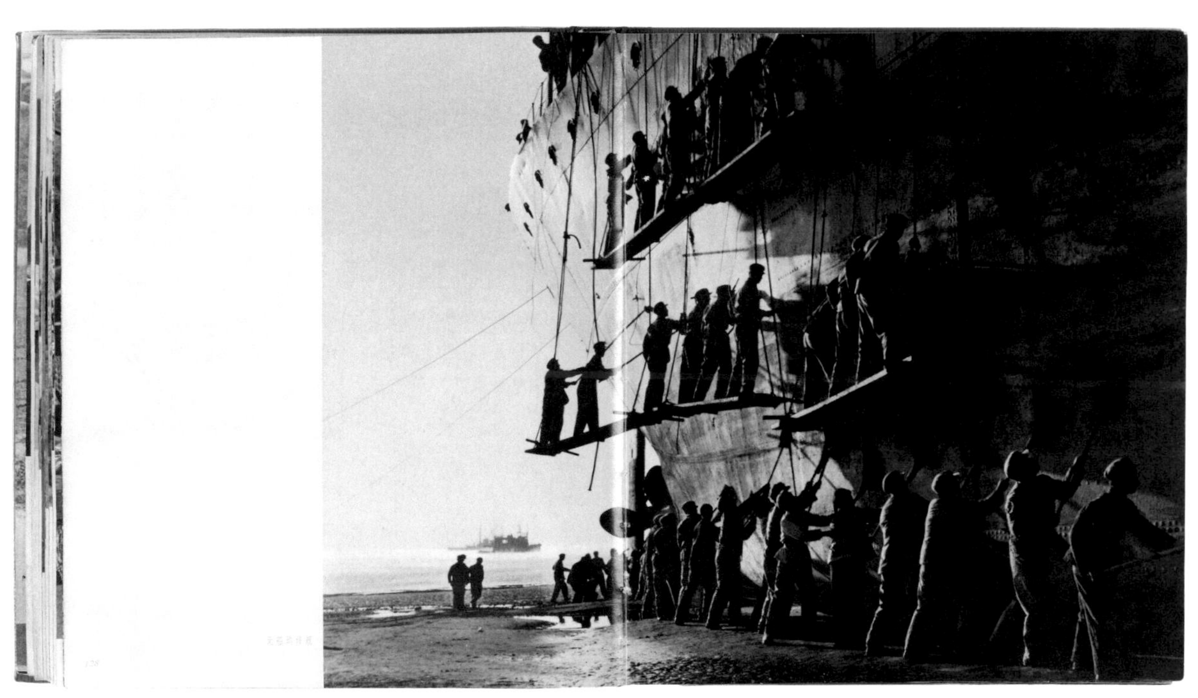

plate 68 无船坞修舰 - Repairing the Ship Without a Dock

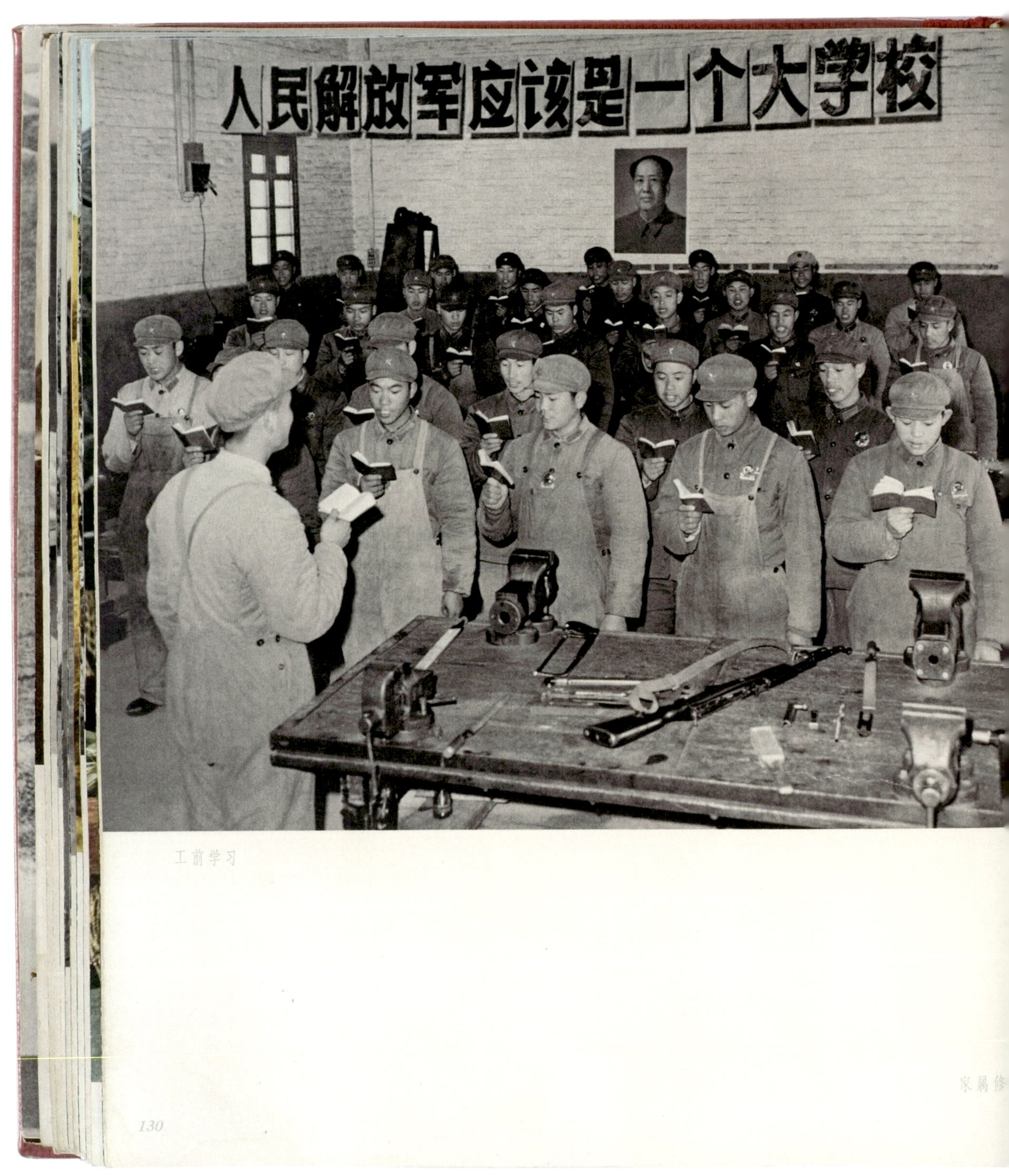

plate 69 (Above) 工前学习 - Studying Before Work (Opposite) 家属修飞机 - The Relatives Are Repairing a Plane

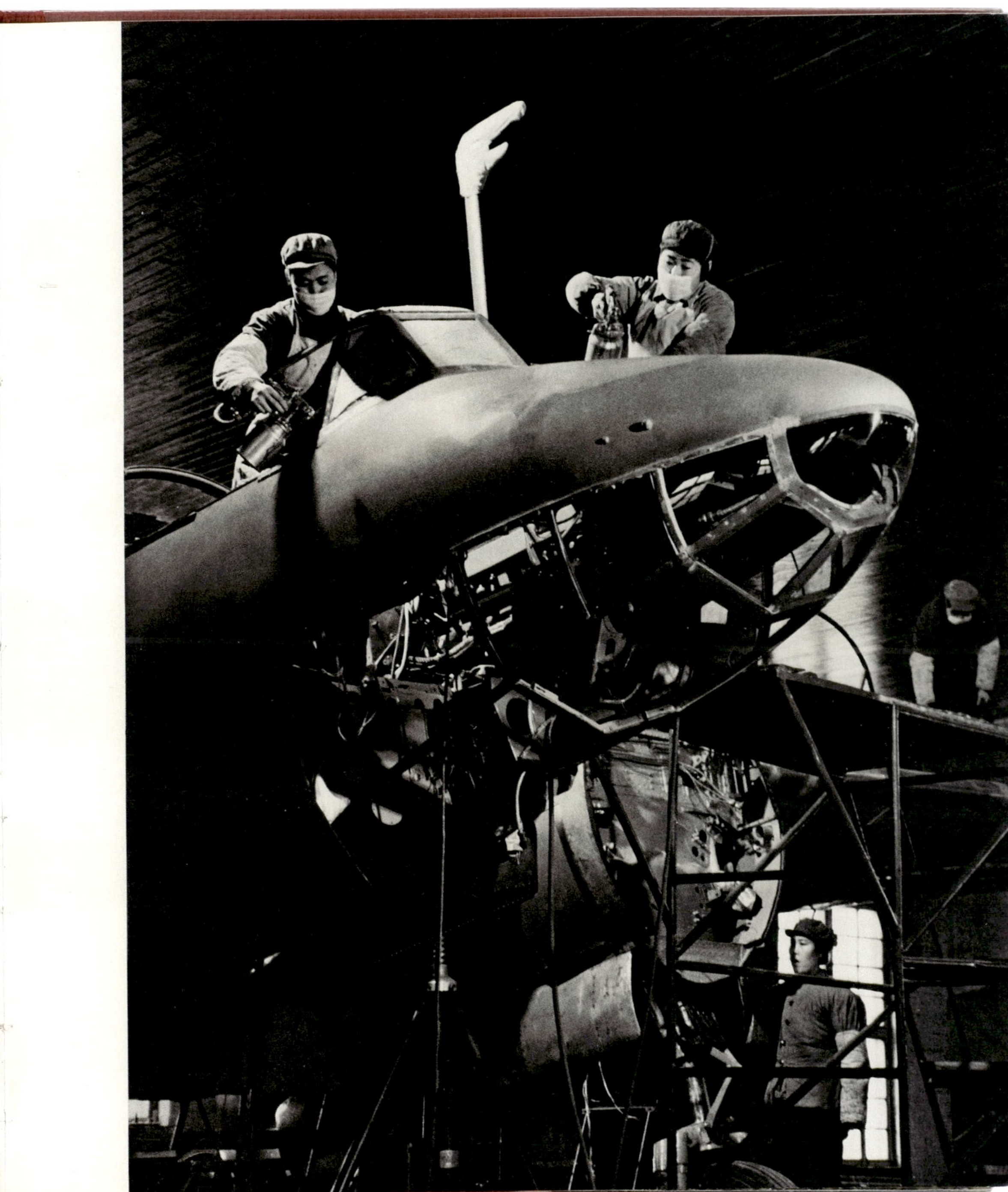

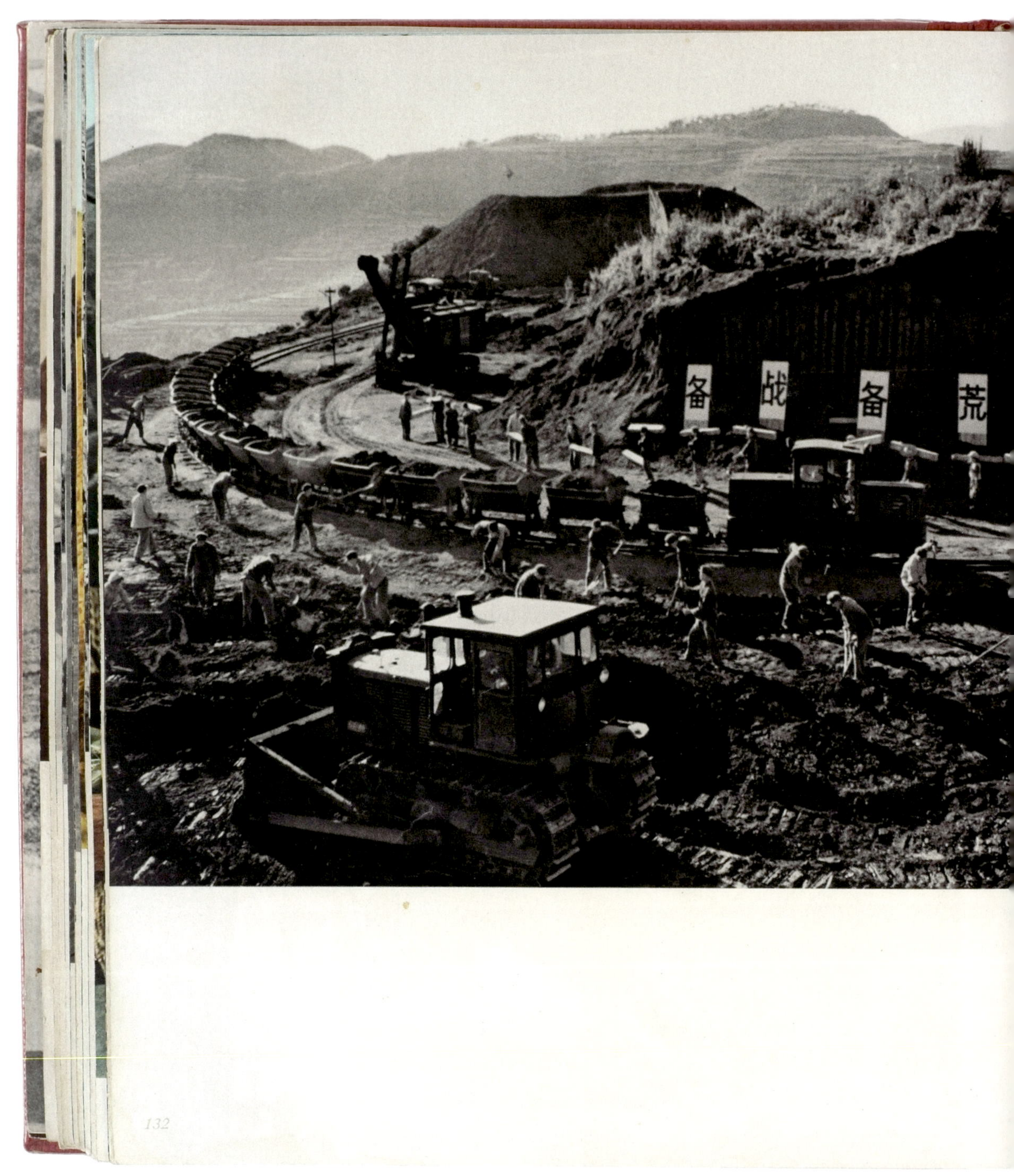

plate 70　多快好省开采锰矿 - Develop Manganese Mining to Be Better, Faster, and Cheaper

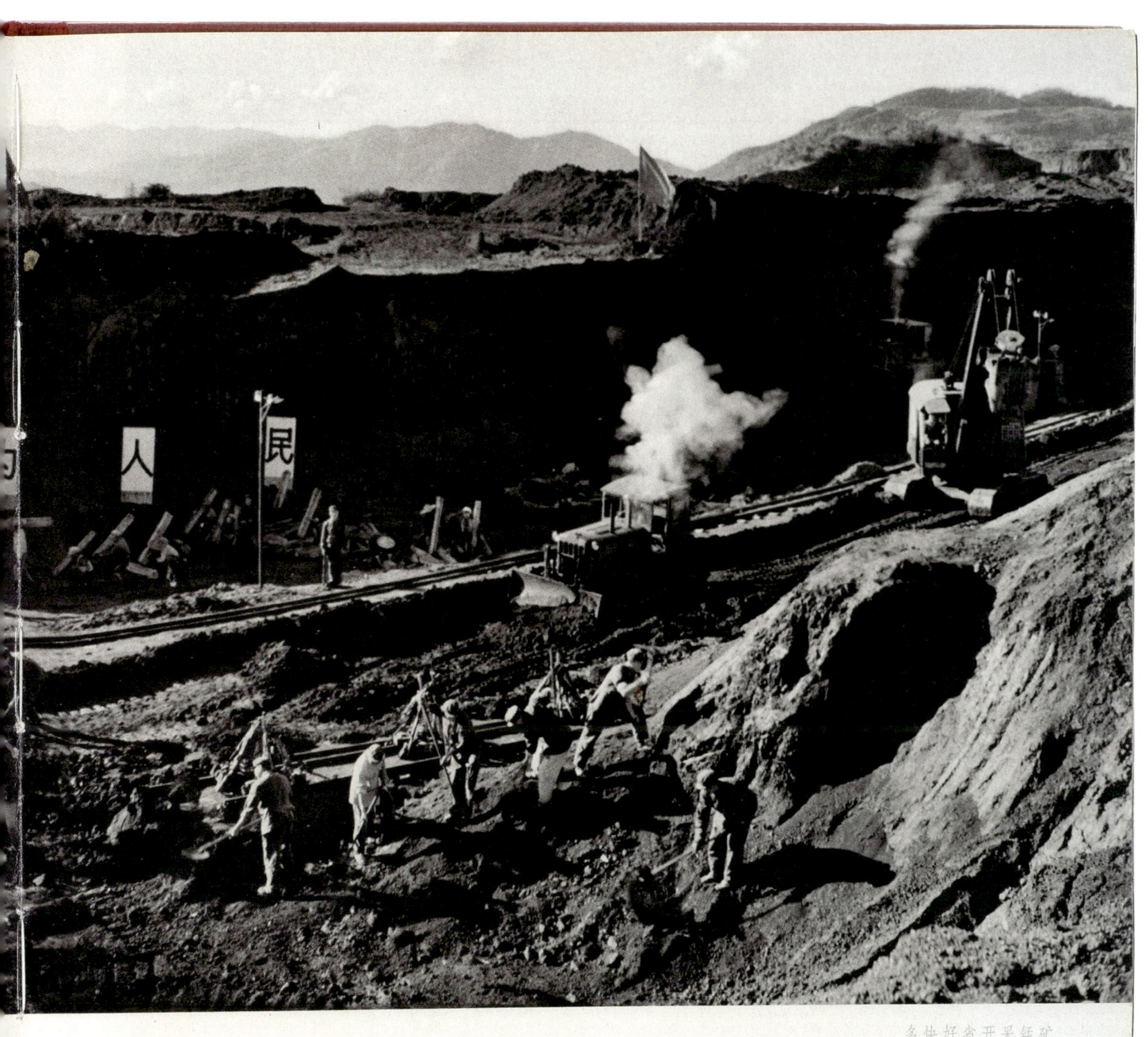

多快好省开采锰矿

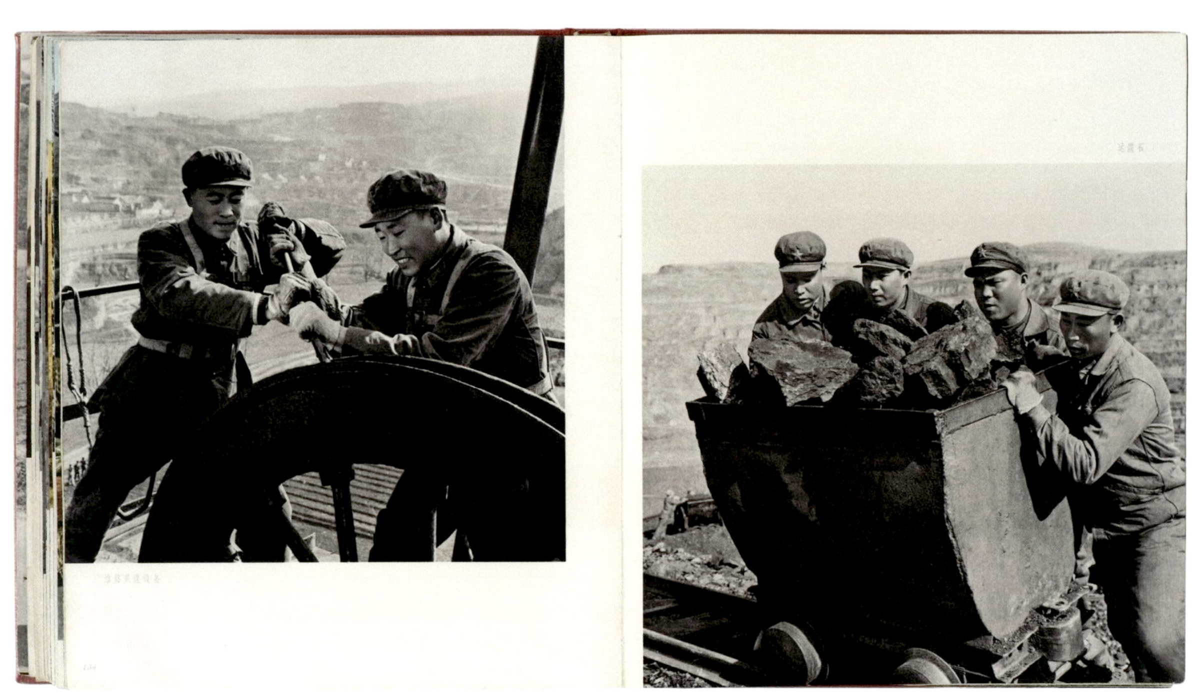

plate 71 (Left) 维修采煤设备 - Repairing the Coal Mining Equipment (Right) 运煤石 - Transporting Coal

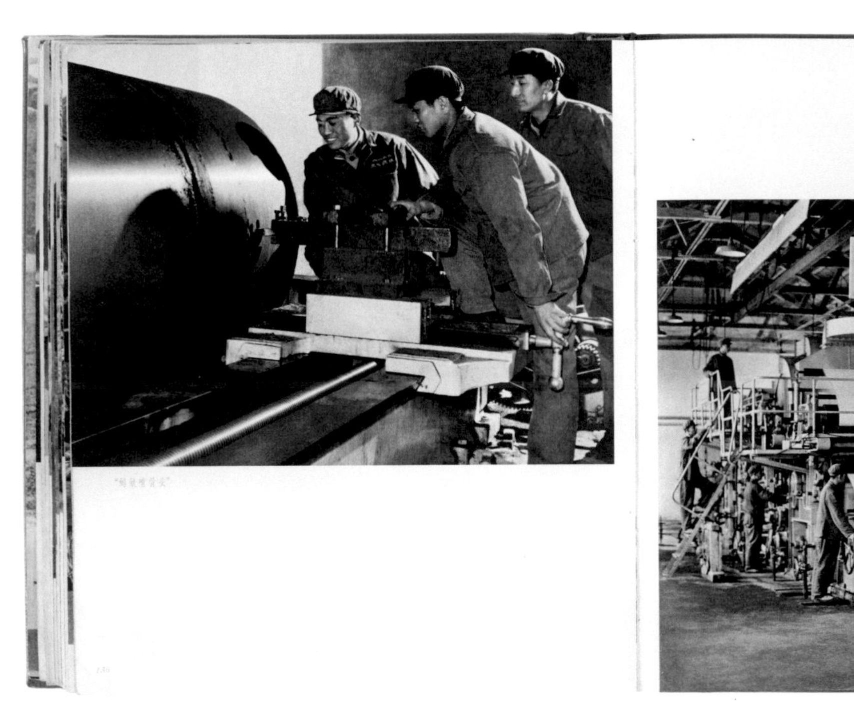

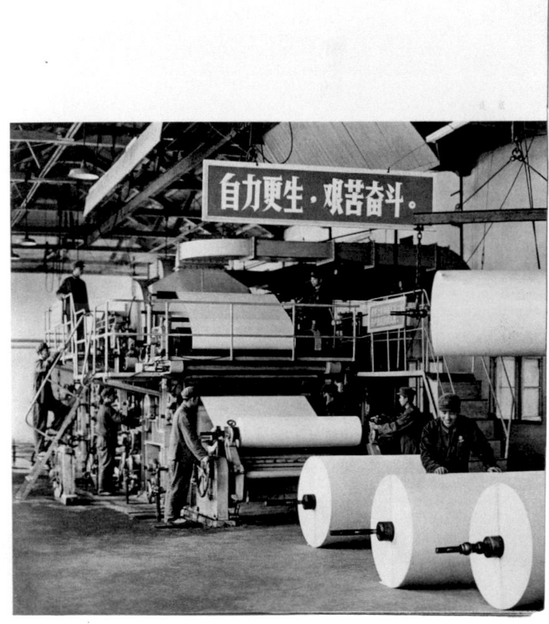

plate 72 (Left) "蚂蚁啃骨头" - "Like an Ant Chewing a Bone" (Right) 造纸 - Making Paper

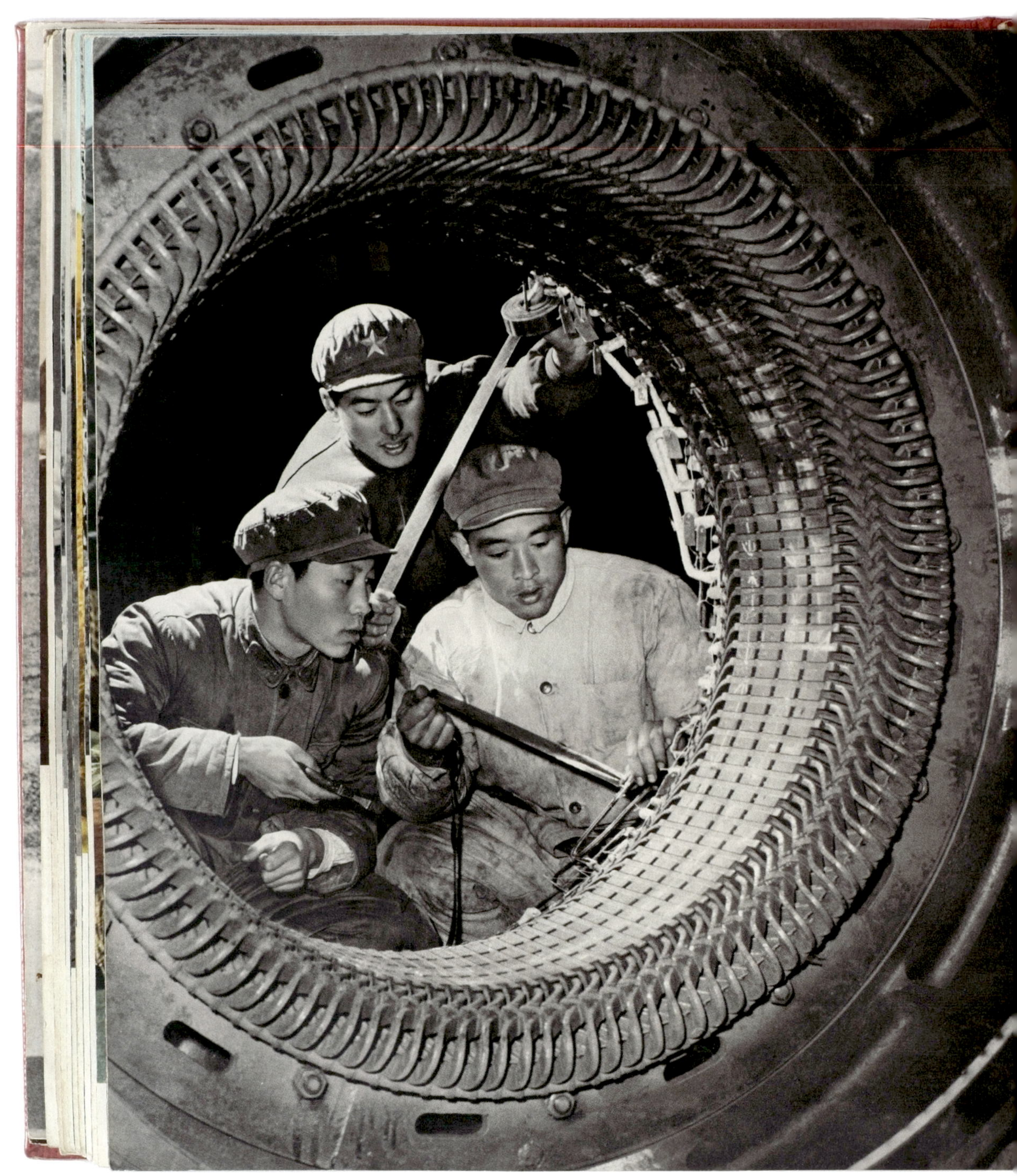

plate 73 (Above) 绕线圈 - Winding the Coils (Opposite) 土法炼钢 - Traditional Steelmaking

土法炼钢

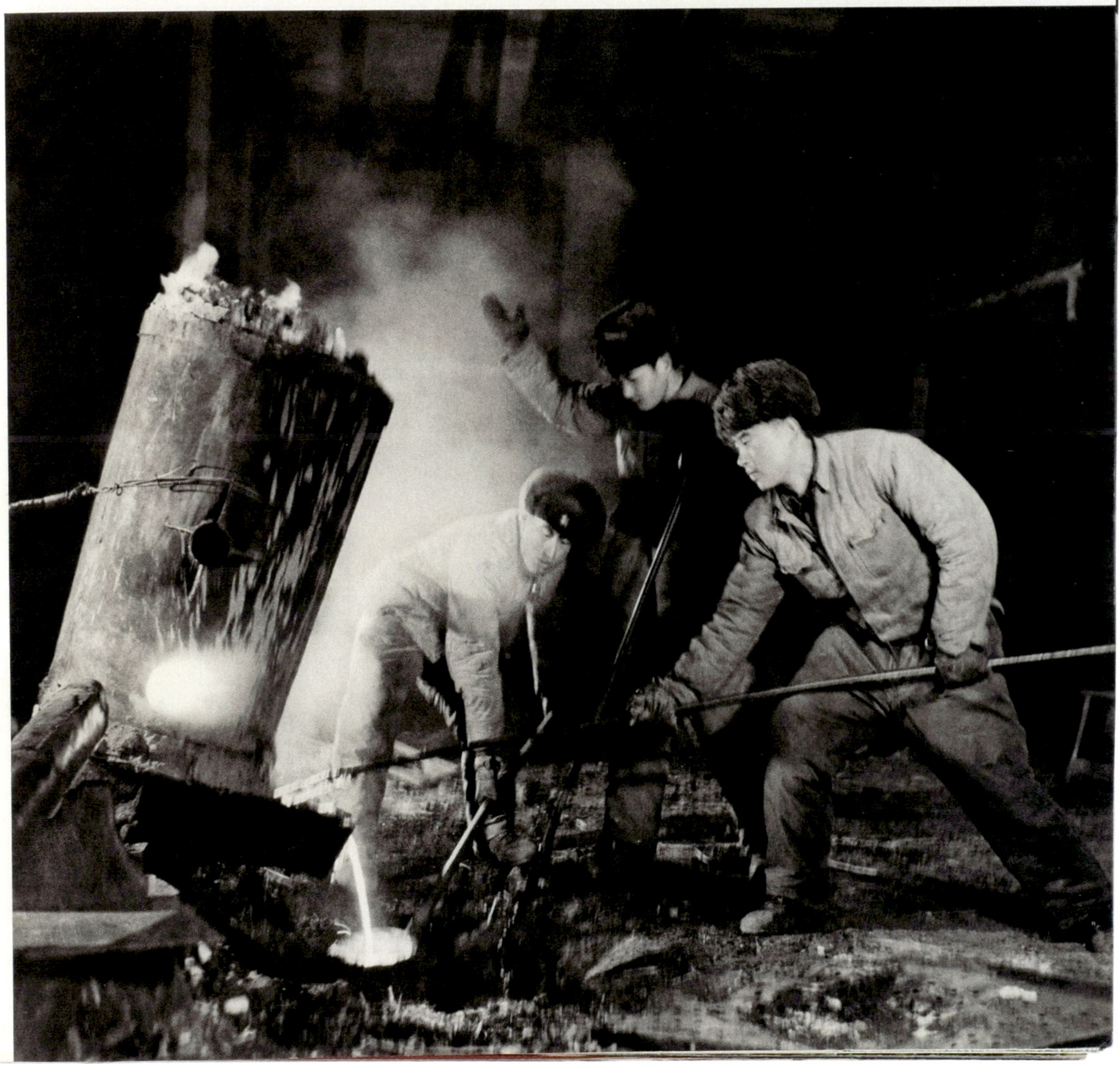

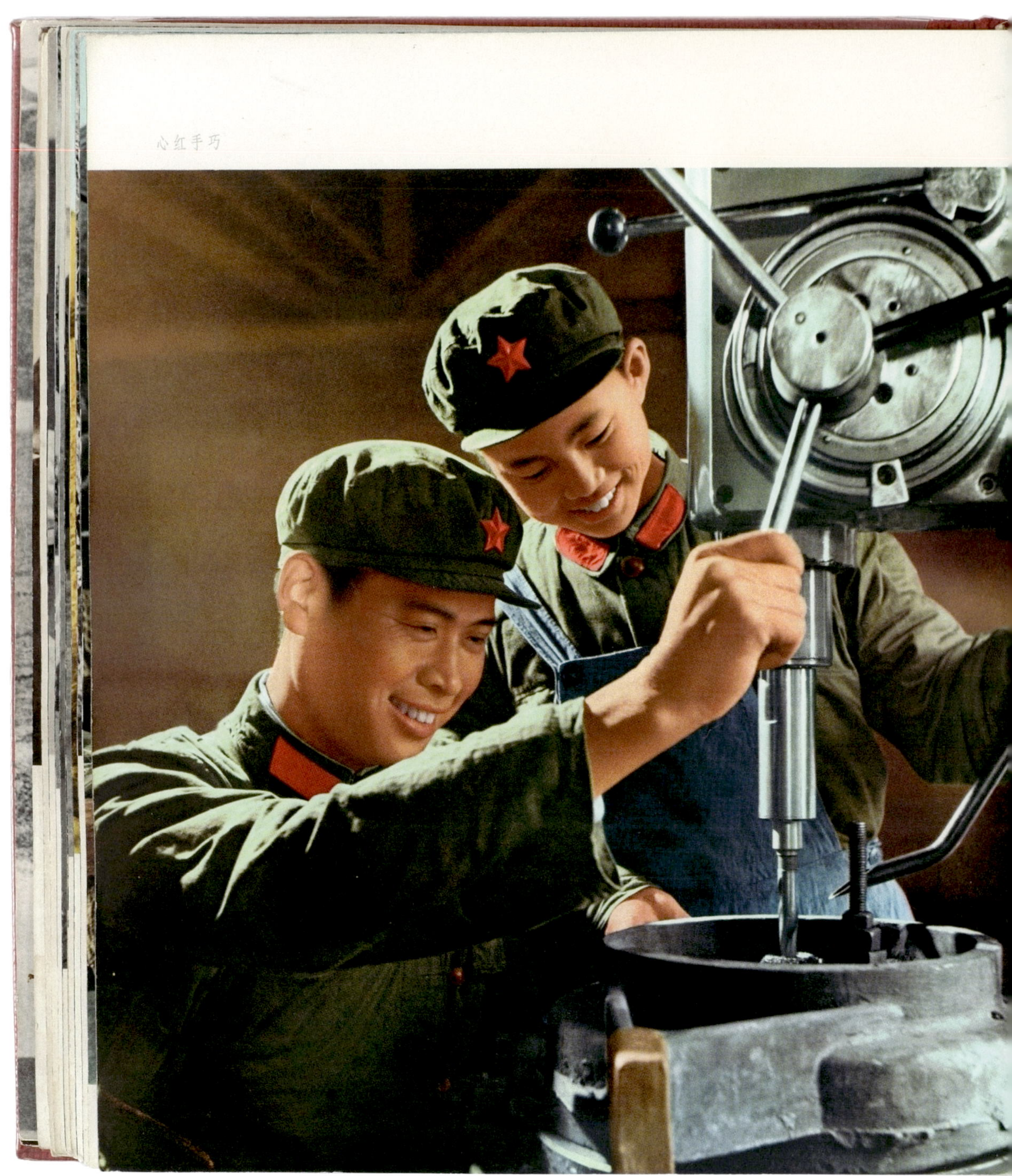

plate 74 (Above) 心红手巧 - Dexterous Hands, Red Heart (Opposite) 领导深入车间 - The Leader Visits the Factory

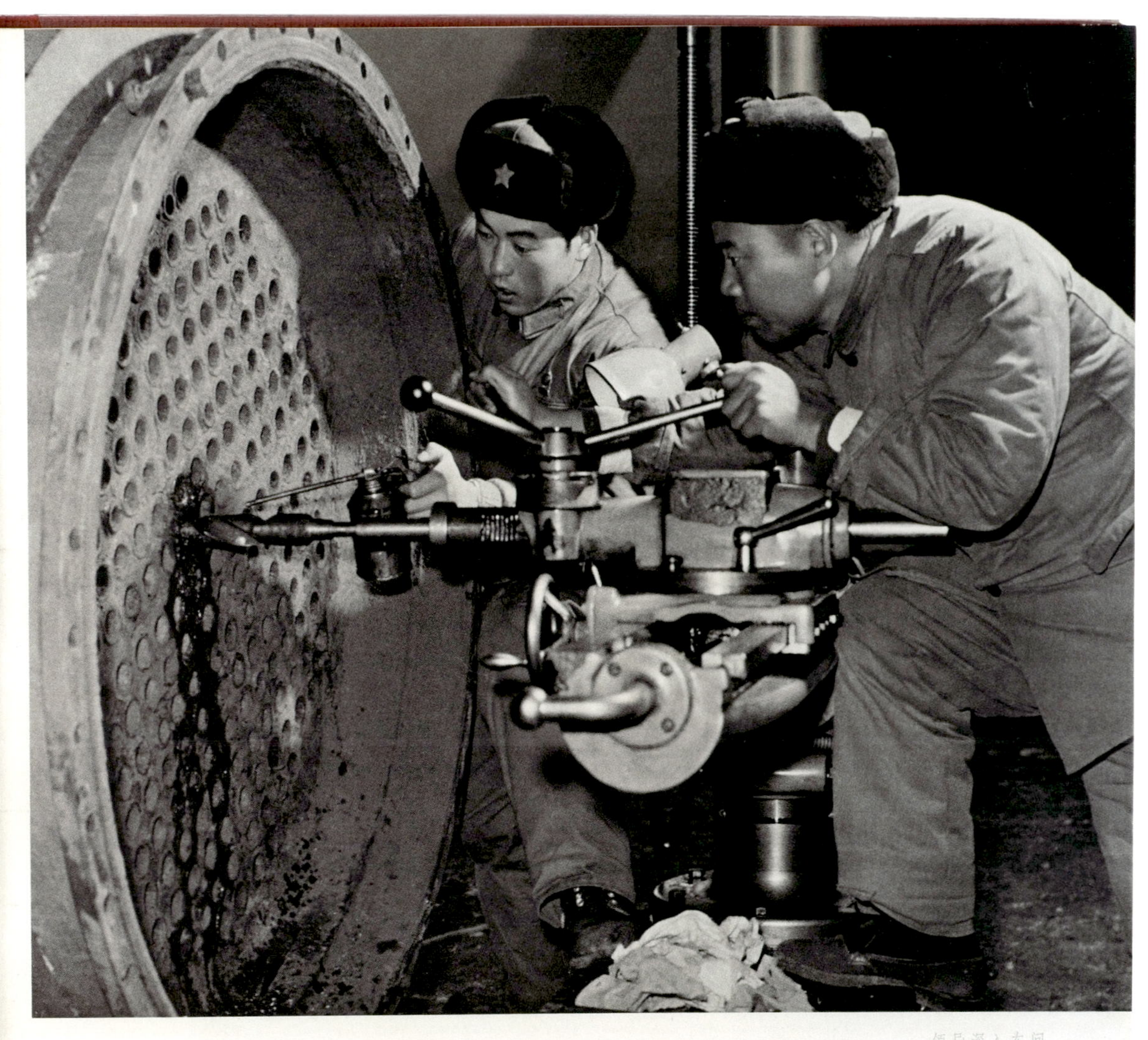

领导深入车间

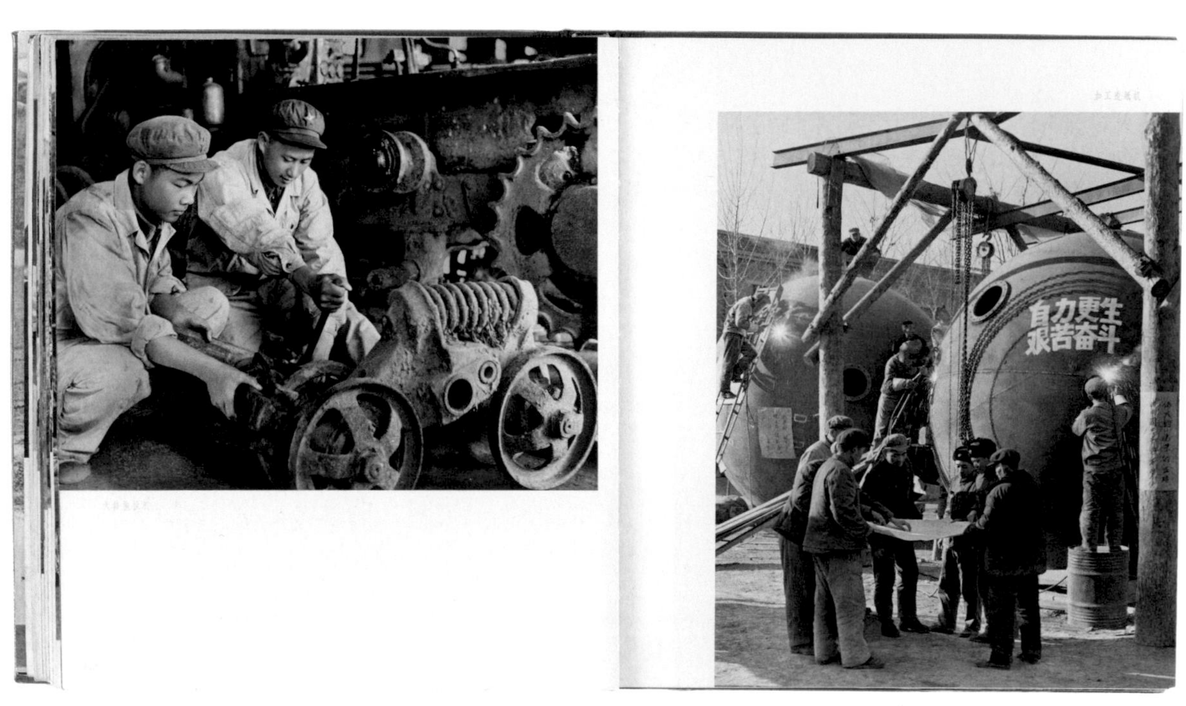

plate 75 (Left) 大修拖拉机 - Doing Major Repairs on a Tractor (Right) 加工造纸机 - Modifying the Papermaking Machine

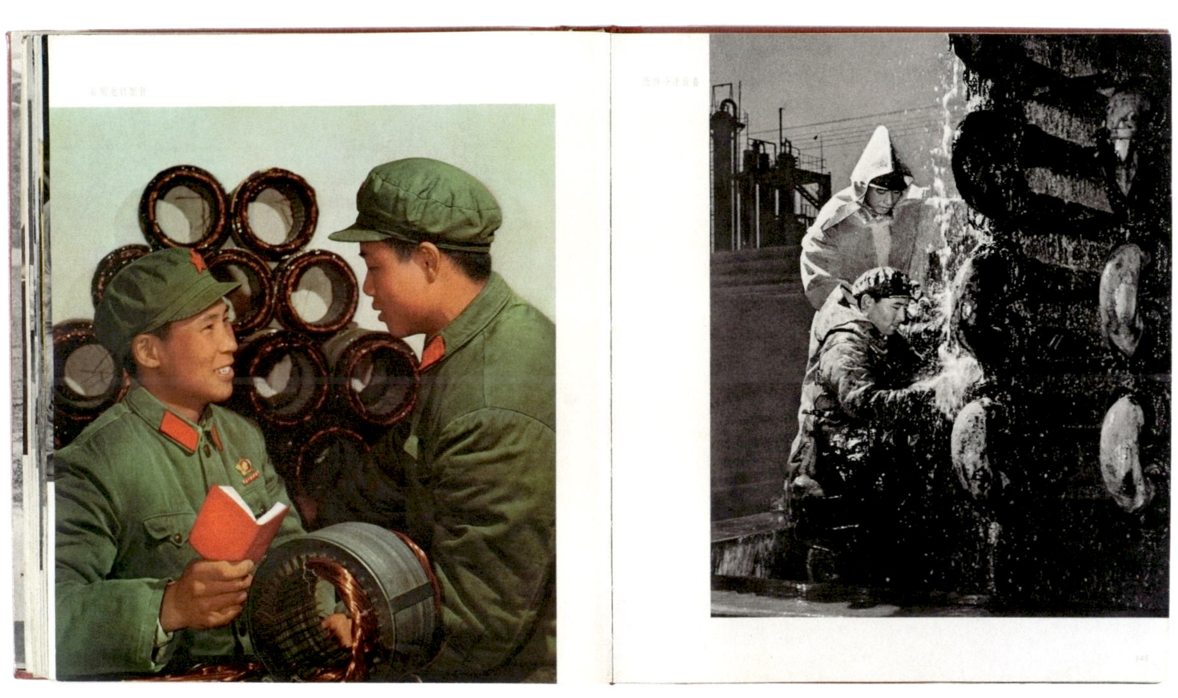

plate 76 (Left) 自制电机配件羊 - Self-Made Parts for an Electric Motor (Right) 抢修冷冻设备 - Urgently Repairing the Refrigerating Equipment

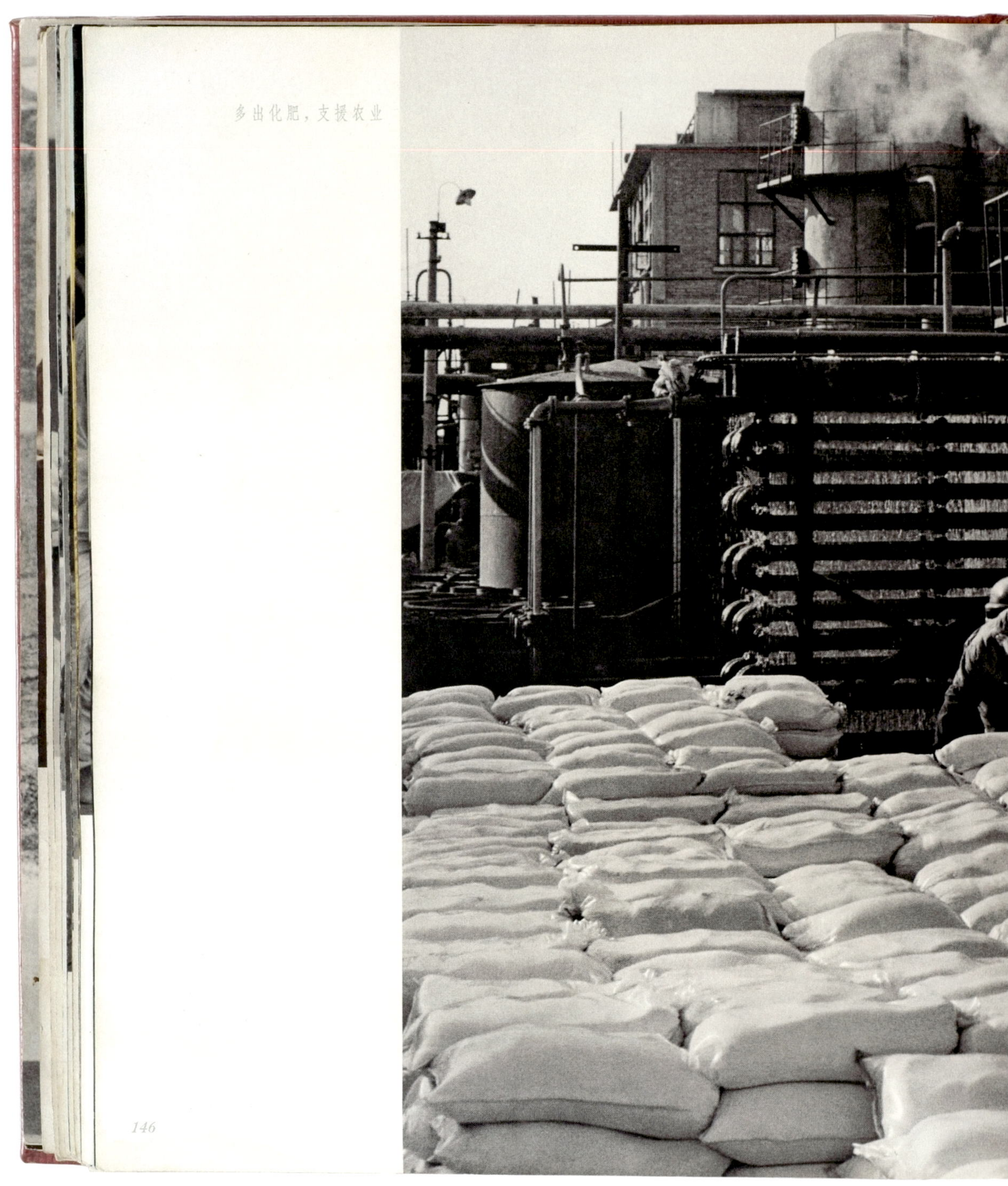

plate 77　　多出化肥，支援农业 - Produce More Fertilizer to Support Agricultural Production

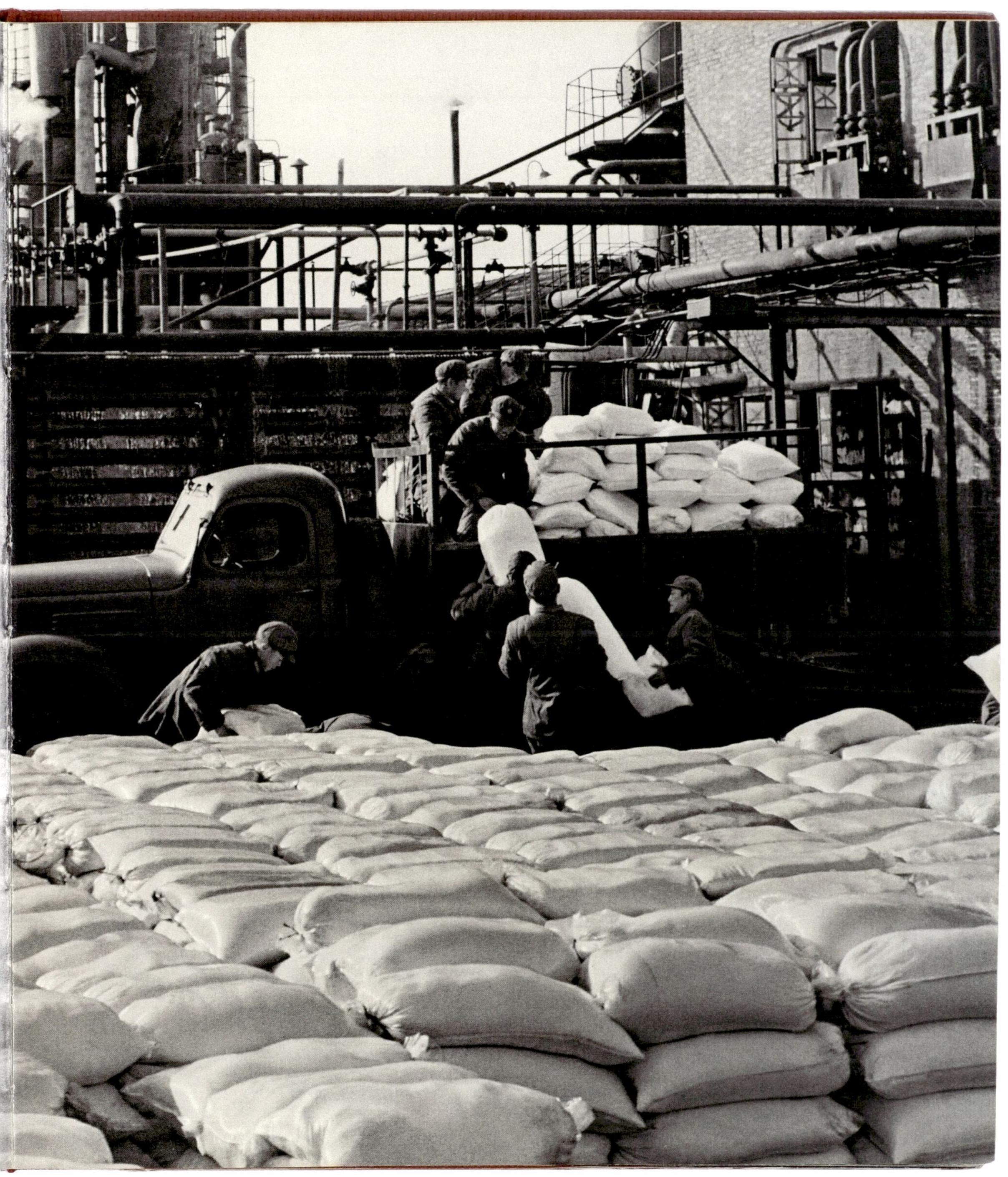

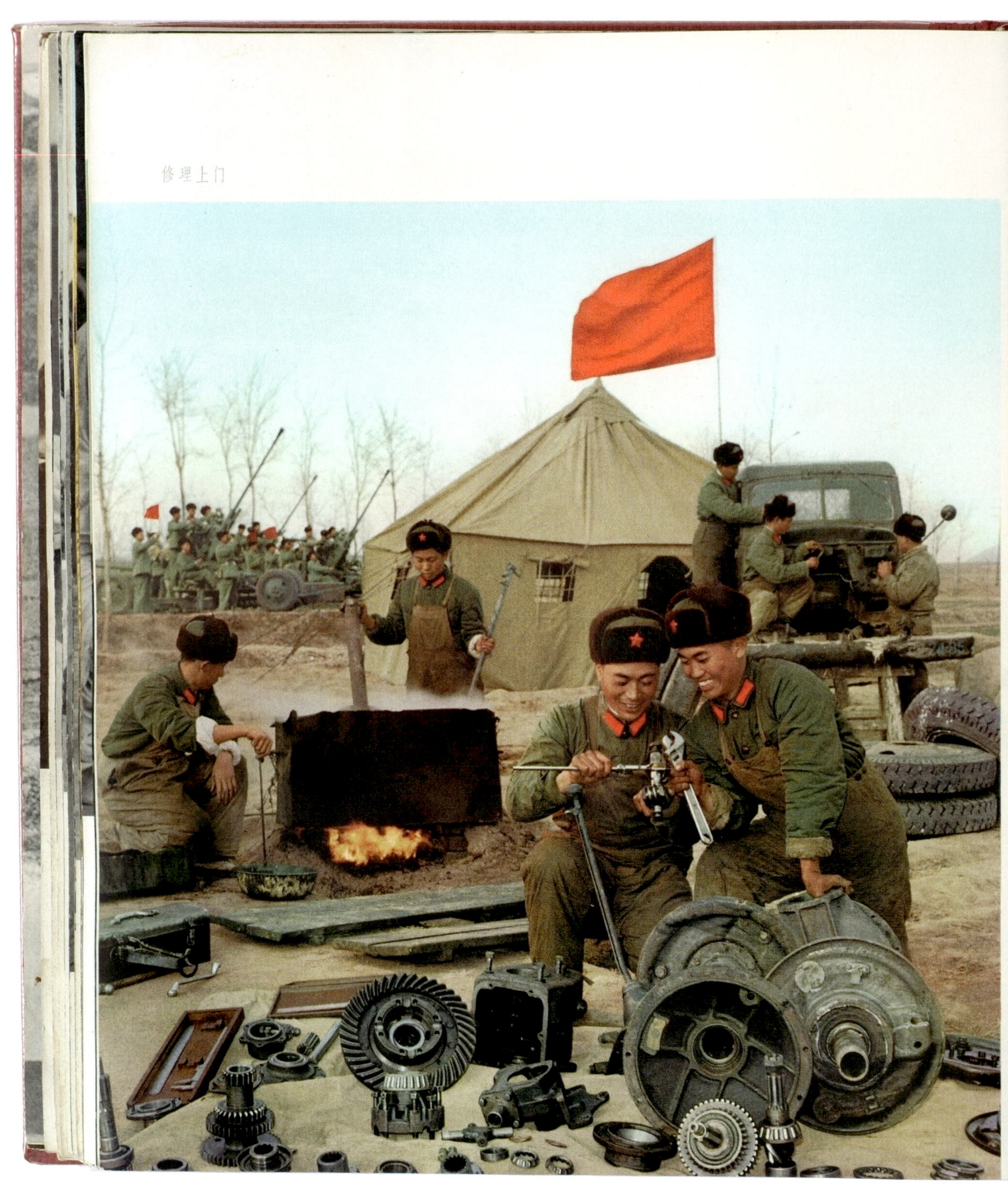

plate 78 (Above) 修理上门 - Repairs (Opposite) 想连队所想, 帮连队所需 - Thinking What the Company Thinks, Helping to Meet the Company's Needs

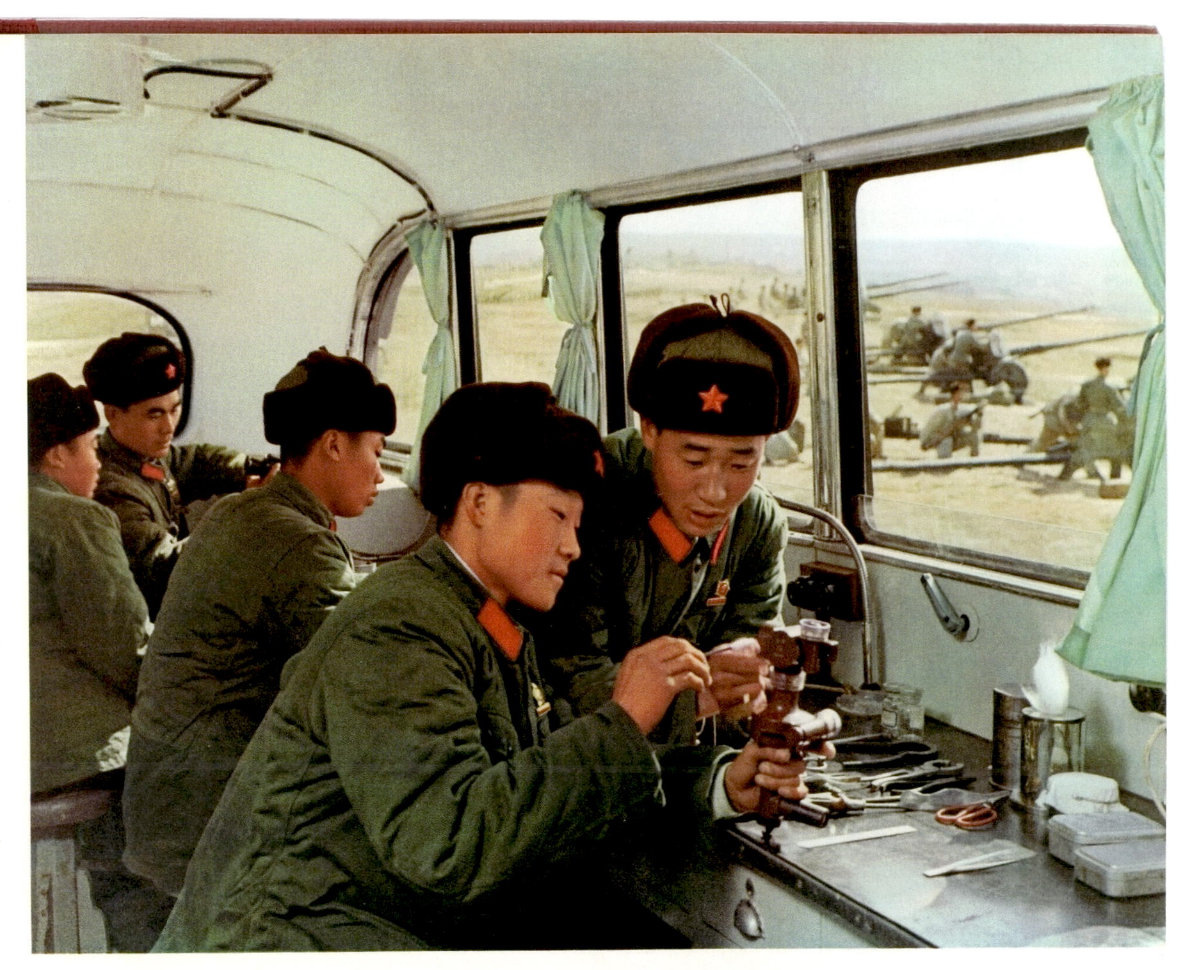

想连队所想，帮连队所需

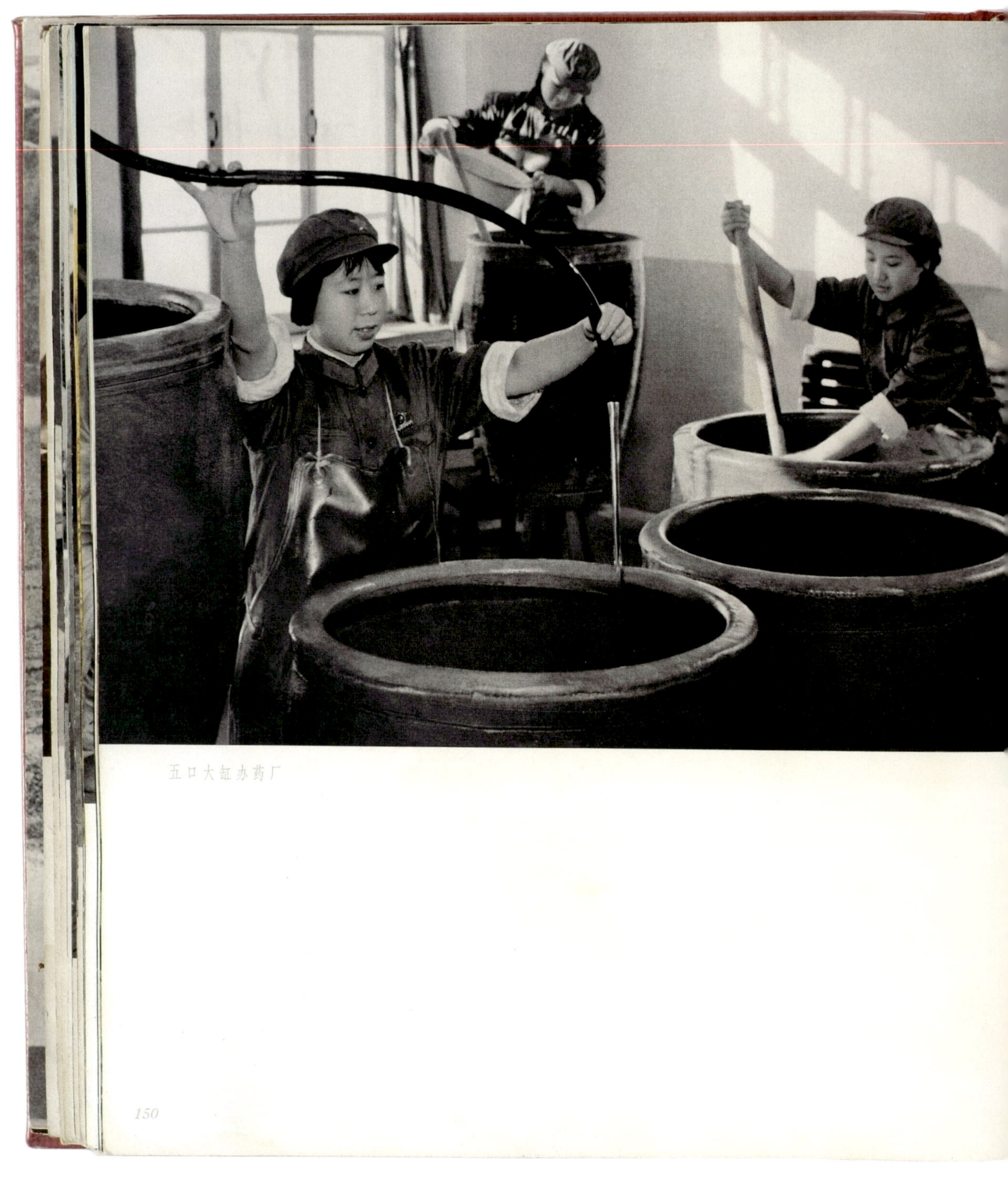

plate 79 (Above) 五口大缸办药厂羊 - Five Big Vats Make a Pharmaceutical Factory (Opposite) 小药厂的新产品 - The New Products of a Small Pharmaceutical Factory

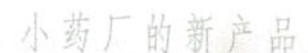

小药厂的新产品

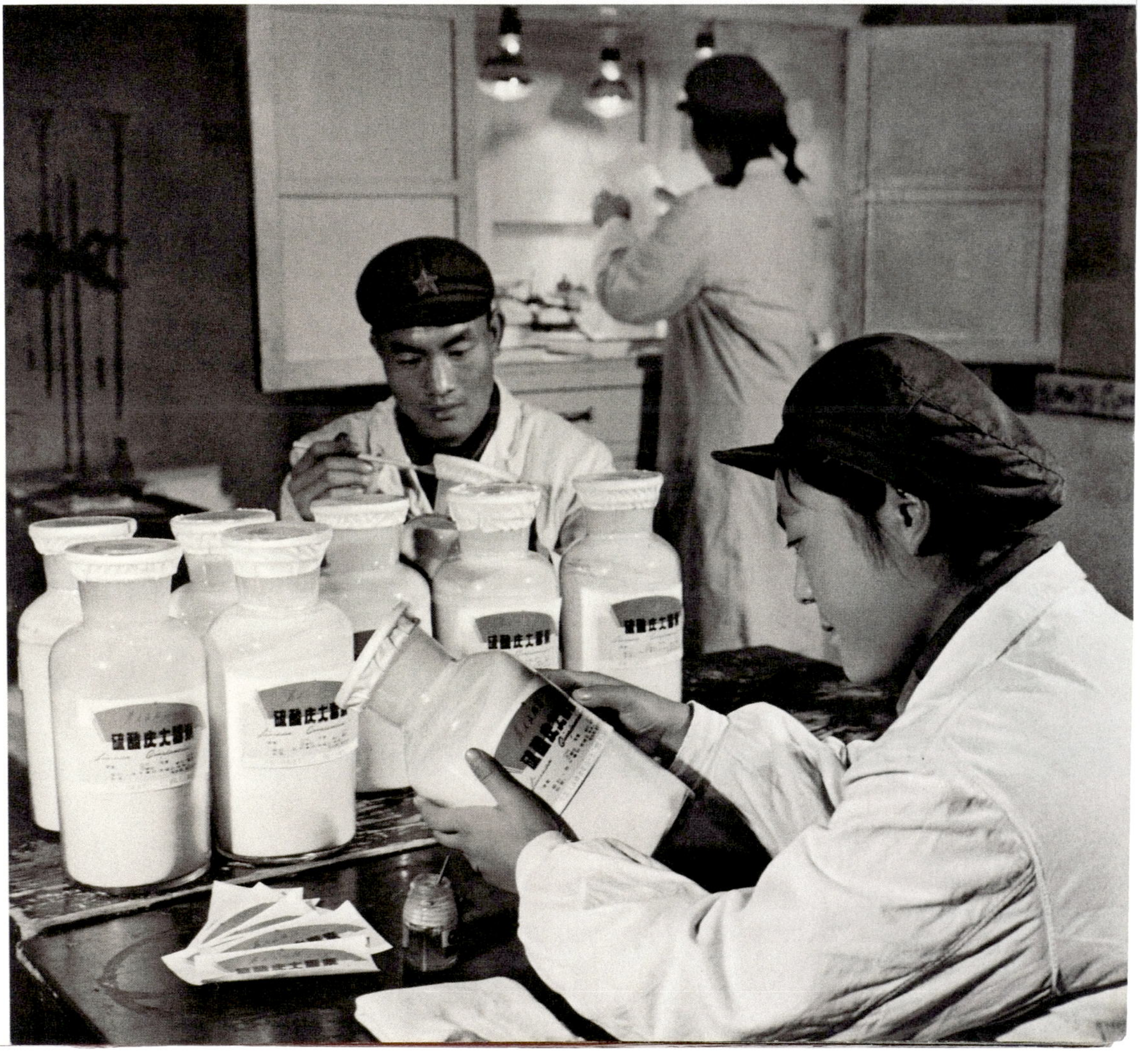

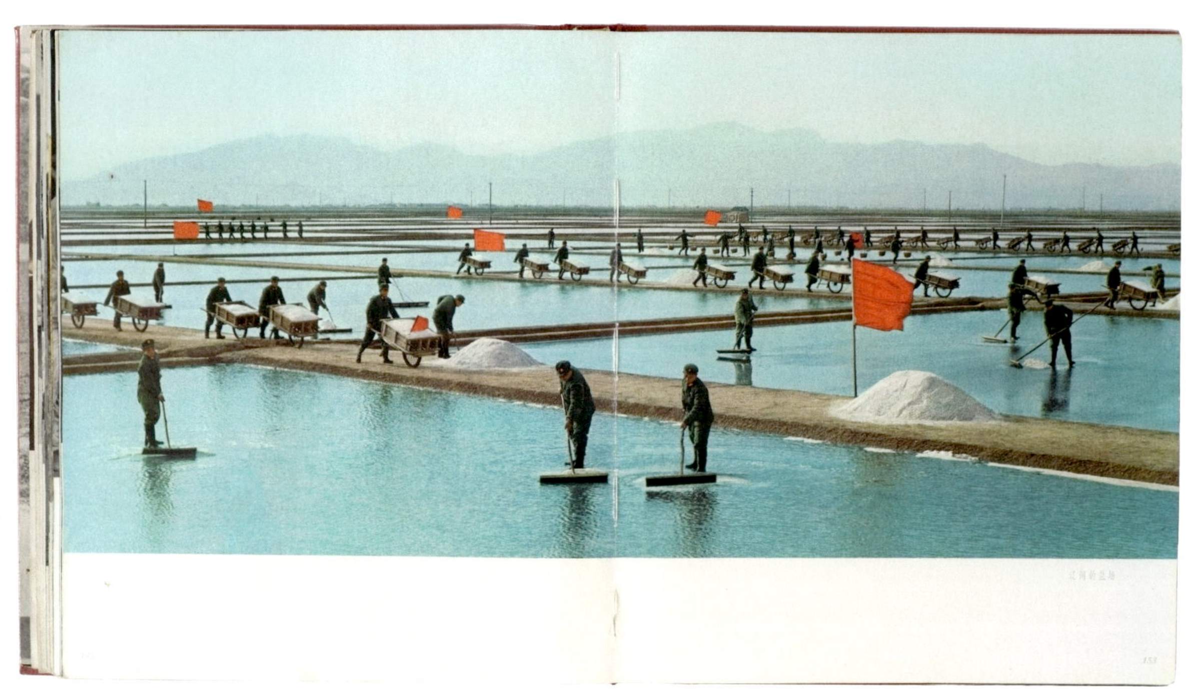

plate 80　辽阔的盐场 - A Vast Salt Field

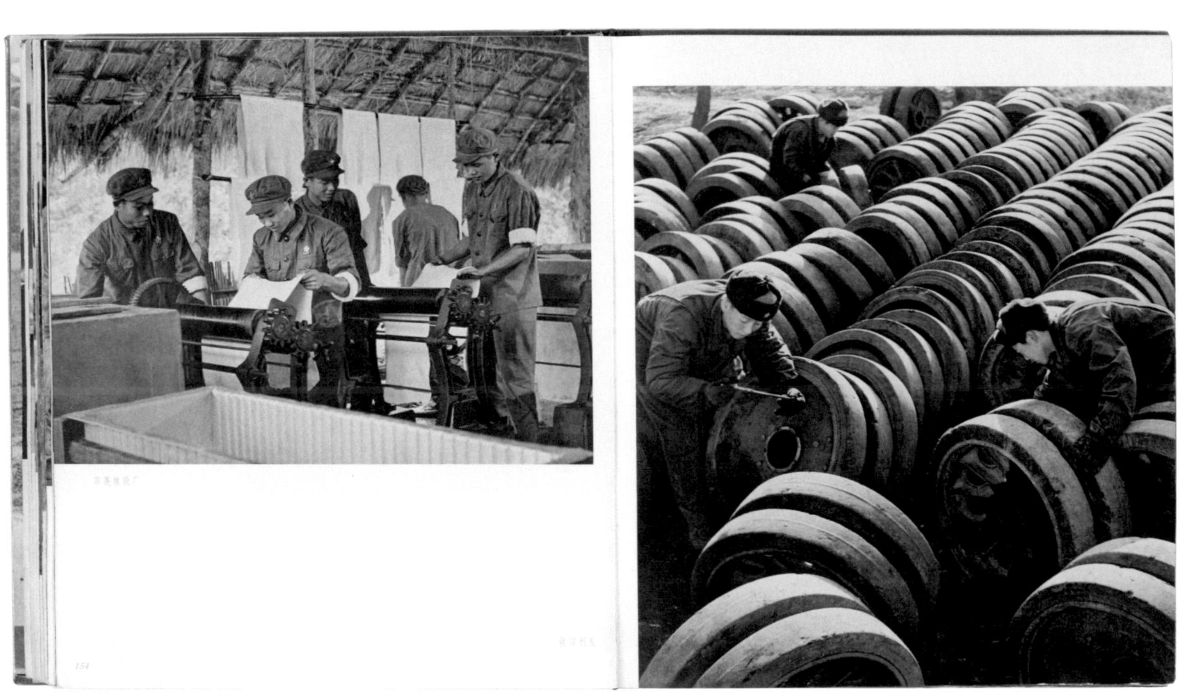

plate 81 (Left) 草蓬橡胶厂 - A Rubber Factory in a Thatched Hut (Right) 收旧利废 - Collect and Recycle Old Things

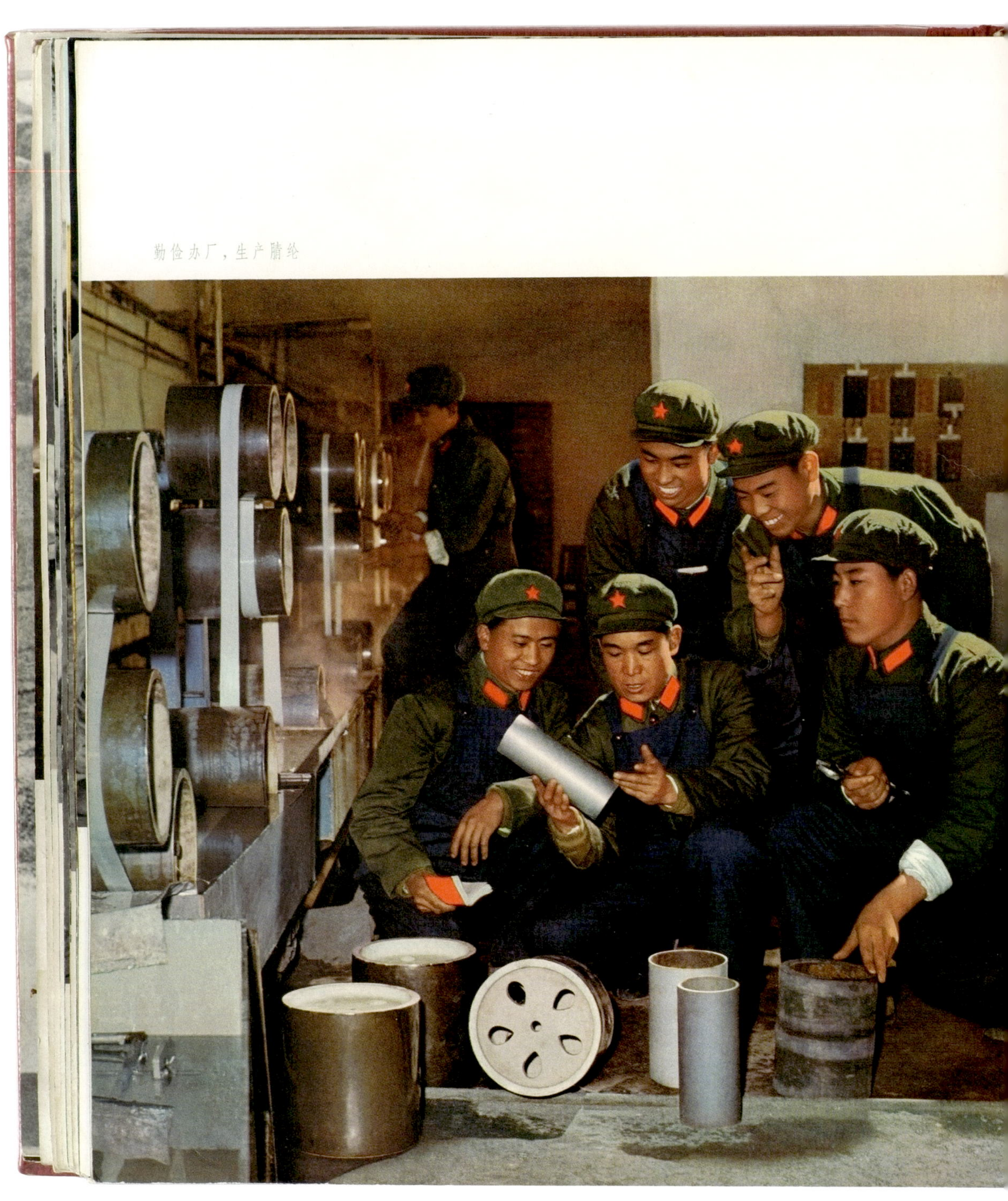

plate 82 (Above) 勤俭办厂，生产腈纶 - Run the Factory with Frugality, to Produce Acrylic Fibers (Opposite) 单晶硅提炼成功 - Successful Extraction of Monocrystalline Silicon

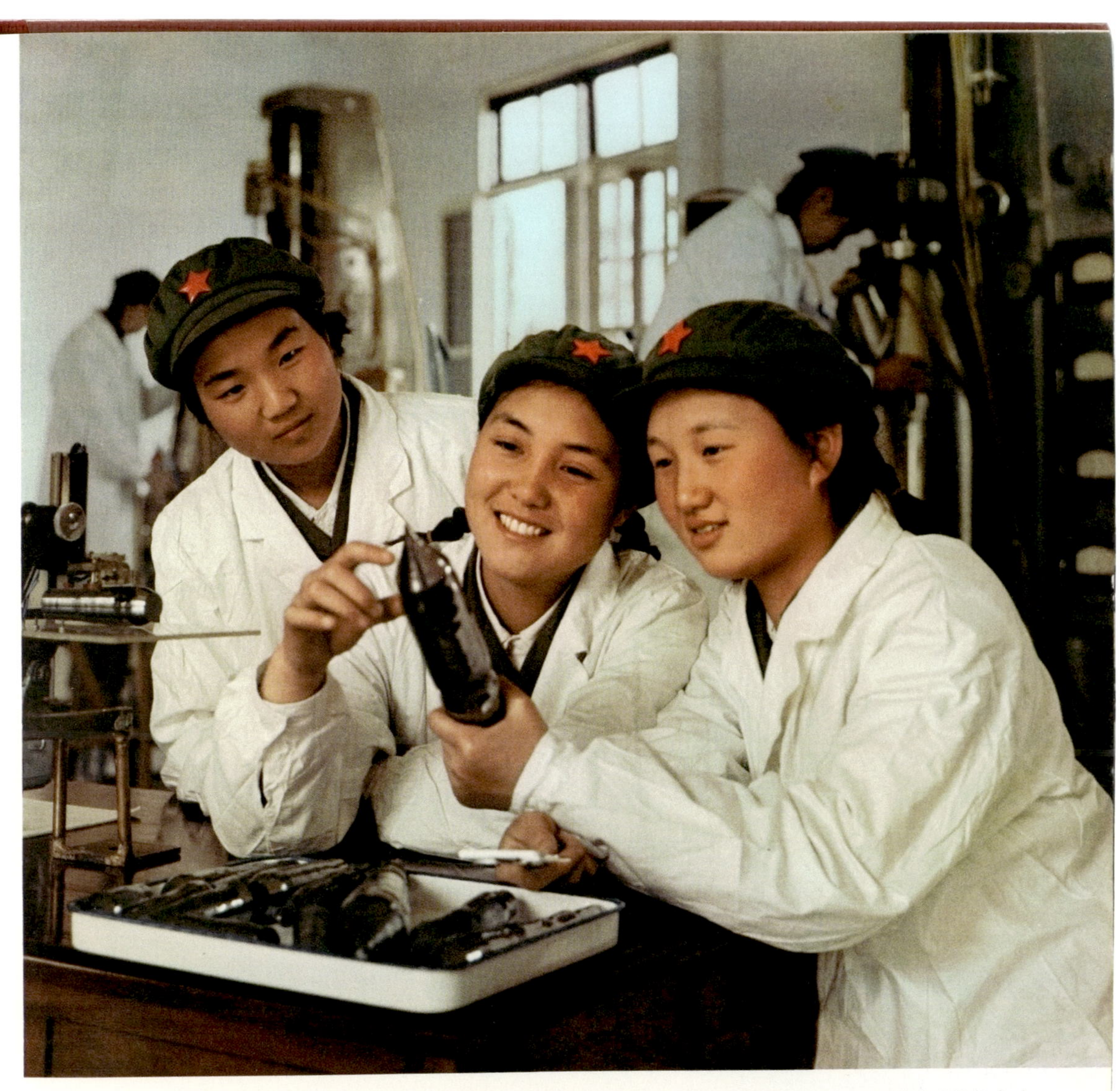

单晶硅提炼成功

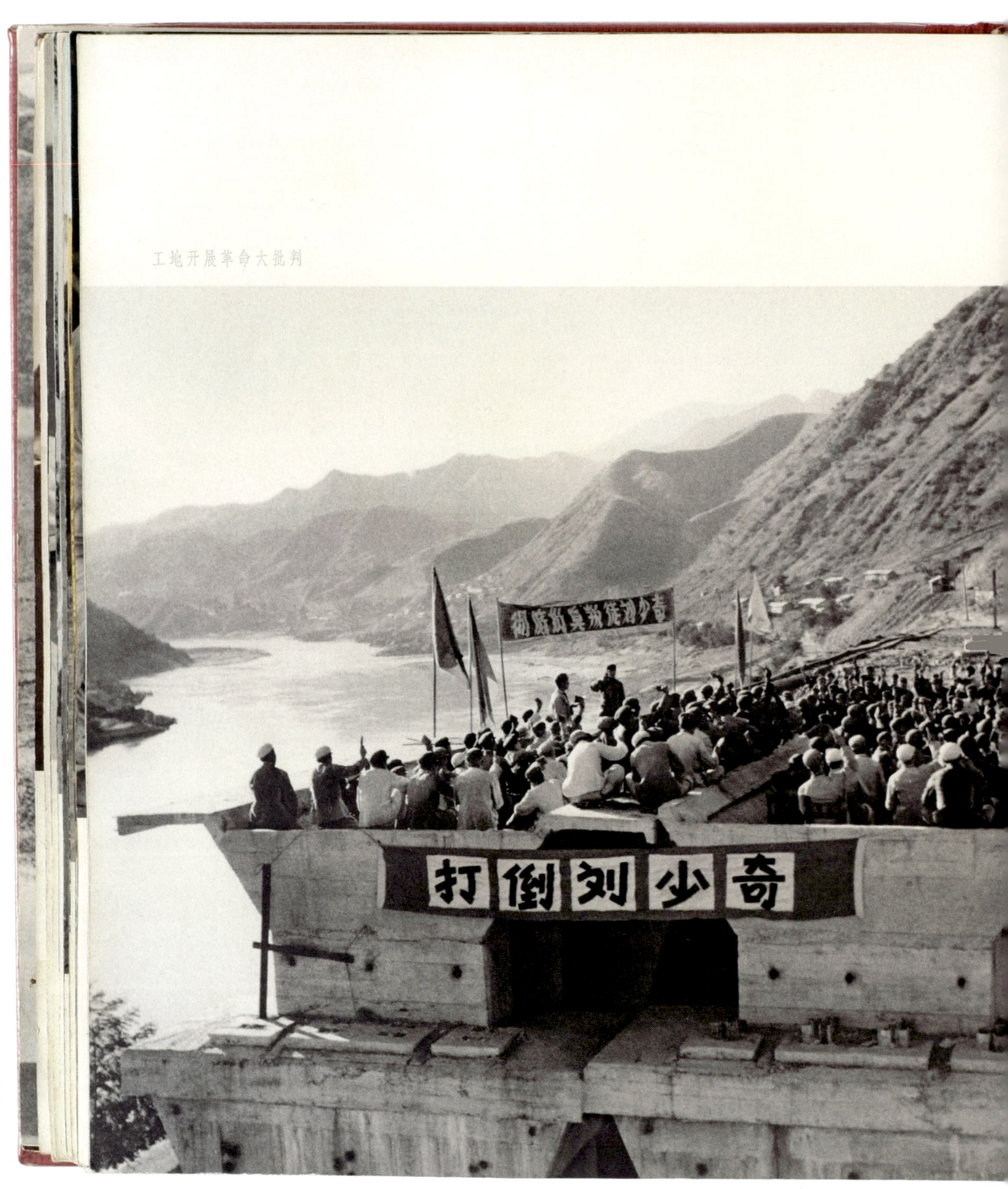

plate 83 (Above) 工地开展革命大批判 - Revolutionary Mass Criticism on the Building Site (Opposite) 争分夺秒为战备 - Race Against Time to Prepare for War

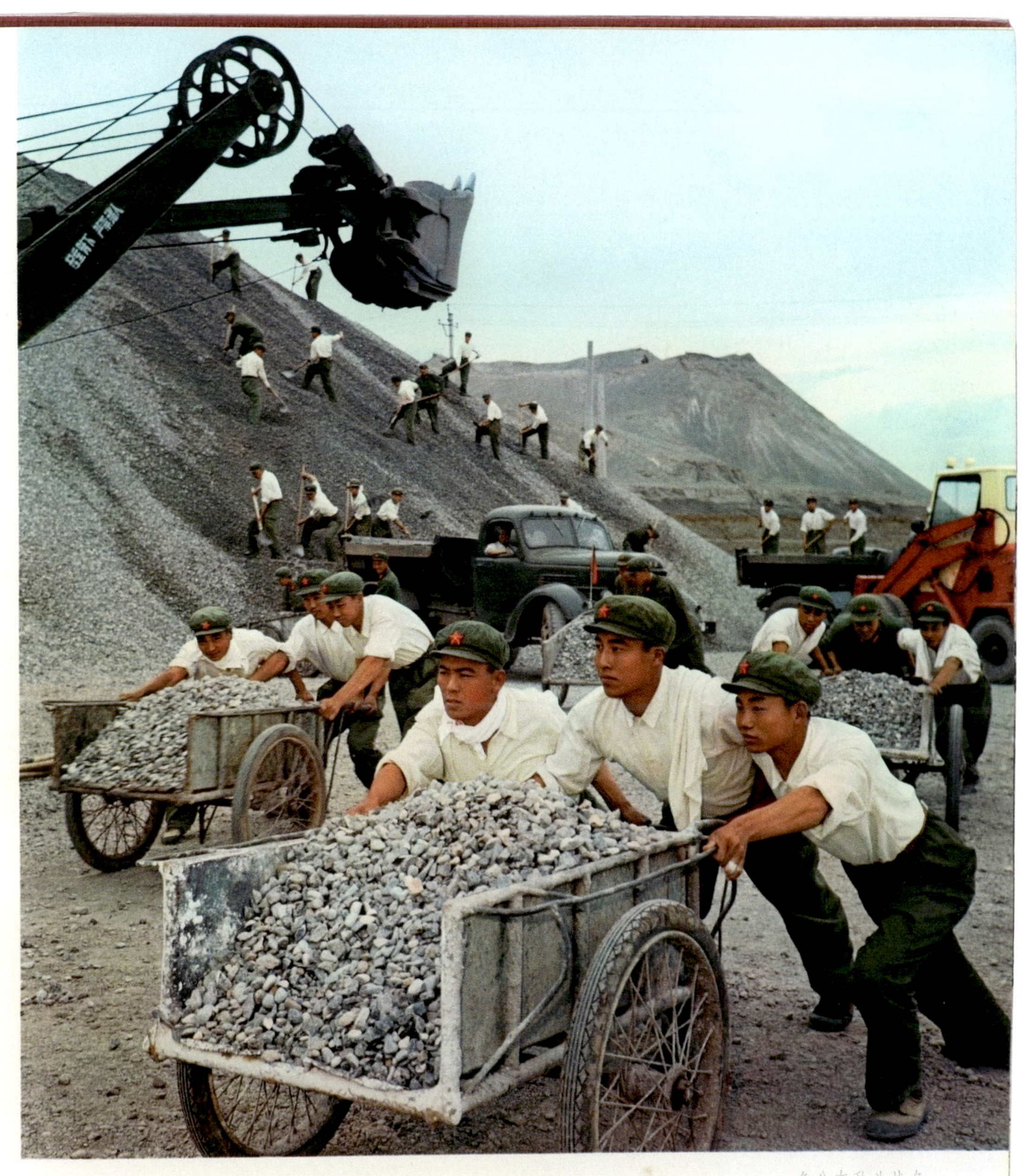

争分夺秒为战备

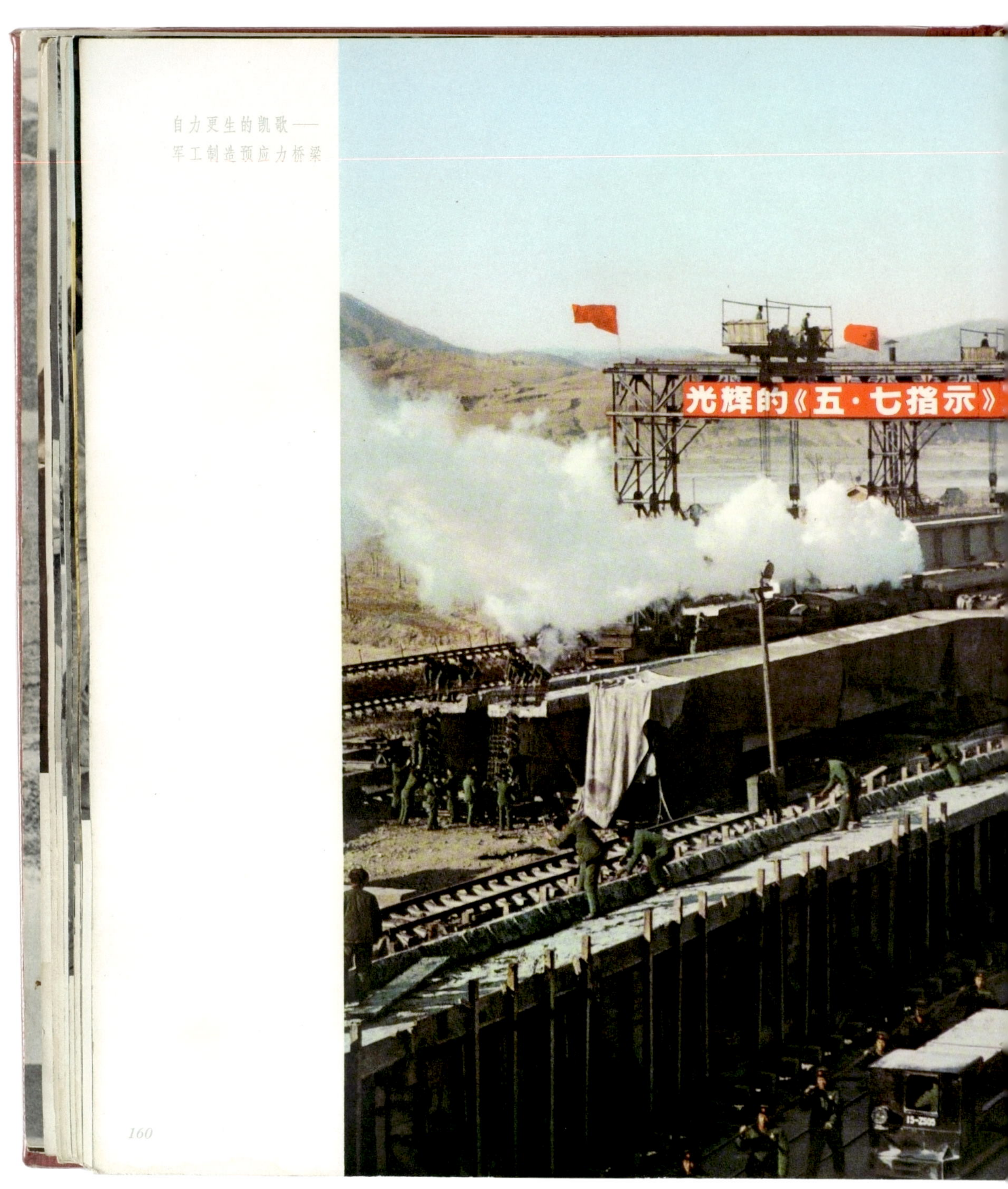

plate 84　自力更生的凯歌 - 军工制造预应力桥梁 - A Song of Triumph for Self-Sufficiency - a Pre-stressed Bridge Made by the Military Workers

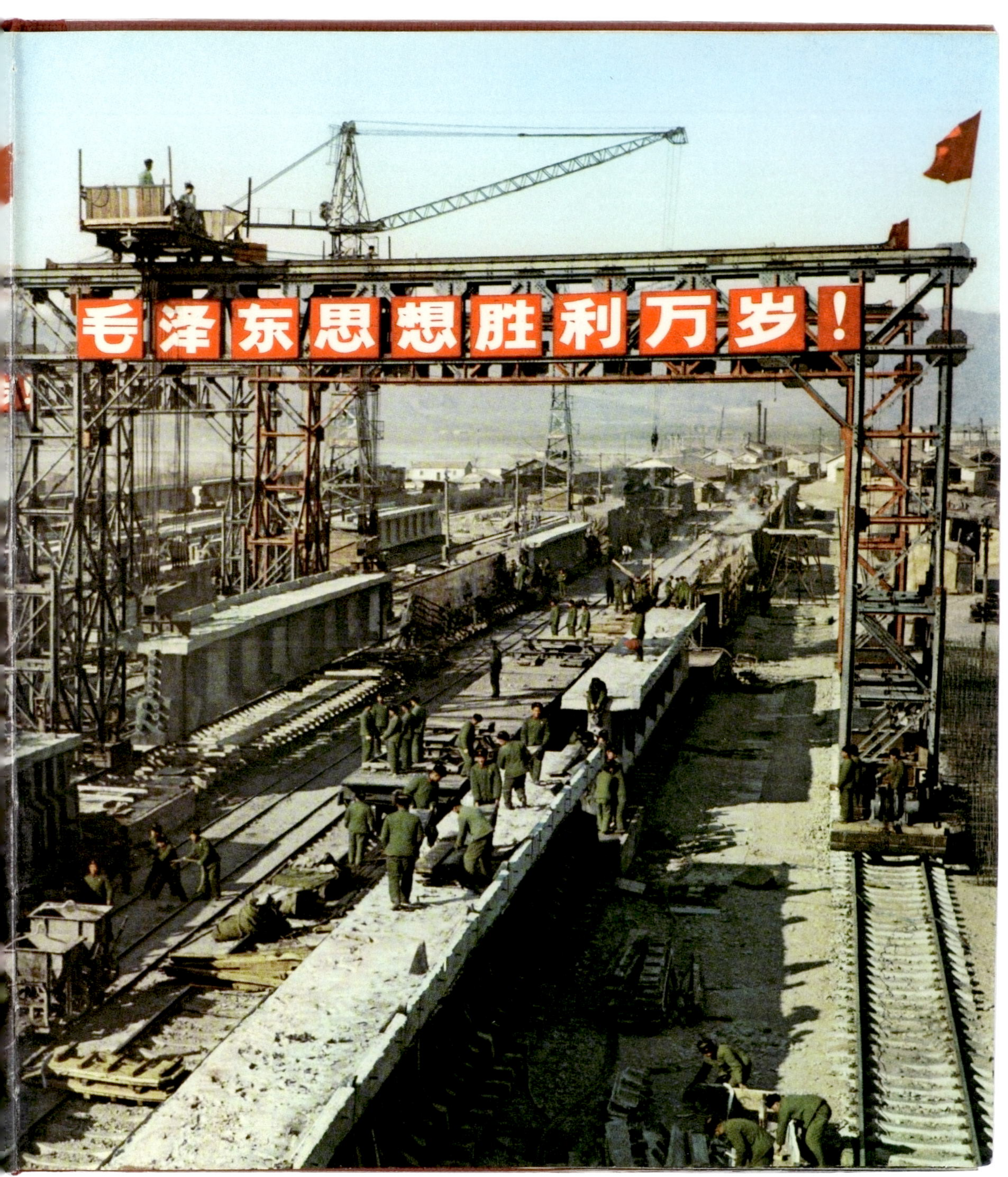
毛泽东思想胜利万岁！

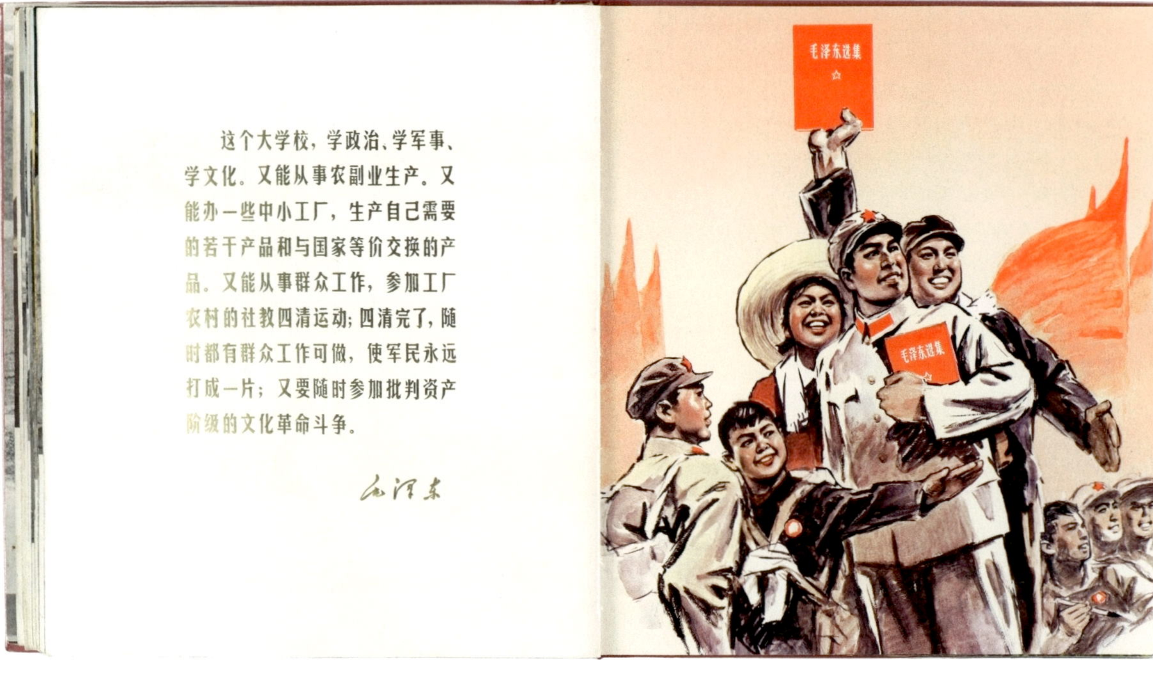

这个大学校，学政治、学军事、学文化。又能从事农副业生产。又能办一些中小工厂，生产自己需要的若干产品和与国家等价交换的产品。又能从事群众工作，参加工厂农村的社教四清运动；四清完了，随时都有群众工作可做，使军民永远打成一片；又要随时参加批判资产阶级的文化革命斗争。

毛泽东

plate 85 (Left) 这个大学校，学政治，学军事，学文化. 又能从事农副业生产. 又能办一些中小工厂，生产自己需要的若干产品和与国家等价交换的产品. 又能从事群众工作，参加工厂农村的社教四清运动; 四清完了，随时都有群众工作可做，使军民永远打成一片; 又要随时参加批判资产阶级的文化革命斗争. - In this great school, troops study politics, military affairs and culture. They can engage in agricultural production and related occupations. They can also run some small or medium-sized factories to make certain products for their own needs or for exchange with the state at equal value. They can engage in mass work as well as the Socialist Education "Four Clean-ups" Movement in the factories and countryside. Once the "Four Clean-ups" is complete, there will still be work to be carried out with the masses, in addition to continuing the cultural revolutionary struggle of criticism against the bourgeoisie.

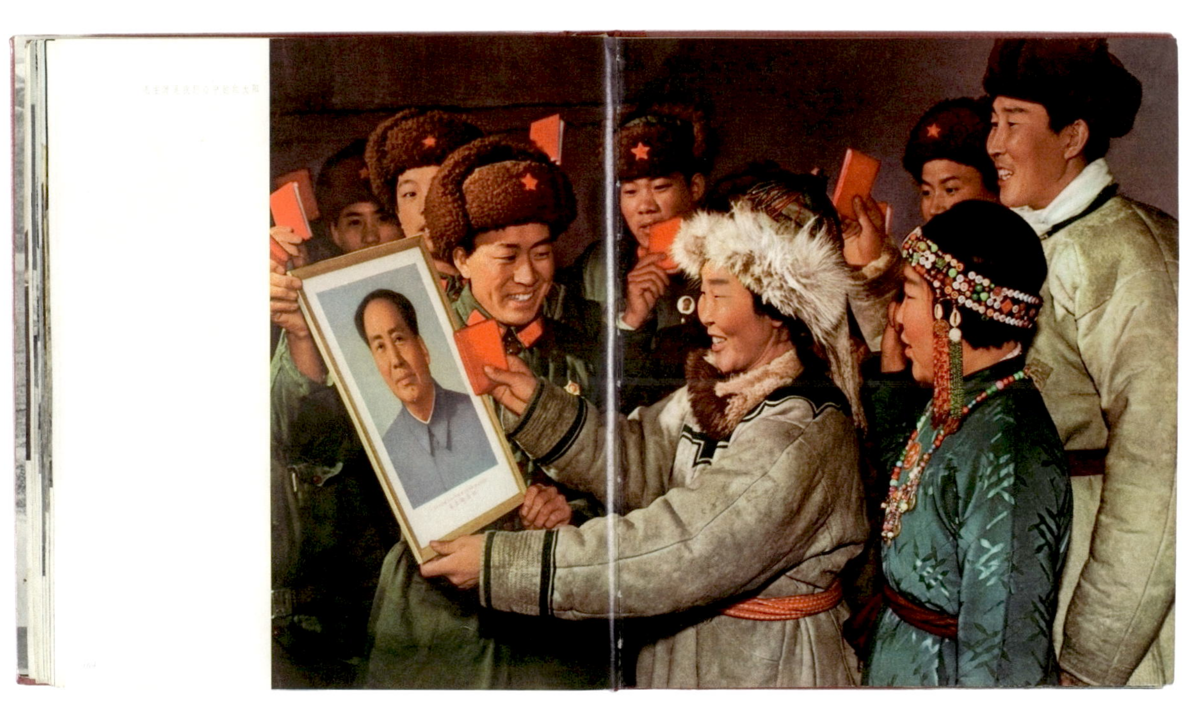

plate 86　毛主席是我们心中的太阳 - Chairman Mao Is the Sun in Our Heart

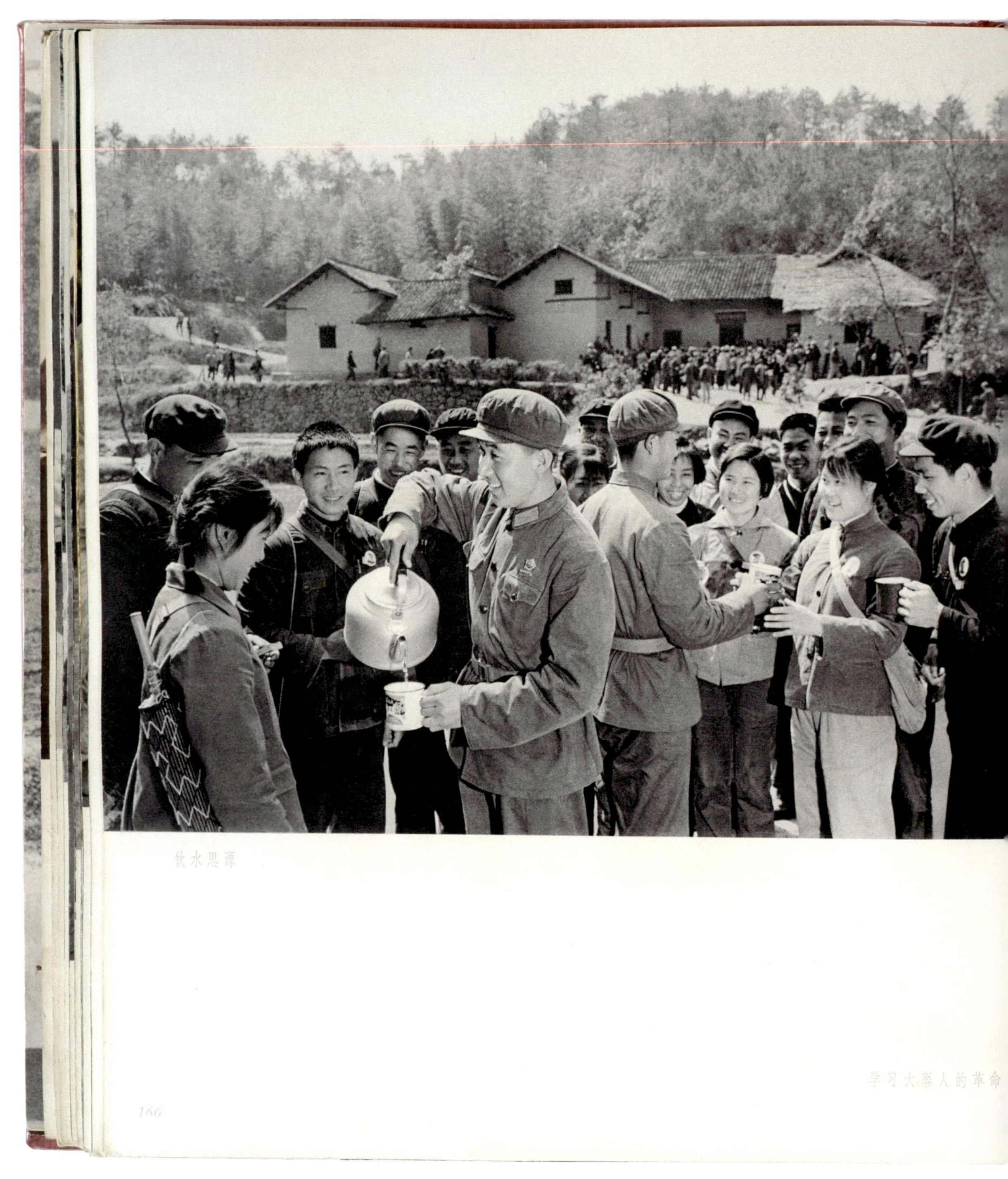

plate 87 (Above) 饮水思源 - When One Drinks Water, Think of Its Source (Opposite) 学习大寨人的革命精神 - Learn from the Dazai People's Revolutionary Spirit

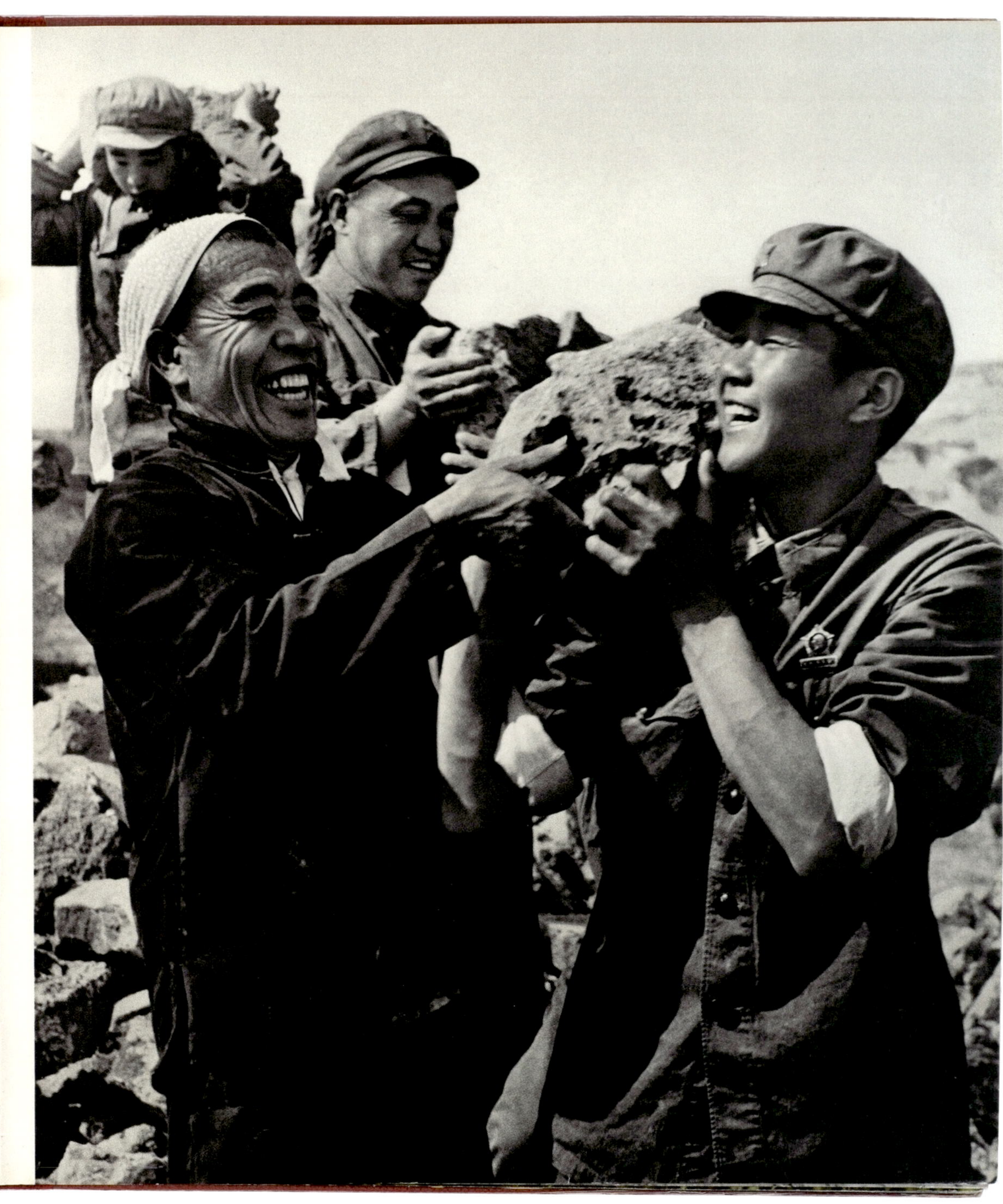

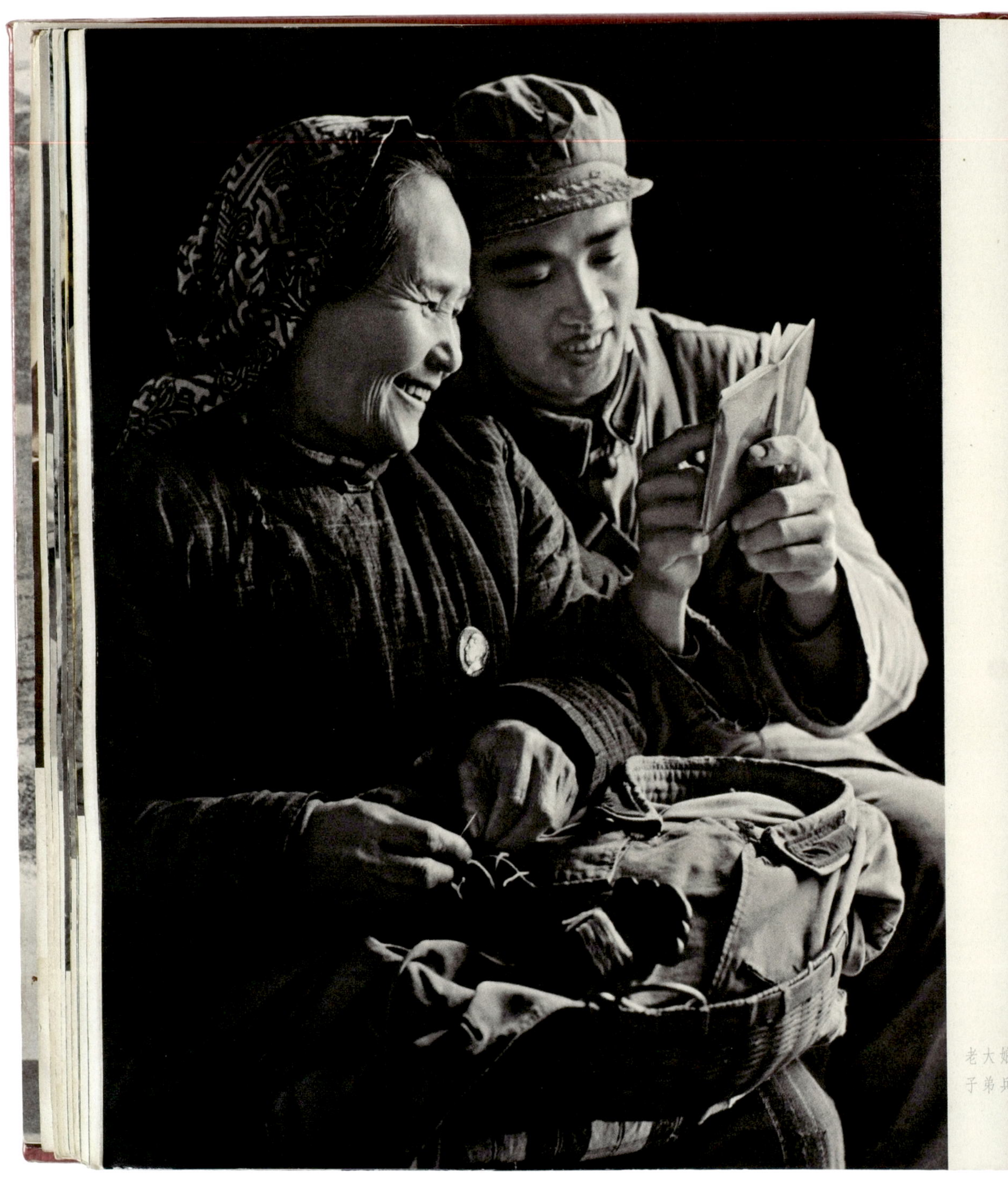

plate 88 (Above) 老大娘和子弟兵 - A Grandma and a PLA Soldier (Opposite) 果香情谊深 - Aromatic Fruits and Sincere Friendship

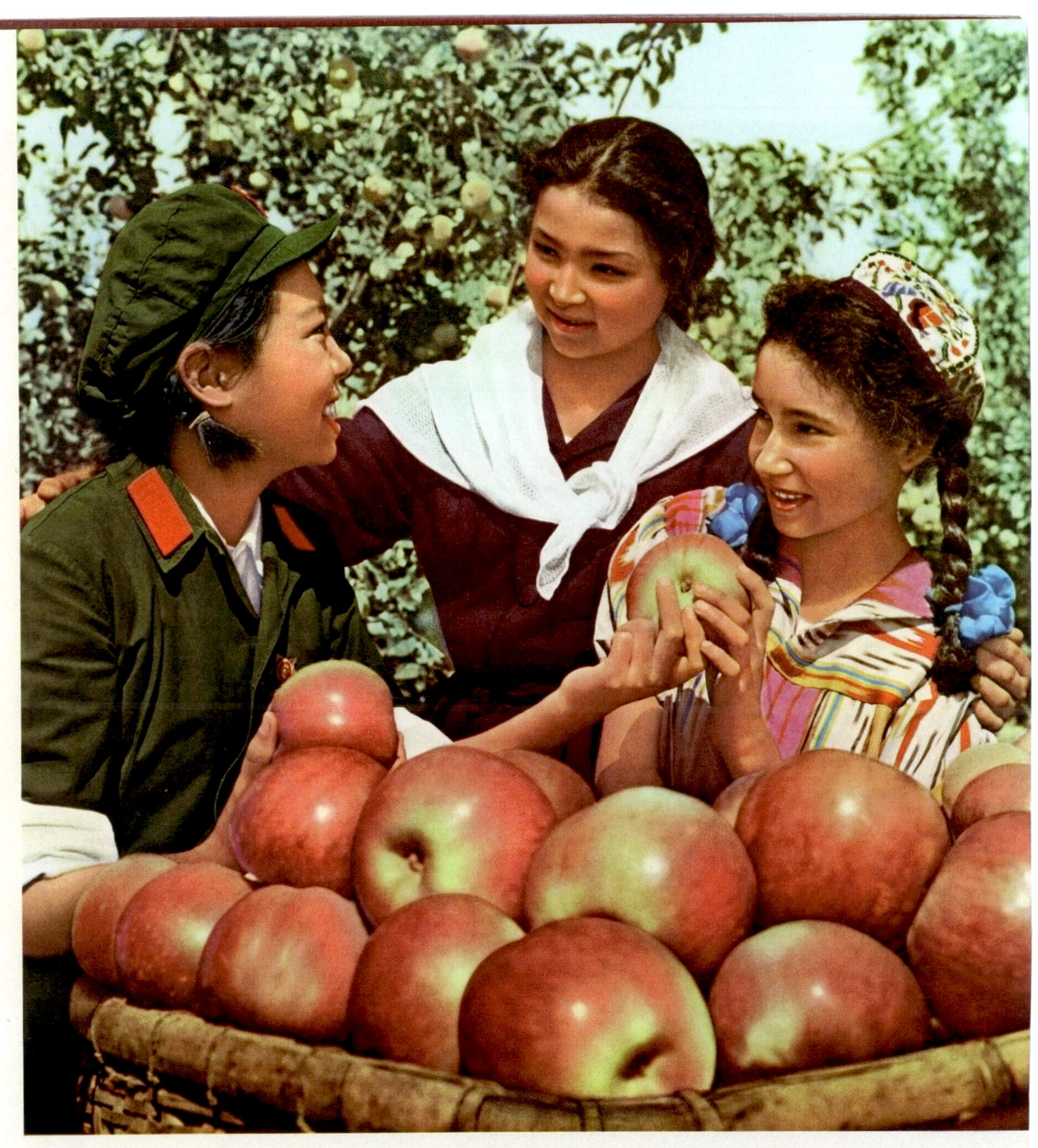

果香情谊深

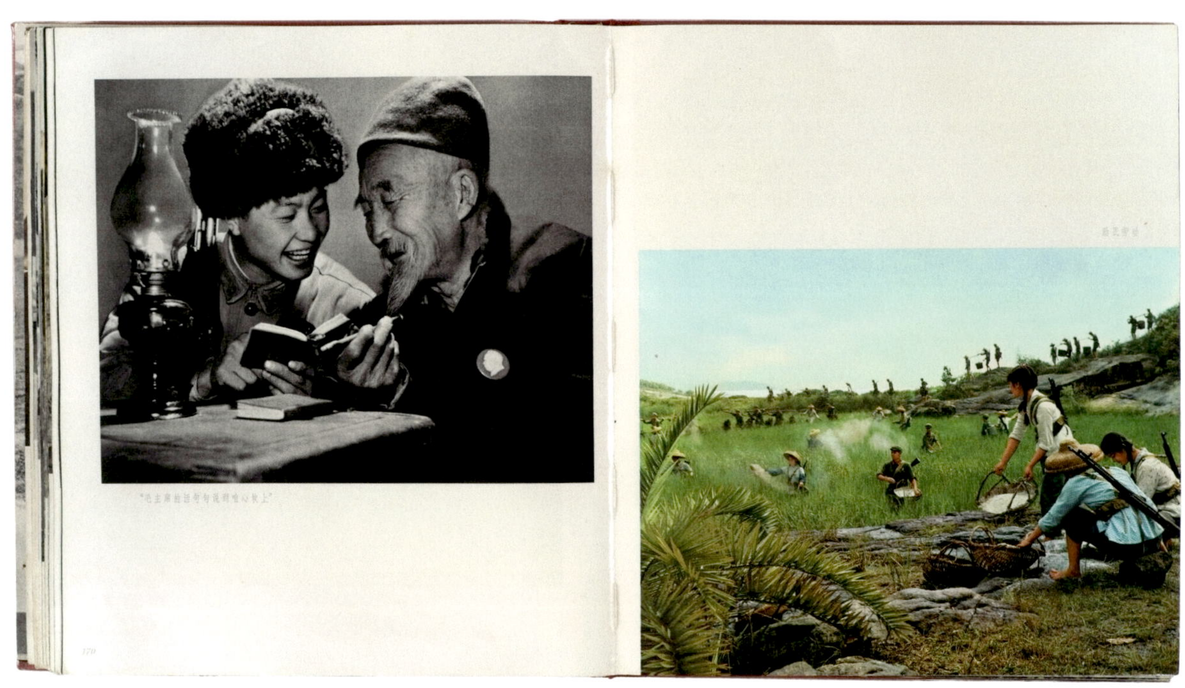

plate 89 (Left) “毛主席的话句句说到咱心坎上” - “Chairman Mao’s Every Word Touches Our Heart” (Right) 助民劳动 - Help the People to Work

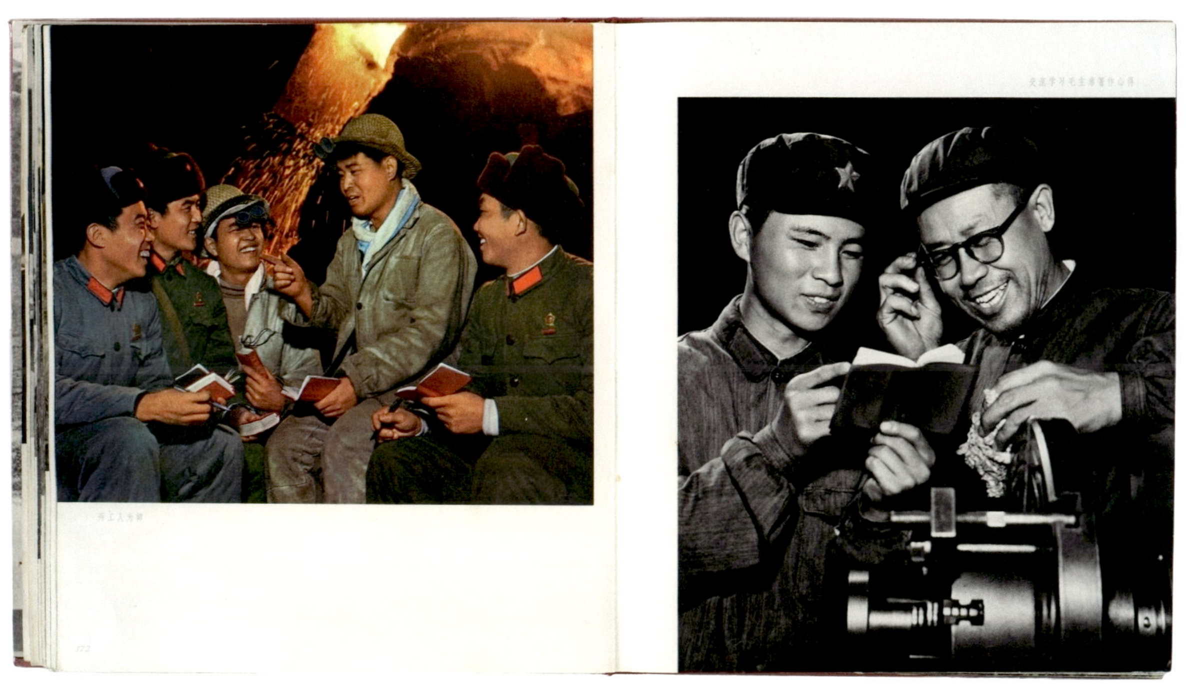

plate 90 (Left) 拜工人为师 - Taking the Workers as Teachers (Right) 交流学习毛主席著作心得 - Exchanging Study Notes on the Works of Chairman Mao

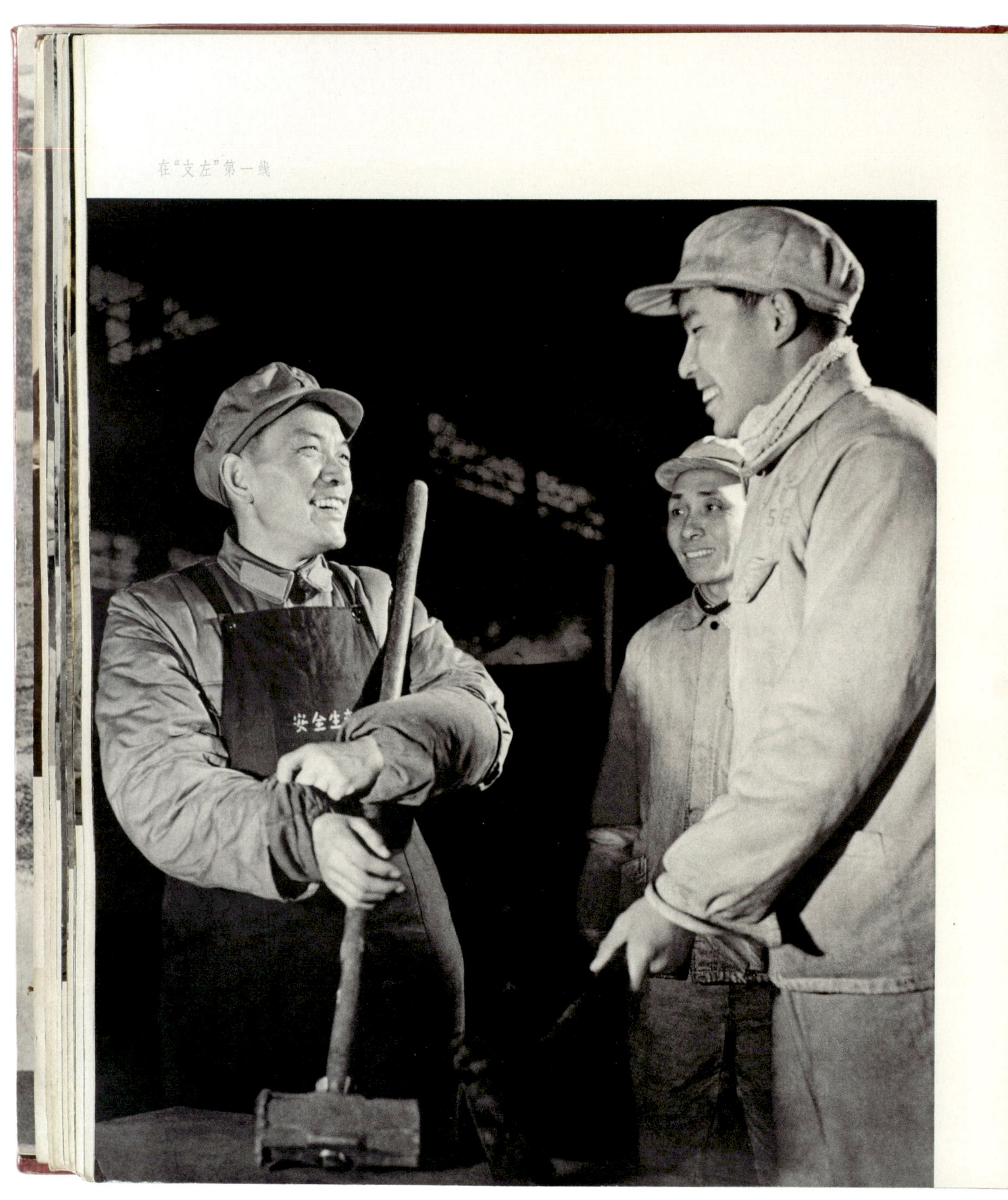

plate 91 (Above) 在"支左"第一线 - At the Frontline of the "Supporting the Leftists" Movement (Opposite) 军宣队虚心听取群众意见 - The Propaganda Department of the Army Listens to Feedback from the People

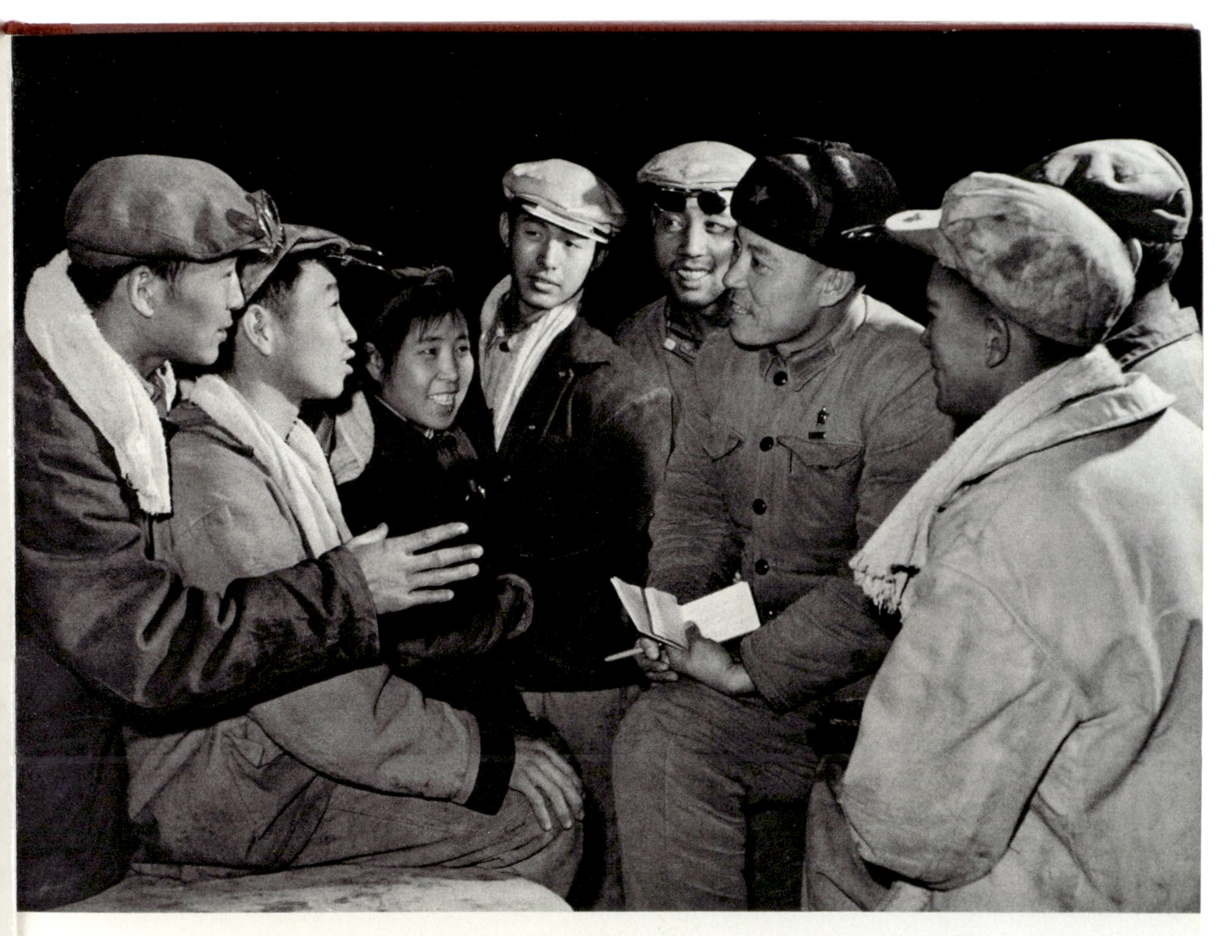

军宣队虚心听取群众意见

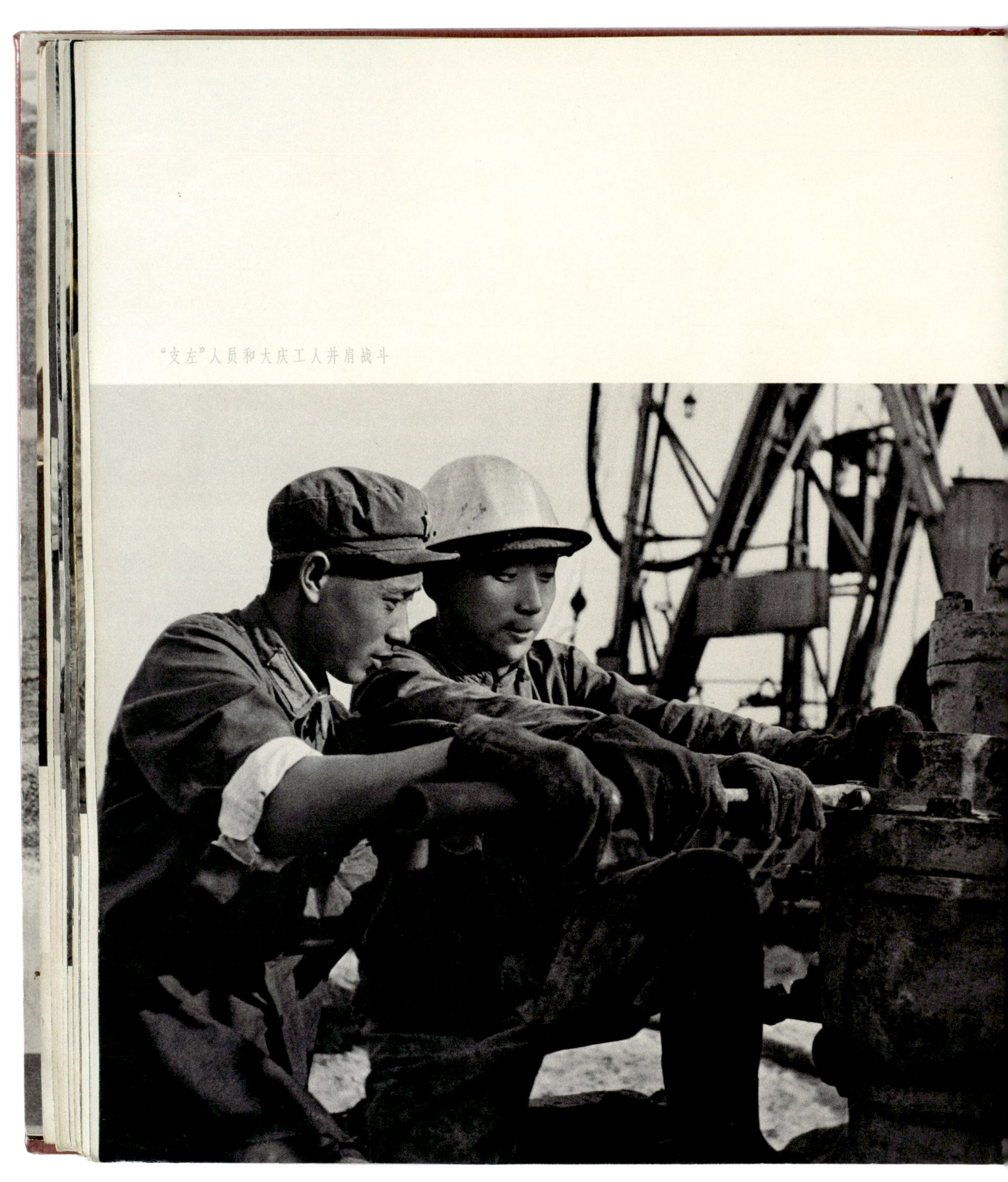

plate 92 (Above) “支左”人员和大庆工人并肩战斗 - An Officer of the “Supporting the Leftists” Movement and a Daqing Worker Work Side by Side (Opposite) 军民同批修 - The Soldiers and the People Are Criticizing the Revisionist

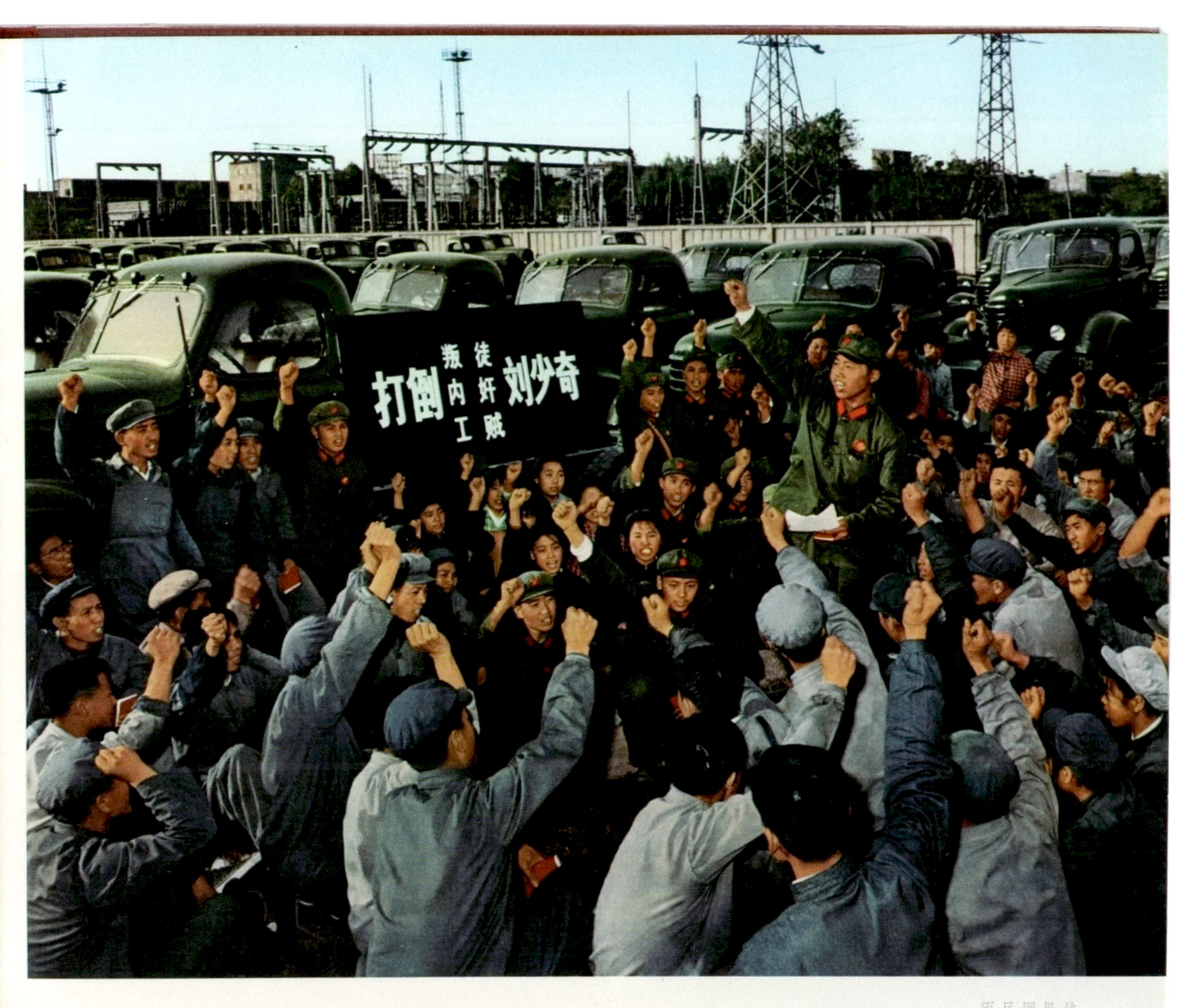

军民同批修

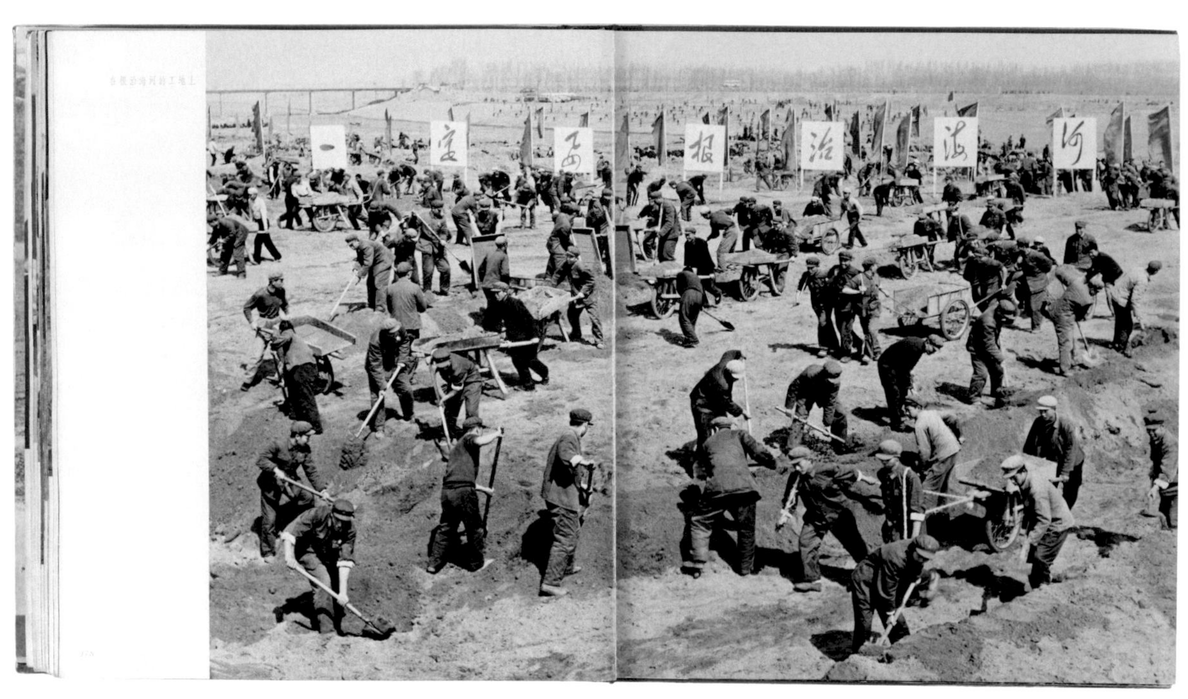

plate 93　在根治海河的工地上 - At the Site of Harnessing the Haihe River

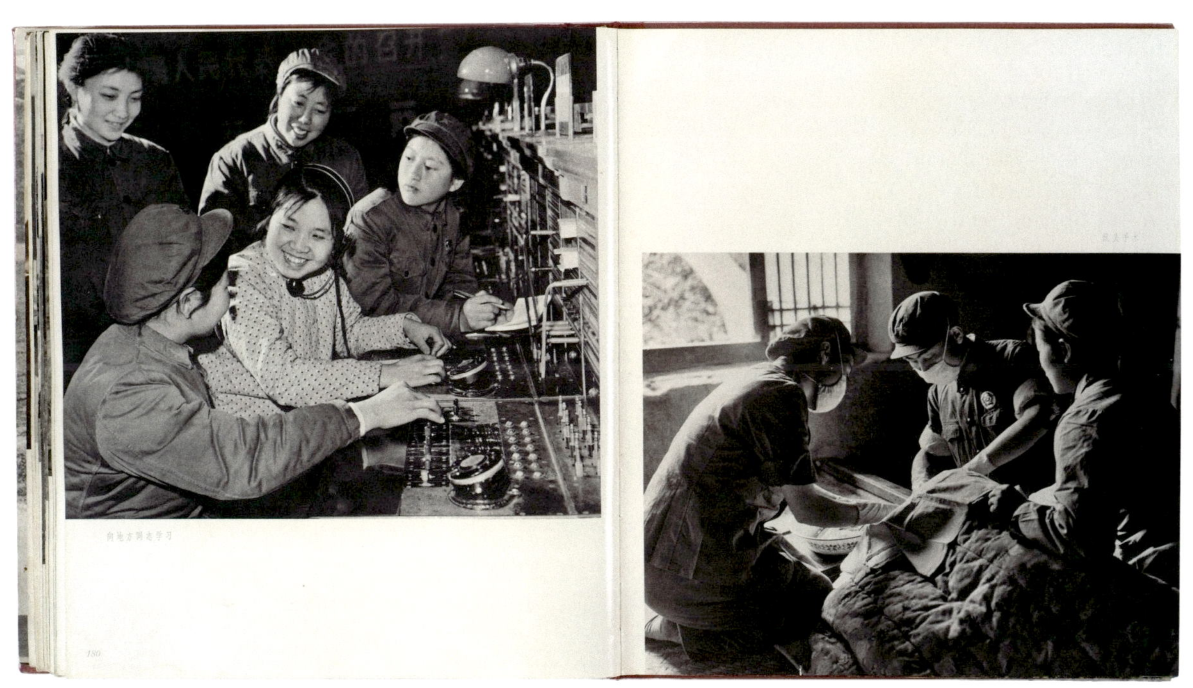

plate 94 (Left) 向地方同志学习 - Learn from Locals (Right) 炕头手术 - Surgery on the *Kang* bed

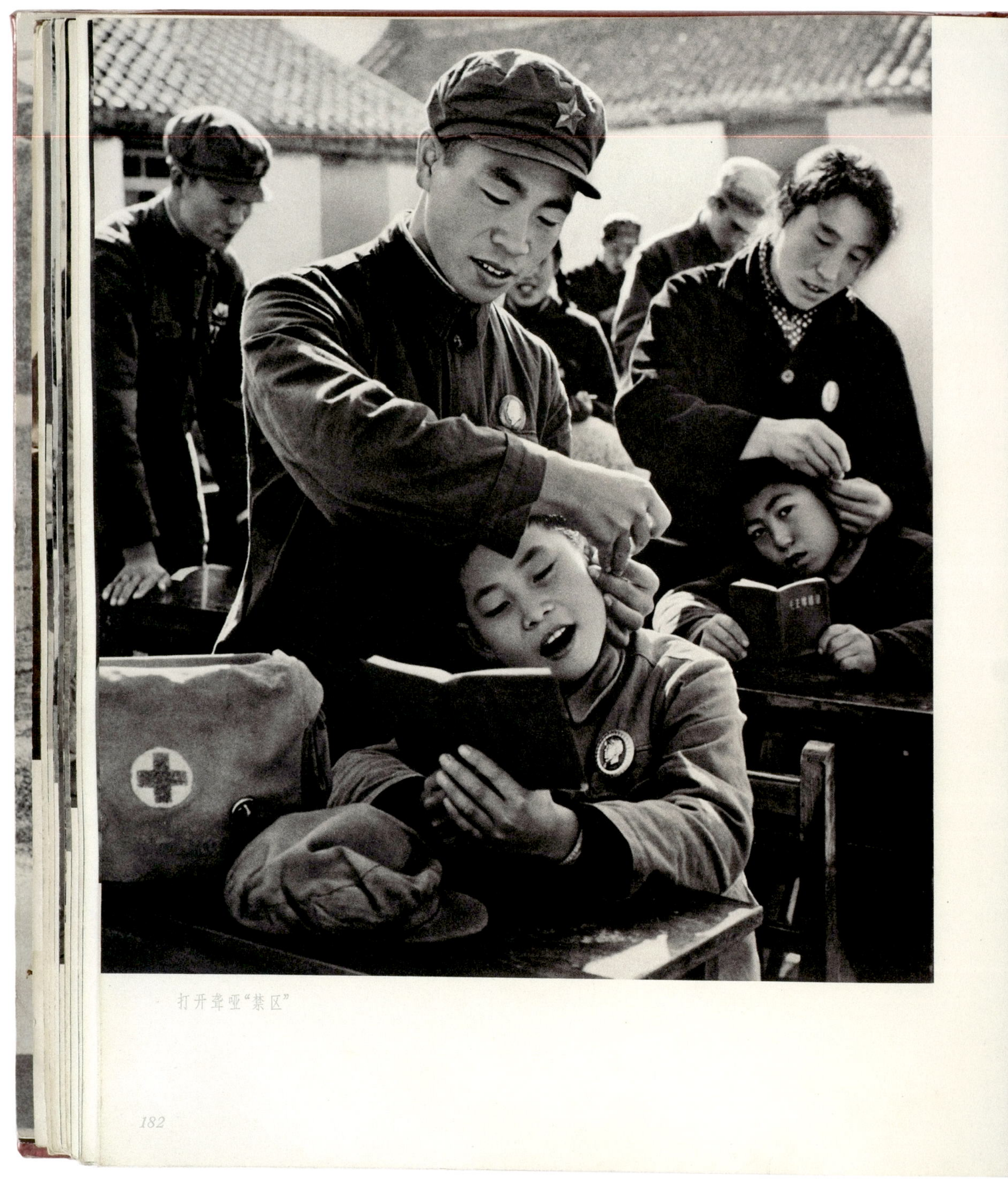

plate 95 (Above) 打开聋哑“禁区” - Opening Up the “No-Go Zone” of the Deaf and Mute (Opposite) 五指山下鱼水情 - Friendship Under the Five-Finger Mountain

五指山下鱼水情

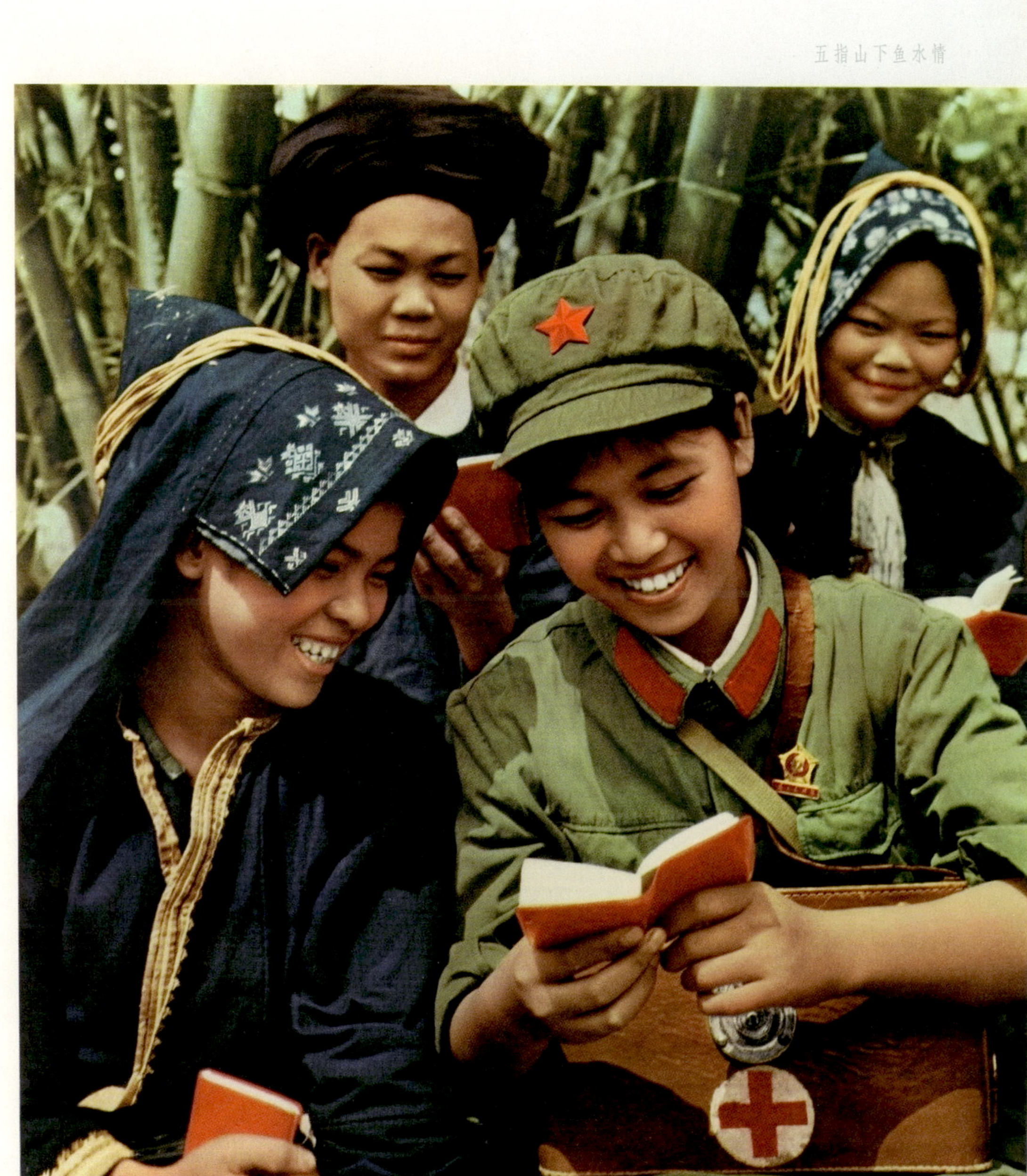

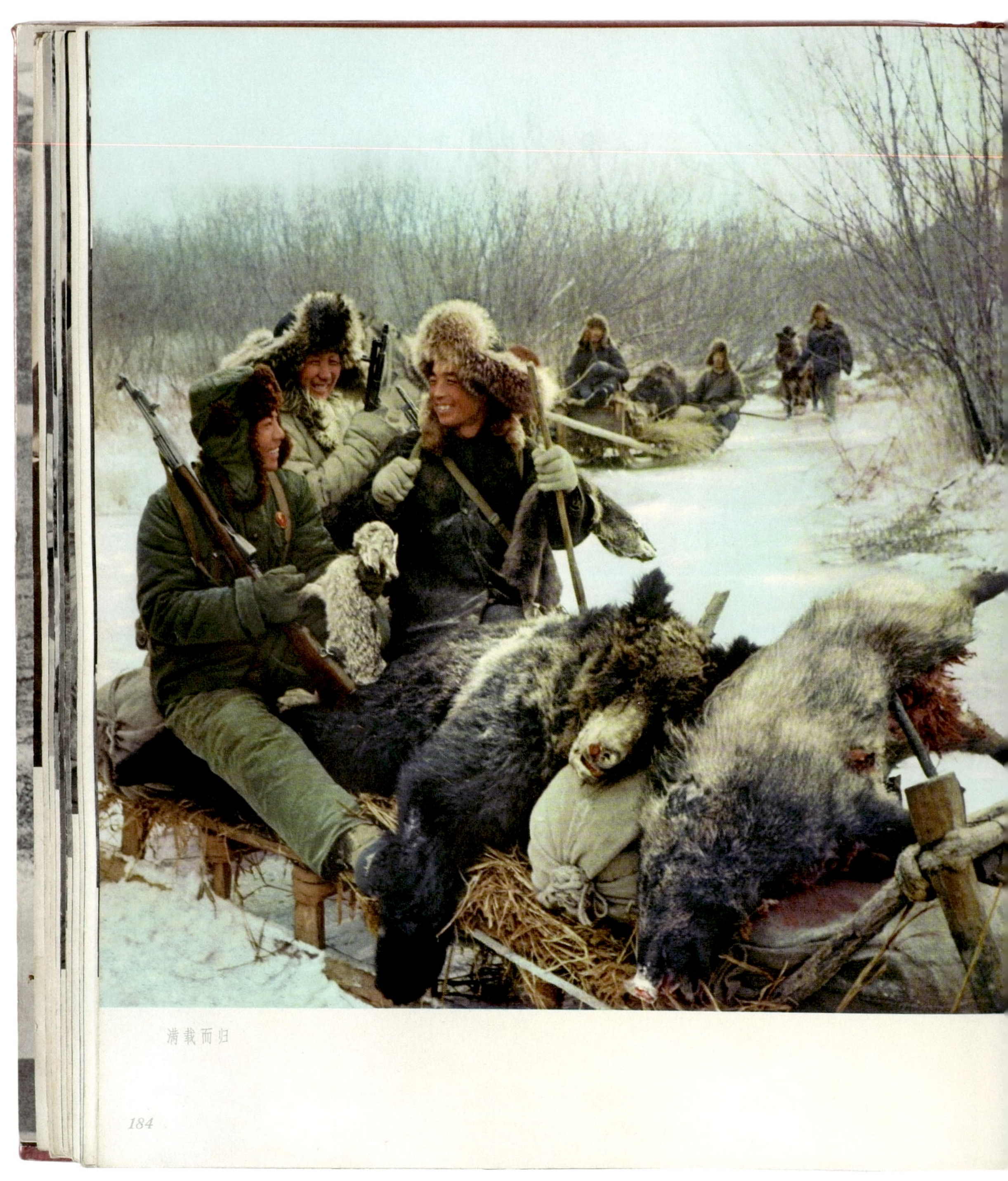

满载而归

plate 96 (Above) 满载而归 - Return Fully Stocked (Opposite) 毛主席教导传苗寨 - Chairman Mao's Guidance in a Miao Village

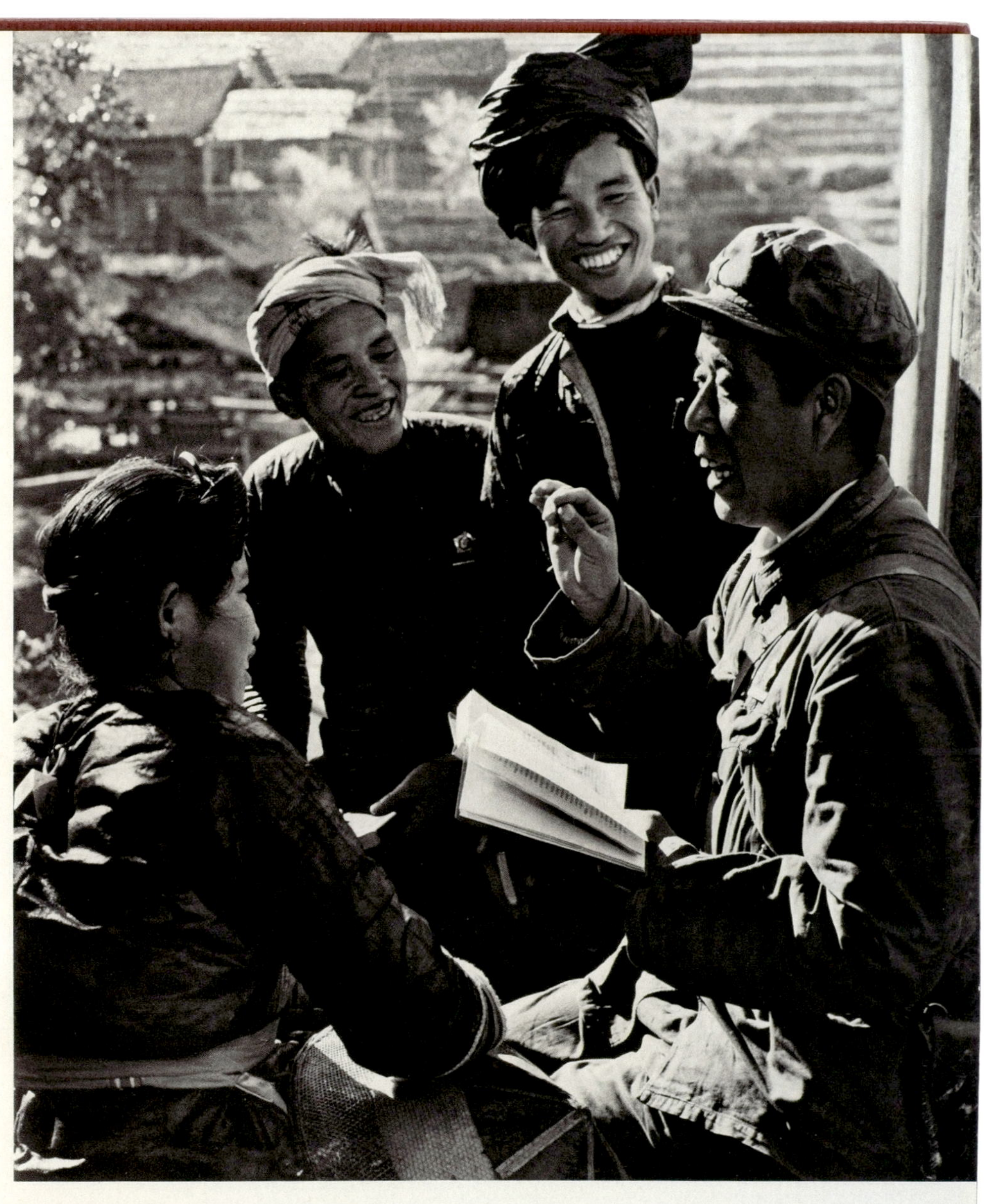

毛主席教导传苗寨

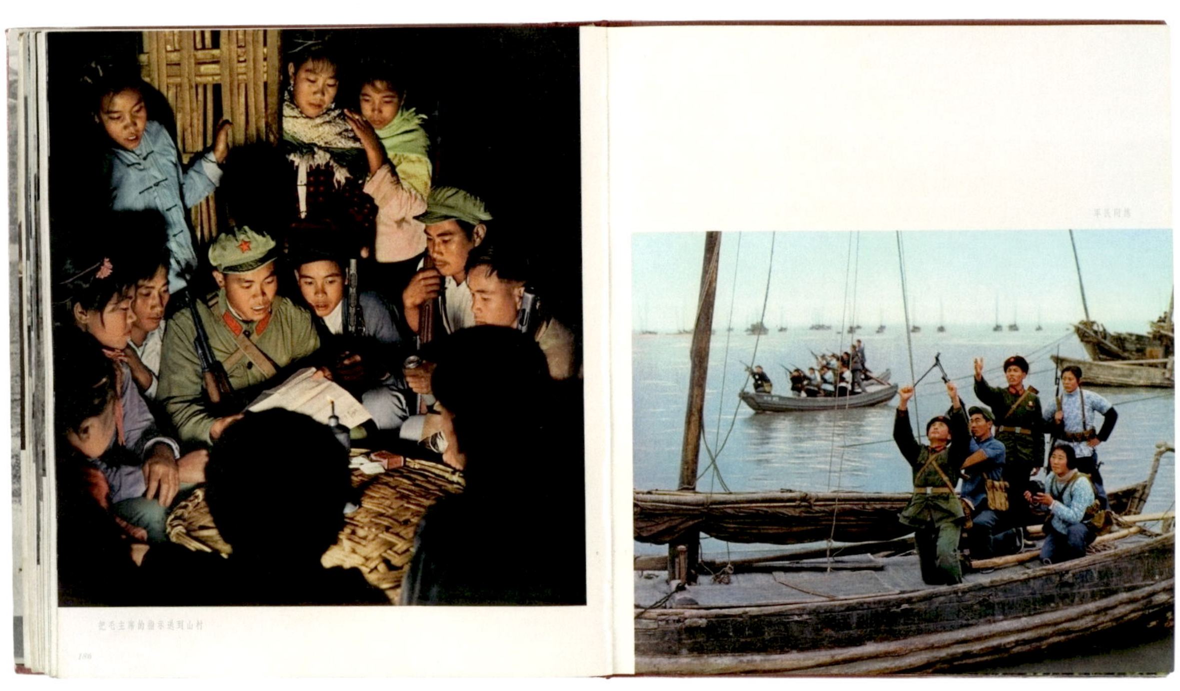

plate 97 (Left) 把毛主席的指示送到山村 - Send Chairman Mao's Instructions into the Mountain Villages. (Right) 军民同练 - The Soldiers and the People Practice Together.

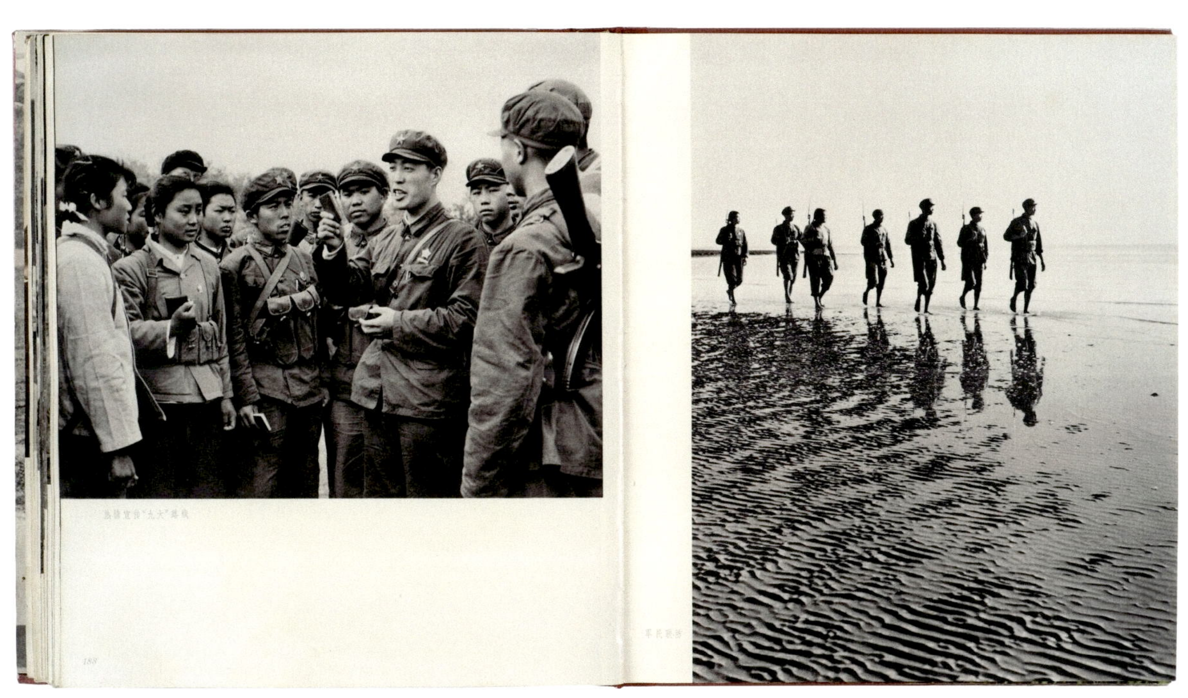

plate 98　(Left) 热情宣传“九大”路线 - Passionately Propagating “the Ninth National Congress of the Communist Party of China” Route
(Right) 军民联防 - Joint Defense by the Soldiers and the People

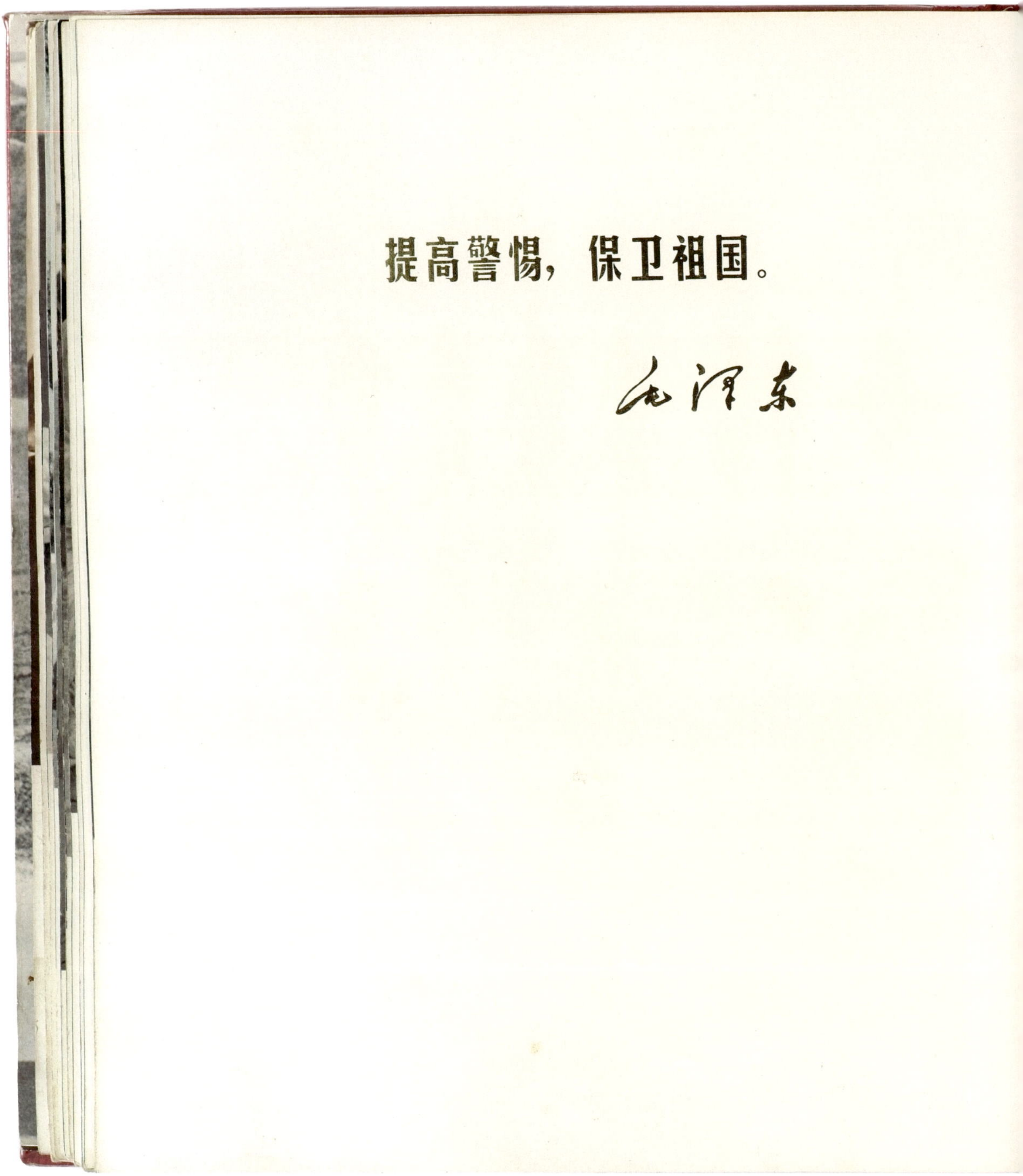

提高警惕，保卫祖国。

毛泽东

plate 99 (Above) 提高警惕, 保卫祖国 - Raise Vigilance, and Defend the Motherland (Opposite) 高度警惕 - On High Alert

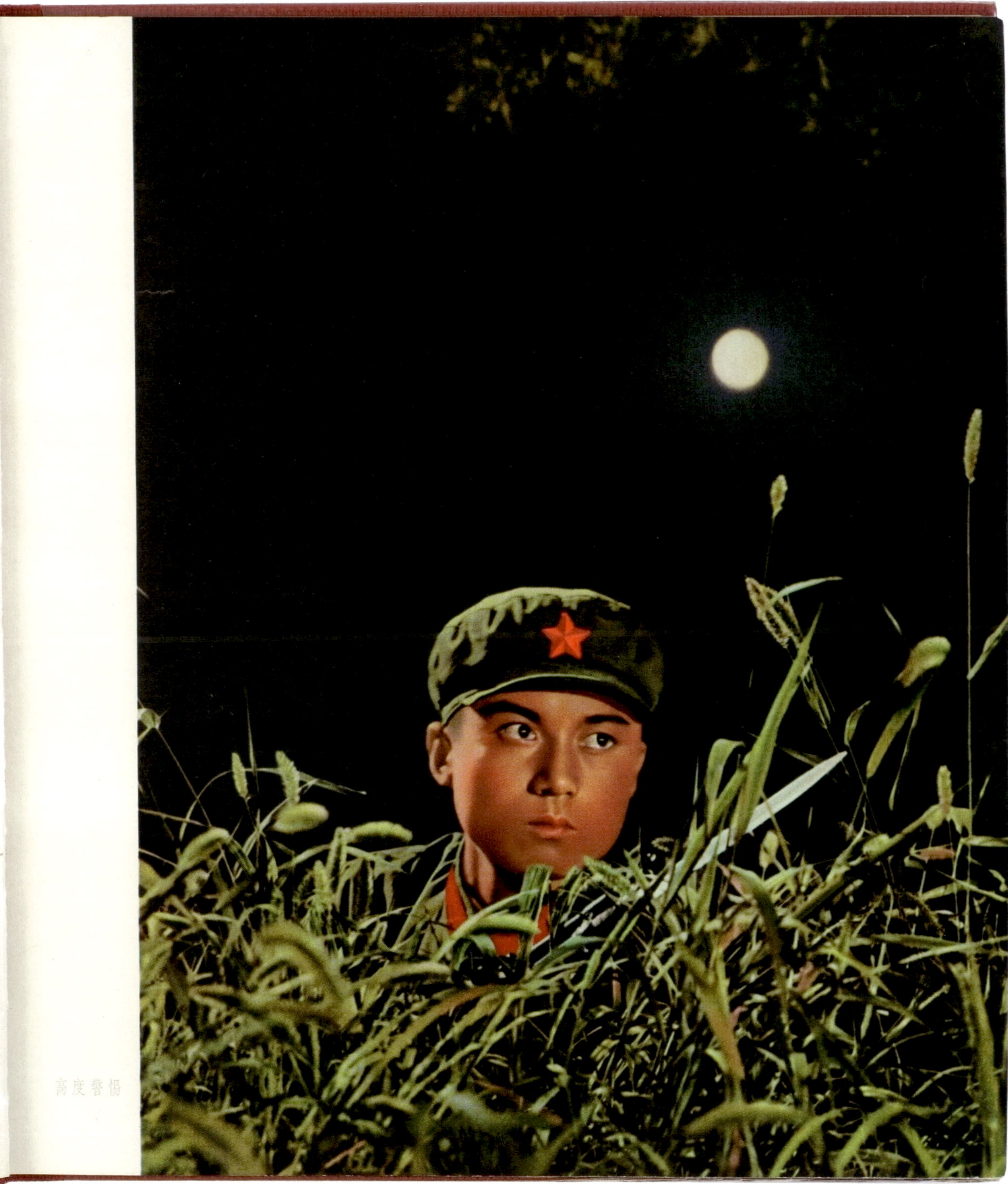

高度警惕

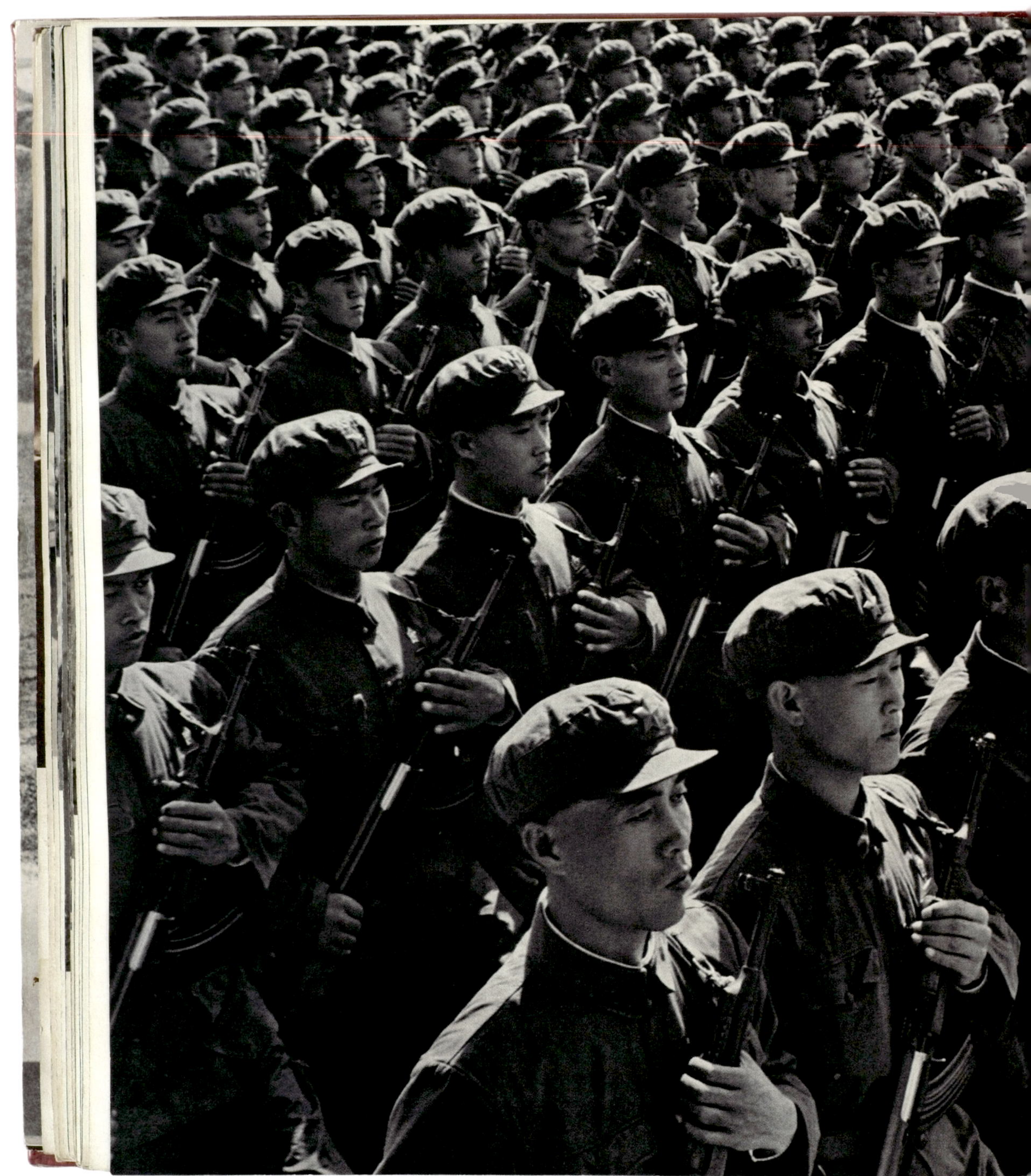

plate 100 一往无前 - March Forward

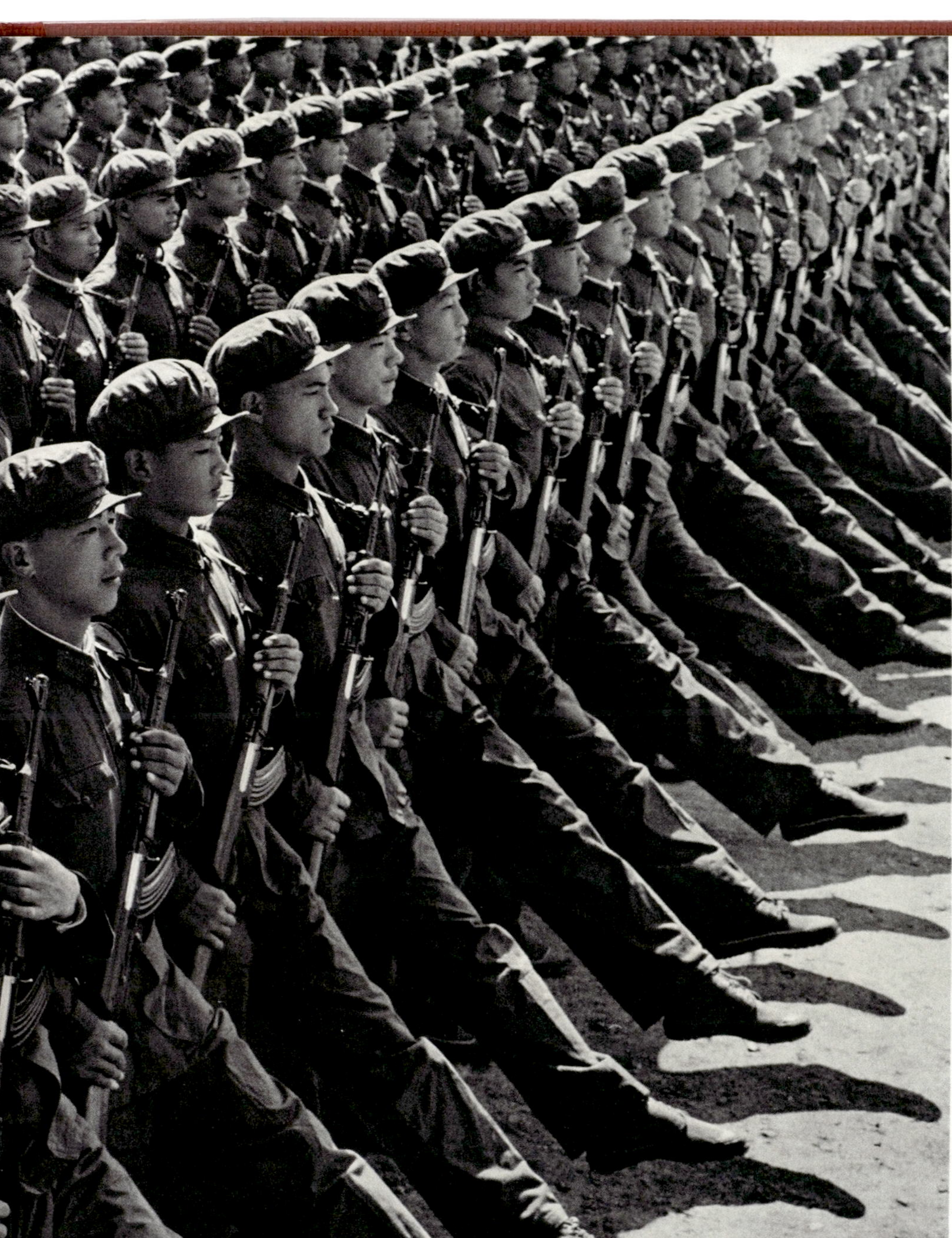

一往无前

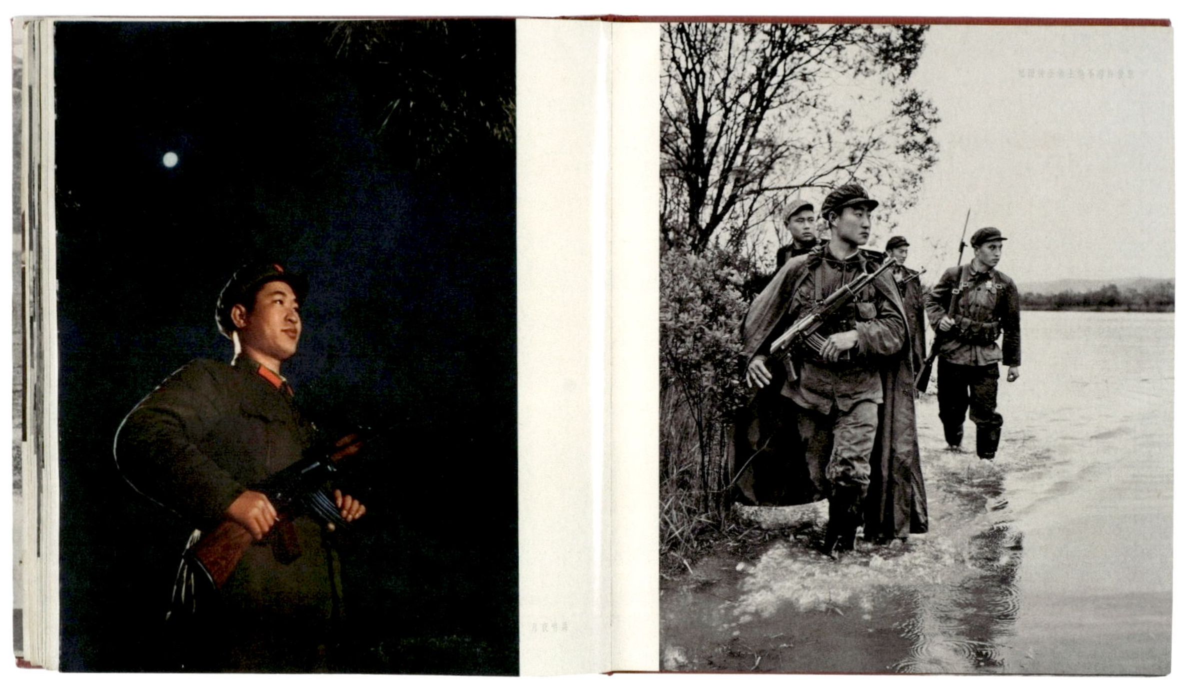

plate 101 (Left) 月夜哨兵 - A Guard Under the Moonlight (Right) 祖国神圣领土绝不容许侵犯 - The Motherland's Sacred Territory Must Never Be Allowed to Be Violated

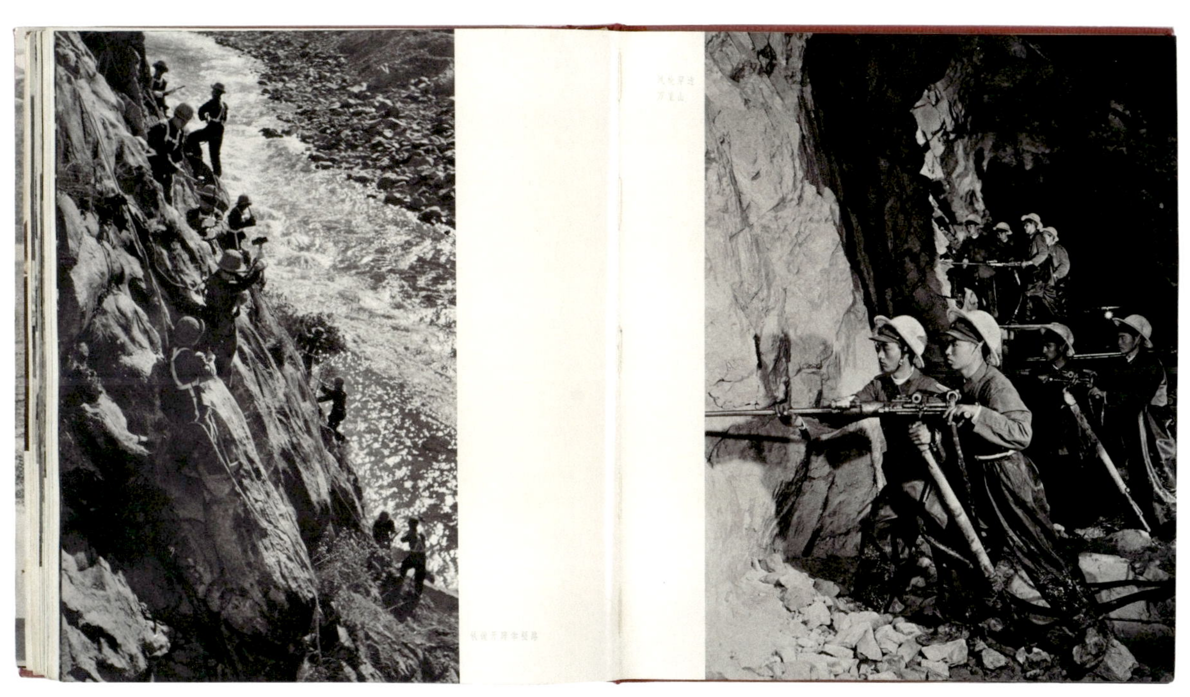

plate 102 (Left) 铁锤开辟幸福路 - Hammering Out a Path to Happiness (Right) 风枪穿透万重山 - Drilling Through the Mountains

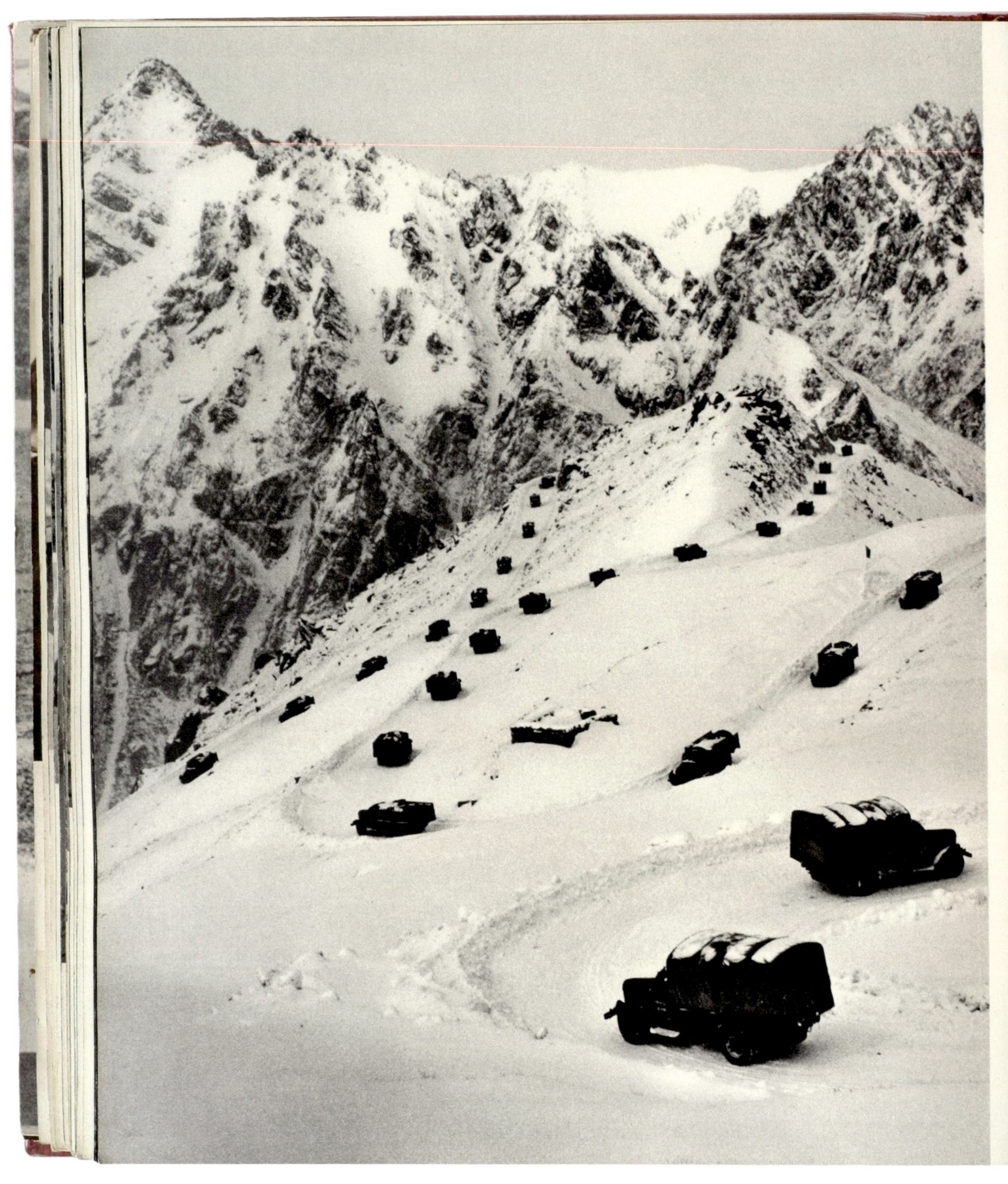

plate 103 (Above) 雀儿山上练硬功 - Acquire Masterly Skill on Mount Que'er (Opposite) 革命大批判开路 - Clear a Path for Revolutionary Mass Criticism

雀儿山上练硬功

革命大批判开路

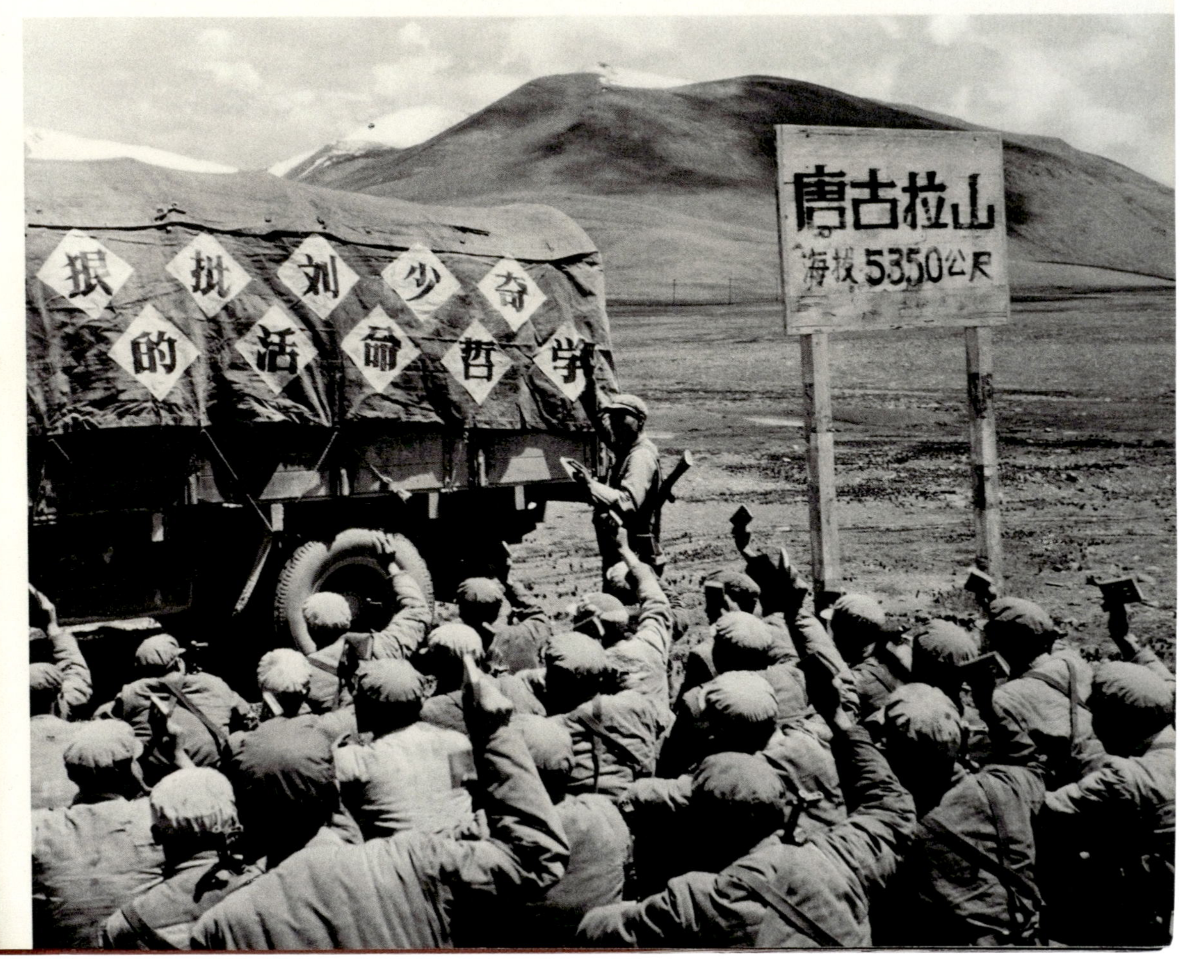

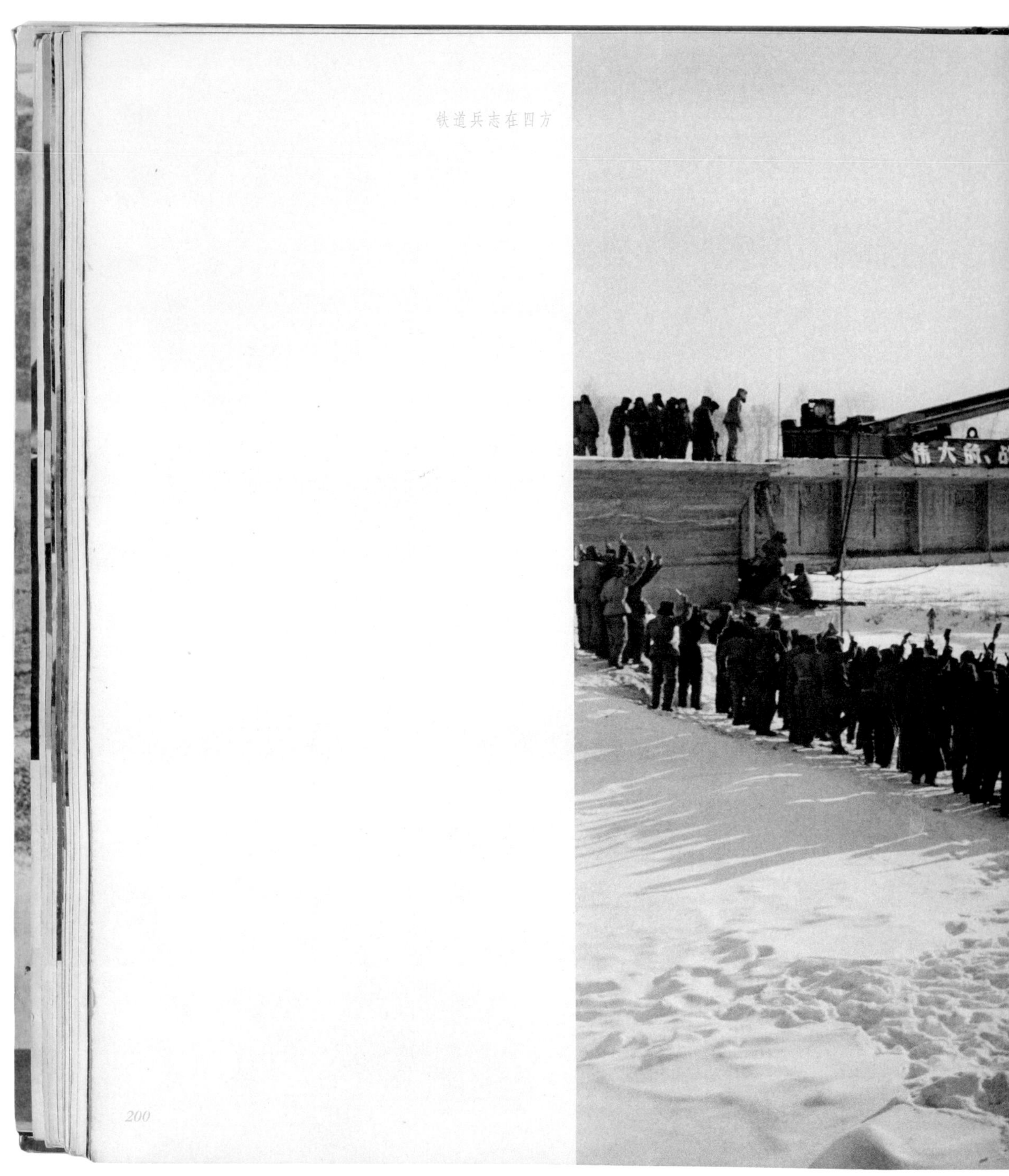

plate 104　铁道兵志在四方 - The Railway Corps Is Eager to Serve Anywhere

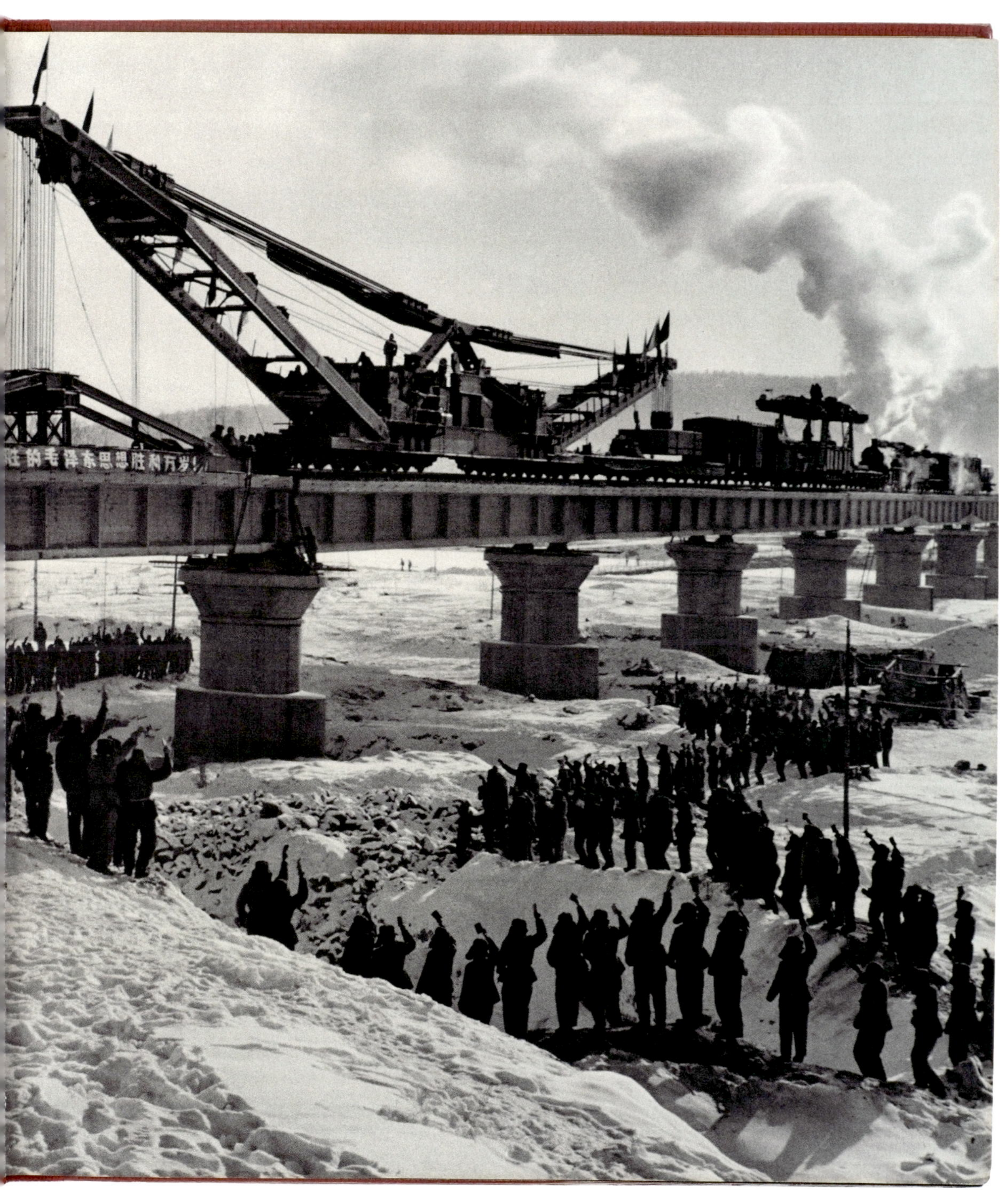
的毛泽东思想胜利万岁！

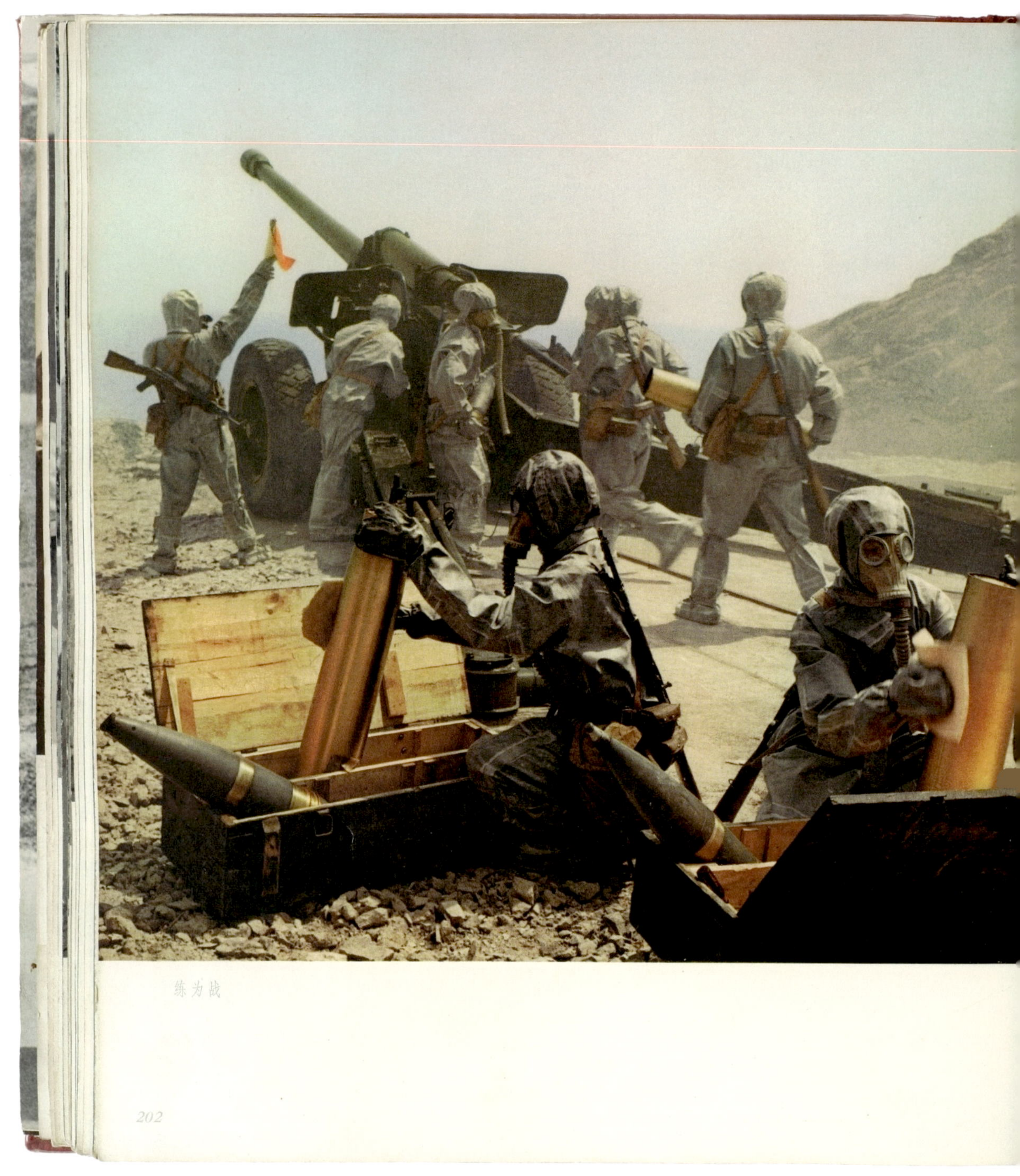

plate 105 (Above) 练为战 - Training for Battle (Opposite) 日夜守卫 - On Guard Day and Night

日夜守卫

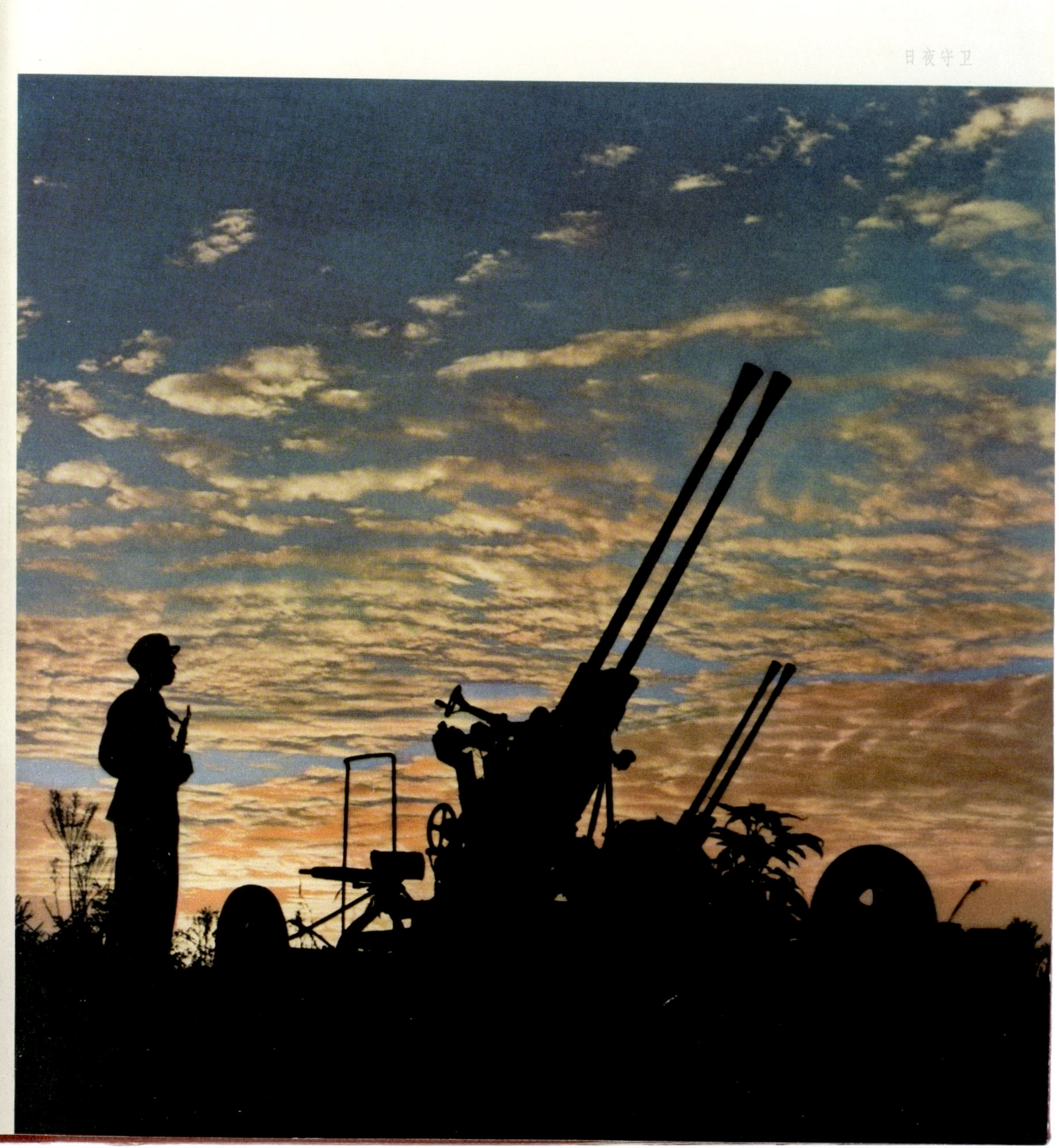

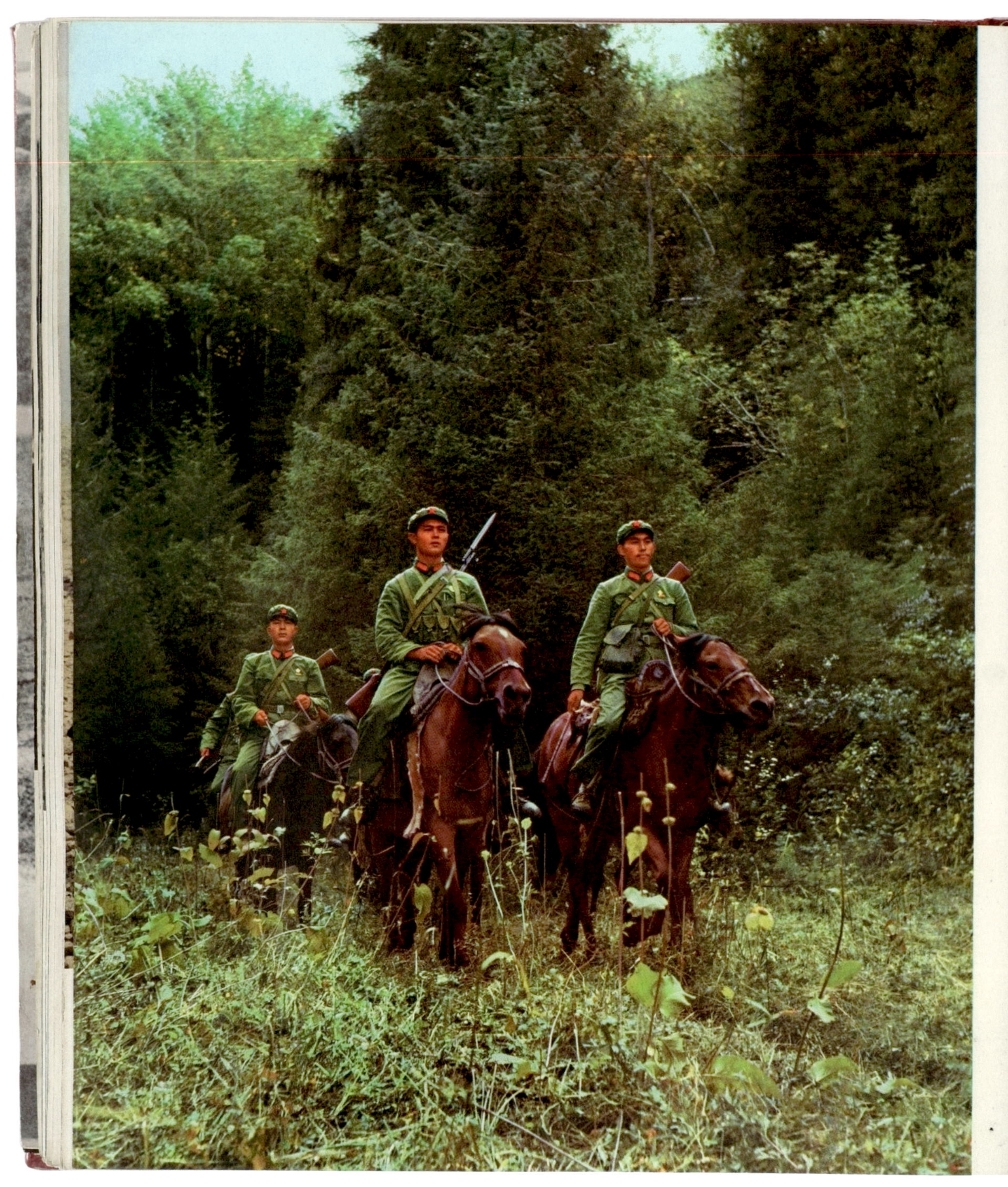

plate 106 (Above) 边防铁骑 - Troopers at the Border (Opposite) 冰山巡逻 - Patrolling Ice Mountain

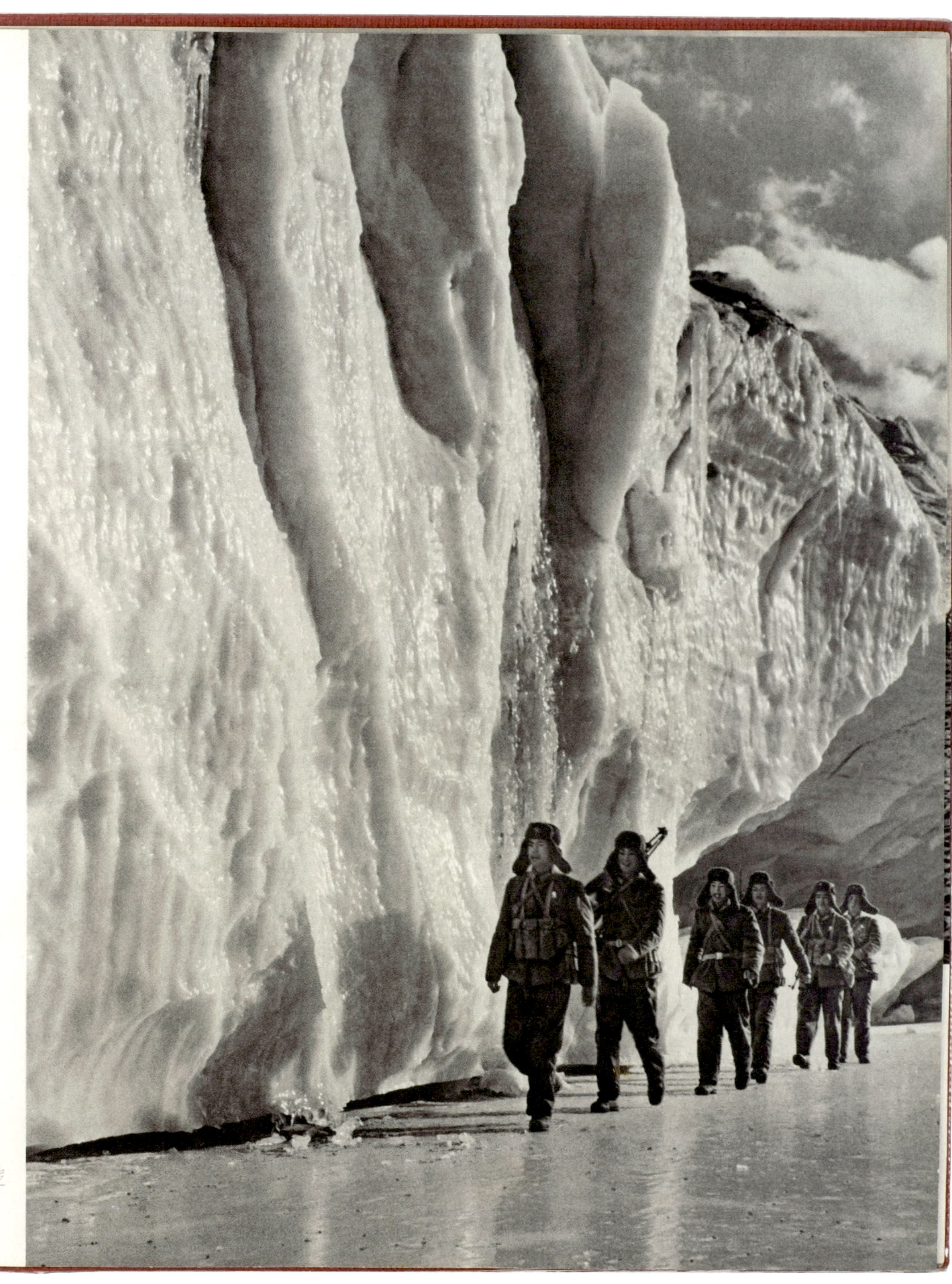

冰山巡逻

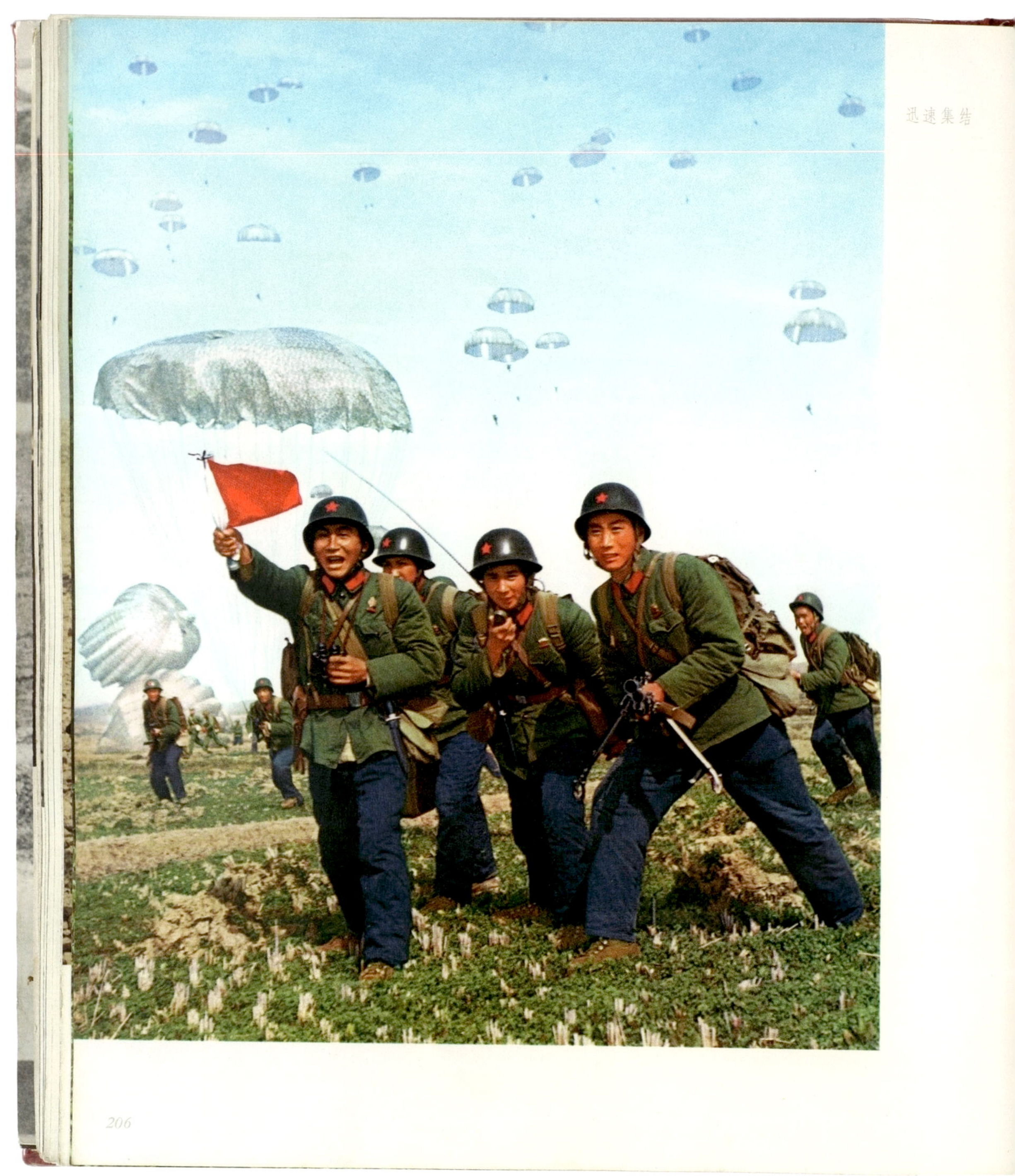

plate 107 (Above) 迅速集结 - Assemble Quickly (Opposite) 步坦协同演习 - A Collaborative Maneuver Between Infantry and Tanks

步坦协同演习

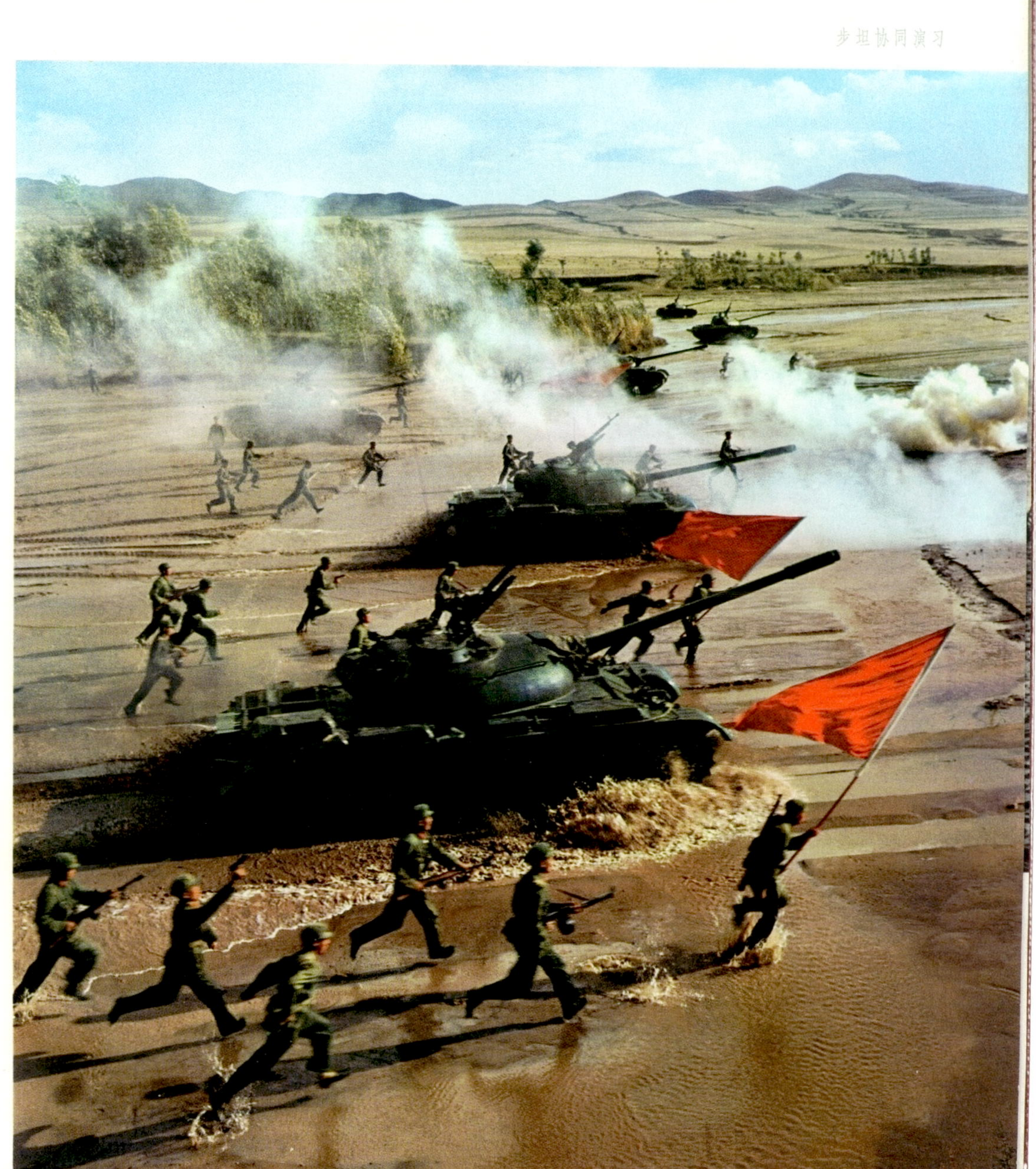

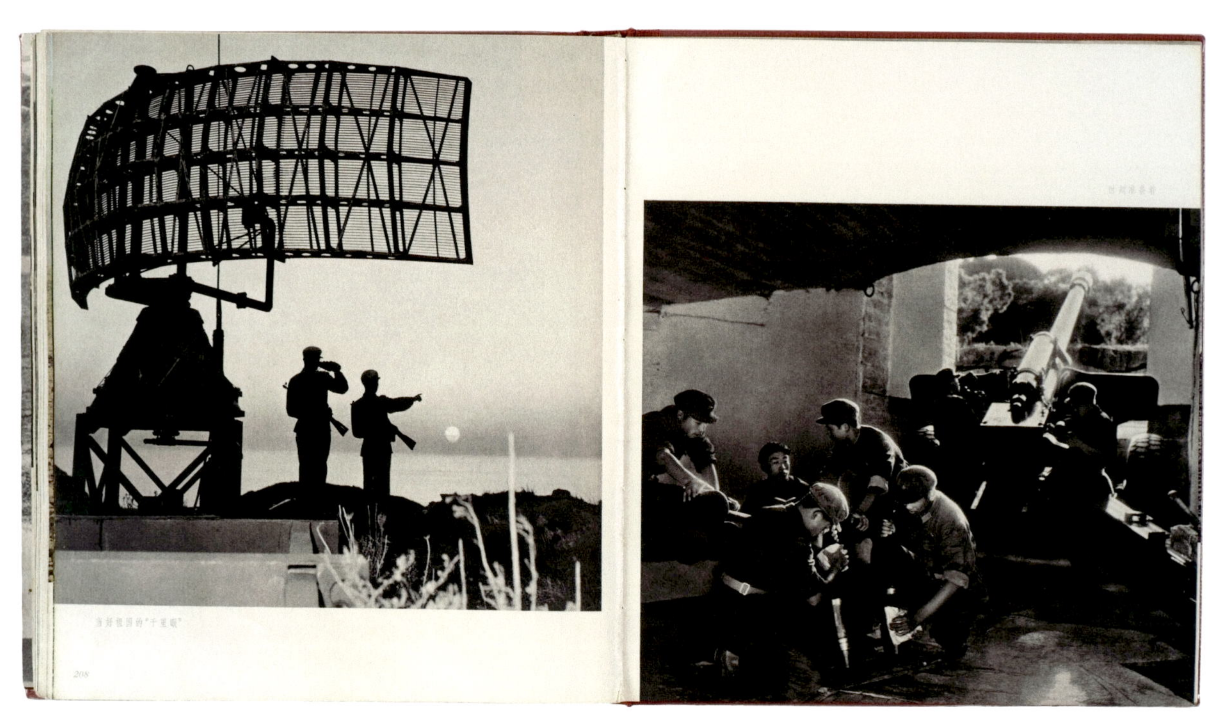

plate 108 (Left) 当好祖国的"千里眼" - Become the Motherland's "Third Eye" (Right) 时刻准备着 - Always Be Prepared

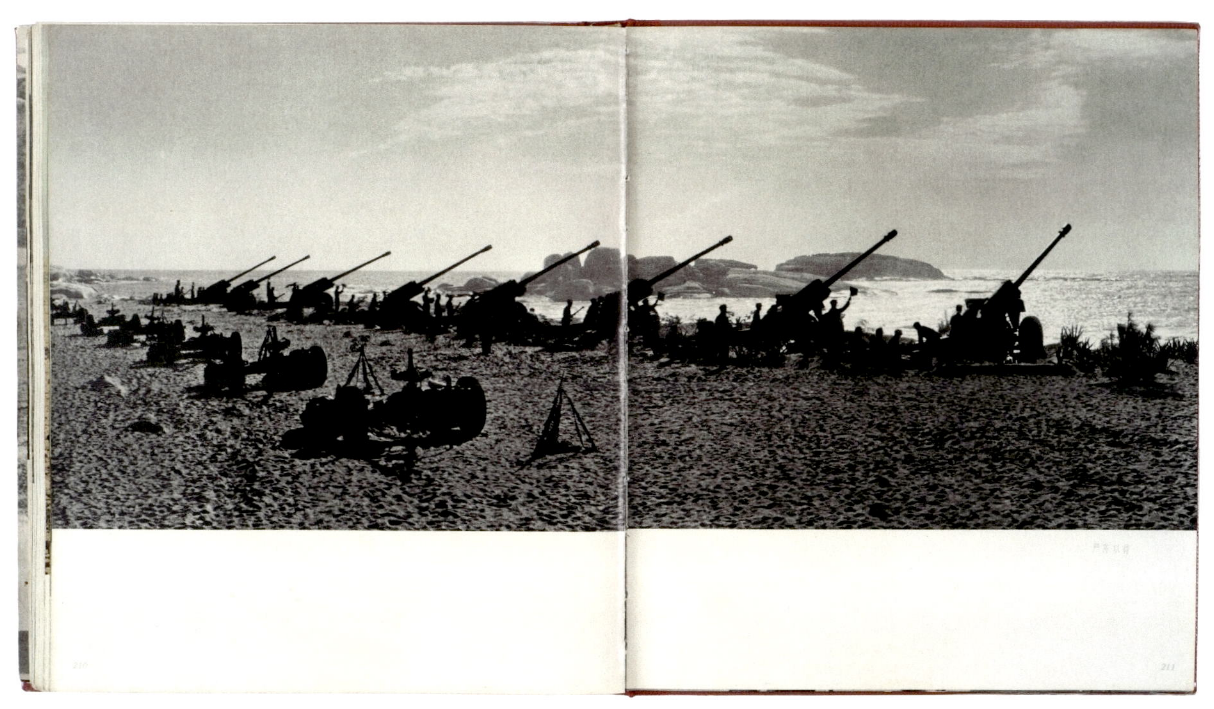

plate 109　严阵以待 - Embattle

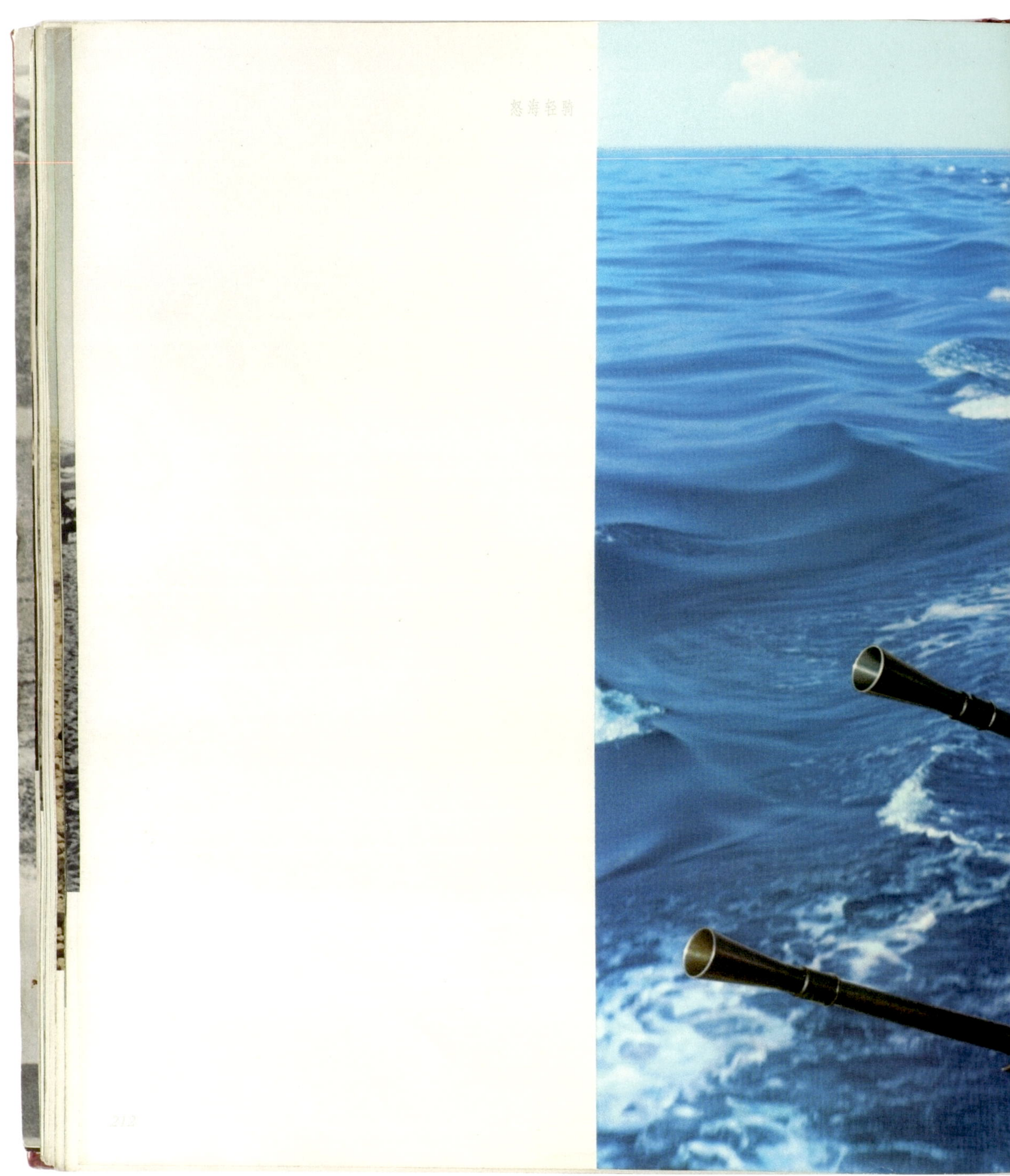

plate 110 怒海轻骑 - Troopers in a Turbulent Sea

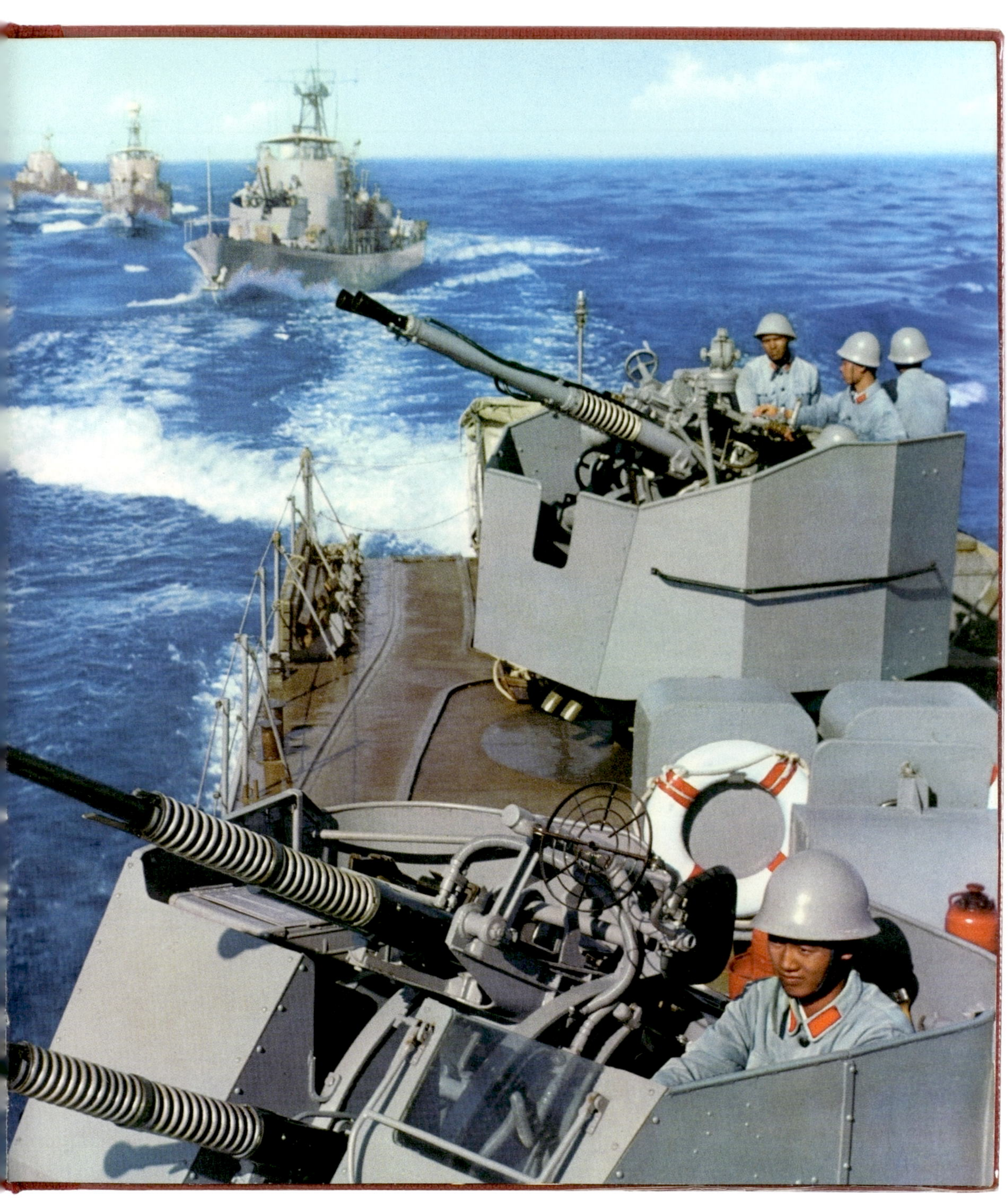

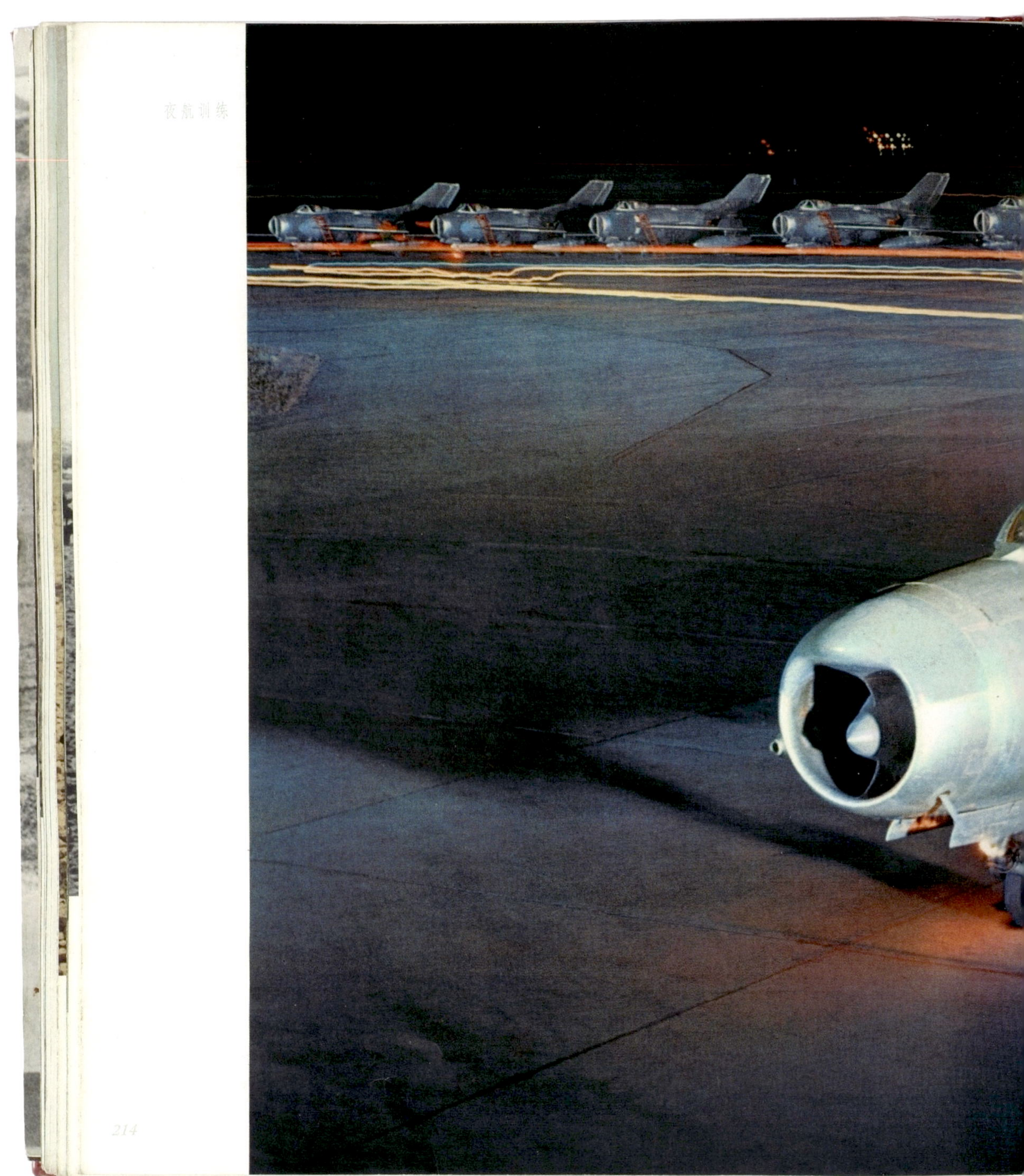

plate III　夜航训练 - Night Flight Training

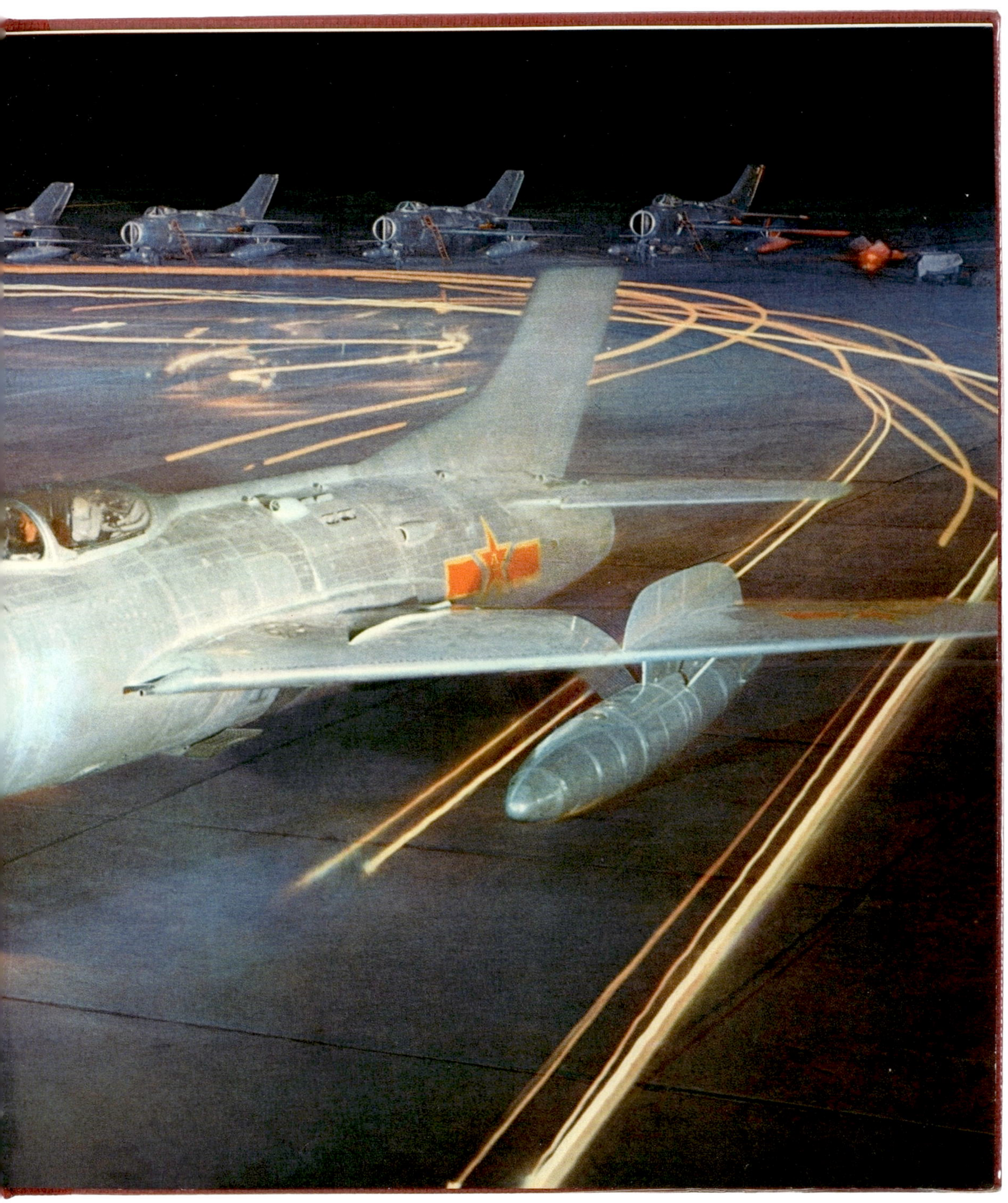

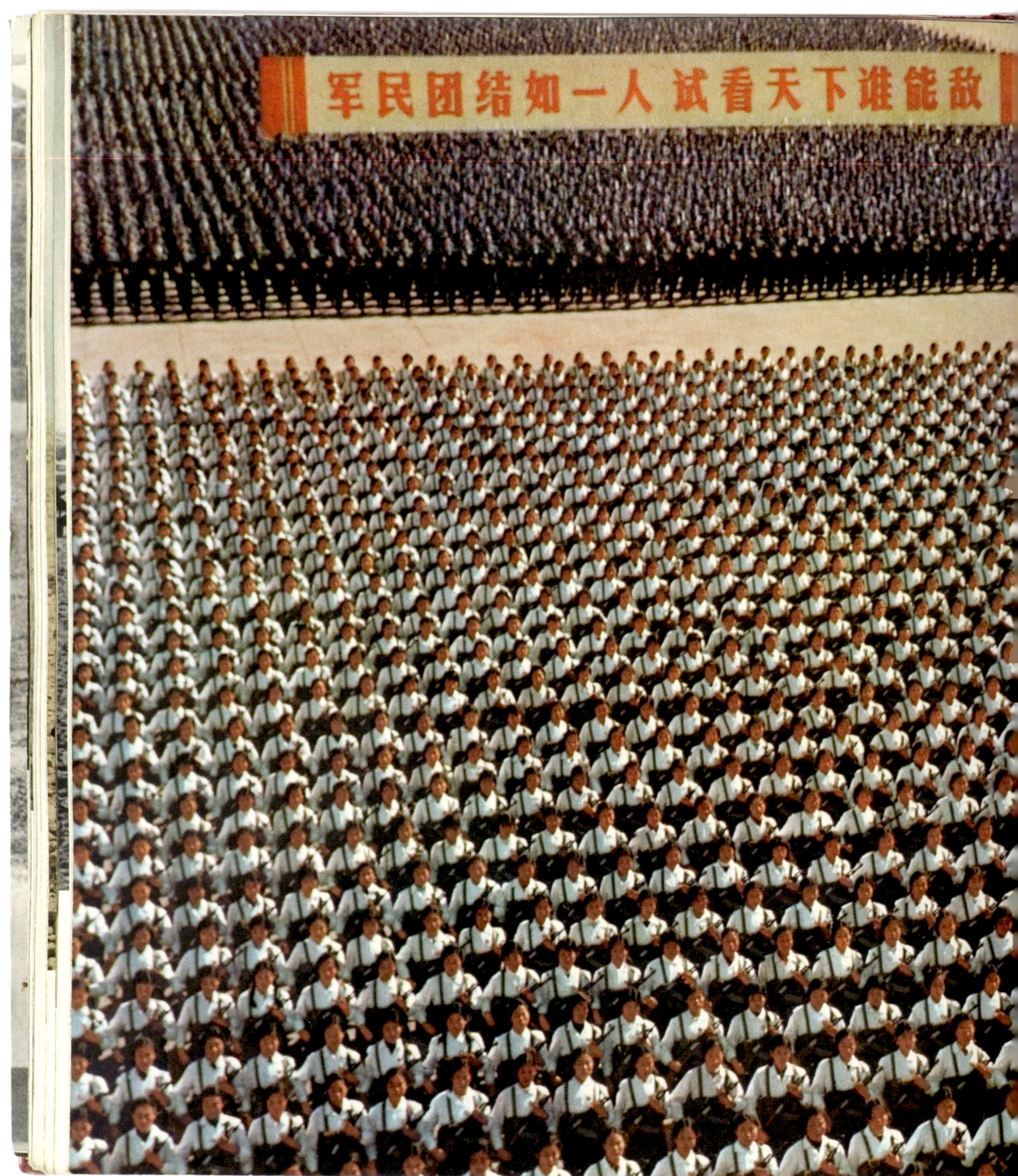

plate 112　全民皆兵 - Anyone Can Be a Soldier

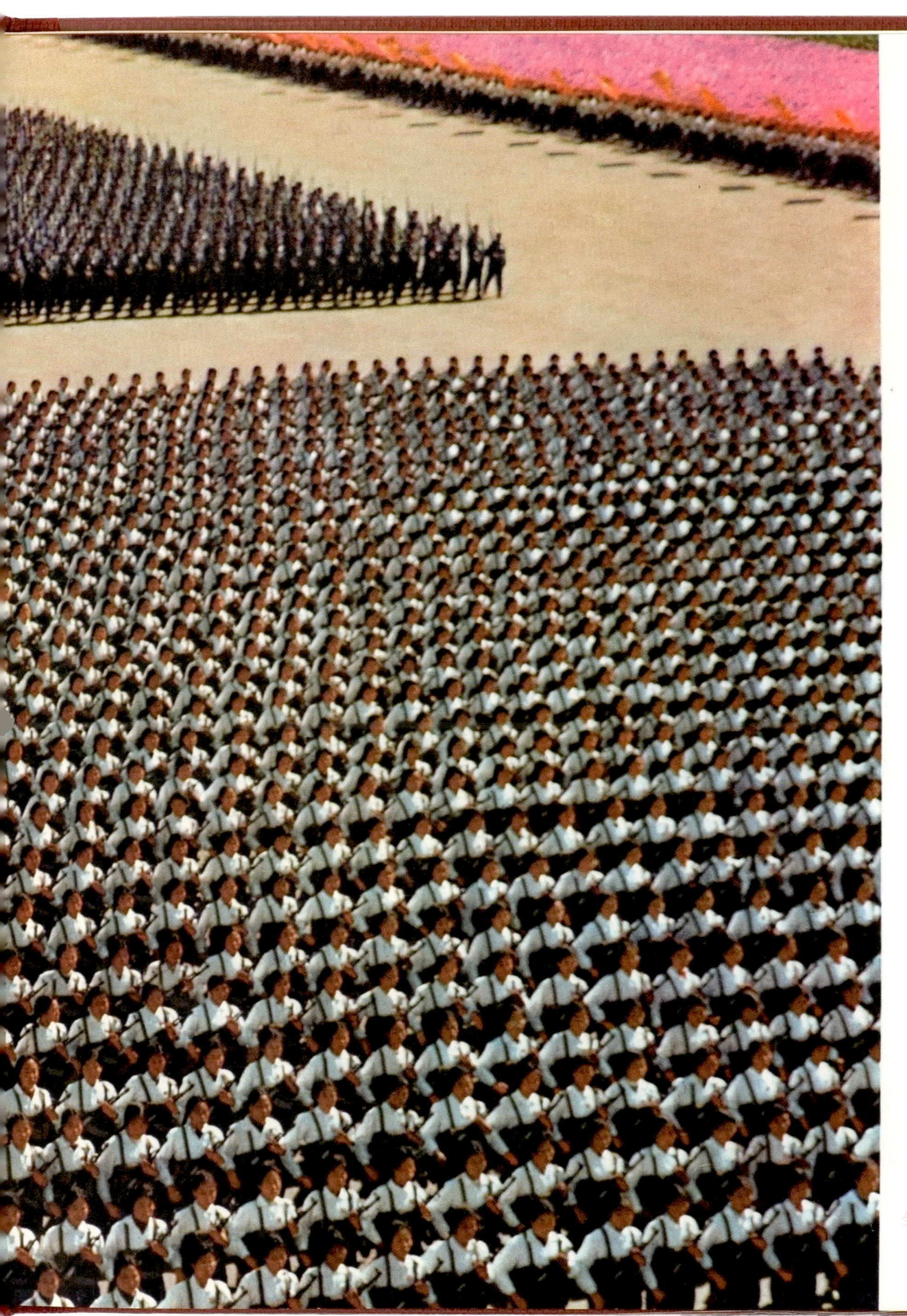

全民皆兵

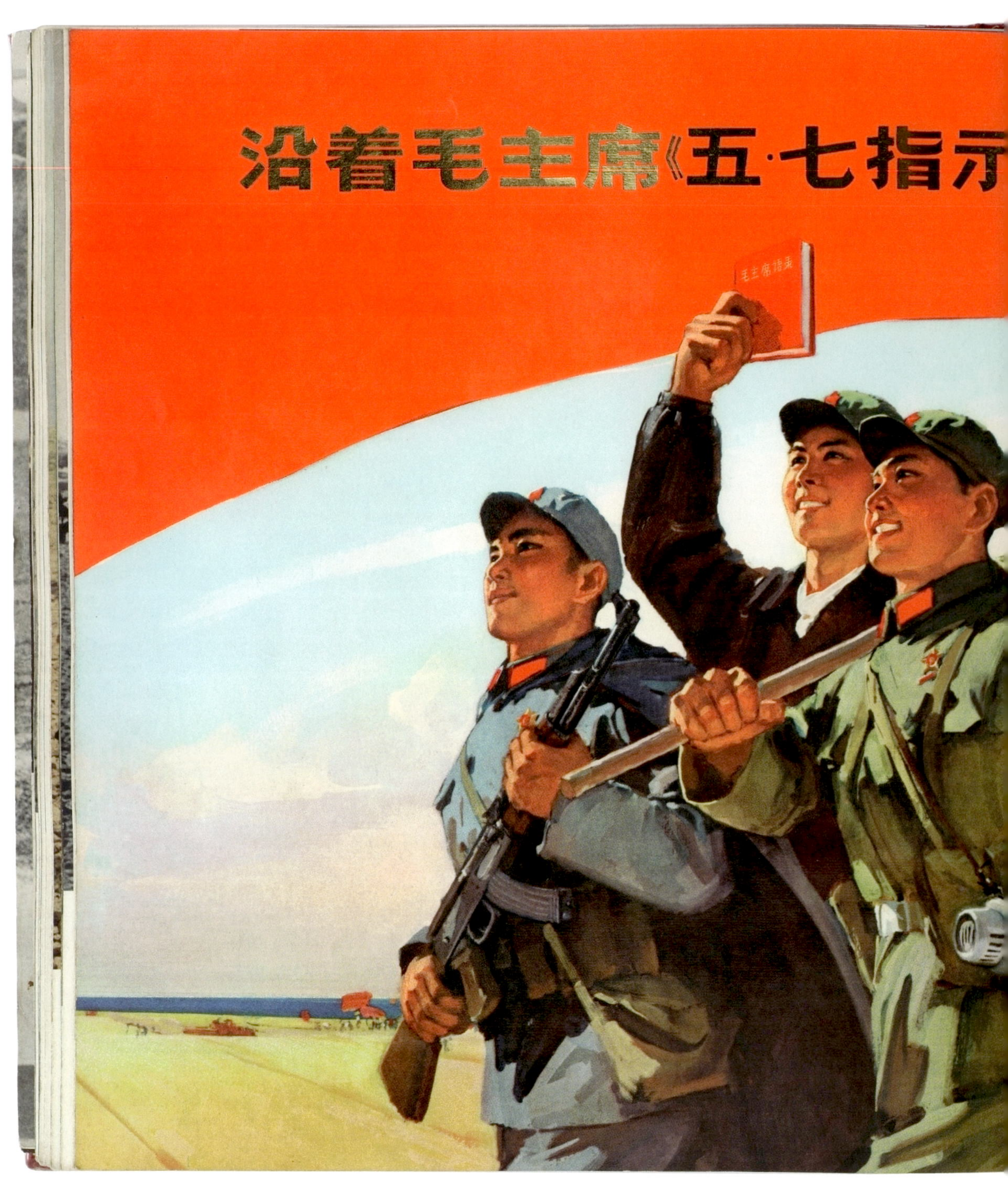

plate 113 沿着毛主席《五•七指示》的光辉道路奋勇前进! - Forge Ahead on the Glorious Road of Chairman Mao's "May Seventh Directive"!

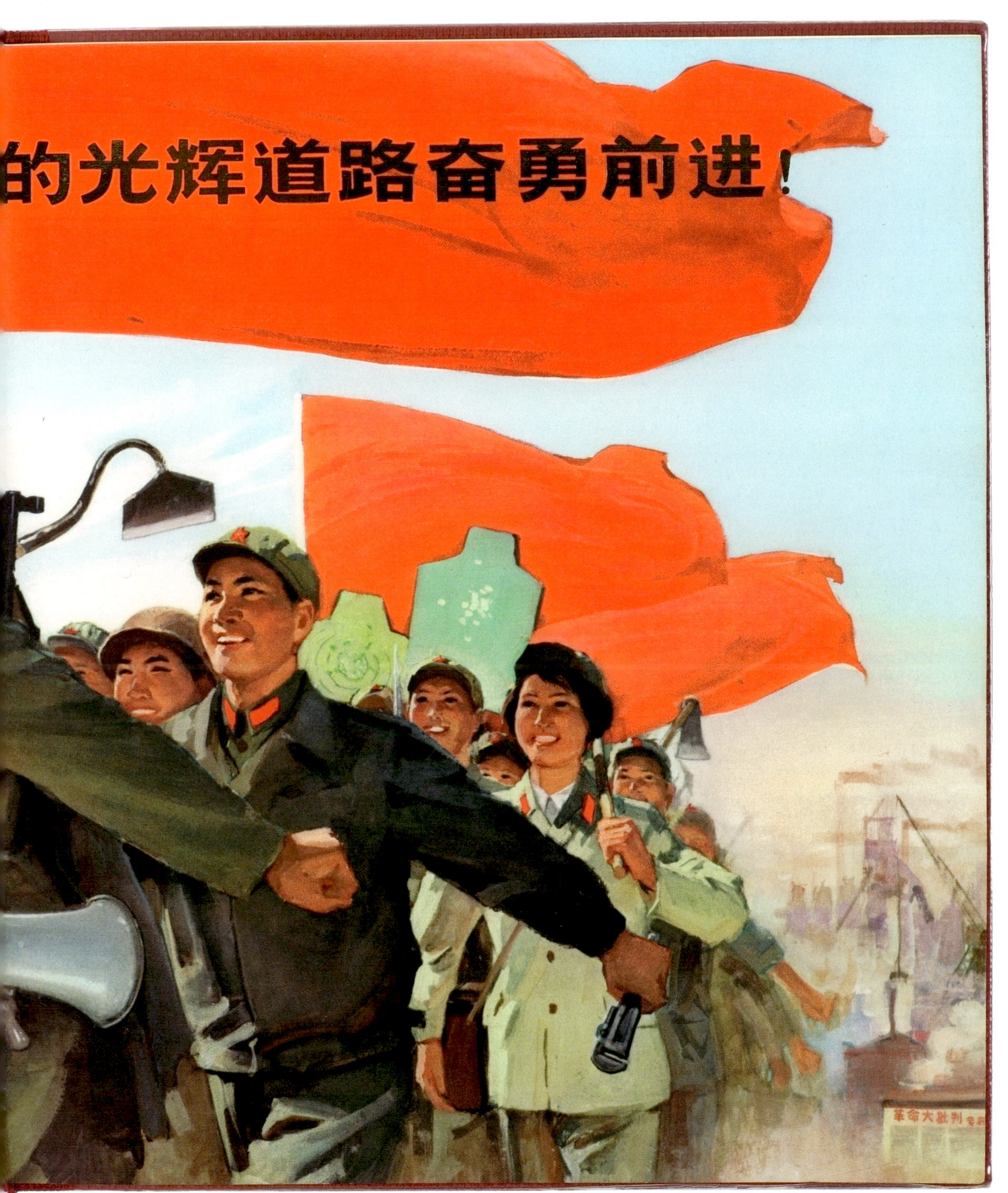
的光辉道路奋勇前进！
革命大批判

目 录

plate 114

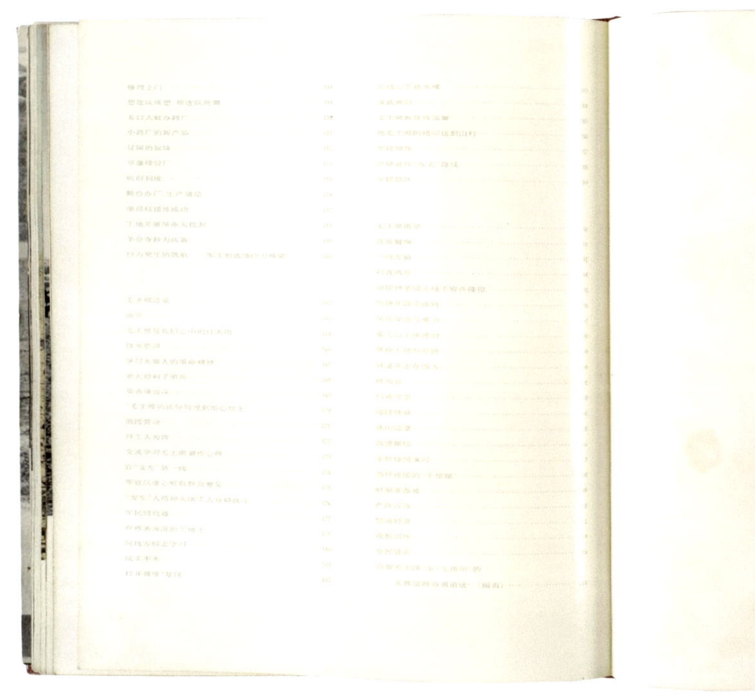

plate 115

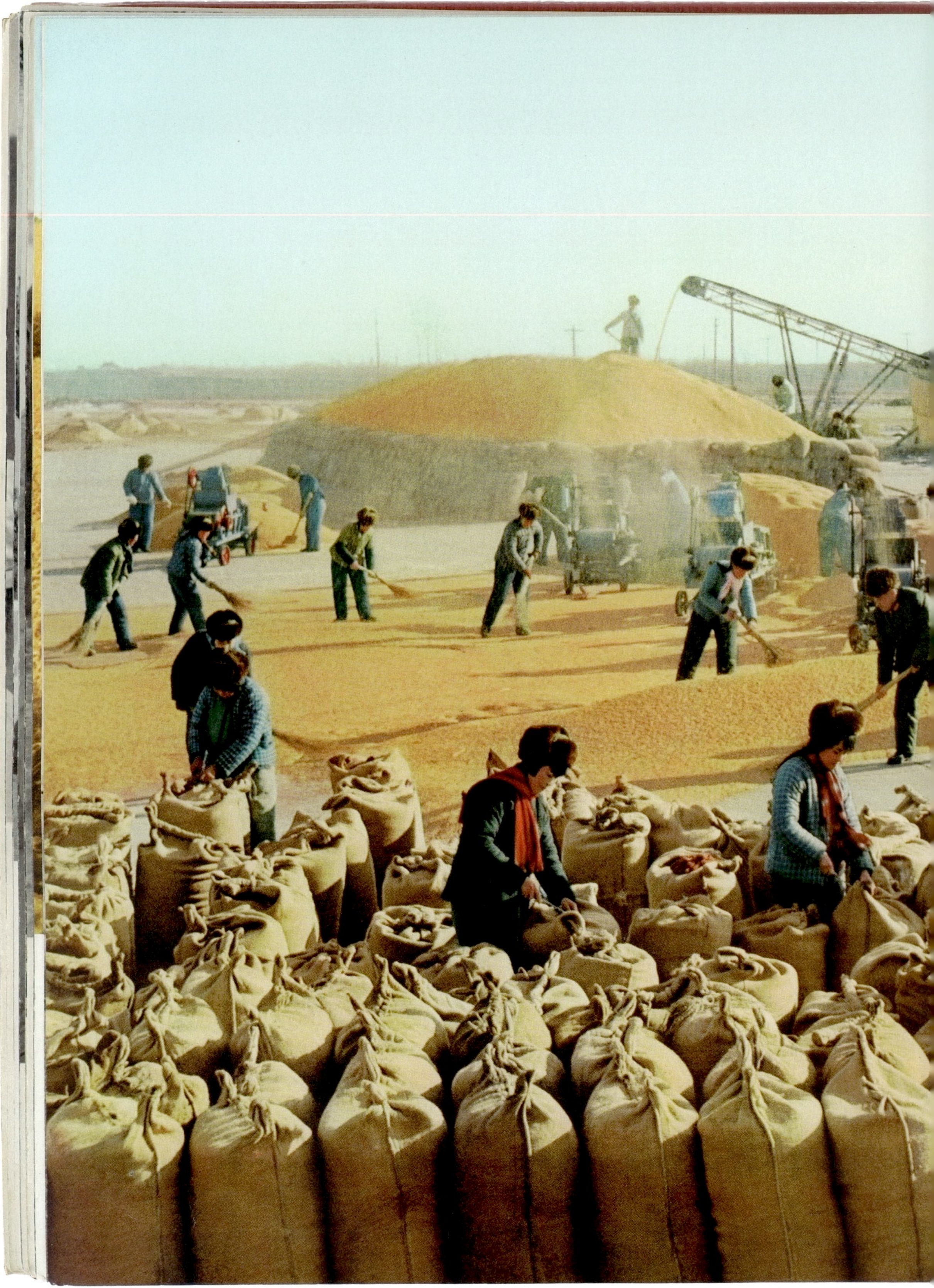

Labor Together: A tentative study of *Long Live the Glorious May Seventh Directive*

Liu Ding and Carol Yinghua Lu

Long Live the Glorious May Seventh Directive was a photobook published and circulated in the Chinese army on May 7, 1971, as a tribute to Mao Zedong's May Seventh Directive, issued in 1966. The Directive took the form of a letter addressed to his handpicked successor, Lin Biao, minister of national defense. Five years later, this photobook was published at the critical juncture when Mao Zedong was growing suspicious of Lin Biao's oversized political ambition. On September 13, four months after this photobook was printed, Lin Biao died in an airplane crash together with his wife and son, allegedly after a botched coup against Mao. This incident led the Communist Party to officially condemn Lin as a traitor.[1] This explains the subsequent obscurity of this publication, which celebrated Lin's alliance with Mao from 1966 to 1971. Nowadays random copies of *Long Live the Glorious May Seventh Directive* turn up with images of Lin Biao crossed out or cut out entirely (see illustration).

The May Seventh Directive was actually composed collectively by three party members, Chen Boda, Yang Chengwu, and Qi Benyu, on May 13, 1966, based on Mao's draft letter to Lin Biao on May 7 and a face-to-face discussion with Mao in Shanghai on May 13. This document was soon authorized and issued by the Political Bureau of the Central Committee of the Communist Party on May 15 as a directive to be distributed and studied within the Communist Party. This document and his plans for it were part of Mao's painstaking plotting to win back his political authority following several years of withdrawal from the public eye after the failure of the Great Leap Forward, his drastic social and economic experiment.[2] By the end of 1959, it was painfully clear that the unrealistic leap and the commune programs were utter failures. Under enormous political pressure, Mao was forced to back off from some of his more radical policies. His hold on the national leadership began to slip.

During Mao's strategic retreat, Lin and his People's Liberation Army (PLA)[3] had turned themselves into ardent supporters of the disgraced leader. Under Lin Biao, the PLA continuously bolstered the personality cult around Mao and became the driving force behind the campaign to study Mao's

(Opposite) Detail of a photograph from *Long Live the Glorious May Seventh Directive*, 1971

thoughts. The army supplied most of the behavioral models that embodied the "spirit of a cog" by unconditionally following instructions from the Party and/or superiors and by loyalty to the larger group. The army also promoted art forms that visually represented Mao's revolutionary legend and vision and contributed to the deification of Mao. Thus, the army became a critical institutional power and instrument for the realization of Mao's communist ideal. By 1966, Mao had the full support of Lin Biao and the People's Liberation Army and was ready to regain his throne.

The May 7 Directive was prompted by a report submitted on May 2, 1966, by the General Logistics Department to the Ministry of National Defense on the political and economic significance and promise of the military participating in agriculture and other areas of production. After receiving this report from Lin, Mao further developed the idea of engaging the army in production into the vision of a "big school." In Mao's conception, this school model should be applied to all lines of work, so that everyone could be involved in studying politics, military affairs, and culture and simultaneously in production. The application of such a model to the society could then produce a holistic system, echoing his initial plan for establishing the People's Commune in 1958.[4] Mao saw this as an opportunity to revive his early scheme, which was foiled by disastrous outcomes.

In this letter to Lin, Mao spelled out his grand vision for the army: As long as there is no world war, the army should function as a big school. Even if the Third World War were to take place, the army would likely become such a big school that could carry out all kinds of work besides fighting the war. Hadn't this been done in the areas where the Sino-Japanese fighting took place during the eight years of the Second World War? In such a big school, one studies politics, military affairs, and culture. One can engage in agriculture and other kinds of production as well. One can run some small- and medium-sized factories, manufacturing dozens of essentials and products that could be bartered with the state. Thus millions of military personnel can play a productive role.[5] In essence, this letter outlined Mao's utopian dream for a socialist country, less than one month before the launch of the Cultural Revolution[6] and his return to Beijing, where he reclaimed the center of power. It was his articulation of the communist society he intended to build after the Cultural Revolution. In this blueprint, he called for the military to maintain readiness both for war and for class struggle, and in the meantime, to make

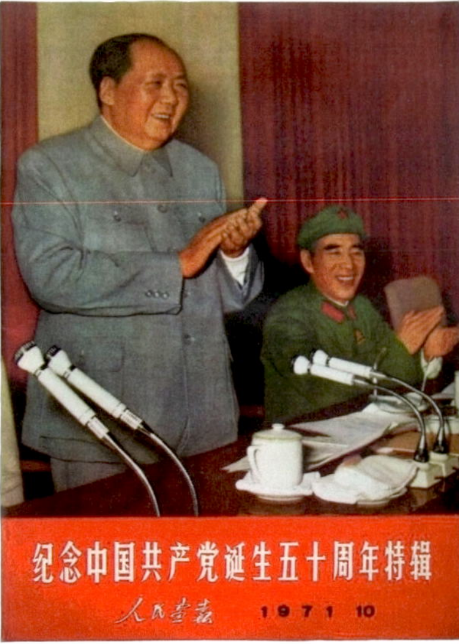

Cover of an issue of *People's Pictorial* magazine from 1971 which features a variant of a photograph that appears in *Long Live the Glorious May Seventh Directive*.

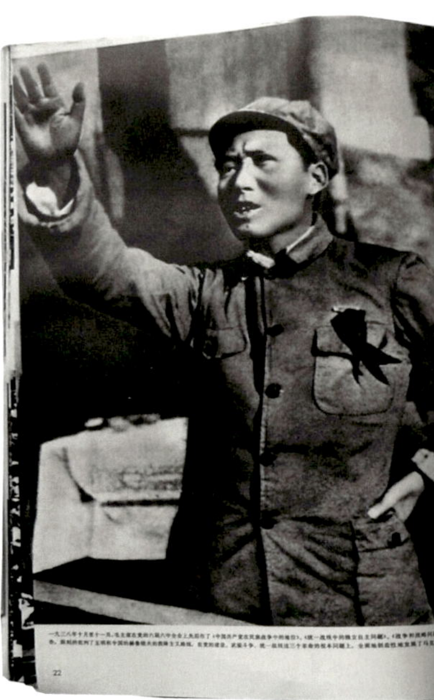

Page spread of an issue of *People's Pictorial* magazine from 1971. The upper right image appears as a handcolored version in *Long Live the Glorious May Seventh Directive*.

themselves useful in all lines of work.

Long Live the Glorious May Seventh Directive was brought out as part of the 1971 commemoration of the May Seventh Directive, a celebration that had taken place annually since 1966. In light of the shifted political dynamic soon after Lin's futile attempt to escape, this photobook was likely to be the last testimony of Lin's pledging his loyalty to Mao. Published by the People's Liberation Army Picture Press, it consisted of 169 photographs (68 in color and 101 in black and white), yet none of the featured photographs was credited to any specific photographer and the entire photobook remained anonymous. The only certainty is that it was a collective effort by photographers working in state-run news agencies. A survey of state-controlled pictorials published around the period from 1966 to 1972, such as People's Pictorial, revealed the names of the photographers for some of the photographs in this book. This research also made it clear that the book is largely a selective sampling of the very same images that filled the pictorials published at this time. Images that had appeared in the pictorials were reprinted either with the same title or a new one. Some of the images here are virtually identical to what appeared in the pictorials, perhaps with a slight change of composition, reduction in size, or transformation from color to black and white. It was not far-fetched to conclude that these pictorials and this very photobook were tapping into the same pool of images. The consistency in their narratives is hard to miss. However, in the official history of the Liberation Army Pictorial Press that could be accessed publicly, there is no mention of this photobook at all.

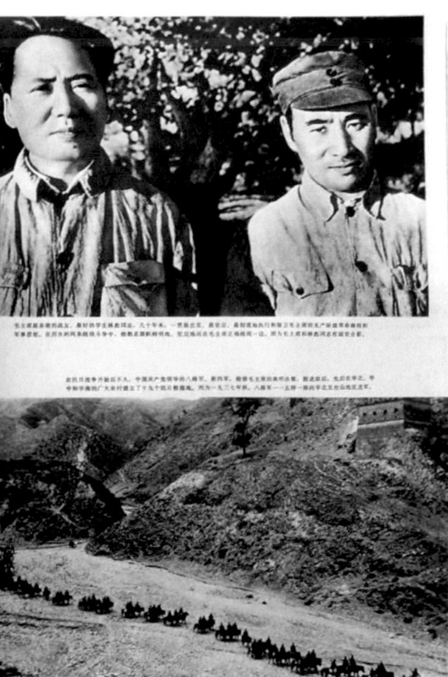

This 232-page photobook of *Long Live the Glorious May Seventh Directive* consisted of seven sections in total, providing a carefully conceived and crafted visual narrative throughout. It opens with two portraits of Mao, and two of Mao accompanied by Lin. Of the photos of the duo, one features the power couple greeting the Red Guards from the Gate of Heavenly Peace in Beijing at the outset of the Cultural Revolution, and the other was taken of them sitting next to each other at the Ninth Congress of the Chinese Communist Party in April 1969. It was at this congress that the victory of the Cultural Revolution was celebrated and Lin emerged as the primary military power and Mao's second in Party rank. Even the Party constitution was modified to name Lin as Mao's successor. These four photographs were followed by a reprint of the May Seventh Directive and a series of photographs recounting the genesis of the Communist Party from its time in Yan'an through the Sino-Japanese War to the Ninth Congress in 1969. In merely nine photographs, a vivid image emerges of a military force as a big school led and lectured to by Mao and armed with Marxist and Leninist thought. The photographs of the army from its Yan'an stint were included to confer historical legitimacy on this notion of the army as a school. The images show that, as was its tradition, this army kept study at the top of its agenda along with national defense and agricultural production, all the while continuously and closely interacting with the people.

From the third section onward, every chapter in this book features an opening double-spread with a quote from the May Seventh Directive on the left-hand page and a propaganda poster on the right. The quote at the beginning of the third chapter reads: "In this big school, one studies politics, studies military affairs, and studies culture."[7] The propaganda poster opposite depicts members of the navy, army, and air force each holding up the red-covered Collection of Mao Zedong's Selected Essays, with the slogan "One must truly grasp Mao Zedong's thoughts." During the phase of Lin's ascendance from 1959, Lin had worked laboriously and closely with Mao, creating a cult of personality around him. One of Lin's efforts was the compilation of some of Mao's writings into a handbook, Quotations from Chairman Mao Zedong, which became known as "the Little Red Book." The first version was published on May 1, 1964; this little red book had since become an emblem of Mao's thoughts.

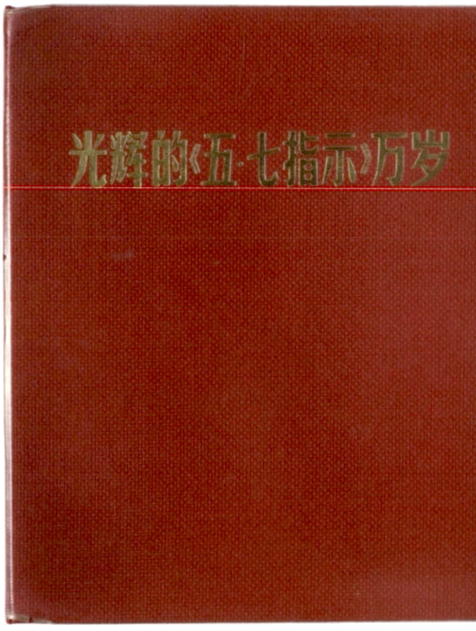

Cover and slipcase from *Long Live the Glorious May Seventh Directive.*

The subsequent nine photographs depict groups of soldiers studying "the Little Red Book" conscientiously in a variety of locations, in Yan'an, on a naval vessel, on an air force airfield, in a military library, in a tent on a road trip, beside a field during a break from plowing, or during a work break inside a mine. The narrative then moves from depictions of ideological studies to another form of study, learning from role models, such as fellow soldiers and villagers. This is exemplified by two photographs. One is of a soldier revealing a knee wound to the group of fellow soldiers surrounding him, with some looking over his shoulder. The other image is of an old villager recalling his suffering during the Sino-Japanese War and begging the young soldiers who are gathered round listening attentively to remember the deeds of the enemy. Then there appears a double-spread of a panoramic and romantic view of Jinggang Mountain where a number of red flags are blowing in the wind, amidst a sea of exuberant green. In 1927, Mao led his thousand remaining men here, fleeing a

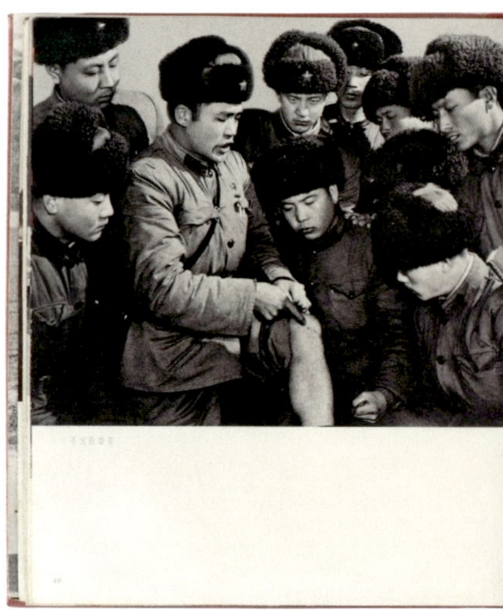
Book spread from *Long Live the Glorious May Seventh Directive.*

violent suppression by his opponent, the Nationalist Party in Shanghai, and set up his first peasant soviet. From then on, Jinggang Mountain was considered the birthplace of the Chinese Red Army, the predecessor of the People's Liberation Army. This image heralds a stroll down memory lane and offers a third approach for study: to learn from the revolutionary history of the Communist Party, through photographs of soldiers revisiting key historic sites and moments. The fourth study method recounted in this chapter is vigorous training and exercise.

Having covered these four approaches to learning—to study ideology, in particular Mao's thoughts; to learn from role models; to learn from history; and to learn through exercise—the book then uses the following images in the same section to illustrate such habits of study as diligence, persistence, self-discipline, and vigilance as well as to emphasize the importance of studying current political situations. This chapter ends with photos of beginners receiving their first lessons in the army and of the recreational moments of singing and engaging in a game of tug of war that punctuate the soldiers' study life. The structure of this chapter is precise and compact, its content thorough. The same ingenious conception can be seen throughout this photobook.

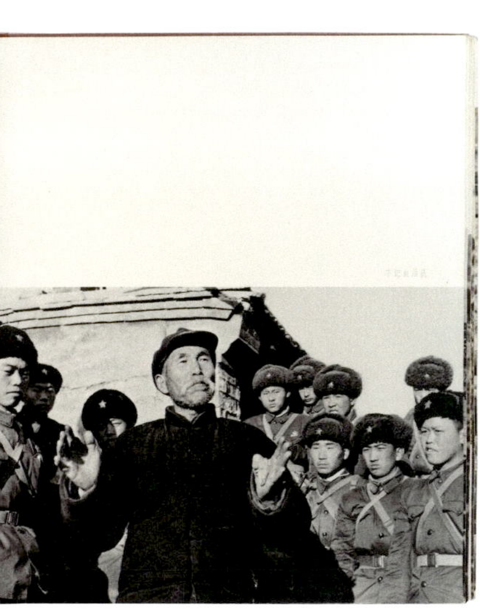

The fourth chapter starts with a quote that extends the previous one. It reads: "In this big school, one studies politics, military affairs, and culture. One can engage in agriculture and other kinds of production as well."[8] The central image of the propaganda poster opposite this quote features two soldiers holding up A Collection of Mao Zedong's Selected Essays together while each carries a hoe in the other hand, against a backdrop of some golden ears of wheat. As this image suggests, this section focuses entirely on creating an image of a military force that is capable of being at war and in production simultaneously and is at once self-reliant, self-reflective, and inventive. The photographs crystallize the image of the military force as actively involved in agriculture, forestry, livestock, fisheries, medicine, and subsidiary business in addition to national defense and warfare. The broad spectrum of images represents the soldiers simultaneously engaging in research and production. They are unafraid to challenge the extremes: they plant vegetables on plateaus. They are well informed of the latest developments in science: rice seeding and pig breeding are carried out with scientific methods. They are unconstrained by geography: their footsteps are found all over the country, from the southern sea of Hainan Island to the forests in northeastern China, from the cold lands to the tropical.

As one chapter leads to the other, the same quote that has appeared as the opening line of the third chapter continues to appear, each time with extra content that expands one's understanding of the role of the military. Likewise, each chosen propaganda poster reflects the concept articulated in the quote for its chapter. The fourth chapter portrays the military as an active participant in agricultural production, capable of being self-reliant both in supply logistics and in scientific inventions. The fifth chapter focuses on the ability of the military to run factories and to manufacture quality goods. This chapter's narrative emphasizes the involvement of the people in military production and the close collaboration between the army and the people. Finally, the publication closes with a chapter of photographs that remind us of the army's undying commitment to protecting the country and its borders.

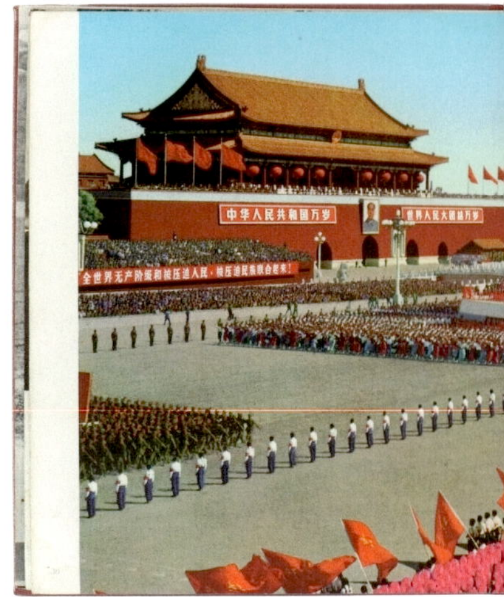

Book spread from *Long Live the Glorious May Seventh Directive.*

Apart from a small number of historical photographs taken during the early years of the Communist Party in Yan'an, most of the images in this publication came into existence around 1966 and in subsequent years. They were consistently theatrical and exemplified the height of revolutionary realism and revolutionary romanticism that was a predominant artistic dogma perpetuated throughout this time. After the founding of the People's Republic of China in 1949, the main group of photographers working in state-owned news agencies and creating the majority of photographs in the official media had commenced their artistic practice, or been exposed to pictorials and photographic training, during the Sino-Japanese War. The system of visual tropes and discourse on photography was formulated and developed in the Yan'an period through the 1940s. Their photography made visible the shifting revolutionary ideology in Yan'an. Through their practice, they gradually developed a system of rules for photography that was consistent with the ideology of the revolution, in that the role and expressions of photography were meant "to penetrate into the masses," "to awaken the masses," and "to educate."[9] The official photographs taken after 1949 absorbed, transformed, and reformed the photographic language from the war period of 1936–1949. Besides the continuous idolization of the leader, photographs taken after 1949 shared such key concepts as "labor,""transcendence (of the reality)," and the image of the "new man"[10] with the photographs taken earlier, all the while practicing and perfecting the same set of visual characteristics. For instance, photo-

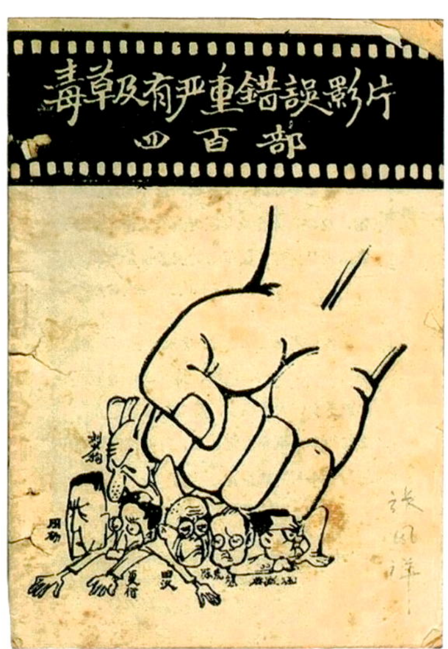

The cover of *Wild Grass and 400 Films of Serious Mistakes*, a book listing Chinese and Western films that were harshly criticized and banned from screening.

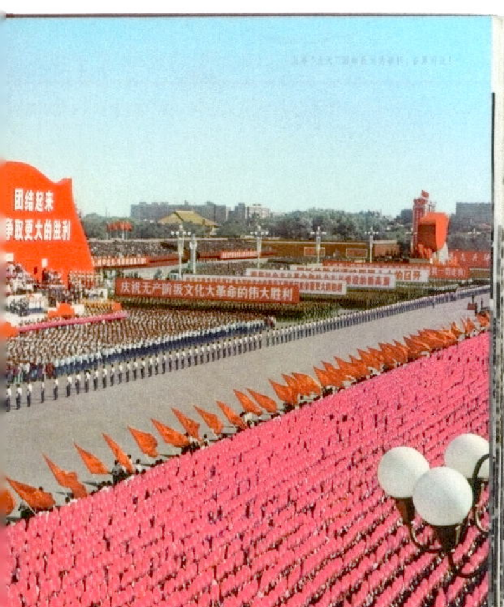

graphs of figures were often taken from a downward perspective of 45 degrees, while landscapes were often presented as expansive and epic vistas. The same visual prose of landscape photographs was evident in ink wash landscape paintings from this time, as, for instance, in Fu Baoshi's paintings.

If we were to consider this artistic dogma as a formal sequence in George Kubler's sense, one of the primary sources of the aesthetic code exemplified in these official photographs was the "model operas," a creation of Mao's wife Jiang Qing that was part of Mao's reclaiming of his power over national political, literary, and artistic matters. From 1962 to 1965, Jiang Qing managed to reform Peking operas, symphony, and ballets with revolutionary content, narrative, and contemporary styles. In Shanghai, Jiang Qing had completed her review and revision of four Peking operas on contemporary themes. In the spring of 1965 she declared that these were "model operas" that could be taken as examplars for the further development of revolutionary Peking opera. Jiang's "model operas," with their clearly defined artistic features, acquired the status of a primary object which others could emulate and, in doing so, generate a sequence and a system of visual codes and artistic principles. Jiang Qing's efforts were firmly backed up by Lin Biao. The army became responsible for promoting art that embodied such messages as proletarian ideology, communist morale and spirit, and revolutionary heroism. The endorsement of the army propelled such an art form to obtain institutional power and thus the status of an institution or that of "a closed sequence" in itself. To consolidate the exclusiveness of such a sequence of visual codes, other forms of practice were censored. For instance, in September 1967, the Jinggangshan Literature and Art Soldier Troupe of the Beijing Film Academy published Wild Grass and 400 Films of Serious Mistakes, listing four hundred Chinese and Western films that were harshly criticized and banned from screening.

The conceptual dogmas and theatrical conventions exemplified by the "model operas" became the standard in the visual arts. For the stage, Jiang had formulated "three prominences": to stress positive characters; their heroic quality; and the centrality of the main characters. Depictions of characters on stage became highly generalized and symbolic. In the arts, this was translated to mean that the subjects were to be portrayed heroically, and they were always to be in the center of the action, flooded with light from the sun or from hidden sources. The subjects were often larger-than-life peasants, soldiers, workers, and educated youth in dynamic poses. Their strong and robust physical presence functioned as a metaphor for the vigorous and healthy productive classes the state wanted to promote. The postures and actions in which these subjects were portrayed seemed to be taking place upon a stage so that the spectators would feel that they were looking upward.

As part of the propaganda campaign orchestrated by Mao and his close allies, this photobook was embedded in the visual culture of idolizing and romanticizing Mao's communist design through a combination of realism and romanticism. On one hand, it eulogized and elevated the army as a model for such a big school; on the other hand, it was didactic at its core, preaching and encouraging the internalization of the communist vision that was Mao's ultimate political ideal. In stunning contrast to this photobook's glorified depiction of Mao's idealized transformation of the society into a big school and the thousands of photographs produced around this time entirely from the perspective of the state, the turbulent reality remained nearly out of sight. Brutal suppression of intellectuals and cadres was effected partly through the propagation of May Seventh Cadre Schools as a result of the May Seventh Directive. The latter half of the Directive had urged workers, farmers, students, and those working in the commercial and service sectors, as well as party and governmental staff, to emulate the example set by the army, engaging in the study of military affairs, politics, and culture while carrying on the revolution against the bourgeoisie. From 1968, the Central Committee and the State Council built 106 May Seventh Cadre Schools in 18 provinces. Over 100,000 officials from the central government and 30,000 family members were sent there for hardship posting and labor. Lower-level government offices set up tens of thousands more cadre schools, where an unknown number of middle- and lower-ranking cadres were sent for reeducation. This became a favored method to remove cadres and intellectuals from the cities and thus prevent the potential rise of class difference, as well as to exercise Mao's wariness about the bourgeois tendencies. After Lin's fall in 1971, the revolutionary fanaticism of the Cultural Revolution gradually faded and a certain order was re-established. In this sense, this photobook could very well be one of the last testimonies to the height of socialist realist aesthetics and ideology before the end of the Cultural Revolution.

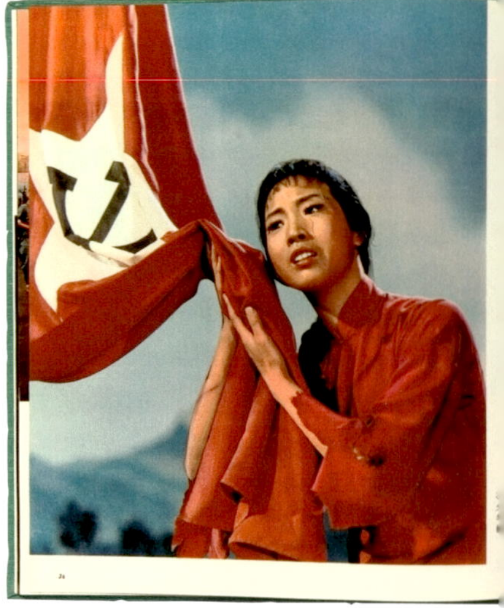

Book spread from *Selected Stage Photographs from Revolutionary Model Operas* (Beijing: China Photographic Publishing House, 1976)

Notes:

1 The news of Lin Biao's plot and disappearance was withheld from the general public for nearly a year. On August 20, 1973, the Central Committee of the Communist Party publically expelled Lin Biao from the party. On January 25, 1981, he was denounced by the High Court of the People's Republic of China as the primary culprit of the anti-revolutionary group.

2 The Great Leap Forward was an economic and social campaign by the Chinese Communist Party from 1958 to 1961. The campaign was led by Mao Zedong and aimed to rapidly transform the country from an agrarian economy into a socialist society through rapid industrialization and collectivization. In 1960, the difficulties created by the Great Leap and too rapid collectivization were compounded by the worst natural disasters China had experienced in a hundred years and the Soviet Union's withdrawal of its aid and technical assistance. With the nation on the brink of economic collapse, Mao was forced to allow a retrenchment of some of his more radical policies.

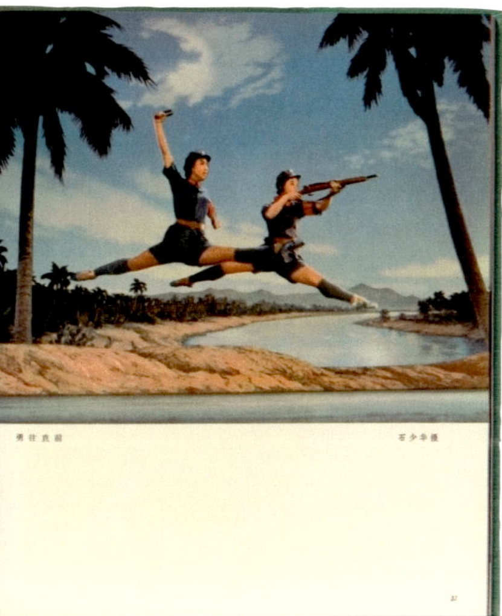

3 The People's Liberation Army was founded on August 1, 1927. It was originally known as the Chinese Workers' and Peasants' Red Army. It has been the armed forces of the Communist Party since 1927 and of the People's Republic of China since 1949.

4 The People's Commune came into existence during the Great Leap Forward, when Mao Zedong had a vision of surpassing the United Kingdom and the United States in a short period of time in terms of steel production. Mao wanted to mobilize peasants to undertake huge water projects during the winter slack seasons in order to improve agricultural productivity. The Peoples' commune was made official state policy in 1958 after Mao Zedong visited an unofficial commune in Henan. Each commune was a combination of smaller farm collectives and consisted of 4,000-5,000 households. Larger communes could consist of up to 20,000 households.

5 Mao, Zedong. "May Seventh Directive." May 15, 1966.

6 In 1966, Mao Zedong launched what became known as the Cultural Revolution, in full the Great Proletarian Cultural Revolution. Frustrated by the direction China was going in, Mao called on the nation's youth to purge the "impure" elements of Chinese society and revive the revolutionary spirit that he believed could lead to his vision of a communist state. The Cultural Revolution continued in various phases until Mao's death in 1976.

7 Mao, Zedong. May Seventh Directive. May 15th, 1966.

8 Mao, Zedong. May Seventh Directive. May 15th, 1966.

9 Gao, Chu. "Chinese Photography During the War Period (1936-1953)," *Chinese Photography: Twentieth Century and Beyond*, ed. Rong Rong (Beijing: Three Shadows Press Limited. 2015. 85.

10 Ibid., 85.

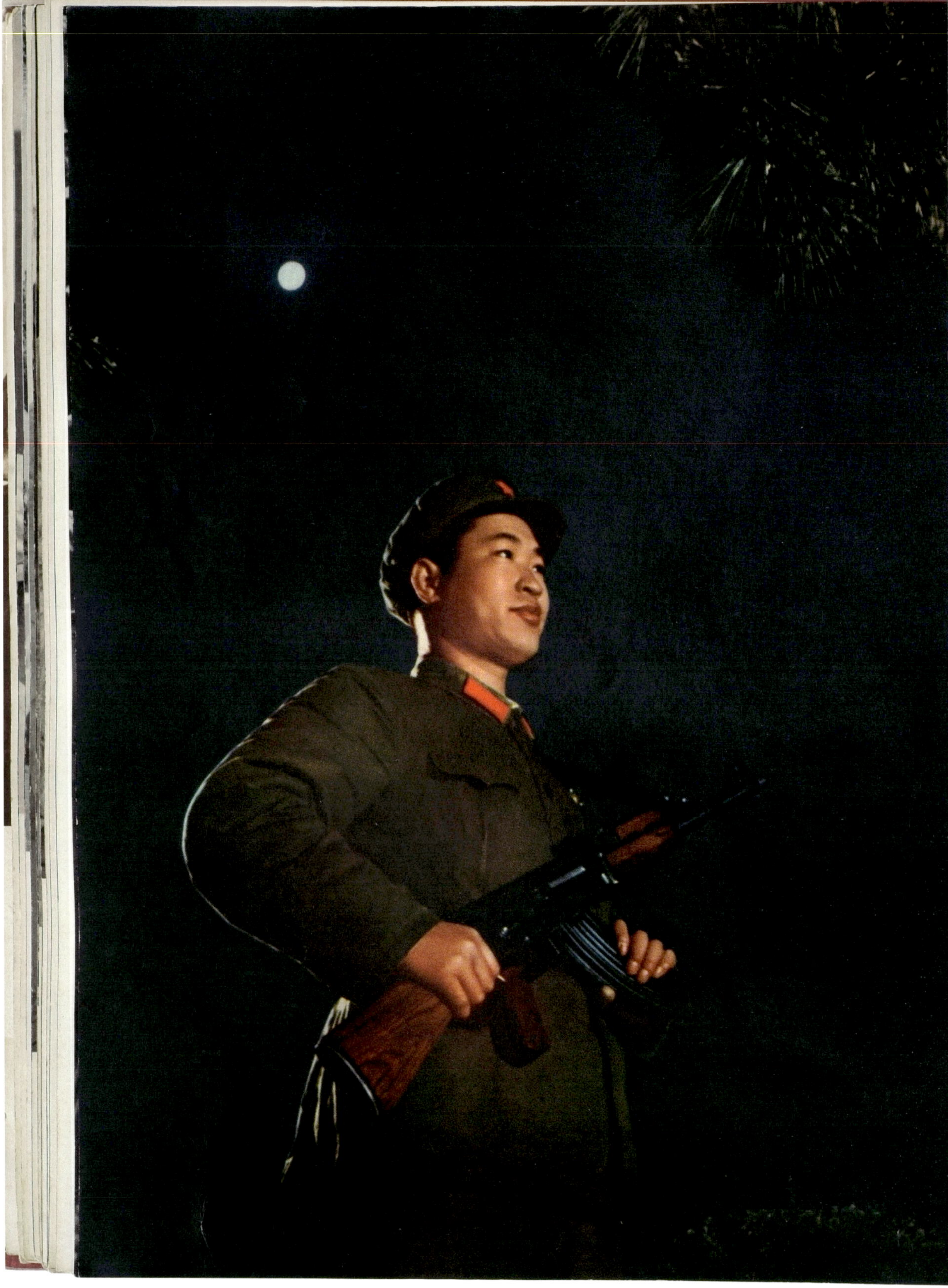

Image from the book *Long Live the Glorious May Seventh Directive*, 1971.

Authentically Socialist: A Window on a Communist Utopia[1]

Chen Shuxia

Publisher: P.L.A. Picture Publishing, Beijing

Year of publication: 1971

Binding: Hardback with red cloth and acetate dustjacket

Size: 292 x 260 mm (11 ½ x 10 ¼ in)

Number of pages: 232

Number of illustrations: 68 color and 101 b&w photographs

Type of reproduction: Offset

Print run: Unknown

Printer: Unknown

Design:

Editor:

The turmoil of the Cultural Revolution reached a climax in the late 1960s and took a dramatic turn in 1971. That year marked the fifth anniversary of a letter dated 7 May 1966 from Mao Zedong to Lin Biao, Minister of Defense and deputy leader of the People's Liberation Army (PLA). Lin was extolled as the Chairman's "closest comrade-in-arms and hand-picked successor." In the letter Mao outlined his view of the role that the army should play in transforming the country as part of China's ongoing revolution. His remarks formed the basis of what is known at the "5.7 Directive," or "May Seventh Directive."

Mao declared that "the army should be a great school.... In this great school, our army should study politics and military affairs, raise its educational level, and also engage in agriculture and side-occupations and run small or medium-sized factories.... Our army should also do mass work.... Also our army should always be ready to participate in the struggles to criticize and repudiate the bourgeoisie in the Cultural Revolution."

The letter formed the basis for the army's essentially taking over Chinese society and becoming the model for everyone. It would also be the document behind the mass rustication of party cadres sent to undergo labor reform in the countryside.

Shortly after this collection of photographs extolling the "5.7 Directive" appeared, Lin and most of his immediate family died in a mysterious plane crash in Mongolia, supposedly during an attempt to flee China for the Soviet Union. Lin was immediately excoriated as a traitor to the revolution, an arch-reactionary, a threat to Mao himself. The happy camaraderie depicted in this book was obliterated in a nationwide campaign of vilification.

Long Live the Glorious May Seventh Directive appeared on the eve of Lin's death, and for many Lin's denouement marked the real end of Cultural Revolution zealotry and idealism. This volume records in the highly stylistic fashion of hyper-socialist realism an imagined real and then an immediately lost world.

Like all publications during the period that Geremie R. Barmé calls "High Maoism" this book starts with beatific images of Mao Zedong in isolated sanctity. These are followed by pictures of the Chairman in the company of Lin Biao, either standing on the rostrum of Tian'anmen Gate overlooking the square in the center of Beijing or during some significant party-state meeting. The book contains 169 black-and-white and color photographs, as well as a double-page spread accompanying the introduction, which reproduces the text of Mao's 7 May letter to Lin Biao.

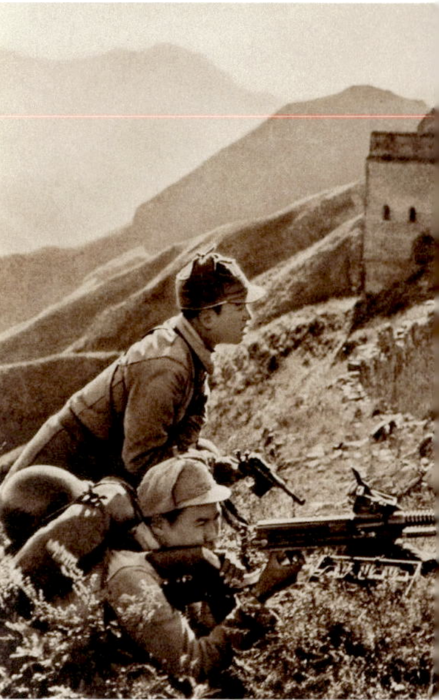

The photograph "Attacking the Japanese Invaders" by Sha Fei taken in 1937.

Each section of the book features a quotation from the letter. Apart from photographs of Mao, the images feature scenes of army life and achievements, including soldiers studying Quotations from Chairman Mao (also known as "The Little Red Book"), farming, fishing, smelting steel, teaching Mao Zedong Thought to peasants and ethnic minorities, working at heavy industrial sites, marching in military parades, and participating in large-scale military maneuvers.

The book is divided into seven parts, an introduction and six sections representing the main points of the "5.7 Directive." The first section focuses on the "army as a great school to learn politics, military, and culture" and features photographs of soldiers studying Mao's Quotations in various situations; section 2 shows scenes of the soldiers engaging in agricultural production and other forms of small-scale agriculture (such as fishing and raising chickens); the third section shows soldiers working on modern industrial production; and the fourth section emphasizes the responsibility of the army in engaging in mass work, featuring images of soldiers enthusiastically visiting and helping minorities in rural and ethnic areas. The concluding section reaffirms the main responsibility of the army "to be vigilant and to protect the motherland," and shows military maneuvers on sea, land, and in the air, using high-tech weaponry.

The photographs in this book, like those produced in other publications at a time of "collective creativity" in which authorship was eliminated, did not acknowledge individual photographers. Everything was presented as being a collective effort. Individual photographic styles, indeed the very concept of self, were done away with. The work in this book dates from the 1930s through to 1971 and, despite the intentions of the editors of the book, we can discern over the decades the evolution of an aesthetic approach that changed according to the political climate and the tastes of party leaders and propagandists.

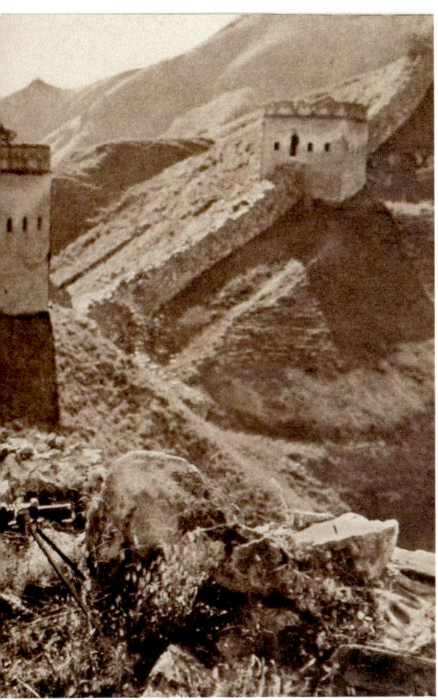

The introduction features photographs by the noted party cultural workers Wu Yinxian (1900–1994) and Sha Fei (1912–1950), which were taken from the late 1930s. The Communist Party and its Red Army had retreated from East China and, following what is known as the Long March through the country's hinterland, set up a revolutionary base at Yan'an in Shaanxi province. Images of Mao at different revolutionary sites in Yan'an and scenes of party soldiers at work illustrate the core May Seventh vision that the military should act as a great and collective school for the whole nation. It's a vision that dates back to the late 1930s, one documented by these photographers. The early work of Sha Fei and Wu Yinxian established an aesthetic and style for all later Chinese socialist photography.

Reflecting what was extolled as "authenticity" 真实性 became a central task of socialist cultural production. This kind of authenticity does not refer to some truth or the originality of an artwork; rather, it is about adhering to a socialist norm of what was "accurate" 正确 and "typical" 典型 within the context of a Marxist-Leninist view of reality and history. Any so-called "fact" that deviated from party policy or failed to conform to this principle was one that betrayed the principle of authenticity in photography.[2] This understanding of photographic authenticity was, of course, based on party ideology and discourse, and the use of the "typical" and "accurate" in the choice of subject matter ensured that photographers would align themselves with party interests and policies. The search for "authenticity" was undertaken entirely within the framework of a constructed, highly stylized form of socialist "reality"—in other words, one that reflected current political needs. Photography was used from the 1930s to depict a truth that served politics. Both Wu Yinxian and Sha Fei were advocates and practitioners of this approach.

Sha Fei, who joined the party in 1937, founded the Communists' first image-oriented magazine, Jinchaji Pictorial (1942–1947). In his preface to Wu Yinxian's 1939 book Photographic General Knowledge 摄影常识, Sha Fei wrote unequivocally: "Photography is a propaganda tool. It is duty-bound to report important political events and it is an incisive weapon with which to carry on the struggle."[3] In his artistic practice Sha documented the heroic activities of the party-army in North China, reflecting in his work many facets of army life, including such everyday scenes as farming activities, soldiers spinning thread, and engaging in various other forms of productive labor.

Carefully chosen for this anniversary book, Sha's photos positioned Mao's idea of the army as a great school within the Yan'an tradition. Such images were used to demonstrate the army-centric propaganda at the heart of the socialist enterprise. In "Attacking the Japanese Invaders" 打击日本侵略者 (1937), two soldiers perch on a ridge on the ruins of the Great Wall, which snakes into the background. One soldier is kneeling, gazing ahead while holding a handgun; the other lies on his stomach, looking down the sights of his machine gun. In the twentieth century, the long-neglected Great Wall became a metaphor for China's resistance to the outside world and foreign invasion. This work was originally published in the September 1943 issue of the Jinchaji Pictorial under the title "The Jinchaji Eight Route Soldiers at Battle in Xifengkou" 转战在喜峰口外的晋察冀八路军[4] under the nom de plume Kong Wang 孔望. In it Sha employed the visual rhetoric of the Great Wall to promote the party as the new protectors of the beleaguered Chinese people during the war with Japan.

Sha Fei claimed that "staging a scene will lose the authenticity [of the event]. It will also arouse suspicion and bias when people try to appreciate our work." Despite the apparent contradiction between this statement and his artistic/propagandistic practice, for Sha "authenticity" was more about the thrust of history and the role the Communist Party played in giving hope to China than actual on-the-ground detail. The means—that is, staging— justified the end—that is, an authentic effect on viewers—even if it was based on visual mendacity. "Staging and doctoring" 组织加工 in photojournalism had been criticized in China since at least the late 1930s as a violation of basic principles of authenticity; however, such techniques were still frequently used for ideological purposes, and by all parties, not just the Communists. In the early years of the People's Republic of China (founded in 1949) discussions were organized to debate the issue of photographic authenticity—particularly inside the New China News Agency in the late 1950s—and such deliberations tended to conclude that above all photography had to serve the party line and educate the masses.[5]

Like Sha Fei, Wu Yinxian advocated using photography for political ends. Wu had attended art school and worked as a cinematographer in Shanghai in the 1920s and 1930s. In 1938, he was invited by the party leader Zhou Enlai to make a documentary film on the activities of the Communist Eighth Route

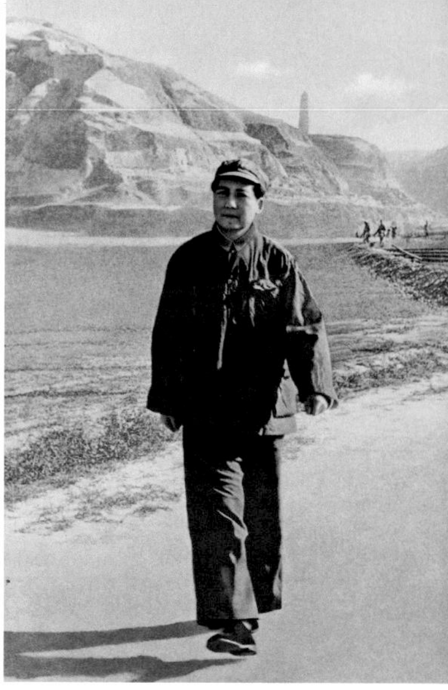

(Above) A retouched version of Wu Yinxian's 1942 photograph "Chairman Mao at the anti-Japanese sacred democratic land: Yan'an" as it appears in *Long Live the Glorious May Seventh Directive*. (Opposite) An original unretouched version. Collection of the International Center of Photography, Gift of Wu Yinxian, 1988.

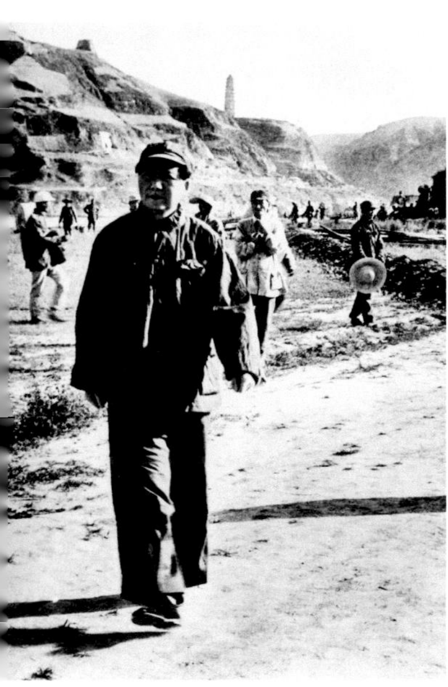

Army. Thereafter, he continued documenting wartime life in the party-controlled Yan'an area. After 1949, as one of the most prominent photographers in socialist China, Wu always referred to Mao Zedong's formulations regarding culture and stressed that photographs "document typical scenes from life" and that they have the capacity to educate the masses in right thinking.[6] In this context, "typical" 典型的 meant idealized or model. The pursuit and representation of the "typical" was a key feature of all artistic practice during the Maoist era (1949–1976). Like other creative men and women during those years, Wu was caught between the requirements of the party and the pursuit of his art. On one hand, he emphasized the "documentary" 纪实的 quality of photography, while, on the other, he advocated in favor of the ideological import of visual culture. This is evident in his work from the Yan'an period. Taken by Wu in 1942, the photograph titled "Chairman Mao at the Anti-Japanese Sacred Democratic Land: Yan'an" 毛主席在抗日民主圣地—延安 shows the party chairman walking alone next to a field, with the Baota Pagoda (by then already a frequently occurring icon in representations of the Communist base area, and later a symbol of the "sacred land" of Yan'an that nurtured the party during the war) in the distance. The composition of the work is reminiscent of a traditional painting and religious iconography. Frequently reproduced after the liberation in 1949, it encouraged a quasi-religious nostalgia for an earlier, ostensibly more peaceful era (even if it was at the height of the war). Mao, the sole figure in this photo (apart from some indistinct peasants working in the far distance), is in army garb, frowning slightly as he gazes ahead with pursed lips and a look of determination. If Yan'an was now figured as the party's "holy land," Mao was the demigod at its heart. The original 1942 photo was subsequently doctored to respond to the needs of the Cultural Revolution, by which time Mao had been made into the inviolable Great Leader. The earlier image shows peasants working and standing in the field near Mao, but here they have been "disappeared," leaving Mao in glorious isolation. His face has also been enhanced and the collar of his jacket painted in to emphasize the fact that he is wearing an army uniform.

In May of the year Wu took this photo, Mao established the basic guidelines for all future party-led cultural and arts production in his "Yan'an Talks on Literature and Art." Following in the footsteps of Soviet cultural policy formulated in the 1930s, Mao declared art and literature to be "part of the revolutionary machinery" and "a powerful weapon."[7] Art had to be "realistic in form and socialist in content."[8] This meant that artistic works could not simply depict reality as it was found; rather, reality was construed by the propagandists and ideologues, based on life but enhanced by the engineers of the human soul. To replicate mere facts as though they were somehow truthful was condemned as crude "naturalism" 自然主义. A fact was not synonymous with truth; the only truth was a socialist truth, "authentic" because it adumbrated progressive socialist life, foreshadowing an immanent communist world. In this sense, no image could be more visually credible than a photograph. Photography as a weapon or tool in China's revolutionary struggle was thus a natural choice of medium, one that was ideally suited for the promotion of the party line and for the enlightenment of the masses.

Wu's 1940s photographs reproduced here reflected this new cultural approach. Mao further modified these guidelines in the late 1950s when the Chinese Communist Party's relationship with the Soviet Union collapsed due to strategic and ideological differences. Now it promoted a "combination of revolutionary realism and revolutionary romanticism" 革命现实主义和革命浪漫主义相结合—a line Mao promulgated during the 1958 Great Leap Forward, thereby outdoing the Soviet concept of "Socialist Realism." Romanticism legitimized the envisioning of an idealized socialist future through the arts, taking cultural production even further away from documentary and revolutionary realism. During the Cultural Revolution, when Jiang Qing, Mao's wife (who following Mao's death in September 1976 was named a member of the counter-revolutionary "Gang of Four"), assumed a leading role in cultural politics, the dogma of revolutionary romanticism further dominated artistic creation. All works were now to be "red, bright, and vivid" 红, 光, 亮 or "tall, imposing, and complete" 高, 大, 全.

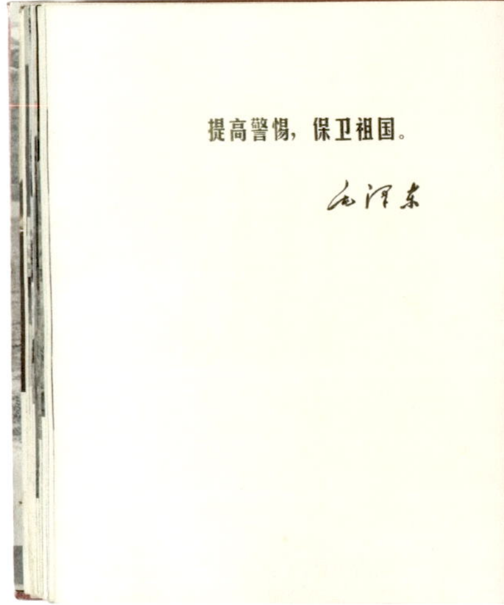

The colorized photograph "To Be Vigilant" by Jiang Qing as it appears in *Long Live the Glorious May Seventh Directive*, 1971.

Jiang Qing was a photography enthusiast herself and her work from this time reflects these garish dicta. "On High Alert" 高度警惕 illustrates her approach. This was most probably made using her favored camera, a German Leica, and it would have been developed and printed at the headquarters of Xinhua News Agency, which worked at her behest. Despite her avowed amateur status, Jiang's prestigious position within the party meant she had access to the best photographic resources in the country.[9] According to the memoirs of her personal nurses, Jiang waited until late one moonlit night and asked a security guard at the Diaoyutai State Guesthouse (Jiang's principal place of residence and work during the Cultural Revolution) to pose for her. The nurses assisted with lighting as Jiang worked through the night to take the shot, which was meant to highlight the unflagging spirit of the guard on duty. Although camouflaged by the vegetation the young soldier is heroically positioned at the center of the image. His dark eyes are alert, red lips tightly pressed together, his cheeks glowing with fervor. The red star on his cap glistens in the moonlight, an orb hanging in a pitch-black sky. His young face displays a solemn glow, like a statue, firm and still.

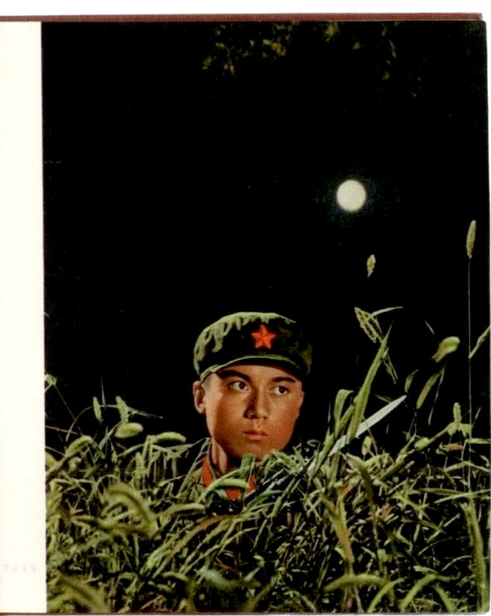

The staged lighting on his face, his thick and dark eyebrows, rosy cheeks, red lips, and the red star and collar of his uniform reflect Jiang Qing's carefully considered production values. The work is, quite literally, theatrical. Nearly every page of *Long Live the Glorious May Seventh Directive* has similarly posed works. Thick eyebrows, dark hooded eyes, and rosy cheeks came to typify the image of the ideal revolutionary soldier; their white, even teeth shine as they study Mao's Quotations or engage in edifying manual labor. Wearing their pristine army caps with shiny red stars, they happily help children, the elderly, the poor, ethnic minorities, and the disabled, all the while determined to fight against the bourgeoise and other enemies. Their images and activities, through staging, airbrushing, and colorizing, represent an ideal socialist reality.

To glorify and maintain such authenticity, a well-funded and all-encompassing propaganda system was established. The fifth anniversary of the "May Seventh Directive" in 1971 was celebrated with a suite of activities including the publication of photobooks and posters, the holding of exhibitions, and the release of documentary films. Besides this photobook published by the People's Liberation Army Picture Press, another book, *Forge Ahead Along the Glorious Road of "5.7,"* was produced by Hubei People's Publishing House. An exhibition, *Long Live the Glorious May Seventh Directive*, was held at the Military Museum of the Chinese People's Revolution in Beijing, appropriately opened to the public on 7 May 1971, and reported by the People's Daily as displaying over ten thousand items, including photos, paintings, posters, books, notebooks, letters, and specimens of vegetables and fruits, the labors of those who had responded to Mao's directive to labor in the countryside.

As in the case of this photobook, the introductory section of the exhibition outlined the traditional role of the army in agricultural and industrial production during the 1930s and 1940s. Again this demonstrated that the May Seventh Directive had been a constant element of Mao Zedong Thought, the crystallization of which was the declaration that the PLA was "a great school of Mao Zedong Thought." The exhibition's content also overlapped with other "May Seventh" celebratory products and included examples of the "advanced" 先进的 model PLA units that were held up to extol Mao Zedong Thought. A technicolor documentary film, *Long Live the Glorious May Seventh Directive*, was produced by the PLA's own August First Film Studio. A poster for the film was featured on the last page of the photobook, but with a slightly different exhortation: "Forge Ahead on the Glorious Avenue of Chairman Mao's 'May Seventh.'"

In this way, content such as photos, slogans, and posters was shared, reproduced, or referred to in different media and cultural forms produced to mark various anniversaries—not altogether unlike repetitive advertising or branding in market economies. Moreover, such prepackaged propaganda was not merely the work of one party-state organ or instrumentality. The party's top-down system required that different offices and agencies be self-motivated and politically astute concerning the need to promote certain images according to particular guidelines issued in advance of such occasions. Such political awareness or consciousness 政治觉悟 was rooted in the system of party values and compelled people to express the correct, formulaic opinion on all matters related to party-state affairs. Such socialist authenticity was the bedrock of a coercive yet widely recognized and internalized system of control that illustrated undeniable party truths, while political awareness required everyone to think and react in lockstep.

Political consciousness, however, despite its "mass" nature (everyone was expected to nurture it), was an uncertain quantity; celebration could easily turn into denunciation depending on the mercurial party line. Following Marshal Lin Biao's mysterious death, for example, he was denounced nationwide as an anti-party, counter-revolutionary traitor. By denouncing Lin in a timely fashion, one validated one's own political consciousness; this held true not only for party members, but also for "the people" as a whole. While party photographers and propagandists had the resources to doctor photographs and erase Lin from the public record, normal everyday denunciations often took a far simpler form as his name and image were crossed out or erased from all books, posters, and diaries. We can see that Lin Biao's name was erased from the index of this book by its owner (Figure 5). Given that Lin was transformed virtually overnight from Mao's closest comrade-in-arms to Public Enemy Number One, it is hard to gauge the extent to which this mass response was a reflection of actual repugnance or of a fear of being seen as a Lin Biao supporter. Either way, it was a correct political awareness that allowed the individual to express an appropriate response to the changing political situation.

This book affords us a glimpse into the changing landscape

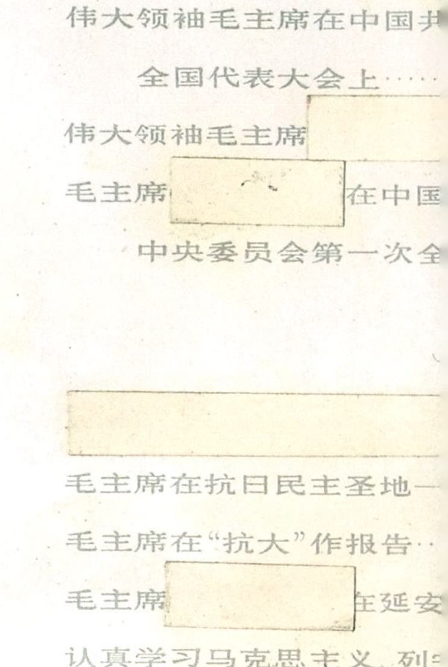
伟大领袖毛主席在中国共
全国代表大会上……
伟大领袖毛主席
毛主席 在中国
中央委员会第一次全
毛主席在抗日民主圣地—
毛主席在"抗大"作报告··
毛主席 在延安
认真学习马克思主义、列

After denunciation of public officials, books and photographs were often defaced by the owners through crossing out or cutting of images. In this particular copy of *Long Live the Glorious May Seventh Directive*, the photographs including Lin Biao are untouched, but on the index pages his name is covered over by white linen tape.

of China's socialist visual aesthetics from the late 1930s to the early 1970s, from the Yan'an period work of Sha and Wu doctored to suit an evolving party line, to the carefully staged and colorized works of the Cultural Revolution. The book was produced to extol the army at the height of its authority and that of its leader, Lin Biao. Ironically, its appearance coincided nearly exactly with the fall of Lin and the declining role of the PLA in China's revolutionary politics. A work painstakingly produced to reflect mass celebration suddenly became an awkward reminder of Lin Biao and his failed ambition, and indeed of the bankruptcy of the Maoist propaganda enterprise as a whole.

A carefully created and maintained aesthetic system and worldview reaches an apogee in this book, and collapses at its moment of maturation. The erasure of Lin's name by the book's onetime owner reminds us how such works were the products equally of celebration and of denunciation, their fate uncertain, prone to precipitous change in a world in which no one was entirely sure what was authentically socialist.

Notes:

1 I would like to thank Geremie R. Barmé for his valuable comments and suggestions.

2 "'On the field forces' September photographic interview (*Dui yezhan budui jiuyue sheyingcaifang de yijian* 对野战部队九月摄影采访的意见)," *Photography Network Communications* 摄影网通讯 9 (1947).

3 Jiang Qingsheng, et al., *Chinese photography history 1937-1949* 中国摄影史 *1937-1949* (Beijing: Zhongguo sheying chubanshe, 1998), 86.

4 This photo was later identified as having been taken not in Xifengkou but in Futuyu 浮图峪. See Si Sushi, "Sha Fei and his series 'Battle at the Ancient Great Wall,'" *Chinese Photographers* 中国摄影家 1(2015).

5 Jin Yongquan, *Red flag studio: debates on Chinese photography, 1956 – 1959* 红旗照相馆: *1956-1959* 年中国摄影争辩) (Beijing: Jincheng chubanshe, 2009).

6 Wu Yinxian, *Expression Methods for Photographic Art* 摄影艺术的表现方法 (Beijing: Beijing Film Press, 1961).

7 Mao Zedong, "Talks at the Yan'an Conference on literature and art," in *Mao Zedong's talks at the Yan'an conference on literature and art: a translation of the 1943 text with commentary*, trans. Bonnie McDougall (Michigan: the University of Michigan, 1980), 58.

8 Boris Groys, "Educating the masses: socialist realist art," in *Art Power* (Cam bridge: The MIT Press, 2008), 141.

9 Zhou Shuying, Zhao Liu'en, " 'Leisure Jiang Qing' and 'Poison Incident,' "休闲江青"与"毒药事件" in *China Through the Ages* 炎黄春秋) 11(2014).

Errata Editions gratefully acknowledges the following people for their generous assistance and support: Carol Yinghua Lu, Liu Ding, Chen Shuxia, David Campany, Sarah Meister, Andrew Lewin, Dennis Santella, Thomas Roma, Jeffrey Hirsch of Fotocare NY, Ruben Lundgren, Lois Conner, John T. Hill, Stefanie Armbruster, Deirdre Donohue, Claartje van Dijk, Sharon Gallagher, Elisa Leshowitz, Malcolm Daniel, Frits Gierstberg, John Gossage, Corey Keller, Thyago Noguiera and Brian Wallis.

A special thank you to Affirmation Arts, Ltd. for enabling the aquisition of camera equipment used in the production of the Errata Editions' *Books on Books* series.

Series Concept: Jeffrey Ladd
Publisher: Valerie Sonnenthal
Editor: Ed Grazda
Book Design: Jeffrey Ladd
Scans: Jeffrey Ladd
Copy Editor: Susanna Sturgis

First Edition 2016

This copy of *Long Live the Glorious May Seventh Directive* from the collection of David Campany.

errata editions
10 Bleecker Street
Suite 7B
New York, NY 10012
www.errataeditions.com

ISBN: 978-1-935004-42-4 (trade edition)
ISBN: 978-1-935004-43-1 (limited edition)

Printed in Germany